W9-BEA-354

ALSO BY BRIAN MACARTHUR

The Penguin Book of Twentieth-Century Speeches (ed.)

The Penguin Book of Historic Speeches (ed.)

The Penguin Book of Twentieth-Century Protest (ed.)

Requiem: Diana, Princess of Wales, 1961–1997

Despatches from the Gulf War (ed.)

Deadline Sunday: A Life in the Week of the Sunday Times

Eddy Shah: Today *and the Newspaper Revolution*

SURVIVING THE SWORD

RANDOM HOUSE
NEW YORK

SURVIVING THE SWORD

Prisoners of the Japanese in the Far East, 1942–45

BRIAN MACARTHUR

Published in the United States by Random House,
an imprint of The Random House Publishing Group,
a division of Random House, Inc., New York.

RANDOM HOUSE and colophon are registered trademarks of
Random House, Inc.

Originally published in Great Britain by Time Warner Books.

ISBN 1-4000-6413-9

Printed in the United States of America

Book design by Jennifer Ann Daddio

For the Far East Prisoners of War

1942–45

and their families

CONTENTS

PART TWO

PART THREE

ACKNOWLEDGMENTS

I owe two profound debts. The first is to James Sanders, who helped with research, particularly in the United States, and who was a constructive critic of the work in progress. The second is to Anne Manson, who typed the manuscript and pursued copyright approval with indefatigable imperturbability.

Equally profound debts are owed to Rod Suddaby, the Keeper of Archives, and his staff at the Imperial War Museum, and to Peter Stanley, Margaret Lewis, David Joliffe, and the staff of the Australian War Memorial. Both are superb institutions.

The idea for this book was sparked by Roland Philipps, and my agent Hilary Rubinstein was a source of constant support and encouragement, as were Ursula Mackenzie, David Young, Stephen Guise, Peter Cotton, Nann du Sautoy, Diane Spivey, and Tamsin Barrack at Time Warner, Alan Samson, and in the United States Robert Loomis, Evan Camfield, and Daniel Barrett. Robin Glendenning (in the Netherlands) and Peter Field (in Australia) helped with research. Duncan Stewart created a new map of the Burma–Thailand railway. Philip Parr was a meticulous copy editor. Much of the writing of the book was done at the French home of Barry Turner and Mary Fulton.

I am deeply grateful to the former prisoners who agreed to interviews: Stephen Alexander, Lewis Altman, Leslie Audus, the late James Bradley, Jack Chalker, Tom Evans, the late Stanley Gimson, Reuben Kandler, Peter Jamieson, Eric Lomax, James Mudie, Ray Parkin, Nowell Peach, Charles Peall, Fred Ryall, Arthur Titherington, John Stewart Ullman (who writes as John Stewart), and Loet Velmans.

Stephen Alexander, Leslie Audus, James Bradley, Tom Evans, Eric Lomax, James Mudie, Fred Ryall, John Stewart Ullman, Tom Eaton, Sears Eldredge, Roy Fullick, Clifford Kinvig, Hank Nelson, David Price, Robin Rowland, Patrick Toosey, and Don Wall read draft chapters and offered helpful advice.

All of the following helped at some stage during the preparation of the book: Claire Baker, Linda Bradley, Carol Broughton, Pamela Britcher, Ian Chapman, Elaine Cleary, Tom Condon, Christopher Elliott, Sibylla Jane Flower, Margaret Gee, Jeni Giffen, Simon Harris, Dennis Hackett, Liz Hughes, A. Jeyathurai, J.D.F. Jones, Igor Judge, Phillip Knightley, Murdoch MacLennan, Steve Martin, Mason Nelson, Ian Norrie, Meg Parkes, Sharon Parmeter, David Parry, Sandra Parsons, Simon Parsons, Qantas, Maggie van Reenen, Tony Rennell, Andrew and Sandra Richman, Alan Rusbridger, Singapore Airlines, the Singapore Tourist Board, William Slape, Robert Stiby, Peter Stothard, Robert Thomson, Rob Tomkinson, Gina Topping, Lucia van der Post, David Wadmore, John Waller, David Whitaker, Tom Wills-Sandford, Charles Wilson, and Jenny Wood.

The book could not have been completed without the continuous encouragement, tact, patience, and tolerance of my wife, Maureen Waller, over nearly four years.

For permission to quote from diaries held by the Department of Documents at the Imperial War Museum, I am grateful to Adrian Abbott, David Barratt, Alan Butterworth, John Chambers, James Chandler, H. DuMoulin, Mrs. V. V. Franks, George Grigs, Hertfordshire Yeomanry and Artillery Historical Trust, Mrs. Y. S. Huntriss, Enid Innes-Ker, Pam Kidner, P. N. Kingwill, Michael Milford, Margaret Nelson, Sally Orman, Miss M. Pollard, Vivien Pringle, J. A. Richardson, S. J. Riley, Lady Sharp, Liz Shields, Harry Silman, Kit Stephens, Susan Tanner, Kate Thraxton, Patrick Toosey, Paul Vardy, and Charles Wild.

For permission to quote from diaries held by the Australian War Memorial, I am grateful to Rosemary Maxwell, W. H. Miggins, John Nevill, and Tom Wragg.

For permission to quote from published sources, I am grateful to Birlinn Ltd., Tim Bowden, Margaret Gee, Hertfordshire Yeomanry and Artillery Historical Trust, Peter Lee, Hank Nelson, Oleander Press Ltd., Pen & Sword Books Ltd., Penguin Group (Australia), Lady Piper, Philippa Poole, Sayle Literary Agency, Socialist History Society, U.S. Army Medical Department Museum, Fort Sam Houston, Josephine Watt, Roy Whitecross, and *Wisden Cricketers' Almanack* 1946.

AUTHOR'S NOTE

I have used "Thailand" throughout instead of "Siam," and "Taiwan" instead of "Formosa." There are many ways of spelling Thai place names; I have decided to standardize the following: Ban Pong, Chungkai, Hintok, Konkoita, Konyu, Nakhon Nayok, Nikhe, Nakhon Pathom, Nong Pladuk, Takanun, Tarsao.

Ranks and ages are generally given as they were at the time of capture.

ABBREVIATIONS

AB	Able Seaman	L.Cpl.	Lance Corporal
AIF	Australian Infantry Force	L.Sgt.	Lance Sergeant
Bdr.	Bombardier	Lt.	Lieutenant
Brig.	Brigadier	Lt. Cdr.	Lieutenant Commander
Btn.	Battalion	Lt. Col.	Lieutenant Colonel
Capt.	Captain	Lt. Gen.	Lieutenant General
Cdr.	Commander	Maj.	Major
CO	Commanding Officer	Maj. Gen.	Major General
Col.	Colonel	MO	Medical Officer
Coy. Sgt. Maj.	Company Sergeant Major	MP	Military Police
Cpl.	Corporal	OR	other ranks
Div.	Division	PO	Pilot Officer
Flt. Lt.	Flight Lieutenant	Pte.	Private
Flt. Off.	Flight Officer	Regt.	Regiment
FM	Field Marshal	Regt. Sgt. Maj.	Regimental Sergeant Major
FO	Flying Officer	2nd Lt.	Second Lieutenant
Gen.	General	Sgt.	Sergeant
LAC	Leading Aircraftman	Sgt. Maj.	Sergeant Major
L.Bdr.	Lance Bombardier	Sqn. Ldr.	Squadron Leader
		WO	Warrant Officer

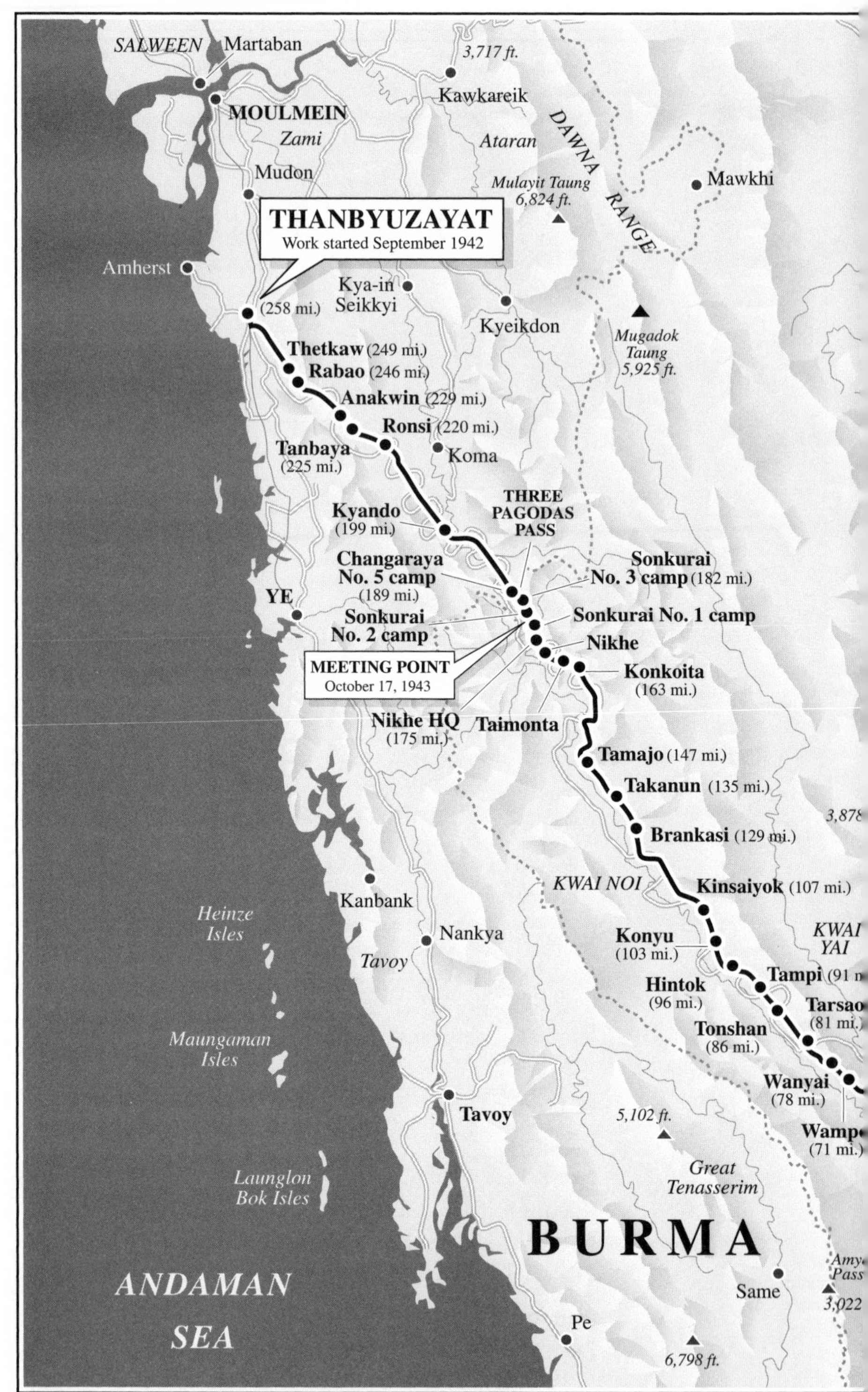

CONSTRUCTION OF THE BURMA-THAILAND RAILWAY

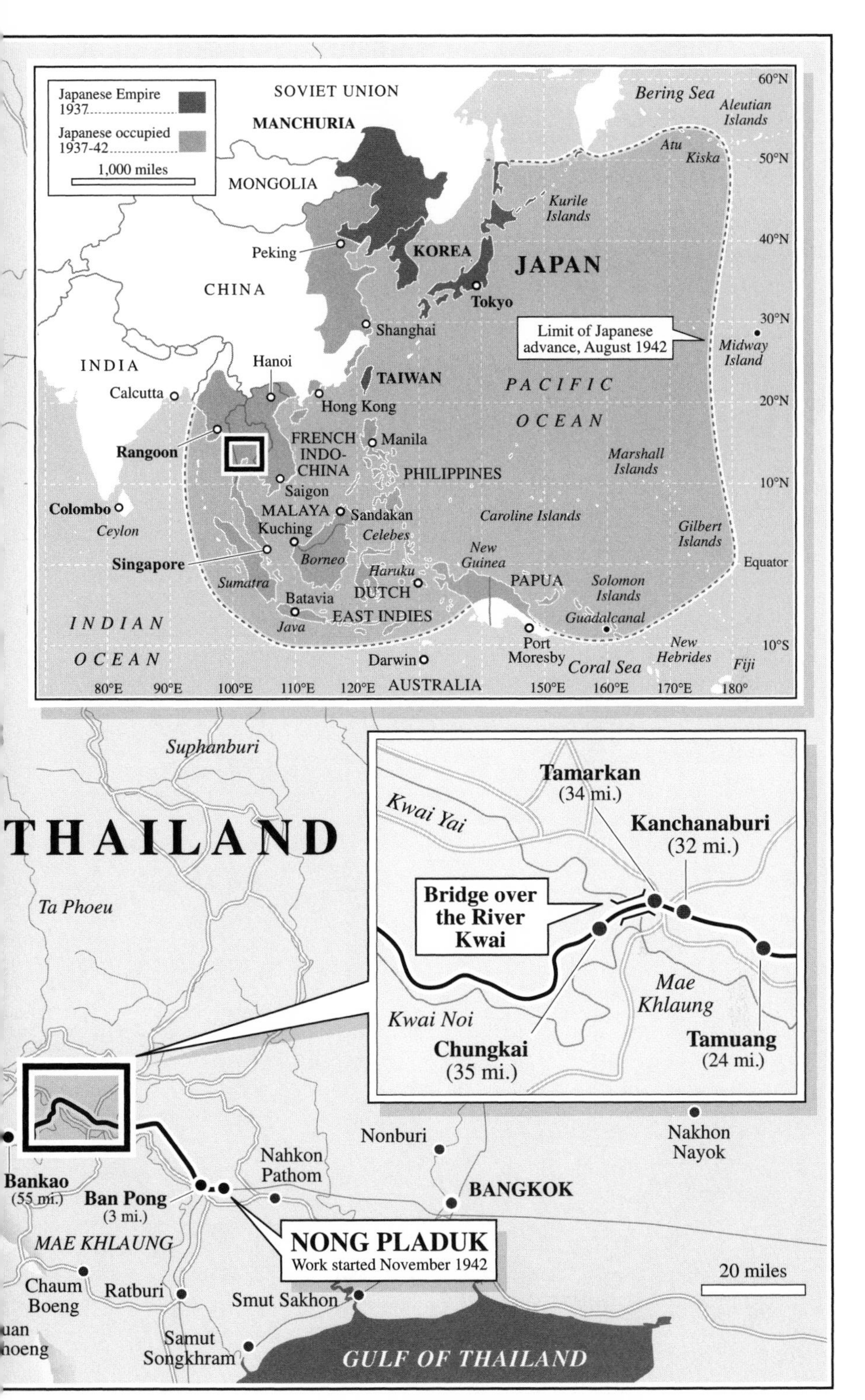

Japanese Empire 1937
Japanese occupied 1937-42
1,000 miles
SOVIET UNION
MANCHURIA
MONGOLIA
Bering Sea
Aleutian Islands
Atu
Kiska
Kurile Islands
Peking
KOREA
JAPAN
CHINA
Tokyo
Shanghai
Limit of Japanese advance, August 1942
Midway Island
INDIA
Hanoi
TAIWAN
Calcutta
Hong Kong
PACIFIC OCEAN
Rangoon
FRENCH INDO-CHINA
Manila
Marshall Islands
Saigon
PHILIPPINES
Colombo
Ceylon
MALAYA
Sandakan
Caroline Islands
Kuching
Celebes
Gilbert Islands
Singapore
Borneo
New Guinea
Haruku
PAPUA
Solomon Islands
Equator
Sumatra
Batavia
DUTCH EAST INDIES
Java
Guadalcanal
INDIAN OCEAN
Port Moresby
New Hebrides
Darwin
Coral Sea
Fiji
AUSTRALIA
60°N
50°N
40°N
30°N
20°N
10°N
10°S
80°E
90°E
100°E
110°E
120°E
150°E
160°E
170°E
180°
Suphanburi
THAILAND
Ta Phoeu
Tamarkan (34 mi.)
Kwai Yai
Kanchanaburi (32 mi.)
Bridge over the River Kwai
Mae Khlaung
Kwai Noi
Chungkai (35 mi.)
Tamuang (24 mi.)
Nonburi
Nakhon Nayok
Nahkon Pathom
Bankao (55 mi.)
Ban Pong (3 mi.)
BANGKOK
MAE KHLAUNG
NONG PLADUK
Work started November 1942
20 miles
Chaum Boeng
Ratburi
Smut Sakhon
Samut Songkhram
GULF OF THAILAND

THE "FEPOW" PRAYER

As we that are left grow old with the years,
Remembering the heartaches, the pain and the tears,
Hoping and praying that never again
Will man sink to such sorrow and shame,
The price that was paid—we will always remember
Every day, every month—not just in November.

Amen

INTRODUCTION

Sixty years on from 1945, we are all too aware of the horror of the Holocaust: the survivors have refused to let the world forget about the atrocities committed in Hitler's concentration camps. Other enduring images of the Second World War are mostly set in Europe, and culled from Hollywood films—*The Longest Day, A Bridge Too Far, The Guns of Navarone, The Dam Busters.* The British and American prisoners of war who were imprisoned in Germany are—justifiably—lauded in stories of how they escaped from captivity in such films as *Colditz, The Great Escape,* and *The Wooden Horse.* There is only one memorable film about the war in the Far East—*The Bridge on the River Kwai*—and its central theme—a British officer connives with the Japanese to thwart the blowing up of the bridge—is fiction, not fact. Although a few attempts succeeded, escape was generally out of the question in the jungles of Thailand, Burma, Borneo, and Sumatra. Most of the prisoners who escaped and were recaptured were executed. And if Hollywood has neglected these men, so too has the official British history of the war. Of its five volumes, only ten pages are devoted to Far East prisoners of war (Fepows), compared with 170 pages in the Australian history.

As we approach the sixtieth anniversary of Japan's surrender in August 1945, and as the surviving Fepows enter their eighties and nineties, it is time their story was told, especially to a new generation, most of whom remain ignorant of the suffering they endured. It is time we remembered the quality, the sacrifices, the suffering, and the courage of the Fepows.

As Japan's army conquered the Far East in 1941 and 1942, prisoners were taken in Singapore, Hong Kong, Malaya, Thailand, Java, Sumatra, Timor, Ambon, New Britain, Celebes, Guam, and the Philippines. According to the Tokyo War Crimes Tribunal, Japan took 132,142 Allied prisoners. More than fifty thousand British and Australians were captured in Singapore alone, forty-two thousand Dutch and ten thousand British in Java, and twenty-five thousand Americans in the Philippines. The worst experience for most British and Australians was the building of the Burma–Thailand railway; for the Americans, the Bataan death march and their journeys by sea to Japan from 1944. Such transportation of human cargo was common: by the end of the war there were significant numbers of prisoners in Taiwan, Sumatra, and Manchuria, as well as the Japanese home islands.

The most striking commentary on the treatment of the Fepows is provided by the death rate in Japanese prisoner-of-war camps: 27 percent of Japan's prisoners died in captivity, compared with 4 percent of Germany's. Twelve thousand deaths occurred during the building of the Burma–Thailand railway; perhaps one hundred thousand native laborers—"coolies," as they were described at the time—died on the same project.

Germany, which showed a brutal barbarity to many of its own citizens, was generally scrupulously law-abiding when dealing with British, American, and Australian prisoners. The commanders of Germany's prisoner-of-war camps followed the rules set out successively in the Hague Convention of 1907 and the Geneva Convention of 1929. Among the many articles in these documents were those stating that all prisoners except officers could be used for non-military work; that prisoners should be paid at the same rate as soldiers of the nation holding them captive; that they should be protected against acts of violence and insults; that freedom of religious worship must be allowed; and that if escaped prisoners were captured they were liable to disciplinary punishment. Japan, however, had never ratified the Geneva Convention (although it was a signatory), mainly because it proposed that prisoners should be treated in a different way from its own soldiers. Under Japanese military law, it was better to die with honor than live in the shame of captivity. Surrender was a punishable offense, and Japanese soldiers were expected to commit suicide rather than accept capture.

The Japanese government made its position known in 1942 through its legation in Bern. Japan was not bound by the Geneva Convention, it said, but would apply the convention as far as was possible—*mutatis mutandis* (with necessary changes)—to its prisoners, taking into consideration the customs of each nation and each race with respect to feeding and clothing. The result of that small phrase *mutatis mutandis,* as this book will show, was that Japan flouted almost all the significant rules of the Geneva Convention, which was why so many Fepows died. By Japanese standards, the men who were captured had shamed themselves; they were contemptible and expendable.

Another crucial factor in Japan's treatment of prisoners was race. Japan was leading a war of the "yellow" races against the hated imperialist "white" races. Its soldiers therefore relished their triumph. Japanese soldiers had been indoctrinated to consider the white nations as oppressors and themselves as descendants of the sons of heaven. Surrender was a shocking experience for all the Fepows who hailed from nations that had regarded themselves as invincible, especially against the "Nips." Singapore was believed to be an "impregnable fortress," but the Imperial Japanese Army outwitted and outmaneuvered the British and Australian forces and conquered Malaya and Singapore in just forty days.

This is not a story of unremitting cruelty. Not all of the Japanese and Korean guards in the camps were brutal, and not all of the camps were hells on earth. There were a few kindly guards in almost every camp, and the Japanese treated their own soldiers—and the Koreans—as brutally as they treated the prisoners. Captivity was a more bearable experience for the officers in Manchuria, Borneo, Taiwan, or Zentsuji in Japan than it was for the men. It was better to be a Fepow of any rank in Java than in Burma, Thailand, Sumatra, Fukuoka, or Sandakan, or on a "hellship" to Japan.

Generally, the prisoners conformed to national stereotypes. The British tried to preserve the class system, with the officers maintaining their privileges—but noblesse obliged, and they contributed some of their pay to support the sick and to establish canteens. The Australians were generous to their "cobbers," but were also considered the most skillful at robbing or tricking the Japanese. The Americans were the most entrepreneurial, but some of their rackets were worthy of the Mafia. There were inevitable tensions between the nationalities. The Americans "offended" the Australians because of their ignorance about other countries and an unsubstantiated superiority complex; they made insulting remarks about the menial status of Australia as a pawn of Britain. The Americans in turn found the Australians smug, opinionated, and inexplicably fond of the monarchy and pageantry. Both Australians and Americans saw the British as arrogant, stiff-necked, inflexible, and superior.

For most Britons, the war ended in May 1945, as was illustrated by the jubilant scenes of VE Day. But if the soldiers of the 14th Army commanded by General William Slim and still fighting in Burma were the "forgotten army," the Fepows were not only forgotten but forsaken. It took them more than fifty years to receive any proper compensation from the British government. Their disillusion was expressed in a poem by Bill Duncan:

I was crucified in Tarsao,
And again close by Hintok—
I was whipped along the River Valley Road;
I was driven, pierced and bleeding,
With a million maggots feeding
On the body that I carried for my load.

Yet my heart was still unbroken
And my hopes were still unquenched,
'Til I bore my cross to Blighty thro' a crowd;
Soldiers stabbed me on that road,
But at home, I dropped my load
When Politicians broke my legs and made my shroud.

At Westminster, my poor body,
Wrapped in linen of fine words,
Was perfumed with their sweetly scented lies,
And they laid me in the tomb,
Of their golden-mirrored room,
With the other lads who had refused to die.

Once their war was over, they were so scarred by their experiences—most for life—that they could not discuss them even with their wives and close family. They believed that their experiences at the hands of the Japanese were, literally, incomprehensible. On his return home, Lt. Eric Lomax wanted to tell his new wife about his experiences, but she brushed aside his attempts to describe the Burma–Thailand railway, where he was tortured. She claimed that she had also had a hard time during the war. So Lomax was expected to behave as though his formative years had never happened. "I am sure," he wrote in *The Railway Man,* "that tens of thousands of returning soldiers walked bewildered into the same incomprehension. It was as though we were speaking a different language to our own people. The hurt I felt silenced me as effectively as a gag." Old friends hadn't really changed, said Ian Watt. "But I had and they didn't know it. But I did."

Only after thirty years—and perhaps with the arrival of grandchildren or the approach of death—did many start to tell or write their stories. One of the most comprehensive diaries was kept by the legendary Australian medical officer Sir Edward "Weary" Dunlop, but it was not published until thirty-three years after he was liberated. One prisoner's name is a pseudonym: before he died he asked his son-in-law to ensure that no other member of his family should read his account; that they should not even know that it existed. What he had written would be "too distressing." That self-effacement reinforced the Fepows' sense of isolation, as the less fuss they made, the more they were ignored.

An incident when a Japanese or Korean guard is beating you or a friend is never forgotten, but after fifty years the memory fades. That is why the most important memorial of the Fepows lies in their diaries and drawings (there are only a few photographic records, most notably taken by the Australian George Aspinall). More than 150 of the diaries and archives kept by British, Australian, and American prisoners form the foundation of this book, and they are complemented by personal accounts published as books, many of them based on contemporary notes. Most of the diaries were written, raw, on the day or within days of the events they described, in the heat of the moment. One of Dunlop's reservations about publishing his diary was that it was a "hymn of hate written in a mood." The men's quarters were constantly being searched and the diarists risked their lives for putting pen to paper, but they were determined that posterity should know how they were being treated. There were many hiding places, including sealed bottles buried in graves. When the guards were searching the men's huts at Tamarkan in Thailand, the Australians hid Roy Whitecross's diary inside a small tin, which was buried under the floor of a toolshed exactly thirty-seven paces south of a well. It was exhumed eighteen months later. John Milford buried his in an old biscuit tin. The Australian doctor Rowley Richards made a summary of his diary on the thinnest paper he could find, rolled it up, and inserted it into the tubing of his stethoscope; the rest he put into the bottom of a beer bottle salvaged from the guards' refuse, sealed it with candlewax, and buried it in a grave. George Aspinall's photographic negatives and prints were hidden down a latrine. When Ian Watt returned to the camp at Tamarkan, where the bridge on the River Kwai was built, on August 17, 1945, two days after Japan's surrender, he found scores of prisoners circling about with their eyes scouring the ground. They were looking for diaries, letters, and pictures they had buried.

In the almost total absence of photographs, it is sketches, drawings, and paintings by such artists as Ronald Searle, Jack Chalker, Charles Thrale, Leo Rawlings, and Philip Meninsky that provide vivid visual records, and these also had to be ingeniously hidden (except for the portraits the guards requested of themselves). The artists used any paper they could purloin—tissue, music scores, cardboard, scrap, stolen sheets of Japanese toilet paper and notepaper. They made brushes from human hair and paint from jungle roots, clay, India ink, crushed pencils, rice water, blood, crushed leaves, and brass polish. Their work was encouraged by the senior officers, who wished posterity to witness the conditions of captivity under the Japanese.

The soldiers' diaries do not tell the whole truth of captivity. This book does not include the stories of the civilian internees and touches only tangentially on the plight of the "coolies." But the diaries reveal the hardships suffered over three and a half years, and the aim of this book is to speak in the voices of the Fepows themselves. They tell inspirational stories of how the men survived nearly sixteen hundred days of captivity, starvation, disease, and torture, and they record compassion to comrades in distress, stories about eating cats, dogs, rats, and snakes, tales of coping with sickness and disease, details of camp "universities," and accounts of entertainment and military discipline within the camps. There are less noble stories, too, about the thieves, robbers, criminals, and black marketeers among both men and officers. They are all intensely human stories.

According to Ronald Searle, when the Fepows' memories of Singapore, Thailand, Malaya, Burma, and Indonesia have vanished, their story will be a mere milestone in history. All the personal misery and suffering that captivity entailed will become simply words on a page. Meanwhile, he says, the Fepows have been described as members of the world's "most exclusive and impenetrable" club:

> This is not as silly as it might sound. When one has touched bottom, become the lowest of the low and unwillingly plumbed the depths of human misery, there comes from it a silent understanding and appreciation of what solidarity, friendship and human kindness to others can mean. Something that is difficult to explain to those unfortunates who are on the outside of our "club," who have never experienced what it means to be dirt and yet be privileged to be surrounded by life-saving comradeship.

PART ONE

Chapter 1

SURRENDER

At 6:15 P.M. on December 6, 1941, Emperor Hirohito presided over a solemn feast with his closest advisers at Omiya Gosho, his mother's palace in Tokyo. They toasted the spirits of his commanders in the field and heard a prayer of supplication and benediction from the Emperor, Japan's high priest. Nine hours later—at 7:40 A.M. in Hawaii—Japan launched its war against the United States with a devastating attack on Pearl Harbor. President Franklin Roosevelt declared that December 7, 1941, was a date that would live in infamy. Attacking with 183 planes, the Japanese sank 3 battleships, destroyed 120 planes and killed 2,403 servicemen. When Roosevelt declared war on Japan, a true world war had begun.

An hour before Pearl Harbor, Japan had attacked British territory in Malaya. Assault boats landed on the beaches at Kota Bharu, quickly overran the Anglo-Indian barbed-wire defenses, captured the airfield, and established Japanese air superiority over northern Malaya. Meanwhile, after landing with his mobile and mechanized 5th Division, the best in the Japanese army, Lt. Gen. Yamashita, the "Tiger of Malaya," had established the HQ of Japan's 25th Army in southern Thailand and had immediately begun advancing down the peninsula that connected Thailand and Bangkok to Malaya and Singapore. On December 11, thirteen miles south of the Thai-Malay border, they quickly overcame the first resistance at Jitra. The town was defended by twenty thousand British and Indian troops, but they abandoned it that evening, allowing food, ammunition, guns, trucks, and armored cars to fall into Japanese hands. The Indians had never seen a tank, and the British armored cars had been made by Rolls-Royce for the First World War.

The task of defending the rest of Malaya against Yamashita and his chief staff officer, the thirty-eight-year-old Lt. Col. Masanobu Tsuji, the fanatical planner of Japan's campaign (who had tutored Prince Makasa, the brightest of Hirohito's brothers), fell to Lt. Gen. Arthur Percival, who had taken command in May 1941. At the age of twenty-six, Percival had volunteered on the first day of the First World War; during that conflict he would win the Distinguished Service Order, the Military Cross, and the French Croix de Guerre. He had been a soldier for twenty-seven years, mainly in staff positions. But in Malaya, now aged fifty-three, he had jumped directly from commanding a division in England to commanding an army, and an independent, multinational, polyglot army at that. As Gen. Clifford Kinvig has observed, it was the most demanding elevation of the war.

Percival commanded 100,000 men in one British, one Australian, and three Indian divisions. They were joined during the campaign by another 7,000 Indian and 30,000 British troops, some of whom would land in Singapore only in January. Set against him were three Japanese divisions, the 5th, the 18th, and the 2nd Imperial Guards, with a front-line strength of 60,000 men. This was the strongest invasion force that Japan had ever sent to war and included most of the army's tank forces and the best artillery, mortar, and machine-gun units, as well as small-boat and jungle commandos, bicycle troops, and bridge and railway engineers.

Inspired by Hirohito, the Japanese were fighting for an Asia for the Asiatics. The aim of the war, according to the Emperor, was to eradicate the "source of evil" and to see an enduring peace established in East Asia. It was a war between the yellow and white races in which the white commanders gravely underestimated the strength, caliber, and fanaticism of their enemy. Before they sailed, all the Japanese troops had been issued an anti-West manual entitled *Just Read This and the War Is Won*. Their job, it declared, was to set Asia free.

> When you encounter the enemy after landing, regard yourself as an avenger come at last face to face with his father's murderer. Here before you is the man whose death will lighten your heart of its burden of brooding anger. If you fail to destroy him utterly you can never rest at peace. And the first blow is the vital blow. Westerners—being very superior people, very effeminate, and very cowardly—have an intense dislike of fighting in the rain or the mist or at night . . . By jungle is meant dense forest in which a large variety of trees, grasses and thorny plants are all closely entangled together. Such places are the haunts of dangerous animals,

> poisonous snakes and harmful insects . . . This type of terrain is regarded by the weak-spirited Westerners as impenetrable, and for this reason—in order to outmanoeuvre them—we must from time to time force our way through it . . . You must demonstrate to the world the true worth of Japanese manhood. The implementation of the task of the Showa Restoration [the reign of Hirohito], which is to realize His Imperial Majesty's desire for peace in the Far East, and to set Asia free, rests squarely on our shoulders.
>
> *Corpses drifting swollen in the sea-depths,*
> *Corpses rotting in the mountain-grass—*
> *We shall die. By the side of our lord we shall die,*
> *We shall not look back.*

That warrior spirit of the Japanese had also been celebrated in the Japanese Field Army Service Code of January 1941. "You shall not undergo the shame of being taken alive. You shall not bequeath a sullied name," it said. "After exerting all your powers, spiritually and physically, calmly face death rejoicing in the eternal cause for which you strive."

At Jitra, Tsuji used the tactics which were followed throughout the Malaya campaign. Soldiers forded rivers and infiltrated behind enemy lines, enabling engineers to repair damaged bridges. Tanks then moved forward until stopped by another unbridged river. The infantry used collapsible bicycles which could be carried on their backs across streams. Using bicycles in war was incomprehensible to the British, but the bicycle troops moved so quickly that they put pressure on the retreating British. They could also clear derelict armor from the road. Yamashita, meanwhile, used flanking movements in which troops proficient in jungle fighting turned British lines by getting through swamps and other "impassable" terrain. Small-boat parties moving down the west coast infiltrated deep behind the British lines, creating a fear of encirclement among the British.

By February 1, twenty thousand Indian troops had surrendered, and Percival withdrew the British troops to Singapore. The rear was brought up by the ninety survivors of the Argyll and Sutherland Highlanders, with bagpipes defiantly playing "Highland Laddie" and "Jeannie with the Light Brown Hair." The landward end of the causeway linking Singapore and Malaya was dynamited, but the Japanese arrived by night a week later. Gen. Wavell, the British Commander in Chief in the Far East, who had moved to Java, attempted to stiffen the British resistance in an order of the day on February 10. Britain's fighting reputation and the honor of the British Empire were at stake, he said. The Americans had held out in the Bataan Peninsula against far heavier odds, the Russians were turning back the Germans at Stalingrad, and the Chinese, with an almost complete lack of modern equipment, had held the Japanese for four and a half years.

> It will be disgraceful if we yield our boasted fortress of Singapore to inferior forces. There must be no thought of sparing the troops or civil population and no mercy must be shown to weakness in any shape or form. Commanders and senior officers must lead their troops and if necessary die with them. There must be no question or thought of surrender. Every unit must fight it out to the end and in close contact with the enemy . . . I look to you and your men to fight to the end to prove that the fighting spirit that won our Empire still exists to enable us to defend it.

In spite of the exhortation from Wavell, the Japanese continued their relentless advance. By February 13, Percival and Lt. Gen. Sir Lewis Heath, Commander of the 3rd Indian Corps, had agreed that the British might be forced to surrender. Maj. Cyril Wild, one of Heath's staff officers, who had worked in Japan before the war and spoke fluent Japanese, was asked to be ready to go through the lines and contact the enemy. That day a Japanese force invaded the Alexandra Barracks Hospital and bayoneted to death 323 people, including 230 patients, many in their beds or on operating tables. It was a chilling demonstration by the Japanese army of their merciless brutality. Afterward, survivors were returned to the British lines as a warning of what might happen in the future if the British did not surrender.

At 9 A.M. on February 15, Percival held his final conference in the underground "battle-box" of the British HQ in Fort Canning. The situation was grim. The meeting was told that ammunition would run out that day and water the next. There was no dissent when the decision to surrender was made. Wild was with the first party that drove through the front line to meet the Japanese at a small villa off the Bukit Timah Road and then accompanied Percival to the meeting with Yamashita at which it was agreed to surrender at 8:30 P.M. Yamashita had been preparing to launch his final assault on Singapore two hours later. "Few acquainted with the situation could doubt that had Yamashita attacked that night he would have broken clean through to the sea, splitting the garrison in two," Wild said later. "The half million citizens of Singapore would then have shared the fate of those of Nanching and Hangchow. As it was, Yamashita never allowed his three divisions to enter the city after the capitulation." Within seventy days, Yamashita's army had marched 650 miles down a road through the jungle, repeatedly overcoming the Allied troops, crossed the Johore Strait, and conquered Singapore, the "impregnable fortress." (Wild was to have the satisfaction of being the sole member of the surrender party who witnessed the formal surrender of the Japanese to Lord Mountbatten in September 1945. He also interrogated Yamashita in Manila on the day before the latter's trial. Yamashita was hanged in February 1946.)

Judged against what occurred elsewhere as the Japanese army advanced, the prisoners taken in Singapore were fortunate. On New Britain Island there were at least four separate massacres of prisoners on February 4, in which more than 140 Australians were shot or bayoneted to death at the Tol Plantation, where the Japanese had set up their headquarters. The prisoners' thumbs were tied together behind their backs, then they were bound by cords or belts passed between their arms, grouped into twos and threes, and led into the jungle. The Japanese stood over the prisoners to stab them, said Pte. Bill Cook, who was serving with the 2/10th Field Ambulance:

> I received six wounds in the back—two just missing the spine, two more breaking ribs, one under the shoulder blade and the other sliding across the shoulder blade. My two companions had not uttered a sound. I think one of them must have died very quickly and the other lingered a short time because, when the Japs started to leave us, he groaned a little and one of the Japs returned and stabbed him again. I had been holding my breath and feigning death but could not hold it any longer. When I breathed again, I either made a noise or moved, and the Jap started on me again, stabbed me another four times in the neck and another through the ear, which entered my face at the temple, severing the temporal artery, and the point of the blade finished in my mouth. Each of the wounds which I received had not hurt a great deal, except the last, which grated across the cheek bone and, when he withdrew the bayonet, it lifted my head. Blood spurted from my mouth. He then covered the three of us with palm leaves and bushes, and left us. I just lay there waiting to die and I heard two distinct shots followed by a scattered volley of rifle shots which meant that the last two had been shot.

When the guards left, Cook managed to free himself by chewing through the cord and then staggered fifty yards to the sea to let the salt wash his wounds. The next morning he found a small party of his countrymen and eventually escaped to Australia.

The Americans on the Bataan Peninsula in the Philippines suffered an even more pitiless and brutal introduction to captivity under the Japanese. The treatment of prisoners on the "Bataan death march," although it lasted only days, was as vicious as the treatment of the men on the Burma–Thailand railway and was the worst atrocity committed by the Japanese against U.S. prisoners. When the Americans on Bataan surrendered on April 9, between eleven thousand and twelve thousand of them became prisoners, as well as more than fifty thousand Filipinos. There are no exact figures, but at least six hundred Americans and five thousand Filipinos died as they marched seventy-five miles in temperatures of 90°F from Balanga to San Fernando, where they were put on trains to Camp O'Donnell. Another one thousand Americans and sixteen thousand Filipinos died within the following six weeks.

When Gen. Edward King had negotiated surrender with Lt. Gen. Masaharu Homma, he had asked if his troops would be well treated. "We are not barbarians," Homma's interpreter had snapped. The prisoners would be given "humane and honourable" treatment. Some were indeed aided by a few sympathetic guards, and a few thousand men escaped the march to be transported to San Fernando in trucks. But they were the exceptions. King had reserved enough transport and petrol to get his troops out of Bataan. He offered them to the Japanese, but his offer was ignored. In spite of the promise of "humane" treatment, the marchers, most suffering from malaria and dysentery compounded by malnutrition, some wounded, set out without food or water. What food they received was thrown at them by sympathetic Filipinos. As they marched they were beaten, bayoneted, starved, and kicked with hobnail boots. Men who lagged behind were immediately, brutally, beaten and bayoneted.

One marcher was Maj. William "Ed" Dyess, a twenty-six-year-old, six-foot-tall Texan from the farming community of Albany, a fighter pilot who had become an infantryman on Bataan. After his stay at O'Donnell, Dyess was imprisoned first at Cabanatuan and then at Datao, from which he was part of a daring escape that eventually got him back to America. He became a hero after his story of the march was told in newspapers and alerted Americans to the crimes that were being committed against prisoners. The first murder on Dyess's march from Balanga occurred when Japanese yen were found on an officer during the initial search of the prisoners' possessions:

> The big Jap looked at the money. Without a word he grabbed the captain by the shoulder and shoved him down to his knees. He pulled the sword out of the scabbard and raised it high over his head, holding it with both hands. The private skipped to one side. Before we could grasp what was happening, the blackfaced giant had swung his sword. I remember how the sun flashed on it. There was a swish and a kind of chopping thud,

> like a cleaver going through beef. The captain's head seemed to jump off his shoulders. It hit the ground in front of him and went rolling crazily from side to side between the lines of prisoners.

After that the guards beat and hit the men and looted their watches, pens, and money. Then the men, who had not eaten for four days, started marching. Coming toward them were "seemingly interminable" columns of Japanese infantry, truck trains, and horse-drawn artillery moving into Bataan for the assault on Corregidor. Dyess, reasoning that it would help morale, mustered the 110 officers and men of the 21st Pursuit and they marched together. When they tried to help some sick and wounded American soldiers found in the ruins of a bombed hospital, they were kicked or jabbed with bayonet points by the guards. They were marched into a clearing and seated on the scorching ground, many with no protection from the sun:

> When I thought I could stand the penetrating heat no longer, I was determined to have a sip of the tepid water in my canteen. I had no more than unscrewed the top when the aluminum flask was snatched from my hands. The Jap who had crept up behind me poured the water into a horse's nosebag, then threw down the canteen. He walked on among the prisoners, taking away their water and pouring it into the bag. When he had enough he gave it to his horse.

Dyess had marched another mile when he stumbled over a Filipino soldier writhing in the dust of the road after having been bayoneted through the stomach. A quarter of a mile farther on there was another who had been crushed beneath the trucks. Soon such smashed corpses became commonplace. They marched until midnight, when they were herded into a paddy field—but there was no room to lie down. Some of the men tried to rest in a half squat; others drew up their knees and laid their heads on the legs of men next to them. Japanese guards stood around the edges of the field, their feet almost touching the outer fringe of men. Dyess heard a cry, followed by thudding blows at one side of the paddy. "An American soldier so tortured by the thirst that he could not sleep had asked a Jap guard for water. The Jap fell on him with his fists, then slugged him into insensibility with a rifle butt."

Soon the roadside was littered with dead bodies; the marchers eventually stopped trying to count them.

Until the war was over, Dyess was the main witness to the horror of the death march. But at the Tokyo War Crimes Trial in 1946, other marchers described equally barbaric scenes. Staff Sgt. Samuel Moody reported that a friend of his, Sgt. Jones, fell sick with dysentery after drinking muddy water and had to stay behind on the roadside. He was bayoneted several times, beaten, and killed. Col. Stubbs, who was on Gen. King's staff, saw Japanese guards start to bury five uniformed Filipino soldiers after throwing them in a latrine. Another Filipino was made to eat his own excrement. The wounded soldier D. F. Ingle was lying on a stretcher with a temperature of 105°F when he was prodded with a bayonet and ordered to sit up. A Japanese soldier looted his watch, ring, and wallet, and ordered him to march. The only water he received for the next nine days was from ponds and ditches. It was so polluted, Ingle testified, that it was highly dangerous:

> That which came from the artesian wells was of such a small amount that when great numbers of men tried to get it, the Japanese troops would simply raise their rifles and fire into the group, and when the smoke and dust had cleared away it showed that pure water could cause your death as well as that which was polluted.
>
> The Filipino civilians tried on many occasions to give us food, but they did so at the risk of their lives and, indeed, many lost their lives so doing. Apart from that, only an occasional sugar cane patch offered the chance of food, but to try and get some was courting death.

The second day's march resumed at dawn. More American and Filipino prisoners were struck down. Others simply reached the end of their endurance and, as Dyess witnessed, were shot by the guards as they fell:

> There was a sharp crackle of pistol and rifle fire behind us. Skulking along, a hundred yards behind our contingent, came a "clean-up squad" of murdering Jap buzzards. Their helpless victims, sprawled darkly against the white of the road, were easy targets. As members of the murder squad stooped over each huddled form, there would be an orange flash in the darkness and a sharp report. The bodies were left where they lay, that other prisoners coming behind us might see them. Our Japanese guards enjoyed the spectacle in silence for a time. Eventually, one of them who spoke English felt he should add a little spice to the entertainment. "Sleepee?" he asked. "You want sleep? Just lie down on road. You get good, long sleep!" On through the night we were followed by orange flashes and thudding shots.

As the men approached Orani they were overwhelmed by the stench—ever-increasing numbers were suffering from dysentery and fouling the ground with diseased excrement. Dyess and his comrades had marched thirty miles in twenty-one hours and were like zombies. They "rested" for a day, but the heat of the sun turned many delirious and they began lapsing into comas and dying. Then the grave-digging began. The men marching with Dyess thought that they had seen every atrocity that the Japanese could offer. But they were wrong.

> The shallow trenches had been completed. The dead were being rolled into them. Just then an American soldier and two Filipinos were carried out of the compound. They had been delirious. Now they were in a coma. A Jap noncom stopped the bearers and tipped the unconscious men into the trench. The Japs then ordered the burial detail to fill it up. The Filipinos lay lifelessly in the hole. As the earth began falling about the American, he revived and tried to climb out. His fingers gripped the edge of the grave. He hoisted himself to a standing position. Two Jap guards placed bayonets at the throat of a Filipino on the burial detail. They gave him an order. When he hesitated they pressed the bayonet points hard against his neck. The Filipino raised a stricken face to the sky. Then he brought his shovel down upon the head of his American comrade, who fell backward to the bottom of the grave. The burial detail filled it up.

On the fourth day the men with Dyess got a saucerful of sticky gray rice, but many were still delirious or dying. At sunset they marched again along a road lined with artesian wells but weren't allowed to drink (though men with cups profited from rain). Men continued to fall—a flash and the crack of a shot announced that they were being executed. Dyess stopped counting. After a short rest before dawn, they were prodded awake and started again, now marching through the flat, marshy land of Pampanga province. The splashing of an artesian well was too much for six Filipinos:

> Jap guards all along the line raised their rifles and waited for the six to scramble into the grassy ditch and go up on the opposite side, a few feet from the well. Most of the Filipinos fell at the first volley. Two of them, desperately wounded, kept inching toward the water, their hands outstretched. The Japs fired again and again, until all six lay dead. Thus did our fifth day of the death march start with a bloodbath. I needed all the control I could muster. Men had been murdered behind me all night, but the deeds had been veiled by darkness. There had been nothing to veil the pitilessness and wantonness of the murders I had just seen. I walked a long time with my head down and no doubt my cultivated ability to do

> this saved my sanity on more than one occasion in the days to come. I remember little of the two miles we walked after the six murders at the well. We were at the outskirts of Lubao, a sprawling city of 30,000 before mutterings about me brought me back to earth to look upon a new horror.
>
> I saw that all eyes were directed toward an object hanging on a barbed-wire fence that paralleled the road. It had been a Filipino soldier. The victim had been bayoneted. His abdomen was open. The bowels had been wrenched loose and were hanging like great grayish purple ropes along the strands of wire that supported the mutilated body. This was a Japanese object lesson, of course. But it carried terrible implications. The Japs apparently had wearied of mere shootings and simple bayonetings. These had served only to whet the barbaric appetite. What might lie ahead for all of us we could only guess.

As they passed through Lubao, sympathetic Filipinos tossed food—bread, rice cakes, eggs, lumps of sugar, chocolate—and cigarettes to the men. The guards retaliated by beating them with their rifles, stamping on the food, and attacking the marchers. When they finally reached Guaga, and could see the railway, they had marched seventy-five miles on a single saucerful of rice. Two soldiers near collapse were put into a cart by an American colonel who noticed there was no guard nearby. But they were soon discovered:

> Yammering Jap guards pulled the three Americans from the cart and dragged the Filipino from the driver's seat. A stocky Jap noncommissioned officer seized the heavy horsewhip. The enlisted men were flogged first. The crackling lash slashed their faces and tore their clothing. The searing pain revived them for a moment. They fell to the ground. The blows thudded upon their bodies. The colonel next. He stood his punishment a long time. His fortitude enraged the Jap, who put all his strength behind the lash. When the American officer finally dropped to his knees his face was so crisscrossed with bloody welts it was unrecognizable. The trembling Filipino driver fell at the first cut of the whip. He writhed on the ground. The lash tore his shirt and the flesh beneath it. His face was lacerated and one eye swollen shut. When the whipper grew weary, he ordered the driver on his way. The colonel, bleeding and staggering, was kicked back into the line of American prisoners.

Dyess never saw the two soldiers again.

When Sgt. Earl Dodson reached San Fernando there was a seemingly endless queue for water. He spent most of the night in line. When he reached the tap he had crawled on all fours for the last hour. At San Fernando the men were put in a barbed-wire compound packed with sick, dying, and dead marchers, sprawled amid the filth and maggots that covered the ground. Nearly all had dysentery, said Dyess. Malaria and dengue fever were rife, too. The worst cases were put beneath the floors of a dilapidated building. On April 16 they were marched to a railway siding where they were packed 115 men to each truck for the three-hour journey to Camp O'Donnell. They looked so wretched when they got out of the trucks that there were cries of compassion from Filipino civilians lining the tracks. For the Americans, as for the British, Australians, and Dutch, the years of captivity had begun.

> As we stood, staring dazedly, there came to me a premonition that hundreds about to enter O'Donnell prison this April day never would leave it alive. If I could have known what lay in store for us all, I think I would have given up the ghost then and there. Sharp commands by the Jap guards aroused me. We started moving.

The fall of Singapore a few weeks before the Bataan death march had shattered Britain's pretensions as an imperial power. It was the worst disaster and largest capitulation in British history, said Churchill. The Japanese had conquered the British within a week of first setting foot on the island. A special correspondent of *The Times* reported in a famous dispatch that time and time again the Japanese had shown that natural features such as rivers, creeks, and swamps, which the Allies regarded as obstacles, were avenues of penetration. There were not enough Allied troops, he wrote, while those who were fighting were exhausted, dispirited, unfit, and relentlessly bombarded because the Japanese had complete ascendancy in the air. "The absence of forceful leadership," he added, "made itself felt from the top downwards. The material of the men was potentially good. Something was lacking to crystallise it, to co-ordinate it, to infuse it with the fire of confidence." He excepted the Australians from this assessment.

Many junior officers agreed with his analysis. They believed that untrained men, unblooded in jungle warfare, had been sacrificed in a lost cause to placate American and Australian public opinion, which was more concerned by the Japanese in the Far East than by the Germans in Europe. Lt. Stephen Abbott had seen the "muddled incompetence" surrounding Percival when he was briefly drafted to the Combined Operations Room, an analysis endorsed by Cyril Wild's experience during the surrender negotiations. Orders were given, countermanded, then renewed, Abbott observed, often within the hour. Off-duty officers were usually found at the Tanglin Club, the Swimming Club, or Raffles Hotel, and twice Abbott had to cycle to locate officers for whom he had urgent messages. His faith, morale, and optimism were destroyed on January 28 when he discovered that no final decisions had been made on the location of defensive positions on the island. As he and three colleagues toured the north shore they learned that no preparatory work had been done. Nowhere did they find a single trench, strand of wire, or fortified post. The beaches were bare. Behind lay the dense, untouched jungle.

The days that followed were a nightmare of weary confusion for Abbott—a succession of bewildering conferences, orders, counter-orders, contradictory orders, and long treks through the jungle and swamp in search of obscure map references. The area his battalion was to defend was altered five times. On February 14 he collapsed by the roadside and slept for sixteen hours. When he was woken up the next day, Percival had surrendered.

More than one hundred thousand troops were now prisoners of the Japanese in Singapore, and more than eleven thousand had been captured during the fighting in Malaya, mostly Indian officers and men. They had failed to act by Japan's code of Bushido, the "Way of the Warrior," and had shamed themselves by surrendering rather than dying in battle. There were 38,496 British, 18,490 Australians, 67,340 Indian, and 14,382 volunteers recruited locally. The contempt of the Japanese military for prisoners of war was all the greater because they regarded captivity as the final degradation of the male spirit, said Laurens van der Post, who became a prisoner in Java. The Japanese would take their own lives by the hundreds of thousands rather than endure the disgrace of falling into enemy hands. Whether consciously or subconsciously, moreover, they saw themselves as instruments of a kind of accumulated revenge of history on the European for his invasion of the ancient worlds of the East, and his arrogant assumptions of superiority that had seen him bend the lives and spirits of the Asian people to his inflexible will. The fact that the European had brought also to the Far East his great Roman virtues was for the moment forgotten, said Van der Post:

> All that mattered was that for centuries his powerful presence had prevented the peoples of the Far East, so diverse in character and culture, from being their own special selves. These processes of frustration indeed had been carried on for so long that it was almost as if the peoples of Asia had only to come into the presence of a European to be hypnotised out of being themselves, and forced to live a kind of tranced life in his presence that was not their own. But now the spell was broken, and the built-up flood of resentment following centuries of frustration had

> broken through all restraints. Out in full spate, in the open at last, it swept the Japanese, normally so disciplined, but now drunk on what for the moment appeared to be invincible military power, into a chaotic mood of revenge on those who belonged to the world which had been responsible for that resentment.

Within five months of the attack on Pearl Harbor, Japan had conquered Hong Kong, Malaya, Singapore, Burma, Java, Sumatra, Borneo, the Philippines, and all the islands in the western Pacific. By May 1942, its new empire embraced 110 million people across five time zones and stretched four thousand miles in each direction. Over the next three and a half years the spirit of Bushido was to dominate the lives—and the deaths—of the men who had become prisoners of the Japanese.

INTERLUDE

"We Feel Let Down Rather"

Another young junior officer who reflected on the extent of the British defeat at Singapore was 2nd Lt. Louis Baume, who came from a well-known Swiss watchmaking company with offices in London's Hatton Garden. Baume had been posted to the 137th Field Regiment, 11th India Division, Royal Artillery, at Larkshill in England in July 1941. Now, seven months later, at the age of twenty-two, he was a prisoner of the Japanese.

> So it is all over. Prisoners; defeated we feel let down rather—no planes, no ships, no tanks, except in half-penny numbers; outnumbered, out-manoeuvred and out-bluffed by those little yellow bastards. Was it Churchill or Roosevelt (or just Malaya Command?) who said "Hold on until February 15th and the skies of Singapore will be darkened with our planes?" Yes, they are dark, dark with the thick black clouds gushing from blazing petrol dumps and the acrid smoke of many fires burning in the town

and docks—black clouds stretching miles across the Island and far out to sea, blotting out the sun. Night has come. I foresaw all sorts of possibilities except this one—just waiting to be collected by the enemy; waiting for what? We prefer not to think. Gloom, disappointment, relief, resentment, uncertainty, bewilderment—these are our mixed feelings this evening. It seems incredible that we are finished, that it's all over; everything seems so deathly still now: only the distant crackling of flames and the steady drone of bombers flying over the city, a stillness punctuated by the occasional bursting of burning petrol drums.

Chapter 2

CHANGI

On February 17, 1942, the captured British and Australian troops of Singapore were ordered to gather all the food and clothing they could carry and march fifteen to twenty miles into captivity in the Changi area, at the northeast tip of the island. The march was a humiliation for all of them. As they tramped through sweltering tropical heat, Japanese soldiers stood guard along the route, their rifles and bayonets often taller than they were. Some forced the "dirty, thirsty, sweaty and demoralised herd of losers," as Signaller Ronald Searle described them, to surrender watches and rings until word went down the line and the men started hiding them. The local population—Chinese, Malay, and Indian—stood on the roadside waving Japanese flags. Where Union Jacks had been flown a week earlier, the red orb of the Japanese standard now hung from many buildings.

The men marched through the streets of Singapore, littered with the detritus of war, then through the swamps and trees, passing native villages and coconut and rubber plantations, hour after hour, until all that could be seen to the end of the road were troops, troops, and more troops, in step, out of step, heaving and swaying, khaki as far as the eye could see. "Where have all these sprung from?" wondered twenty-six-year-old Capt. Richard Sharp, who had landed at Singapore only ten days earlier but had been mentioned in dispatches for conspicuous gallantry. "How were we defeated, and these still fit? And past them all, lorries career by in defiance of Jap orders, carrying stores, provisions and anything they think will come in handy."

For Lt. Stephen Abbott, still angry about surrender and disillusioned with the British leadership, it was a dismal parade:

> As the long columns of prisoners marched by, we were greeted only by pitiful looks and silence. Here and there a Chinese would raise his thumbs with a faint smile and an understanding wink; but suffering, and the fear of greater suffering were too deep in the hearts of these people to allow them a show of friendliness or loyalty. Who could blame them? Who had assured them of their safety within this "fortress"? Like most of my fellow prisoners I felt a terrible weight of personal guilt. The disgrace of the Malayan campaign could never be exonerated or forgiven.

An estimated 41,500 men arrived at Changi that night, followed by another 10,700 the next day. Their new prison camp had been a military showcase. The four three-story barracks were set in almost ten square miles of green, undulating parkland, overlooking the sea and dotted with trees and ornamental shrubs—bougainvillea, temple flowers, and yellow cassia. It seemed almost palatial to some of the men, and had been one of the most popular military stations in the world. Each barracks had its own officers' quarters and mess, married officers' bungalows, quarters for married warrant officers, sergeants, and men, all with verandas, and regimental stores. There were churches, canteens, theaters and cinemas, garages, squash courts, playing fields, workshops, piers and jetties, bathing beaches, yacht clubs and tennis courts, swimming pools and guardhouses. Near by was the forbidding Changi Jail, Singapore's main prison. It was easy to see where much of the money voted for the "Great Island Fortress" had been spent, Capt. C. F. Blackater, still disillusioned after the surrender, reflected: it had gone not on fortification, but on Changi and the naval base.

British engineers had deliberately destroyed the water supply before the surrender; water was therefore rationed while wells were dug. There was also no power and no sewer system. The barracks, moreover, had been "bombed to hell"; the ammunition dumps had been blown up and the ground was littered with unexploded mortar shells and bombs. The roads were cratered, the walls were pitted and scarred, and there were craters on the parade ground at Selarang Barracks, which the Australians occupied. The British were at the Roberts, India, and Kitchener barracks. The sick and wounded were crowded into Roberts Hospital.

The Japanese were overwhelmed by the number of prisoners they had taken. For the first days at Changi, the men saw few guards and came and went as they liked. It was left to the British and Australian officers to sort out the chaos, maintain discipline, and organize the cooking and distribution of food. The men could wander unsupervised over a large area of one of the most delightful parts of Singapore. There was a sense of "freedom" which confounded normal expectations of captivity and which did not exist at most of the other Japanese prison camps. Within a year, as men moved on to Burma and Thailand, Changi came to be regarded as a "paradise." But the Japanese did introduce some abrupt changes to the prisoners' way of life. They forbade the singing of the national anthem and ran all their prison camps, including Changi, on Tokyo time. Singapore was an hour and a half behind Tokyo, but reveille was blown according to the time in Tokyo, even if the men were woken up in the dark. The Japanese also insisted that there would be no segregation of officers and men. Allied officers would be responsible for discipline and administration of the prisoners: Gen. Percival was in command, assisted by Lt. Gen. Lewis Heath, Maj. Gen. M. B. "Becky" Beckwith-Smith, Gen. B. W. Kay, and the Australian Maj. Gen. C. A. Callaghan, AIF.

The Japanese were determined to humiliate the officers. On March 4 they issued a written order that officers were to remove their badges of rank and wear only one star on the left breast. All protests were ignored. They then made examples of Percival and Heath, the latter a veteran who had served with the King's African Rifles before the First World War. After refusing to obey an order from Yamashita that British gunners should be provided to teach the Japanese how to use Allied weapons, Percival was shut in a cell at Changi Jail without food for four days. Heath, aged fifty-six, was interrogated at the jail after refusing to answer questions about the defenses of India. He was punched under the jaw and seized by four soldiers, who took him to an underground room within Fort Canning. There was an inch of water on the floor. The Japanese major who had punched him turned off the water supply and left him in the dark for forty-eight hours.

It was also made brutally clear that escape would not be tolerated. When three gunners from the 9th Coast Regiment put on civilian clothes and made their way to Singapore, they were accused of being spies and sentenced to death. The men were marched outside the Changi perimeter wire and made to dig their own graves. Their commanding officer, Lt. Col. C. A. Heath, and a priest were compelled to watch the execution, which was so bungled by the Sikhs that a Japanese officer was forced to shoot the men with his own revolver. Heath was so horrified that he needed a powerful sedative. Five days later, six Australian privates who had tried to cross to Johore on the Malayan mainland were also executed.

At the end of March an order was issued that all ranks had to salute all sentries, Japanese or Sikh. The Free Indian troops—renegades from the Sikh, Punjabi, Dogra, and Hyderabad regiments, led by Capt. Surbatesh Singh, an Indian commissioned officer—took over all guard duties in April. If a sentry did not consider a salute smart enough, he was allowed to administer instant punishment, usually a slap in the face but often a severe beating while the man was tied up.

The renegade Free Indians enjoyed humiliating their former masters. Some Indian army officers were struck by men who had been in their own units. Prisoners arrested for infringements of orders were employed to do menial tasks for the Sikhs. To men who had been reared as masters of the British Empire, this was a humiliation that was deeply felt, and one sadistic Indian guard who inflicted crippling cuts and bruises with his rifle butt and bayonet met an unpleasant death. He was ambushed by British prisoners, carried to the latrines, and lowered in slowly, head first. "The perpetrators of this action were not violent men," said Capt. A. K. Butterworth, who had joined the Oxford and Bucks Light Infantry in 1939 rather than going to Oxford and entering the Church. "They were ordinary people who had been driven over the top into hatred."

The men concentrated on making their quarters habitable, finding food, and digging latrines. They also scoured the camps for any useful articles. With his batman, Capt. John T. Barnard made two big handcarts by removing the axles and wheels from an overturned truck. They were similar to the trailers that the Australians had used for the march to Changi, which had been constructed by stripping abandoned cars and trucks and substituting a wooden platform for the body. A strong rope or wire hawser was tied to the front axle and wooden poles attached at regular intervals. Each pole gave pulling space for four men. The spectacle of a fully loaded heavy trailer "preceded by a phalanx of brown and sweat-streaked backs, the rhythmic crunch of eight feet and the bored nonchalance of the helmeted guard riding like a potentate on top of the load" was to become for many the striking memory of Changi, remembered the Australian Sgt. David Griffin. The trailers were usually loaded with vegetables and rice or fuel, but they were also used to transport the sick and the dead.

Robert Reid, a second lieutenant, enjoyed being out and about. He feared that officers would soon be segregated from the men and confined within the jail, so he volunteered for the "exalted" post of sanitary officer and became responsible for the success of the latrines or "boreholes." The first priority was to dig slit trenches. Reid's men worked four-hour shifts night and day to accomplish this, using earth augers:

> With a waiting list, we worked flat out. The courtesy of putting in an appearance on each shift meant I did not get much sleep. The men drilled and emptied the augers, often in pouring rain in the darkness, the rain making the soil heavy and turning it into soft mud. As this was progressing, the carpenters made banks of seats, with lids, and others wove atap screens. In a few days, we passed on the augers to the next on the list. Banks of six seats were fitted, screens erected and paving slabs laid to keep the places clean and dry. The same gunners who had groused while the hard, dirty work was in progress, now boasted they had by far the best loos in the division.

Five days after the men had arrived at Changi, the Japanese brought in a party of Chinese, drove them into the water near Changi Point, bound some to the barbed wire that had been erected, and sent away spectators. They then opened fire on them: seventy were killed. Another hundred bodies were buried on a different beach by parties of Australians and British. Some had their hands bound; all had been shot. Hundreds of Chinese in Singapore were executed without trial. Louis Baume heard the guns as he and his men disentangled miles of barbed-wire fences with their bare hands. "We are voluntarily sending out burying parties to bury the hundreds of Chinese and Indians butchered by the Nips on Changi beaches. We see them, half naked, hands bound behind their backs and ropes round their necks, being marched off to their deaths. Later we hear the machine guns." The gruesome task of cutting the corpses from the barbed wire, dragging them off the beaches, and burying them in mass graves went on every day for nearly three weeks.

Meanwhile, the smartest units had come prepared and quickly adapted to their new conditions: some doctors had smuggled in medical supplies; Australian gunners scavenged and purloined from the bombed buildings the necessary materials to build walls within walls. Within a day of the arrival of Capt. Rowley Richards, AIF, his orderlies had removed all the medical supplies, "liberated" rations from his truck, and stowed them behind false walls. Staff at the hospital concealed pills along the picture rails of the dormitories—too high for the Japanese to reach. Within three weeks another Australian medical officer, the Melbourne doctor Glyn White, had tricked the guards into letting him use seventy-six vehicles to transport the sick from Singapore. The men who drove them scrounged forty-five hundred hospital beds, seven thousand mattresses, medical supplies and even two pianos.

Nowhere else within the Greater East Asia Co-Prosperity Sphere, as the Japanese described their new empire on posters around Singapore—now renamed Shonan—were so many prisoners concentrated together as at

Changi. Over the next few months the prisoners suffered paralyzing hunger, sickness, disease, and death, but also developed compassion and camaraderie. All human life was to be found at Changi, the noble and the ignoble, the diligent and the shirkers, the good, the bad, and the indifferent. Some men explored their capacity to survive by resorting to spivvery, cunning, petty theft, and crime, but most showed a compassion for their fellow men, especially when they were sick, and discovered innate skills and crafts that alleviated the misery of the camps and helped them to survive the harshest of conditions. The men summoned up their civilian skills and spent their days building shacks from discarded lumber and fitting them with bunks. Inch-piping was stolen for showers, bedding fashioned from old rice sacks, eating and drinking utensils made from soup tins and filing cabinets, and cooking kettles devised from old oil drums. It was so hot that they did not need much clothing. Sifted wood ash made toothpaste and, when combined with palm oil, produced enough soap for an issue of one cake per person per fortnight: its appearance and smell were foul, but it was as effective as real soap. Brushes, brooms, and toothbrushes were made from coconut fiber. Rubber was tapped, and some was used for patching tears in uniforms until the men began to make their own thread; it was also turned into adhesive plasters and was used to mend boots or to make sandals (which were also cut out of old car tires). Other sandals were made of hard wood with a webbing strap across the toes. Men who were less fit wove palm fronds and made atap (thatch) to patch any damaged roofing and screens around the latrines.

A variety of palm, when tapped high up in the early morning, yielded the liquid that Asians fermented and drank as "toddy." It produced an alcohol good enough for surgical purposes. Deep laterite clay, washed, dried, and powdered, furnished a cure for diarrhea. Castor-oil plants grew locally, and their oil was used as the traditional laxative, as an ingredient for ointments, and as lubrication oil. Vehicle springs made good hollow-ground open razors and surgical instruments. Enough old bayonets were found to make products that needed high-grade steel. As cigarette lighters ran out of petrol and flints, they were replaced by hundreds of tinder boxes, some of which were works of art.

In a camp at Sime Road, Lt. Col. Alfred "Knocker" Knights devised an ambitious plan to restore electricity after he found a hut in which there was a live transformer connected to a 6600-volt supply. Knights, a short, quiet, but fearless man, had won the Military Medal in the First World War and then worked in the electricity-supply industry. At Sime Road he launched the so-called "Bukit Timah Electric Light Company," with himself as general manager and chief engineer, and recruited officers and men who knew about electricity. Engineering gangs set about repairing the electrical installations in the huts, strung lengths of cable to the huts with faulty underground distributors, and located and repaired faults in the cable. Light bulbs were smuggled in with the medical supplies. Most of the huts soon had electric lighting and ceiling fans. Knights had worried about the Japanese reaction to his scheme, as the jailers themselves were still in darkness. But when he was summoned, Knights learned that the camp commander was not worried about how he had made an unauthorized connection to the Singapore mains supply; he simply wanted the blessing of light extended to the guardroom and Japanese living quarters. Knights had made a friend, and he was allowed to roam free outside the camp during the day.

Knights and his gang of engineers dealt next with the water supply. They located a pumping station and a large underground water tank that was connected to a water supply. They traced the pipeline, mended the fractures, and piped water to the cookhouses. Soon the men were also able to take showers when they returned from work: men on working parties stole as many lengths of piping and showerheads as they could find and two banks of showers were created.

Yet, although such examples of ingenuity cheered the men as they settled into captivity, the shame of surrender still rankled. The men had lost some of their self-respect because of the capitulation, noted Richard Sharp:

> The feeling that British arms had failed again, the disappointment, all the reaction to the surrender, possibly deep down the feeling of disgrace, brought about a breakdown of discipline and a collapse of morale. Men, who had let down themselves, their officers and their regiment, felt themselves let down, and were contrarily assertive. Hunger added wings to a self-discipline already in flight, and thieving of money and food became widespread. Disobedience was common and mutiny not unknown.

One popular wisecrack was that there was going to be a medal for the Malaya Campaign—a white ribbon with a yellow streak through it. Capt. Harry Jessup, a general staff officer at the 8th Australian Division headquarters, noted the same reaction among the Australians. They thought they had been sold out in Singapore and vented some of their bitterness on the officers. But many officers were equally bitter: junior officers blamed their seniors, and senior officers blamed Malaya Command. The other ranks blamed all of them.

It was mostly officers who kept diaries, but the few diaries kept by the men all hint that some officers, even within the conditions of a prison camp, were determined to maintain their privileges and class distinctions. Signalman Walter Riley remarked on the "ludicrous" establishment of an officers' mess, much to the amazement of the Japanese guards and the chagrin of the other ranks:

> Various barrack blocks and latrines were prominently marked "Out of bounds" and "Officers only." The dignity, privacy and privilege of the British officer and gentleman must be maintained. "This is good for discipline and morale," they said. "It will show the Japanese that we are not a common rabble as they are." The Japs responded to this fatuous order and class distinction by contemptuously and promptly decreeing that all PoWs, regardless of rank, would salute every Japanese guard, regardless of his rank. If a prisoner was not wearing any headdress when encountering a guard, and therefore was not expected to salute, he would stop, face the guard and bow deeply from the waist and remain thus until the guard had passed by.

Aware of the men's disillusion and of the danger of a breakdown in order, Percival and the Allied Command insisted on maintaining strict military discipline to avoid anarchy. They organized full days to avoid boredom, another threat to morale. The atmosphere of a disciplined camp kept morale high and stopped any tendency to drift into a mob of prisoners instead of a body of soldiers, said the Australians. Officers insisted on maintaining differences of rank, refused to tolerate sloppy appearance or behavior, introduced fatigue duties, and punished infringements of regulations by placing offenders under guard on reduced rations.

The maintenance of military discipline was often a chore for the men, but at least it kept them busy, collecting fuel and water, cutting down trees, digging latrines, doing calisthenics, sweeping paths clean, attending endless roll calls and drill parades. There was a routine to the days: reveille was at 8 A.M., breakfast at 9:30, a work period from 10:30 to 1:30, an hour of rest, followed by work and free periods until 6 P.M., a meal at 6:30 and roll call at 9 P.M. By the end of March a forestry company had been set up to cut firewood for the kitchens (by December they had cut 2,150 tons for the Australians alone), the first concerts had been staged, the water supply had been restored by the engineers, and a regulated community life had begun to emerge from the early confusion and chaos. The reason, said Capt. David Nelson of the Singapore Volunteer Corps, who became the archivist of Changi, where he remained throughout captivity, was the guidance of senior officers combined with the cheerful help of men with special skills and trades whose days were filled with a mix of work and play. In the area occupied by the British 18th Division, that meant a routine of gardening and drill, a university for fairly advanced students and secondary and preparatory schools for beginners, music, concerts, and theater, and church for those who sought spiritual solace. Each of the four divisions was within barbed-wire fences, guarded by Sikhs. If men wished to visit another area, they went as an organized party and carried a white flag with a scarlet edge.

But in spite of these efforts to make it bearable, captivity weighed on the men's minds, and they were haunted by memories of home. The British medical officer Lt. Cyril "Pop" Vardy missed the simple things most: the ring of the telephone, the tinkle of ice in a glass, the whirl of a fan, the sound of a filling bath, the distant noise of a train, the swish of a woman's dress, a waft of scent, the sight of a woman making herself up. "It must stop, it *must* stop," he wrote in his diary, "much too dangerous a game."

Food rapidly became a daily obsession. The greatest atrocity committed by the Japanese against their prisoners, according to the Australian historian Hank Nelson, was that they did not feed them enough. The Australian army ration of 1941 gave the men a daily intake of 4,220 calories; they could survive and work on three thousand, but in Changi they got just over 2,000, with the result that they lost weight and started to become ill. The Japanese provided no food at all for the first week, the men having to feed themselves from the supplies they had brought with them. Breakfast might be half a sausage, lunch two hard biscuits and a slice of sausage meat, and supper half a mess tin of stew. For the first time in their lives, many men began to know hunger. So there was great relief when the first Japanese rations arrived—sacks of rice, sweet potatoes, pumpkins, the leaves and tops of plants, and a kind of Chinese radish. But when the men realized that rice—often full of broken grains, husk and gravel, occasionally dyed yellow, which stank of sulphur, and harboring maggots and weevils—was going to be their main diet, their relief quickly evaporated. Richard Sharp noted:

> When the rations arrived they were rice. Bags and bags of it, and we looked dumbly at each other and said, "Now what?" For the next few months, rice was the main topic, all the jokes (not many) were about rice and when they weren't they were about that other complaint—the "trots." "Rice and Shine" was the name of the first small show attempted with a thin plot about stealing a handful of rice. . . . Some said they were allergic to rice, and some were, and they tried to do without it; they either learned better or died. Twice a week we got frozen meat from the cold storage, and on the third day it was usually rice . . . if they weren't ill, they were hungry, and if they were ill, well, they were hungrier still when they became better.

The sacks of rice provoked visions of gargantuan feasts when they first arrived, said David Griffin, AIF:

> Memories of fine white rice cooked by expert Chinese and served at delicious curry tiffins flashed through many minds. And a nice piece of fish; nothing better than a nice piece of fish! The dismay, the bitterness of disappointment which followed the first efforts of army cooks to cope with rice defy description. It appeared on the plate as a tight ball of greyish gelatinous substance, nauseous in its lack of flavour and utterly repulsive. The fish, when it came, which was not often, proclaimed its arrival by an overpowering stench and massed squadrons of flies. To gaze on a sack of rotting shrimps moving slowly under the impulse of a million maggots was a poor prelude to the meals which followed, meals which were nothing but a series of gastronomical disasters.

A month after he moved to Changi, the rations issued per person to Cyril Vardy's unit at the hospital were 8 ounces of rice, ⅙ ounce of tea, ⅔ ounce of sugar, ½ ounce of milk, ⅙ ounce of salt and butter, 2 ounces of flour, ½ ounce of cheese, and 1 ounce of vegetables. Vardy lost fourteen pounds in the first month. He sat in "utter misery" trying to force down the rice. His diary conveys the woeful nature of his diet:

> Breakfast. Rice with ½ sardine, or rice alone, or 1 small piece of cheese. Strong black tea. Lunch. Rice and milk (very little milk) ALWAYS. Dinner. Rice and a little stew, or curry or small piece of vegetable or one small piece of meat about that size. We twice a week get bread (2 slices, one with butter, one with jam). Once a week Army biscuit. Once a week sugar—teaspoonful. But there is always RICE.

An instruction on cooking rice issued in July demonstrated that although the men might have been hungry, they were still fastidious about their food. Rice should not be rejected because it contained mealworms or weevils, it read. One day's rice ration should be placed in a thin layer on newspaper and exposed to the direct rays of the sun. "Both mealworms and weevils will walk out of the rice and make their way to the end of the paper and then will take cover under the paper. Do not arrest the progress of the mealworms whilst they are walking off the paper, as they will return to the rice and die (almost immediately making it most difficult to find and remove them thereafter)."

With four fellow officers, Lt. Jim Richardson, who had worked in Malaya as a geologist, decided to teach the "cooks" how to deal with rice. They had seldom seen a group of Europeans so pleasantly surprised when they served an edible portion for dinner. Over time, the cooks learned how to make rice palatable by boiling, steaming, frying, or roasting it and flavoring it with dried fish, dehydrated meat, salt, curry powder, vegetables, pineapples, coconuts, chilies, and occasionally "gula malacca," a sticky brown sugar. Eventually, said Murray Griffin, the Australian war artist, the cooks could almost make rice sit up and beg: "It was coloured bright green, orange, pink, red and just plain white." The men made their own salt by boiling seawater collected in big oil drums, and learned to make flour by grinding down the rice. Then, using ovens (again made from oil drums or other containers), they could bake rice bread. But it was still rice, and would remain so for the next three and a half years, for breakfast, lunch, and dinner. Reg. Sgt. Maj. Peter Neild calculated that he had thirty-eight hundred consecutive meals of rice during his captivity.

At first the rice diet led to widespread constipation. A few men went thirty days without a motion, and a week to ten days was commonplace. The high water content of cooked rice also made the men urinate copiously until their metabolisms adapted to the new conditions. Another side effect of the lack of food was a drop in libido: "It was just as well as there were no women," wrote Lt. Jim Richardson. "Our excellent Squadron Leader said to me one day, 'If my wife had had any idea of the debilitating and deflationary effects of a low rice diet, she would have been spared much worry and apprehension!' " There were more serious effects too, though, and the hospital that had been established in five blocks of Roberts Barracks was hardly up to the task of treating them. "No water, no WCs, people using any trench, septic tanks bust, staff difficulties, equipment short, water carts late—chaos," Cyril Vardy noted in his diary. Order was restored by the end of March 1942, but in the first hundred days the hospital had admitted 16,043 patients, more than half with dysentery. There had been 223 deaths. By August, 22,342 patients had been admitted, again more than half with dysentery, but 926 with beri-beri and 1,314 with malaria. Another effect of the lack of vitamins, particularly B_2, was Changi Balls or Rice Balls (or Java Balls in Java). One Changi victim was Bdr. E. S. "Art" Benford:

> Rice Balls was not an elegant term. It was not, however, an elegant complaint. Rice Balls to us meant not one of the favourite dishes of the Japanese, but the ripping raw of a man's scrotum and genitals. There was at first a faint discomfort, then the skin split and peeled off an area which

> might spread from the genitals right down the inner thighs. This entire surface then became raw and sticky and painful. By refusing us a spoonful a day of the worthless polishings taken off rice—and they could easily have given us sacks full—the Japs condemned us to years of living with a scrotum that was red weeping flesh. Happy Feet was another symptom of lack of vitamins. This scourge struck only about half the prisoners but made up the balance by striking them with pain twice as severe as any of us had ever seen. It inflicted them with a persistent series of searing stabs in the soles of their feet. The pain was like fire. But when they put their feet in water, the coolness immediately tore at them like ice. So that once again they moaned for warmth. As you looked at them, the flesh dropped: the light of youth from their eyes: the life from their faces. Boys of twenty became suddenly old men—shrunken and desperate.

But the starvation diet meant that the men savored the occasional treat. Roy Whitecross, AIF, paid three dollars for a tin of condensed milk. He had recently recovered from a serious bout of diarrhea and thought that the milk would help him regain his strength. He decided to eat one teaspoonful a day, and the next morning opened the tin:

> Ah! The exquisite sensation as the sweet, sticky milk flowed over my tongue! I rolled it round my mouth, savouring every drop, reluctant to swallow it. I wallowed in the very smell of the tin. I was careful not to have a drink for some time after, so that I would not wash away the lingering trace of the taste which clung about my mouth. Every time I opened the cupboard for lotions or pills, there was my tin tantalising me. I put it right at the back of the shelf where I couldn't see it. But the next time I opened the door I smelt it. My mouth watered. It was some hours after breakfast and I was famished. I had one more teaspoonful. Then my will broke and faded like a morning mist. I grabbed my spoon and the tin, sat down on a box, and ate the lot.

He swore that when he was a free man again he would line up ten tins of condensed milk and keep eating until he was sick.

Whitecross's tin of milk was bought on the black market which flourished as the men became desperate for any food other than rice. Officers always had more money to spend than the men. From August 1942 they were paid by their captors at the same rates that applied in the Japanese army. But deductions for board and lodging and sums held back for repayment after the war meant that they got much less than they were due. The official scale, paid in the local currency (ticals in Thailand, rupees in Burma), ranged from 220 Straits dollars a month for lieutenant colonels to 85 for lieutenants. But in practice, lieutenant colonels got thirty dollars a month, while lieutenants received ten. At least the officers were paid regularly. Other ranks were paid only if they worked or did camp duties, and then very little. After February 1943 warrant officers got forty cents a day, NCOs got thirty, and privates got twenty-five, enough to buy perhaps one egg and four cigarettes. Pay, as will be seen, was to become an issue that rankled with both officers and other ranks throughout captivity. Starting at Changi and elsewhere, officers did, however, make contributions from their pay to establish funds for the hospitals and messes and to buy extra rations for the canteens.

But the men were still hungry, and entrepreneurs and spivs flourished. Naturally, the men could buy on the black market only if they had the money, so thieving was rife—from the sick as well as the fit. Fusilier Harry Howarth noted one macabre occasion when a few of his friends even stole the cakes and bottles of beer that had been placed on a grave after a Malay funeral. One prisoner, despite being searched twice by the British military police and once by the Japanese guards, walked out of the camp with a typewriter that he sold in Singapore for $8,000. Another borrowed ten dollars, bought food in Singapore, sold it at a 300 percent profit, paid back his loan, and eventually accumulated $4,000. "How could any man so exploit the distress of his comrades?" wondered Lt. Wallace Marsh.

There was a thriving trade in selling razors to the Japanese. These were hollow ground and highly polished, made from crossbars, swords, and bayonets stolen from the Japanese themselves and engraved, inscribed, and encased in ebonite. "Parker" pens were made, while inferior watch movements were put into deceased Rolex Oyster cases and sold for $2,000.

Other black marketeers left the camp at night and brought back sacks full of tins which they sold at a profit to compensate for the risks they had taken. The penalty, if they were caught by the Japanese, was at best a severe and merciless beating. When a party of thirty-five Australians led by Lt. Ramsbotham were accused of stealing tobacco, they were paraded and beaten fifty times each across the face and body with a leather riding crop. They were then placed in two small vans in the sun with the doors open about an inch and kept there for six hours without food or water. Two of the men were kept tied up until the following morning, and several had to be treated in the hospital.

In spite of such disincentives, the black market boomed when the men started going into Singapore on working parties. Some "merchants" could not resist making exorbitant profits from hungry men. If the trade had been controlled, it would have been a godsend, but "As it was, it became a curse and gave rise to a lot of crime," said Harry Jessup. Not all officers thought like Jessup, though, and some participated in the racketeering. The black market was often run by British Malay officers who had contacts outside the camp. Small tins of milk, fish, and cheese, which cost about fifty cents in Singapore, were sold for as much as six dollars inside. Other officers even managed to lay their hands on boxes of chocolates. The Japanese joined in, too, according to 2nd Lt. John Milford:

> More and more working parties are going in to Singapore these days, and the Japanese now appear to connive at their bringing back in to the camp whatever they have been able to purchase. The result is an increasing supply of tinned foods, which fetch fantastic prices after passing through several hands. We are never in a position to deal direct with the actual "importers," but one of the other ranks will sidle up to one of us and ask if we would be interested, say, in a tin of milk for $5, and according to the state of one's funds and the gnawing pain in one's tummy, one absurdly accepts or regretfully refuses. Early this week, we four purchased communally three 12 oz tins of jam, two of herrings and one of bully beef, for the shocking sum of $42, or very nearly £4. By any civilised standards, these prices are intolerable, but here we come to realise the truth of the fact that the value of money is measured by what it will buy, not by the number of monetary units it represents.

"What a meal!" 2nd Lt. W. H. Baillies wrote in July after tiffin with some Australians—soup and steak with two fried eggs and chipped sweet potatoes, served with home-brewed beer. "Split a tin of pilchards and had half at lunch and dinner," FO Denis Dodds wrote in his diary. "Rolls, butter and marmalade too! Afterwards a little cocoa." After lunch he went down to the black market: two hundred prisoners were waiting at the side of the road to bargain with the drivers of twelve lorries. This sort of trading was the greatest source of irritation to the Japanese and the greatest source of income to the prisoners. Many lived comfortably; few suffered to any great extent. Without the black market, more men would have starved to death. "Strictly ethical it may not have been but Changi owes much to its black market," said one anonymous prisoner.

Despite the incessant bartering and black marketeering, many men were still malnourished. The doctors and scientists among the prisoners were forced to think of new ways to supplement the diet and combat disease. One early discovery was that hibiscus leaves were a good source of vitamin C.

"Those of us who followed this advice from imprisoned doctors munched away on the slimy tasting leaves whenever we came across them," wrote A. K. Butterworth. "Others scoffed and paid for it later with scurvy and ulcers." A daily teaspoonful of red palm oil, opaque, thick, and greasy, which was usually used to make soap and purchased outside the camp, was employed by some units as a prophylactic for running sores. Axle grease was used as the base of sulfur ointment for scabies. When the medical officers started worrying about the lack of vitamin B_2, they made a machine from a modified lawn mower, chopped and rolled grass, percolated it with water, and produced a foul drink which was nevertheless a godsend. Centers devoted to nurturing yeast cultures were also established. Some used a peanut mulch that was supplied as manure and served as biscuits. At Selarang, yeast grown on potatoes, flour, sugar, and later rice polishings was produced continuously for two years by the Australians. More than thirty thousand gallons were made in twenty months.

Another way to cultivate yeast was described by 2nd Lt. Robert Sutcliffe:

> By boiling 1 lb of rice and 1 lb of sugar in water, diluting and exposing to the effect of sunlight for 48 hours, fermentation is started and a yeast culture commenced: the yeast itself is creamed off the top and used to start the next day's brew and so on whilst the cloudy liquor is issued daily to all ranks (5 dessertspoonsful) and is a most pleasant drink, with a good "brewery" aroma about it. We are using the accumulator jars from the naval radio power plant which was here—two gallon rectangular glass vessels—placed on concrete where they get mild sunlight. The small quantities of raw materials develop a sufficient amount to issue the daily ration to 200 men . . . a happy way of avoiding a dread disease.

Soya beans were dried, ground to flour, and used for bread and pastry. The Dutch used fungus to break down the beans before they were cooked, which not only made them more digestible but created another source of vitamin B. They were as unpleasant to chew as hibiscus but helped to cure beri-beri. Extracts from the leaves of passion fruit, teak, and rhododendrons, or buffalo grass, dried in the sun and rendered to powder, were percolated and used to treat other illnesses. A thousand pounds of grass and leaves were being processed daily at one time.

Among the British and Australians, a levy was taken from the officers' and other ranks' meager pay to help buy food for hospitalized men—an early example of the compassion that was to be shown throughout the next three years. The Australians decided to give twenty-five cents each for the men in the hospital, which bought soap, food, and the occasional treat for them. "No money was ever better invested," said Gunner Russell Braddon, who later wrote *The Naked Island* about his experiences during captivity. "It was sheer delight to see the faces of those near-corpses who for weeks and months had been living a life of the most complete squalor." The Japanese eventually allowed the purchase for the hospital of eggs, peanuts, dates, pineapples, bananas, dried fruit, and coconut oils. "It was surprising how tasty a banana skin pie could be," said the British medical officer Lt. Col. L. Fernley.

A. K. Butterworth learned a lesson—and compassion toward others—after he had volunteered to climb coconut trees for food:

> The rationing of a coconut was a serious business. The milk of one coconut and then the flesh was meticulously measured and divided into nine sections. These were put in a line on the window sill and the order of choosing your flesh and milk was changed in rotation daily. I foolishly and half jokingly suggested that as I had expended my talent and much energy in obtaining the nuts I should be entitled to an extra portion. To my surprise this was seriously debated by the eight officers, the final verdict being that we must work together as a team and share whatever talents and expertise we possessed for the benefit of all. This was a good lesson in survival—when the chips are down, you cannot go it alone.

When the Japanese allowed the men to start vegetable gardens, they watered them partly with their own urine, as water was still scarce. Flt. Off. Denis Dodds became an enthusiastic allotmenteer:

> 15 April. I arranged the cucumbers and filled the rest of the garden with potatoes, kankong, chillies and radish.
>
> 18 May. Dug three holes for pumpkin seeds and planted two pots of chillies. Had four brindgels and 6 small cucumbers for dinner. Very good fare!
>
> 24 May. Took three cucumbers and 2 loofahs and had a good stew.
>
> 26 May. Rain again last night. My word how the plants enjoyed it. I took 7 cucumbers and some potatoes and spinach leaves. Planted out potatoes and kankong.
>
> 3 June. Roast potatoes for lunch! Great joy!

Lt. John Coast's battalion had an acre and a half of garden laid out in long, shallow beds of kankong and sweet potatoes. The soil was so sour that the potato tubers would not form, so they ate the unpalatable tops as greens.

Cucumbers and tomatoes had a habit of being snatched by night and were discontinued, but the men had some success with spinach, radishes, and shallots. Louis Baume's party also planted tapioca, ginger roots, papaya trees, pineapples, and banana plants as part of a four-year plan. By the end of March one banana tree had been successfully fertilized and was being guarded to prevent its kidnapping. The gardens covered more than 120 acres, and at times more than 85 were under cultivation. By October 1943 they had produced 410,000 pounds of vegetables. Chickens and eventually pigs were kept as well. Wallace Marsh bought a dozen chickens that laid two or three eggs a day. The officers took turns for an egg in alphabetical order.

The quality of the food improved when the first Dutch prisoners arrived from Java in September 1942. They taught the British and Australians how to cook rice and how to use blachang, the Malay fisherman's equivalent of Gentleman's Relish, a powerfully fishy paste of prawns and small fish, dried and powdered, and a good source of protein. It was made by spreading out in the sun the remains of inedible fish, sprinkling them with sea salt, and letting them rot into a soft, putrid mass. The British turned this substance into fish cakes, merely adding it in its raw state to give an anchovy flavor to soggy rice balls. It was sold in the shape of a loaf, and looked like a piece of toast when cut and grilled. The Japanese recipe was to fry it in palm oil with hot chilies and garlic (bought on the black market and later at the canteen set up by the Japanese) and to add it in small amounts to boiled rice. The mixture was then pushed into a short length of bamboo, sealed at both ends with mud plugs, and baked under hot coals. "With such skills the Dutch and their East Indian cooks were the first prisoners to make money from 'manufacturing' rather than by trading on the black market," said L.Cpl. John Stewart Ullman.

As well as being adept black marketeers, the Australians were notorious racketeers, and tricking the Japanese boosted spirits. One "prank," according to Lt. Austin Ellerman, AIF, was to steal petrol from Japanese trucks and then sell it to the Chinese for four dollars a gallon. One engineer in charge of a diesel-powered steamroller told the Japanese he needed 44 gallons of petrol, a gallon of oil, and 44 gallons of diesel oil each morning. The diesel was used in the roller, but the petrol was sold to the Chinese, from whom the Australians in turn bought medical supplies stolen from the Japanese or obtained from pre-war supplies.

The Australians, however, were caught one day by one of the guards, who was nicknamed "the Brooklyn Kid" because he spoke his halting English with an American accent. As he sat in the front of a truck going into Singapore for supplies, the prisoners in the back were discussing the prospects for scrounging food. When the truck stopped, one man said, "I wonder if this little yellow bastard will stop somewhere for a woman. While he does we can nip off and find some grub." The "Kid" appeared at the back of the truck and drawled, "Say, you guys, this little yellow bastard has pulled up, but not for a woman. Now you get to hell and find some food!"

Having cottoned on to the Australians' scams regarding fuel, one high-ranking Japanese officer harangued them about the amount of petrol that was going missing during the building of a shrine at Bukit Timah. He suggested that severe punishment would be meted out to anybody caught stealing petrol in the future. Having delivered his oration, he returned to his car, started it up, but rapidly came to a halt. While he had been talking, somebody had siphoned the petrol out his tank. Unfortunately for the smirking Australians, though, all future petrol deliveries were thereafter more closely supervised, restricting black-market activities and subjecting the more unwary participants to the usual Japanese form of punishment. One to suffer was L.Cpl. Ennett, AIF, who was suspected of stealing petrol at Bukit Timah. He was taken to the camp HQ and struck with a malacca cane across each side of his face. He was then paraded before the commanding officer and struck again, whereupon he fell backward onto concrete steps. He died soon afterward at Changi.

"Knocker" Knights, for one, was impressed by the attitude of the Australians. They would take abnormal risks to raise money by stealing from the Japanese, he said, but they invariably used the money not for their own benefit but to provide for sick "cobbers." The British, meanwhile, were aiming for bigger scores with their rackets, according to 2nd Lt. Geoffrey Pharaoh Adams:

> With the active co-operation of one or two of the Japanese quarry-truck guards, the nearside ten-gallon fuel tank of the 15-cwt Bedfords was disconnected from the engine, and fitted with a motor-cycle stop-cock; the offside tank was left undisturbed. Each morning the trucks' tanks would be filled with petrol, of which the Japs had found ample supplies in Singapore, and when a suitable rendezvous had been fixed with a Chinese, the Jap would leave the vehicle and take a short walk, and the truck would be pulled into the side of the road. The driver remained in the cab. The customer would drain off the contents of the one tank, and leave the money under the truck. The British driver retrieved it, handed 50 per cent or less to the Jap, and pocketed the rest.

At the end of March 1942 there were 45,562 men at Changi, and another 5,812 fit prisoners were in Singapore on working parties, mainly at the docks and railway station, where they handled food supplies, ammunition, and military equipment. By now they had become involuntary subscribers to an extraordinary lottery, according to Bdr. Hugh Clarke. They could remain hungry and bored in Changi but relatively undisturbed by the Japanese, or they could grow fat and work on the wharves and food dumps if they were prepared for the bashings they received if caught stealing. According to Richard Sharp, the view at Changi was that it was better to remain there, while the men on the working parties loathed Changi as the seat of smart uniforms and self-interest: "Here was the settled calm, undisturbed by Japs, leisure to enjoy bookish things, play games and potter gently—and for that you were willing to put up with less food."

The first parties of men were now sent from Changi to work in other countries conquered by the Japanese. The first 1,125, under Lt. Col. F. E. Hugonin, left on April 3 for Saigon, and were followed in May by three thousand Australians of A Force, who went to Burma under Brig. A. L. Varley. Three thousand British left for Thailand in June and fifteen hundred Australians for Borneo in July. As men were moved around Japan's new empire, and others arrived, mainly from Java, the camp varied in size. It fell to fifteen thousand in June but had 18,790 inmates in August, when the biggest upheaval occurred: all officers above the rank of lieutenant colonel were sent to Japan. Maj. Gen. Beckwith-Smith died of diphtheria on the journey. He had won the DSO in the First World War and survived the evacuation from Dunkirk in this one, but the trip killed him at age fifty-two. He was mourned as much by the men, who called him "Becky," as by the officers.

At Changi, Lt. Col. E. B. Holmes took over from Gen. Percival, and Brig. Galleghan, AIF, replaced Maj. Gen. Callaghan. Galleghan, who was universally known as "Black Jack" or "B.J.," now became the senior Australian officer. He had commanded the 2/30th Battalion, the first to meet the Japanese army in combat in Malaya in January 1942, when eleven hundred Japanese were killed in a single ambush in the Gemas area of north Johore. Upright and soldierly, Galleghan, who always carried his swagger stick, was a ruthless disciplinarian and a stickler for military etiquette, but he also possessed a streak of sentimentality. He was to play a crucial role in maintaining morale and discipline among the Australians in the months to come.

Within three weeks, Holmes and Galleghan would have to deal with the biggest crisis of the men's first year at Changi—the Selarang Incident. On Sunday, August 30, the commanders of the British and Australian divisions were summoned by the Japanese, who complained that four prisoners were in jail after trying to escape. Holmes and Galleghan were warned that they were being held personally responsible for the discipline of the prisoners and were then handed a form stating that the prisoners promised not to escape. The two officers were asked to sign it, but they refused on principle and were supported by the men when they returned to camp. Maj. Gen. Shimpei Fukuye, the Japanese officer commanding Malaya's camps, told Holmes that the prisoners had therefore admitted that they intended to try to escape. Two days later he announced that the prisoners were to be punished, and on Wednesday, September 2, all men were ordered to move from Changi to Selarang Barracks, taking with them only what they could carry. At 1:45 P.M., sixteen thousand men started making their way—they had been warned that anybody who was not at Selarang by 6 P.M. would be shot. (The sick at Roberts Hospital were not moved.) As the men marched to Selarang, Holmes, Galleghan, and area commanders were forced by the Japanese to watch a display of brutality on the beach. They had been invited to witness the execution of the four soldiers—Cpl. R. E. Breavington, Pte. V. L. Gale, AIF, Pte. Eric Fletcher, and Pte. Harold Walter. Two padres were allowed to speak to the men, but the officers were not allowed to approach them. Soon a burial party of Sikh guards with chunkols arrived, followed by a Sikh firing squad under an Indian officer. Capt. N. G. Macaulay, a general staff officer at the Australian headquarters, described what happened next:

> The British and Australian Officers present were commanded to take up a vantage point where they could watch the proceedings, and Koriasu, an IJA Interpreter, informed them that they were to witness the execution. The condemned men were then fallen in, with their backs towards the sea and four Sikhs took up their positions approximately ten paces in front of them . . . Okasaki then offered Cpl. Breavington a piece of cloth with which to bandage his eyes, whereupon he refused. Subsequently all the condemned men refused to be blindfolded. Cpl. Breavington then made an appeal to the Japanese to spare the life of Pte. Gale, and explained that as he was a non-commissioned officer, he had ordered Pte. Gale to accompany him in his attempt to escape. He pointed out that in any army it was the duty of a junior to carry out the orders given by his senior in rank and therefore he accepted the full responsibility and was prepared to take the consequences. Lt. Okasaki refused to consider the appeal. Breavington then shook hands with the condemned, came to attention and saluted the British and Australian Officers. Lt. Okasaki then gave the Indian Officer in charge of the firing squad the order to fire, and at this juncture, the Indian officer

> walked to the firing squad, took a rifle from one of the squad and himself knelt with the three other Sikhs. He gave the command to fire and each man fired at his target. The four condemned fell immediately but it was obvious that at least three had not been killed. Cpl. Breavington sat up and asked the firing squad to shoot him through the heart as he had been shot through the left arm. They immediately fired again, smashing his kneecap. As each body moved, a member of the firing squad would again fire. As the condemned men were on slightly higher ground and the firing party were in a kneeling position, their targets were the crutch and lower portion of the anatomy of the condemned men. Each of the executed men had received at least five shots and the firing squad reloaded and approached their targets where, at the slightest movement of finger or joint, they fired into their bodies, Cpl. Breavington receiving at least eight shots. The witnessing Officers were then approached by Okasaki, who made a speech in Japanese, which was translated by Koriasu, who said, "You have just seen four men put to death for attempting to escape. This is the punishment which will be meted out to any persons in future making a similar attempt!"

Meanwhile, at Selarang, the sixteen thousand English and Australians who had arrived were "corralled up like cattle waiting to be slaughtered" in seven barracks blocks designed to house about eight hundred, Capt. David Nelson wrote. Each building was about 120 feet long by 80 feet wide and held over one thousand men, with nine thousand sleeping on the parade square and hundreds on the flat roofs. Indian guards stood at intervals with fixed bayonets as squads of Japanese soldiers marched around the square; machine-gun posts were dug at all corners. No food was issued by the Japanese, and the men were on half rations. A latrine was dug in the middle of the parade ground and the men had to squat in full public gaze; the stench was appalling. There was one tap to each barracks block, but water was allowed only for cooking. Bdr. G. D. Austin described how the situation soon deteriorated:

> Washing was obviously out of the question, no food was issued by the Japanese for four days, diphtheria and dysentery had broken out. Nobody was allowed to step on to the road encircling the guns mounted at each corner. In order to lay down and sleep it was necessary for two men to sleep opposite one another with their feet under each other's armpits. Squads of men were working in shifts all night and day digging latrines

> on the concrete square. At all times there were great queues of men at the latrines and urinals, mixed up amongst which were the cookhouses and livestock, ducks, chickens and pigs—and also men sleeping.

As Holmes haggled with Fukuye, Galleghan's medical officers advised him that half the men would die within two weeks if the conditions did not improve. Fukuye simply tightened the screw on Selarang, though, by threatening that the sick from Roberts Hospital would be brought there if Holmes remained defiant. Holmes was finally persuaded. A few more days in Selarang would lead to an epidemic of something, probably diphtheria, and the inevitable death of many. It was his duty—"under the duress imposed by the Imperial Japanese Army"—to order all personnel to sign the form promising not to escape. He was convinced, he wrote, that the British government would approve if the circumstances in which they were living were known to it: "I am fully convinced that his Majesty's Government only expect POWs not to give their parole when such parole is to be given voluntarily. This factor can in no circumstances be regarded as applicable to our present conditions, the responsibility for this decision rests with me, and me alone, and I fully accept it in ordering you to sign." Answering anxious enquiries from the men, he added that they would not lose pay, pensions, or allowances. All the signatures were delivered by 11 P.M. on Saturday, September 5. When the men returned to Changi, some found that their possessions had been looted by the Japanese.

Conditions at Selarang had been pitiful, but David Nelson had a "wonderful experience" there. On the last night, the Southern Area Concert Party put on a show which ended with the crowd singing "Land of Hope and Glory," "There'll Always Be an England," and "Waltzing Matilda." Capt. Harry Malet's barracks had a huge lighted "V for Victory" made of small oil lamps in a wooden frame. "The singing and laughter and gramophones must have puzzled the guards," Malet wrote. When Galleghan addressed the Australians, he commended the spirit of "co-operation, unity and above all of brotherliness" which they had shown toward the British troops. At last, he added, the Australians had shown not the unit spirit, not the brigade spirit, but the spirit of comradeship throughout the force of ten thousand men that had been displayed by the last AIF, during the First World War.

By November 1942 there were "only" 10,942 men at Changi, but the numbers swelled again to 26,300 in December as the men from the Singapore working parties returned.

Eighteen thousand prisoners left Changi for Thailand, Burma, Borneo, and Taiwan in the first three months of 1943, and another sixteen thousand for Thailand and Japan in the following two months. Meanwhile, several thousand Dutch from Java arrived in Changi, but by May there were only 5,550 prisoners left in Singapore. For the rest, the main ordeal of their three and a half years as prisoners of the Japanese had begun, and they were soon longing to return to Changi. Those who went to Thailand would know no further peace of mind or body until they crossed the causeway again from Malaya to Singapore. But thousands were destined never to return.

INTERLUDE

Christmas in Captivity

The men made the most of their first Christmas in captivity. Padre John Chambers, the chaplain at Roberts Hospital, attended a midnight mass. There were six hundred in the congregation and two hundred took communion.

> When I arrived at 11.45, the cinema was already full of quiet, reverent men. The hall was in darkness, the stage lit by blue lights giving a moonlight effect. The altar alone was visible and as I looked the server, with great reverence and only faintly visible, moved forward to light the candles which blazed into light. A really wonderful service. When it began warm sunshine lit the stage and there was just enough light in the hall for the congregation to read the hymns. After each hymn the hall lights were extinguished. Changi was forgotten, Bethlehem remembered and real.

In the 18th Division area, about two thousand men attended a concert with carols on Christmas Eve.

On Christmas morning there were two more services of Holy Communion and a choral Eucharist, and at night a carol service with nine lessons.

The men were fed well and given two cigars apiece from canteen profits, and there was a floodlit, open-air concert at night emceed by Capt. Ronald Horner, which ended with community singing by an audience of about 3,500. Horner described his Christmas meals—"definitely a riceless day"—in his diary:

> Breakfast: Malted porridge with milk and sugar; fish croquettes and chips
> Tiffin: Meat pies, scalloped sweet potatoes and fried pumpkin, guava and banana flan
> Tea: Tea with milk and sugar, hot mince pies (made with white flour and mincemeat)
> Dinner: Clear consommé, herring creole with cream sauce, roast chicken with roast new potatoes and greens, Christmas pudding and aspic savoury cups, served with homemade wine.

The celebrations continued on New Year's Eve when the Japanese gave the 18th Division area 540 bottles of coarse brandy (which was meticulously shared: ten men to a bottle) and tinned pineapple (two tins for every seven men). Each man received a large tot, which most saved until midnight. There was a concert in the Windmill Theatre and then the men marched around the camp led by drummers, passing through the officers' sleeping quarters, beating drums and cymbals and singing at the tops of their voices. Cheering and singing could be heard throughout the camp until the early hours.

Chapter 3

THE RAILWAY OF DEATH

Japan conquered Burma in May 1942, but its army was at the end of a long and vulnerable supply line by sea from Japan. It was critical to the defense of Japan's new empire that its navy could move freely, and that oil and other raw materials from the conquered countries could be imported while manufactured goods were supplied in return. Yet, to reach the Burmese capital of Rangoon, supply ships had to sail five thousand miles across the East China and Andaman seas, exposed continually to attack from Allied aircraft and submarines. It was therefore imperative to build a secure supply line from Thailand to Burma. By using a new railway from Nong Pladuk in Thailand to Moulmein in Burma, the Japanese army could be supplied via Saigon and Bangkok and then by rail to Burma.

The building of a railway from Thailand to Burma (which Britain had annexed in the nineteenth century) had been considered several times before 1942, first by British engineers in 1885, but the idea had always been rejected. It was thought that the terrain of mountain ranges and dense jungle between the two countries would claim far too many human lives, especially during the monsoon. Nevertheless, after the Burmese coastal line from Moulmein to Ye, which had a junction at Thanbyuzayat, was completed in 1925, one route continued to attract attention. It would extend the line from Thanbyuzayat to Three Pagodas Pass, on the border between the two countries, and then down through Thailand; it would provide a more direct route from Singapore and Bangkok to Rangoon. For most of the way the route ran south through Three Pagodas Pass on the border and then through the valleys of the River Kwai Noi (the River Kwai of the film) to the river port of Kanchanaburi, at the river's junction with the River Mae Khlaung (also known as the Kwai Yai) and then to Ban Pong.

The Kwai Yai—the "big stream" in Thai—could not be crossed at Kanchanaburi, so the main bridge was built three miles upriver at Tamarkan. There were 69 miles of railway in Burma and 189 in Thailand.

With so many prisoners, Japan could ignore the seemingly insuperable difficulties of engineering the railway by using them as cheap labor, augmented by native workers recruited from the lands it had conquered. To Japanese eyes, they were honoring the dishonorable, the defeated enemy who had surrendered, by allowing them to work on a project supported by the Emperor. The pool of labor allowed FM Count Terauchi, commander of Japan's Southern Army, to cut the estimated building schedule from five or six years to just eighteen months. Muscle would replace machinery, as Clifford Kinvig, the most authoritative historian of the railway, put it.

The ambition of the Japanese engineers was in one sense awe-inspiring. With one set of prisoners working in Burma and another, much larger group in Thailand, the railway was to be driven 258 miles through some of the most hostile territory on earth, irrespective of the cost in human lives. "In Burma all the dread agents of fell disease and foul death lay in wait," the historian of the British Army Medical Services wrote later. One account in the archive of Capt. C. E. Escritt described some of the hazards faced by the men toiling in the heat of the jungle:

> The heap of fallen leaves were soft to the touch but ice-cold shivers ran evilly down one's back. The centipedes, flies and scorpions were frightening and one encountered snakes of unusual shape. Soldier ants kept falling onto the back of the neck and little flies tormented one, flying into the eyes. For either sense of sight or of hearing there was no relief. In the depth of the deep forest in the undergrowth beneath the trees there was an inch deep thick layer of fallen leaves and the sunlight was obstructed, so it was dim in daytime: visibility was limited and one called out one's position to the next man to confirm it, and they often lost their way. While the sun shone it was day but one's ability to define the period of daylight disappeared.
>
> Squalls broke out suddenly, from between the leaves big drops began to fall. Instantly the rain reached the bamboo grass. The rain splashed up like arrows, hitting everything, and everywhere it was misty and dim. The rain stopped at one metre, did not evaporate, visibility

> was nil. Under one's feet leaves began to pile up and straightaway there was stagnant water. Suddenly, one's whole body crying out for cover, the rain penetrated to one's underwear and uncomfortable shivers attacked one's body. At this time I was made keenly aware of the powerlessness of man made sport of by the violence of nature.
>
> When squalls went over, the rain-clouds were blown away by the wind, and you could see blue sky which made one forget all about that rain. The sun broke out and shone on the tree-tops and in the midst of the deep forest things began to dry up, the temperature and discomfort supervened on our heated, drenched bodies. In such circumstances it became in the end impossible to work.

The Australian journalist Rohan Rivett had been working as a war correspondent for the Malaya Broadcasting Corporation when he was captured by the Japanese. He was not given any special privileges because of his civilian status:

> Serried ranges of precipitous mountains on the Burma-Siam border, scores of streams which became raging rivers in the rainy season, steep ravines and abysses which had to be bridged made this an undertaking which, though often contemplated in the past, had never been effected. It demanded the very latest in modern clearing, engineering, and bridge-building equipment. But the Japanese provided the prisoners with none of these things. The only "mechanical" aid came from a handful of elephants most of whom died from overwork and underfeeding. The plight of white men facing the heaviest coolie labour in such an area was desperate enough. But unspeakable living quarters, denial of medical supplies and a steady worsening of the rations, which at best were never suitable nor adequate, made the death of thousands inevitable.

The aim was to finish the railway by December 1943, after which it would deliver three thousand tons of freight a day. Its construction would involve erecting 688 bridges (a total of over eight miles), building four million cubic metres of earthworks, hauling 60,000 cubic feet of bridging timber and 650,000 cubic feet of timber poles, shifting three million cubic meters of rock, detonating three hundred tons of explosive, creating many viaducts, and blasting through rocky cuttings. The go-ahead for construction to begin was given on June 20, 1942, after the shocking defeat of the Japanese navy at the Battle of Midway, which tilted the Pacific War in America's favor. Two Japanese railway regiments with twelve thousand men were assigned to the project: one was based at Thanbyuzayat, the other at Kanchanaburi. Three thousand Korean and Taiwanese guards, mostly young peasants, clerks, or merchants, were immediately recruited as civilian auxiliaries of the Japanese army; they were to become especially notorious among the prisoners for their brutality. At some small camps the Koreans, who had been told during training not to be too "soft" toward the prisoners lest they lose their respect, were in sole charge. The first party of prisoners destined to work on the railway left Singapore on May 14, when three thousand Australians under Brig. A. L. Varley set off. They were joined by about five hundred members of the British Sumatra Battalion under Capt. Dudley Apthorpe from Padang. This group was sent first to Victoria Point, Mergui, and Tavoy in Burma to work on airfields. They began to move to the Burma railhead at Thanbyuzayat in mid-September.

The main exodus from Singapore began on June 18, when a British party of three thousand men under Maj. R. S. Sykes left for the rail journey to Ban Pong at the head of the Gulf of Thailand. Six days later they started work as laborers at Nong Pladuk, clearing and building the base workshops and sidings for use by the Thai Railway Materials Workshop. From October 9 to November 9 parties of prisoners were leaving Singapore almost every day and being sent progressively further up the line. More followed in 1943, with the last two substantial parties—the ill-starred H and F forces—leaving for Thailand in April and May of that year. F Force went up to camps near the border with Burma, and H Force to the area that became known as "Hellfire Pass" at Konyu. In all, 330,000 men labored on the railway, which was completed within eighteen months. The official figures put the numbers at 30,141 British, 12,994 Australians, 17,985 Dutch, and 686 Americans, as well as about 270,000 native workers, thousands of whom deserted and who as a group suffered the highest death rate.

Work started in Burma on September 15, 1942, when the prisoners at Thanbyuzayat were "welcomed" to their work by Lt. Col. Nagatomo, who commanded the Japanese No. 3 Group on the railway. Sweltering guards ringed the field as he delivered a speech that demonstrated the contempt in which the prisoners were held and the merciless ruthlessness with which the Japanese would ensure that the railway was completed on schedule. The men were a few "pitiful" victims and a few "remaining skeletons" of those who had tried to defeat Japan, he declared. But they were not the only people who were suffering: they were complaining about their conditions, but needy women and children couldn't get sufficient food either. In such an "inconvenient place" even the Japanese Imperial Army was unable to get food, mosquito nets, and cigarettes. How could the prisoners expect to be treated better? He continued:

> I hope that you will rely upon me and render your lives before me. Living manners, deportment, salutation and attitude shall be strict and according to the rules of the Nippon Army because it is only possible to manage you all, who are merely rabble, by the order of military regulations. The rules for escape shall naturally be severe. If there is a man here who has at least 1 per cent chance of escape, we shall make him face the extreme penalty. If there is one foolish man who is trying to escape, he shall see big jungles towards the east, which are absolutely impossible for communication. Towards the west he shall see boundless oceans, and above all in the main points of north and south our Nippon Army is staying and guarding. You will easily understand the difficulty of complete escape. By the hand of the Nippon Army railway works to connect Thailand and Burma have started, to the great interest of the world. There are deep jungles where no man comes to clear them by cutting the trees. There are also countless difficulties and sufferings, but we shall have the honour of joining in this great work which was never done before, and you should do your best efforts. I shall check and investigate carefully your non-attendance, so all of you except those who are unable to work shall be taken out for labour. At the same time I shall expect all of you to work earnestly and confidently every day. Work cheerfully.

The men whom Nagatomo exhorted to work cheerfully—and the same speech was delivered to every new party of prisoners in Burma—were among the first to experience the conditions that earned the project its sobriquet: the Railway of Death.

By December, the Australian driver J. W. Turner was working from Thetkaw, seven miles up the line from Thanbyuzayat, where an area of about twenty-five yards either side of where the line was to be built had to be cleared using just parangs (Burmese knives, about eighteen inches long) and axes. Trees had to be chopped down and rooted out, and the undergrowth of jungle cleared by laboriously hacking at it. After digging down about a foot the men would strike clay, which made the going even tougher. With just picks and shovels they had to dig out cuttings in the hills, as much as sixty feet through clay and solid rock. Some men were temporarily blinded by a combination of the glare from the clay and the lack of vitamins in their diet (their eyes would be too weak to read a book for the rest of their lives). Each night they returned from work, four miles on either side of the camp, completely exhausted.

For lunch and tea they were given watery stews, often containing just melon, pepper, and salt. Occasionally a small bullock was killed and divided among a thousand men. Pellagra, which inflamed the tongue, made eating agony. There was an acute shortage of medical supplies and prisoners had to fashion their own bandages, which were made by cutting up old shirts. Ringworm on the testicles, a common complaint, was treated by applying a coating of wet clay. If a prisoner reported to the doctor with dysentery or diarrhea, the "cure" was not to eat that day and to take a spoonful of powdered charcoal three times a day.

In Thailand, the 0-kilometer post had been planted at Nong Pladuk on July 5, but construction did not start there until November. Nowhere else were prisoners of war concentrated in such great numbers. The "most significant collective experience" of the Allied POWs held by the Japanese during the Second World War was about to begin.

INTERLUDE

A Walk Along the River Kwai

When he was not working on the railway, Maj. Basil Peacock took the opportunity to become a naturalist. The prisoners were surrounded by steep hills and virgin jungle, but the Kwai Valley was beautiful and a paradise for nature lovers. If the sentries were not too vigilant, it was possible to take a country walk outside the camps.

> Sunday afternoon was a time of rest for captors and captives and on one of them I slipped away half a mile upriver from our camp and sat down on the bank to meditate in solitude, hoping to do some bird watching . . . On this Sunday the river flowed cleanly sparkling in the sun, and for a couple of hours it became a dream location for an ornithologist. Within a minute or two of my arrival a tall grey heron stalked round some reeds and quietly and efficiently swallowed several small fish a few feet away from me. Four ground thrushes pushed through short grass to sip the water, brilliant in their plumage of green, red and blue.

Every few minutes several kingfishers darted back and forth over the river, their colours of vivid blue and brown flashing in the strong sunlight. During one flight they flew into an overhanging tree, which caused some commotion and a cackling, and I saw something move and leap up to a branch. It was a large bird and I watched it intensely as it settled on its perch. It fluffed out its feathers and arranged its long tail and I was astounded to recognise it as a peacock, the first I'd ever seen undomesticated or outside a zoo—what I'd seen was a Java peafowl.

For ten minutes or so after the commotion, all was quiet, and the water lapped so temptingly on a few yards of sandy beach that I slipped off the only clothing I had, a pair of tattered shorts, and washed them as I had a bathe. Having no towel, I lay down on a small patch of grass to dry in the sun with my shorts spread out at my side. I was dozing when I was startled awake by a noise like a steam engine puffing in the distance, which seemed very odd as the railway embankments were not finished and had no rails on them. The noise grew louder, then round a bend in the river flew five huge birds—hornbills—their wings making such a commotion that it sounded like an express train steaming at full speed, whump-whump-whump-whump-whump-whump-whump, then a short pause as they glided and whump-whump again. These hornbills, as big as grown turkeys, had bright orange-coloured bills and blue plumage round the eyes and extending down the neck. Their bodies were brown and charcoal grey and their wings charcoal with bits of white. The wingspan was short for the size of the birds, only about four feet. Once seen they can never be mistaken. In the midst of labour and misery, I've seen a party of prisoners and their guards stop working to watch a flight of them passing overhead like acrobatic flying clowns, and burst out laughing.

Back on my river bank, the noise of the five birds overhead disturbed the jungle and a score of chattering parakeets took wing and dived across the water to take refuge at the other side, looking like a cageful of giant red, blue and green budgerigars let loose.

Chapter 4

THE REAL STORY OF THE BRIDGE ON THE RIVER KWAI

When Lt. Col. Philip Toosey left Singapore in October 1942 he did not know what fate awaited him in Thailand. But he and his 690 men of the 135th Field Regiment were off to build the bridge on the River Kwai. After some eight months in captivity, the journey to Thailand itself was a "severe shock," and offered the regiment their first inkling of the very different conditions they were now going to endure. They were packed as many as thirty-one to a railway truck, with all their baggage, for the nine-hundred-mile journey, which took four full days. Each truck was constructed of steel and had two sliding doors, one on either side. When the train departed, the metal of the trucks was already too hot to touch, yet it was far from the hottest part of the day. The men's clothing was soon black with perspiration, and they started a rotation so that all got a turn near the doors, and took turns to sit down. Gunner Stan Henderson explained that the journey was socially awkward as well as uncomfortable:

> We were travelling at between thirty and forty miles an hour and the problem of passing water from the open doorway of a cattle truck is not to be underestimated. We had to communicate with the truck immediately to the rear of our own or men in the open doorway area would have received an unwelcome baptism. The man who was peeing was held by a couple of others so that he could lean out as far as possible to do his business cleanly. The calls of nature became more complicated. The

> procedure was to stand, legs apart and trousers down, in the doorway facing inwards; two men would hold on to each hand so that one could hang one's middle section as far outside the truck as was possible. A shout of warning was then given to the next truck and from then on matters took their own course. Before the night was through the atmosphere in our truck was almost unbearable. Several of the men had badly soiled garments which were too valuable to throw away but too filthy to wear and these accumulated as the night wore on.
>
> On top of this we were unable to sleep for the lack of space, and we were cold. I think none of us had ever experienced or even visualised such acute discomfiture. . . . Many of the men who previous to this journey had gone for long periods without a bowel movement ended the journey with what we then thought of as diarrhoea but which often turned out to be dysentery.

The men arrived at the small station of Ban Pong at 4 A.M. and then marched two and a half hours to their staging camp in a paddy field. It was completely waterlogged. Toosey was shocked by both its filthy condition and the attitude of the British staff. In the hospital the water was in some cases above the level of the bed platforms and mostly only six inches below; the latrines were overflowing and full of filth; no arrangements had been made to receive the party. To Toosey, it was clear that the British officers had lost their grip and given up hope, and that morale was exceedingly low. One of his junior officers, 2nd Lt. Stephen Alexander, witnessed his commander's anger with one of the resident officers: " 'Don't you "my dear man" me!' Toosey stamped his unwontedly tarnished boot and the two parted in mutual animosity, the one secure in the impossibility of his task and the other in the impossibility of sharing a similar defeatism." That denial of defeatism was to become the defining stamp of Toosey's command throughout his captivity.

Fortunately, Toosey and his men stayed in the staging camp for only one night. They left the next day by lorry (they were lucky to be the first party who had not been forced to march) for the thirty-mile journey to Tamarkan, three miles from Kanchanaburi, eighty miles west of Bangkok, and arrived on October 26, 1942. When the Gordon Highlanders arrived the next day, commanded by Maj. R. G. "Reggie" Lees, who was to become Toosey's number two, the Japanese colonel tried to dismiss the parade. But, as Lees reported,

> The men just stood there stubbornly and refused to move. This went on for half an hour and eventually he said to me in perfect English "You carry on." So I gave the order "Fall out the officers." They came forward

> and saluted and fell out behind me. Then I turned to the Regimental Sergeant Major and said "Dismiss the men."

This was a small but important victory in the upcoming battle of wits with the Japanese camp commandants.

Lees and his men found five huts, a cookhouse, and quarters for the Japanese at the camp, which had been built by small early parties of anti-aircraft gunners under Maj. Roberts and Argyll and Sutherland Highlanders under Capt. David Boyle, who later became Toosey's interpreter. The arrival of Lees's party brought the camp strength to one thousand British prisoners. They were joined by another one hundred British in November and one thousand Dutch from Java in February 1943, at which point another four huts were built. Three hundred men were packed tightly in each of these bamboo huts, which had atap-palm roofs and sides, lashed together with a kind of raffia. They slept on bamboo slats, each man allocated about eighteen inches of space.

On the day after his arrival, the British commanding officers agreed that Toosey should be Senior British Officer, and his appointment was confirmed by Lt. Kosakata, the Japanese camp commandant. That same day also delivered an early example of the random brutality Toosey's men would suffer from the Japanese and Korean guards. Maj. Roberts was in the cookhouse when a Japanese soldier demanded that he assemble a work detail. When Roberts refused, he was struck across the face with a stick. Roberts retaliated by punching the soldier and knocking him to the ground. Toosey immediately protested to Kosakata and succeeded in obtaining an apology. It was the first instance of his refusal to be cowed by his captors.

Kosakata told Toosey that the men's job was to build two bridges across the River Kwai Yai which joins the main tributary of the River Kwai Noi ("small stream") at Kanchanaburi. One bridge would be made of wood, the other of steel and concrete. They also had to construct a mile and a quarter of railway embankment on either side of the main steel bridge. The railway would follow the eastern bank of the Kwai Noi. This was the biggest single task in the construction of the railway, a major engineering operation. The steel bridge would be three hundred yards long and set on eleven concrete piles across the river. One hundred yards south, the wooden bridge, one hundred yards long, was designed for light traffic and use in emergencies while the steel bridge was being built. The schedule was nine months to a year, and the higher priority was given to the building of the temporary wooden bridge (as featured in David Lean's film of the project). Until this was built, little work could be carried out on the far bank, so construction of the wooden bridge began at once, and the demands for labor increased week by week. The healthy toiled away, starting on the steel bridge too, while the sick were ordered to gather firewood and prepare food. The work day started as soon as it was light, when the men were woken by reveille, followed by a wash in a bucket and a breakfast of rice and stew prepared by the cooks (in spite of the division of labor, these were the fittest men in the camp, according to Toosey, because they were closest to the food). Then they paraded for the day's labor and were counted—a process which could take half an hour—split into work groups, and marched to collect their picks and shovels. They reassembled, were counted again, and finally were herded in long columns into the forest. They took their midday meal, again of rice and stew, with them in mess tins. When they reached the line, the Japanese engineer might or might not be there to explain the day's task. He had to supervise a long section of embankment or bridge, and he might or might not have told the Korean guard what the men were supposed to do. Sometimes the men received their instructions but they were ambiguous; sometimes they were clear to the men but not to the Korean guard. According to Lt. Ian Watt, the amount of work each man was supposed to do—move a cubic yard of earth or drive in a certain number of piles—was fairly reasonable under normal circumstances.

> But the task often fell very unequally on different work parties: some groups might have to carry their earth much farther than others, or drive their piles into much rockier ground. As the day wore on someone in a group with a difficult task would get beaten up. The task might actually be impossible, but all the guard thought about was that he'd probably be beaten up himself if the work on his section wasn't finished: so he lashed out. Meanwhile many other prisoners would already have finished their task, and would be sitting around waiting, or—even worse—pretending to work. The rule was that the whole day's task had to be finished, and, often, inspected by the Japanese engineer, before any single work party could leave the worksite. So more prisoners would be beaten up for lying down in the shade when they were supposed to look as though there was still work to do in the sun. At the end of the day's work an individual prisoner might well have been on his feet under the tropical sun from 7 in the morning until 7, 8 or 9 at night, even though he'd only done three or four hours' work. He would come back late for the evening meal; there would be no lights in the huts; and as most of the guards went off duty at 6 o'clock, he probably wouldn't be allowed to go down to the river to bathe or wash his clothes.

At first, the working parties cleared the jungle to a depth of fifty yards on either side. They felled and dragged away the trees, including teak and thick clumps of bamboo, by hand. The clumps of bamboo were up to ten yards thick, large enough to stop an elephant or a tank. Each piece had to be separately hauled out by a team using a rope. All the workers then set to building the embankment, which was two yards wide, using pick, shovel, and coolie earth basket or stretcher. Outcrops of rock had to be pickaxed or blasted out using crowbar, hammer, and dynamite. Toosey reported:

> The river had to be bridged using the trees with rope and pulley as a primitive pile-driving device. Great cuttings on the mountainside were engineering feats. Sleepers and rails were hauled up by hand or by elephant. Work went in spasms. Sometimes a normal day's work, sometimes a very gruelling 18 hours or more, near-naked in the baking sun or tropical rain. "Rest days," or yasumis, as they were called, were much less than once a week. In those days the only shop stewards we had were the officers who did their best, in spite of frequent beatings-up, to relieve the pressures on their men, but they met with very little success.

The bridges were built by sheer manpower. Apart from picks and shovels, and baskets and stretchers to carry earth, sand, and pebbles, the only tools were axes and adzes, hand trucks, hand piledrivers, concrete mixers, and grabs. "The pile-driver for the piers of the wooden bridge was slung from a pulley in a wooden scaffolding between two barges and worked by about twenty ropes on each barge; a Nip engineer squatted in the rigging and chanted a little ditty on the theme of *one* and two and *three* four and *three* four! or '*Ich-I ni no san yo, no san yo,*' " said Stephen Alexander.

> In time with this everyone pulled on the ropes with a short pull and a l-o-n-g-e-r pull, crash! And the weight pounded down on the top of the pile. This went on for hour after hour, and the monotony of it and the primitive nature of the tools and the sheer numbers of men slaving away —some digging, some in long snaking queues carrying baskets of earth, some chaining sand and stones from the river bed—made for a positively biblical scene. We felt like the Israelites building a temple to Moloch.

By December 1942, only weeks after the men had arrived at Tamarkan, the wooden bridge was virtually finished. The men were delighted when the river rose to an unprecedented height and swept it away. But their pleasure in this setback for the Japanese engineers was short-lived. They had to work even harder to reconstruct it when the floods receded. It was finished again by February—most of the material could be reused—and was used by light trains, pulled by diesel locomotives, until the steel bridge was finished. First the men had to heave up the heavy rails by hand and then maneuver them up the riverbank. It was grueling, dangerous work, draining for men on a starvation diet. When they could, they slowed, only to be harried by the guards. The situation became critical in February 1943 when the Japanese advanced the date for completion of the railway from December to August. The "Speedo" period had begun.

There were more beatings and longer hours, and the sick were dragged from their beds to work. At first officers were not forced to do the physical labor—though many did voluntarily—but they found themselves caught between the guards and the men. It was easier for a guard who wanted more work out of twenty or thirty men to harangue the officers, and if necessary knock them around, than to lash out at the individual men. They therefore liked to have the officer in a prominent position, within easy reach. The officer's lot was not a happy one, said Stephen Alexander. There were long periods of solitary boredom. He could walk up and down the line chatting to the men, but was not allowed to deflect them from their work for too long. At the end of his patrol he could hobnob with the officer in charge of the neighboring gang, but only until the Japanese took exception to their chatter. The chaotic organization of the work, and the friction between the guards, the Japanese camp staff, and the engineers also helped to poison the prisoners' lives.

Needless to say, life at Tamarkan was proving very different from life at Changi, where the prisoners had largely been left to their own devices by the Japanese. Now their lives were regimented by the Japanese and by the Korean guards, whom the Japanese despised (on one occasion a Japanese soldier dealt with a Korean by knocking him flat on the ground and gouging out his eye with the heel of his boot). The brutality that the Koreans suffered was transferred by them onto the prisoners, who were also expected to adopt Japanese customs, bowing if they saw a sentry or guard and giving orders on parade in Japanese.

The command of prisoners in a Japanese camp was therefore a supreme test of an officer's caliber, and Philip Toosey was one of the first British officers to be tested. For the eleven months he was in command at Tamarkan he was unflinching before the Japanese and steadfast for his men. He was not a career officer, having been a successful cotton broker and banker before the war, and he did not have the blinkered perceptions of the "Nips" held by some of the regular officers. He was young, tall, perhaps a trifle vain—some called him "Champagne Toosey"—and described by his officers as handsome, with one of those English faces that look like skeptical but genial bulldogs. He generally looked stern and sized up men in an instant, said Signaller W. M. Naylor, who worked for him as chief clerk. He was always dressed smartly, though the men were in rags: even when he stopped wearing a shirt, his shorts, sporting at the waistband a tag with his crown and two pips on it, were immaculately pressed, his long stockings clean, his shoes highly polished, and his cap worn straight. Some younger officers mocked this emphasis on personal smartness, as well as his showmanship, his belief in "army bullshit," and his use of a batman who could have been out at work on the railway. He was perhaps too regimental, they thought, but they all recognized that he was astute in his dealings with the Japanese.

Toosey now faced the dilemma that confronted all the Allied officers commanding prisoners in Thailand and Burma. The Japanese were going to build the railway whatever the resistance they met, whatever the Geneva Convention said about the treatment of prisoners, however sick the men were, and by using the most brutal methods if necessary. There were so many prisoners that it was of no consequence if many died in the process. For Toosey, an empty gesture of defiance or citing the Geneva Convention would not serve the men's chances of survival. "It had become clear to me that whether we liked it or not, the work had to be done," he said later. "I therefore addressed the troops and told them that good discipline was essential and that they should work cheerfully and keep their spirits up. We on our part would do our best to ensure that they got good food and fair treatment. They responded as usual—cheerfully." Toosey had acknowledged the truth that in a showdown the Japanese would always win. Ian Watt and his fellows were well aware that their captors had the power and no scruples whatsoever about how to use it. But from the start Toosey refused to kowtow to the Japanese and demonstrated that he had no fear. He did this respectfully, though, and never forced the issue to such an extent that his captors lost face. "Instead he first awed them with an impressive display of military swagger," said Watt, "and then proceeded to charm them with his ingratiating assumption that no serious difficulty could arise between honourable soldiers whose only thought was to do the right thing." He had to deal with three Japanese camp commandants during his time in charge—Kosakata was succeeded by Lt. Takasaki, nicknamed "The Frog," on December 30; the more junior Sgt. Hosomi took over from Takasaki in May 1943. Whenever Toosey met Takasaki, the Japanese commandant usually had his drawn sword on the table in front of him; he was formal and treated Toosey like dirt. Toosey got on much better with Sgt. Maj. Socho Saito, the second in command. He spent hours with Saito discussing arrangements and developed such a rapport with him that he secured a greater role for himself and his officers in the organization of the work. He considered Saito strict but honest.

Toosey deliberately refused to learn Japanese so that he could always say, "I don't understand." He was fortunate, however, to have as his adjutant David Boyle, an Argyll officer who spoke good pidgin Japanese and acted as Toosey's interpreter for the rest of the war. Conveniently, he also shared Toosey's attitudes. (Boyle's appointment as Toosey's interpreter was not appreciated by some of the Argylls. He replaced Capt. Gordon Skinner, who had been a businessman in Japan, was more fluent in Japanese, and had earned a reputation for standing up to the captors.) Boyle and Toosey worked well as a team, and the Japanese soon realized, said Boyle, that if Toosey said no, he meant it and was prepared to go on saying it until they shot him. Toosey was blind to all danger, said Capt. Stanley "Pav" Pavillard, who later served under him as a medical officer. When his eyes glared and he gritted his teeth, it spelled disaster to the enemy who crossed his path. Yet essentially he was a man of peace, unpretentious and full of dignity where often none existed. One result of his constant lobbying was that the men's dilapidated huts were rebuilt by convalescent men, and they did such a good job that Tamarkan eventually became for the Japanese the show camp of Thailand. He was also a good delegator: he recruited "Reggie" Lees as his number two, assisted by Capt. H. S. Wood; two officers of his own regiment were appointed to other senior roles—Capt. Malcolm Northcote oversaw the canteen and Sgt. Maj. Coles became camp sergeant major.

As they labored on the bridges, the men were constantly harassed by the guards. When asked to describe the guards' behavior after the war, Toosey quoted a sentence from *Red Star over Asia* by Edgar Snow: "Nowhere in the world was sadism practised with greater efficiency than in the Japanese army." The normal form of punishment in the Japanese army was corporal and violent. Even the despised Koreans had written instructions that they were entitled to kill the prisoners without reference to higher authority. "Every form of cruelty that an uncivilised mind could invent was used on the prisoners," said Toosey. Capt. J. Gibson observed this cruelty when the guards caught ten prisoners selling tools to the Thais. The guards started beating the men with bamboo shafts and anything else they could lay their hands on. They then held one of the men down on the floor while one of their number repeatedly climbed up on the table and jumped onto his stomach. Eventually Toosey managed to stop the beating. However, the next morning the Kempetai, the Japanese Gestapo, arrived in the camp with their instruments of torture: thumbscrews, handcuffs, pieces of sharpened bamboo, and whips.

> The men who had spent the night in the cells were brought out and subjected to the most fiendish tortures which included sticking lighted cigarettes into their noses and ears. They also gave them what they were pleased to call the water treatment. This consisted of holding a man down on his back, placing a rice sack over his face and pouring water from a four-gallon can into his mouth. The result was that within a few minutes the man's stomach was swollen to an amazing extent with the amount of water which he had been forced to swallow. The next step was to jump on his stomach with dire results. All these were accompanied by continuous face slapping with the result that several of the men broke down and the Japanese were able to procure the information as to which Thais the tools had been sold to.
>
> That evening the Japanese accompanied two of our men to their rendezvous and we heard quite a bit of shooting. When the party returned to camp they brought with them a couple of natives and the beating began anew. A certain amount of the tools were recovered by this method. The "enquiry" went on for about four days and in the end we were told that six of the men had been found guilty and would be taken to Bangkok for trial by the Japanese Military tribunal.

Some of the other punishments suffered by the men were listed by Toosey in a report at the end of the war:

- Beatings up in the face with the open hand or closed fist.
- Beating up on any part of the body with any form of implement available, including iron crowbars and great branches of wood.
- Kicks on the head, in the private parts and the stomach and legs.
- Being made to stand to attention in front of the guard room or anywhere else for hours on end, sometimes holding lumps of wood and other weighty objects above the head.
- Kneeling in front of the guard room on two bamboos.
- Two prisoners being made to beat one another up.
- Doing hand presses for an indefinite period under the eyes of a guard, who would strike the offender if he showed any signs of relaxing.
- Solitary confinement in tiny cells of earth and bamboo for weeks at a time.

Saito, known to the soldiers as "the ball-breaking bastard" (in spite of what Toosey thought of him), built a wooden cross beside the bridge. Men who angered him were tied to it by the wrists. Their hands were left free, and they had to hold a bucket of sand or water in each for up to twelve hours a day.

Punishments were administered for the most minor offenses—failing to salute, having no water in the ashtrays in the barrack rooms, imaginary insults to individual guards, failure to understand one another's language, the slightest movement on roll call, wearing a towel around the neck when passing the guardroom. Until the autumn of 1943, such practices were undoubtedly encouraged by the Japanese officers, said Toosey, and he insisted that all beatings or incidents with the guards be reported to him immediately. If he or another officer could not intervene before the incident was over, it was instantly reported to the camp command. Sometimes the result was that the officer himself received a beating, but the continual complaints tended to reduce the number of incidents, and the men felt that their officers were safeguarding their interests.

Toosey took beatings himself and intervened decisively to stop them, as when Cpl. Lawson (who had been stealing tools on Toosey's instructions and selling them to the Chinese outside the camp to raise money for the hospital) was caught and interrogated by the Kempetai. According to his own account, Toosey heard awful groans and was given permission to intervene:

> There was Lawson standing completely naked, facing the Japanese officer, who had a drawn sword on the table, and his back was raw with weals from a whip, from his neck to his heels. I asked him what the trouble was and he said, "Well, Sir, I have told these little brutes the truth and they won't believe me and I am not going to lie to please them." I said, "Now, Lawson, don't be a fool, do you know what they want you to say?" and he said, "Yes, Sir." I said, "Well say it, and if your conscience is in any way hurt, I will take full responsibility when we get home." This he did and the beating-up stopped immediately. This had included other tortures like cigarette burns and matches under his fingernails. He was a very brave man indeed.

On another occasion, when David Boyle was left with a broken arm and two broken ribs after shouting at a Korean guard, Toosey sent him to bed and stood guard outside, refusing to let the Japanese in and deliberately failing to understand what they said. Boyle by this time was the only interpreter, so the Japanese could not pass on instructions to the working parties. As a result, work stopped. After a day of this, Saito had the guard himself beaten up, an apology was made, and work on the bridges started again.

To try to escape from Tamarkan was futile, as the men had learned in January 1943 when Capt. Eugene Pomeroy, Lt. Eric Howard, and four other men fled. Toosey concealed their absence from roll calls for forty-eight hours, but when their absence was discovered, the Japanese called in the military police, who questioned all the men who had been sleeping near them. Saito kept Toosey standing at attention in front of the guardroom for twelve hours. Ten days later the four soldiers were brought back to the camp under armed escort and confined to the guardroom; Toosey was not allowed to speak to them. They stayed in the camp for two days and were then taken into the jungle in a truck with an escort of six guards. The guards returned without them. On February 20, after being betrayed by Thais for money, Pomeroy and Howard were also returned to the camp under escort. They were interrogated by the Kempetai and again Toosey was not allowed to speak to them. Three days later they were taken into the jungle and beheaded.

Although Toosey was outraged, he was prepared to use tactical compromises to achieve his aims of increasing food and medical supplies, improving working conditions, and allocating tasks more reasonably. Gradually he persuaded the Japanese that the issuing of tools or the allocation of the day's workload would be better handled by his staff. He also persuaded them that morale and efficiency would be improved if the responsibilities of the guards were limited entirely to preventing escapes. Officers in charge of working parties would supervise the construction work, and if the Japanese engineers assigned the next day's goals to Toosey, he and his staff would work out how best to achieve them. The new system completely transformed the men's conditions: much less time was wasted, daily tasks were often finished early in the afternoon, and weeks passed without any prisoners being beaten. "Suddenly the camp became almost happy," said Ian Watt.

Critical to the respect Toosey gained from the men was his belief that officers should not set themselves apart (as many did in other camps). According to Stephen Alexander, there was a "lunatic fringe" of officers who expected Toosey to cover for them, who wanted to make themselves as comfortable as possible, and for whom the idea of any manual work was anathema. But Toosey would not tolerate his officers playing endless games of bridge. He had no respect for those who had wangled themselves off the railway, set themselves up in the best huts, and did no work. (But he was well aware that the lieutenant colonels senior to him, who had retired from the Indian Army and come back to war, were as much as fifteen years older than he—Toosey was thirty-eight—and should not have been on active service at all.) Toosey led the group of officers who cared about the troops against the rest, perhaps the majority, who were willing to let somebody else get on with it. He insisted that officers eat the same food as the men, and there was no officers' mess: he did not want a rift to develop between them and the other ranks. Instead of sleeping and messing in a separate hut, which was the practice at many camps, Toosey's officers slept with their men by the door in the end section of each hut. Toosey led by example and frequently performed labor himself. He also insisted that those who avoided working on the railway spent their days improving camp amenities. It was quite normal, according to David Boyle, to find Toosey digging a new latrine—he seemed to enjoy hard physical work.

At first, the other officers had supervised the work parties, but the guards soon ordered them to work alongside the men. Toosey complained—while he was not averse to physical labor himself, he didn't believe officers should be compelled to do it—but was given an order that officers were also to act as workers. After several small incidents between the guards and officers, the crunch came when Kosakata ordered Lt. Bridge to get into a cutting and work with his men. Bridge refused, and then resisted when Kosakata tried to push him. There was a short tussle, two guards were called, and Bridge was taken back to camp and confined to the guardroom. Toosey was told that Kosakata had the power to execute Bridge. In future all officers would work. That was an order. At a meeting with his officers Toosey argued that they had no real option: "Either you are going to work and we will try to get the best terms we can or you are not going to work and you are going to stand there if necessary until they shoot you. . . . If you refuse I will stand and get shot with you." The decision to work on the best terms that could be secured was unanimous, and Bridge was released. Ultimately a few officers joined Toosey in doing manual work, but Kosakata eventually relented and did not force them into it. Toosey had increased his authority with both sides, the Japanese and his men.

Under Toosey's regime, officers were as liable to be punished as the men. There were one or two "stupid" officers who blurted out the news from the "canary," the camp's secret radio. The penalty for operating a radio was severe: at the least a savage beating and torture; at worst execution. To make them shut up, Toosey stopped the "canary" for a week. Officers as well as men were also put in the "no-good hut," a small cell for disciplining offenders. Corporal punishment was also used for serious offenses: some miscreants were given "a damn good hiding." One man who stole a blanket from an extremely ill patient and sold it to the Thais outside the camp to get money for food saw the strict disciplinarian side of Toosey:

> I had had him up in front of me in the battle [at Singapore] for running away, and I said to him, "I know you," and he said, "No, Sir, I've never seen you in my life." I said, "I have, you know." I said, "I'm just going to tell you this: if you ever dare to step out of line I'll starve you to death and you know I have the power to do it because I've got control of the food. Now you are going to be beaten up by two regimental sergeant majors behind this hut and if you dare to do anything about it or report me after the war, all I can tell you is that you will suffer more than I will." From that moment on he never put a foot wrong.

Toosey's brutal treatment of the man can be explained by the fact that the sick patient had died after his blanket was stolen.

On another occasion Toosey discovered a doctor wheedling extra food from the cookhouse and hit him with one of the legs of his bed. The doctor said he would report Toosey to the British Medical Association after the war. "Go on, do it chum and see what happens," retorted Toosey.

The constant lobbying by Toosey and Lees succeeded in obtaining regular working hours and one rest day a week, but the long hours and meager rations still led to sickness. There were four hundred serious cases, mainly malaria, tropical ulcers, and avitaminosis, and some dysentery. However, a small hospital had been built and opened on New Year's Day 1943, and, although few men had mosquito nets or blankets, there were only nine deaths between October and May, mainly because of Toosey's obsession with hygiene.

His fastidiousness helped in another way, too. The division of food among starving men quickly led to quarrels and resentment if someone got a few more grains of rice than his neighbor. Under Toosey, the food was shared equally:

> I insisted there was x number of men in the camp, officers, warrant officers and other ranks, and that whatever came into the camp in the way of food or money would be shared in so far as was possible equally between every single individual in that camp. There was no question of giving extra people extra money. What I did on occasions was when a man was very sick I would get one of these brave chaps who was prepared to go outside the wire to go and get some special food for him, such as a duck or a scrawny chicken. That was the only extra that anybody got. Otherwise it was completely evenly divided out and I used to go to the cookhouse when the food was being distributed, I won't say at every meal, but regularly, and watch the food being distributed to ensure that nobody got any extra.

Nevertheless, the men's rations were insufficient to enable them to cope with their backbreaking manual labor. The average daily ration was 700 grams of rice, 600 of vegetables, 100 of meat, 20 of salt, and 15 of oil. Saito allowed the purchase of a cow every ten days, which at least helped to flavor the stew. Along with news from the rest of the war and the state of the latrines, food was the men's main daily preoccupation. Almost all the meals consisted of rice and stew. When the rations were increased even slightly, there was an immediate drop in the number of sick. The meager rations, however, were supplemented by buying eggs, fruit, meat, ham, and corn from local traders when out on working parties. Officers were paid thirty dollars a month; an egg cost five cents, corncobs were three for five cents, and twenty Virginia cigarettes could be had for twenty-five cents. The men were paid much less—a week's wages gave them enough for just three duck eggs. As a result, many sold their possessions to raise money for food. They also learned to feed from their surroundings. One dish was tapioca flavored with the leaves of a wild lime tree—known as "lime and slime." Sometimes the river was bombed with dynamite and the dead fish collected. At least one dog went into a stew. Once the canteen was set up in December 1942, the men could buy cakes (made from rice), tobacco, and gula malacca, a sweet made from the sap of a palm tree that looked like brown condensed milk. The local ladies who sold eggs were generally charming, and they spoke an English of their own invention: they called hard-boiled eggs "egg-kok" (eggs cooked) and raw eggs "eggs-no-kok." Obviously, if they had no fresh eggs that day, they would say, "eggs-no-kok-no." At the base-area camps and some of the lower "up-country" camps (those not far from Tamarkan and Chung-Kai), the men could often buy duck eggs. "The ducks must have fed exclusively on fish, for their eggs had all the flavour of a cod fillet—but they saved the life of many a POW," said Geoffrey Pharaoh Adams.

To supplement the rations, Toosey initiated a form of "socialism" by "milking" the relatively rich officers: an average of ten ticals was deducted from their pay of thirty ticals a month to buy food and medicine for the sick. He also sanctioned trading with the Japanese and Thais on the understanding that the canteen would get a cut of the profits. One prisoner collected broken watches, repaired them temporarily, and sold them for relatively large sums to the Japanese.

The arrival of the Dutch in February 1943 added to the variety of Tamarkan life in several ways. When they arrived they were represented by Col. Scheyerer and his adjutant Lt. de Grijs. At first, with their officers waited upon by batmen and so many the products of intermarriage between Dutch expatriates and the native population, they were a source of both amusement and puzzlement. But they had lived all their lives in the East and knew about rice. They also ground peanut butter and made *sambal bajak,* peppery herbs fried in oil that helped to make the rice palatable and added vitamins to the diet. Furthermore, said Stephen Alexander, they introduced the British to an improved form of personal hygiene:

> Nothing excited our mirth more than seeing the Dutch colonials walking to the latrines carrying bottles of water instead of toilet paper. But it was borne in upon us that quite apart from saving our books (or our pay in buying Thai toilet paper) Moslem ablutions cost nothing and were more suitable to the climate. After delicate experiment we were soon following their example and wondering why we hadn't thought of it months before. I got terribly shocked when a padre who had dysentery tore up all his Bible and used it as toilet paper. It was a godsend to us the Dutch coming in and showing us how to use water. You had a bottle of water and soon got into the habit of pouring it down your backside and flicking it up. You can get very neat at it, yet some people went on tearing up books or using leaves for ages.

Since many tropical diseases were borne by flies, hygiene was a worthwhile obsession. Toosey regularly inspected the huts and was particularly concerned about cleanliness in the kitchens. Personal hygiene mattered, too: he made the men shave at night. He would not allow any beards because they became infested with lice, but also a beard, he believed, had a negative effect on morale, certainly in wartime, except in the navy: "The ordinary British soldier has always been clean shaven," he claimed. Most were shaved by a Dutch barber, using soap made of wood ash and palm oil.

With the wooden bridge completed for the second time in February 1943, the men's work was focused on the steel bridge. Work had already begun in 1942 on its foundations. Double ring molds of wood were sunk into the riverbed and filled to make concrete shells. The centers were sucked out with pumps and grabs until the concrete casing had sunk fifteen feet. Then sand, pebbles, and more cement were poured in until the solid foundations were ready for the piles which were to carry the steel girders above. Shaped wooden molds were erected on the foundations, and scaffolding built. At the top were platforms for the concrete mixers, and up long ramps queues of men carried baskets and sacks of sand, pebbles, and cement to feed them and fill the molds. According to Stephen Alexander, it was even more "Cecil B. DeMille" than the building of the wooden bridge because the scale was so much greater, "with hundreds of cursing men and excited 'Nips' milling around, barges pom-pomming up the river, tipper-trucks squeaking along narrow-gauge supply lines, and over all—in this dry season—the blinding glare of the sun above and the white sand below." As the men stood in a long human chain, passing the baskets of stones and pebbles from the riverbed to the concrete mixer for ten or eleven hours each day, they relieved the monotony with spelling competitions, mental arithmetic problems, and telling old jokes. When all the main supporting timbers of the steel bridge had been driven into the riverbed, one work party was transferred to a quarry which was to provide ballast for the railway. Tons of stone had been blasted from the hillside when the men arrived: it was in all shapes and sizes, and the men were given sledgehammers with which to reduce the boulders to more manageable dimensions. It looked simple: the hammer was slammed onto the boulder and at some point the boulder would begin to disintegrate. But when the first strike was made and the hammer hit the stone, "a thousand stinging pinpricks assailed the men's unprotected legs," said Stan Henderson.

Pte. Bob Hislop, who had arrived at Tamarkan with the first party of eighty under Maj. Roberts, helped to sink the concrete columns. He wore an old-fashioned diving helmet fitted with an air pipe, which in turn was fitted to an old airpump. He had to get inside the concrete pillars and go down to the riverbed, then shovel out the rocks and pebbles so that the pillars would sink. It was a dark and unpleasant job: he had to keep his body upright, otherwise water would find its way inside his helmet. "It seemed a hell of a long time before we came up for a spell," he said.

The men—in direct contradiction of the story told in the film *The Bridge on the River Kwai*—did their best to sabotage the bridges by bad workmanship, even though they were under constant surveillance by the guards. Rotten tree trunks were used on the embankments and covered with soil so that there would be subsidence. Huge numbers of white ants were collected and put in parts of the wooden bridge. Concrete was incorrectly mixed, and many of the nuts and bolts left loose. According to Signaller Naylor, Toosey's chief clerk, there was an "accident" when a particularly unpopular Japanese engineer was deliberately pushed into the concrete and killed. "We did our damnedest to sabotage the thing," said Toosey.

Once the second bridge had been completed, most of the fit men were moved up the line to new camps. Toosey wanted to go with them, but the Japanese ordered him to stay at Tamarkan as the camp became a hospital. He now witnessed at first hand the toll that the railway had inflicted on the men who had labored at other camps farther up the line during the first six months—and the worst was only just beginning at the northernmost end of the line, near the Burmese border. "We saw scenes of misery that will live for ever in the memories of all of us," he wrote.

When Dr. Arthur Moon, a gynecologist from Sydney serving with the Australian Army Medical Corps, arrived at Tamarkan from Hintok, sixty miles to the north, on May 1, his immediate reaction was relief at arriving at a clean, well-established camp commanded by a "friendly" and energetic British officer. Toosey appointed Moon as senior medical officer the next day, and he became one of several Australian doctors who saved thousands of prisoners' lives over the coming months. When the first 117 patients arrived on May 5, plans had already been made for their reception, classification, and allocation to separate wards for dysentery, malaria, malnutrition, skin infections, and injuries. But no structural alterations had been allowed in the camp, so sleeping huts became hospital wards. Rations dropped because the sick received only 50 percent of the food given to workers, the supply of drugs that had been brought from Changi was almost exhausted, and new issues from the Japanese were negligible. The first issue for a hospital destined to hold three thousand patients (parties of about one hundred sick arrived nightly, and the camp reached its maximum capacity in July) was a few dozen iodine capsules, three bandages, and eight aspirin tablets.

The sick were often in an appalling state. About 75 percent of the men were stretcher cases; it was common for them to arrive dead. They were brought in cattle trucks on the railway, with up to forty men in each truck. No arrangements had been made for food or treatment on the journey by the Japanese. On one occasion a party of sixty, mostly stretcher cases, was dumped in a paddy field some two miles from the camp in the pouring rain at 3 A.M. They were left without a guard, and a search party had to go out from the camp to find them. Toosey was horrified by their condition:

> As a typical example I can remember one man who was so thin he could be lifted easily in one arm. His hair was growing down his back and was full of maggots. His clothing consisted of a ragged pair of shorts, soaked with dysentery excreta. He was lousy, and covered with flies all the time. He was so weak he was unable to lift his hand to brush away the flies which were clustered in his eyes and on the sore places of his body. I forced the Japanese staff to come and look at these parties, which could be smelt for some hundreds of yards, but with the exception of the Camp Commandant, they showed no signs of sympathy and sometimes merely laughed.

Each party was met by Toosey and introduced to his style of command. L.Cpl. J. S. Cosford was in one of them:

> "This camp," Toosey told the new arrivals, "is the cleanest in Thailand and I want you to keep it so. There has been very little illness here and only nine deaths in as many months. Now that it is to be a sick camp, keep it clean and disease will be kept under control. The Nips here are bastards. Discipline is very strict. Here are their orders and it will pay to obey them:
>
> - No smoking is allowed outside the huts.
> - No sing-songs or lectures are permitted.
> - All games are banned, also books.
> - Nobody must go within two metres of the perimeter fence.
> - All Nips must be saluted and you must stand when they enter the huts."

The new arrivals learned the orders the hard way, by seeing or taking the beatings that came from disobeying them. "The colonel received many a clout himself from trying to save us from the savage punishment the Nips handed out daily," said Cosford. "They were swine. They just had to hit somebody."

After Toosey's introduction, the men were given a mug of hot tea, a smoke—and, perhaps the greatest blessing of all, a cake of soap. Within an hour they had had a hot meal. Next day they were given an extra supply of washing water and a haircut. Those who could walk were taken to the river. Within forty-eight hours their clothes and equipment had been disinfected. When Rabbi Chaim Nussbaum arrived in July from Tonchan, he and his party were stopped and sprayed with disinfectant. But they heard laughter, and the men they met radiated health and enthusiasm:

> There are no hungry thin eyes, no empty begging hands. True, it is a closed camp, but there is civilisation here. Our commandant is a born leader. He seems to be steady and ethical and he attempts to maintain a level of comfort and emotional balance. It is said (a gross exaggeration, of course) that there is little reason to die in this camp if you have not arrived here with a mind set to die. If only you reach here, you will be safe. The canteen is full—cigarettes, drinks, food—none of it spoiled or waiting under dust. Almost everyone here walks as if he is proud of something . . . stepping to a mind-music. In the previous camps, we had moved to the absence of sound—with an emptiness of spirit, slow and dragging.

> The camp is close to immaculate, with large and well-ordered huts, but it seems that with every new contingency, some germ is carried in that must be quelled. Because of our lice, we must leave all of our clothes in a huge pot of boiling water, at the other end of the camp. Our hut has been completely emptied, and we washed every bamboo stick with boiling hot water (an unbelievable luxury in a Japanese POW camp). I wait now to receive my ferociously boiled clothes, after having scrubbed my head and body intensely. I wait to feel better, but then I hear from camp veterans that the lice will return—in about four to six weeks.

The spirit that governed the Japanese attitude to sick prisoners was revealed on June 26, 1943, when Col. Sijuo Nakamura, the commander of the prisoners in Thailand, declared in a general order from his Kanchanaburi HQ that prisoners who failed to reach the Japanese targets "by lack of health" were guilty of a "shameful deed." This disregard for the sick was evident at Tamarkan, where the most prevalent disease was dysentery. Other maladies were malaria, avitaminosis, tropical ulcers, and emaciation, and of course some were suffering from more than one. Many were mere skeletons. Their clothes were tattered or consisted of rags and sacking; they had no headgear, blankets, or bedding. "Dysentery cases were often fouled and ulcer cases arrived with improvised dressings from which pus exuded and maggots crawled." The only issue of clothes for up to three hundred men consisted of 190 pairs of rubber boots, 85 pairs of shorts, and 21 shirts. By the end of July, the peak period in the hospital's brief history, the camp strength was 3,108 with 2,920 in the hospital. There had been 87 deaths since the hospital had opened, mainly from dysentery, though the majority of patients were now suffering from jungle ulcers (650), avitaminosis (600), and malaria (450).

There were dreadful sights in the wards—men who were only parchment and bone. "A wreck was staggering back to his bed, his body emaciated and covered with sores," Capt. C. F. Blackater noted in his diary. "Instinctively I drew back, then pulled myself together and went to him. His breathless, tired thanks shamed me. Three have died in the ward in the last twenty-four hours. . . . Oh for unlimited Emetine [which was used to treat dysentery]." Anesthetics were so scarce that they had to be reserved for amputations and other surgical operations. So the men with ulcers who were taken over to the "theater" for a major cleanup had to take the full pain of the cutting, the scraping to the bone, or the removal of dead bone. Capt. Ralston, working in the dysentery ward, had no drugs, but endless patience. Blackater said:

> Daily he listened to everything the men had to tell him. He knew, and they knew, just how little he could do for them, but that morning talk . . . was a tonic in itself. Men pinned their faith on him, and many were cured. There were, of course, Japanese creosote pills, but they were a joke, as they passed straight through you and reappeared as perfectly good pills. It was suggested that patients might try crunching them. The result was equally ineffective.

One patient who appreciated Toosey's visits to the wards was Pte. George Downes:

> I was the second person to have a leg amputated in Tamarkan in September by Major Moon. Colonel Toosey visited the ulcer ward every day, a great figure, immaculate in uniform. As he walked down the hut this particular day he asked when I could get on my crutches. I told him that I would be allowed to the following day, so he invited me to his office for a cup of coffee at 5 p.m. But on that day I got a dose of malaria and I told the Colonel's batman to let him know that I wouldn't be able to come. But at 5 p.m. along came the Colonel to the hut with a tin plate and cup of coffee in his hands. He sat down on my bamboo-slatted, sack-covered bed and said: "As you couldn't come to see me, I thought I would visit you." And I dined on the fried egg, sweet potatoes, ersatz coffee he had brought me, with a Nippon cigarette to follow.

Moon was forced to practice medicine at the most basic level. Toosey watched him amputate a leg under a mosquito net with a local anesthetic. Moon's main tool was the cookhouse saw, which had been sterilized and sharpened for the occasion. Many cures were inevitably simple and basic. Men boiled water in small tins to clean the bandages for their tropical ulcers. They learned to keep four-gallon tins of boiling water alongside all food points for sterilizing. "Mag-sulph" (a form of Epsom salts) was the universal remedy. Water was chlorinated at the pump, clothes were laundered, bed slats were removed and cleaned. A disinfectant was used on webbing, blankets, and mosquito nets, and virtually exterminated vermin. Toosey instituted a system under which each ward was commanded by an officer who, working closely with the medical staff, was responsible for cleanliness and discipline. Lotions that had been used on ulcer cases were poured down a pit with a fly-proof cover: soiled dressings were burned in an incinerator. When cholera broke out to the north in June 1943, patients admitted to Tamarkan were put in quarantine for ten days, river bathing was banned, and all anti-dysentery measures were tightened. There was no outbreak of cholera at Tamarkan.

Sgt. Hosomi, the Japanese commandant since May, tried to help, but he was powerless to do so because of his inferior rank. The Japanese doctor visited the camp once a month, but entered the wards on only one occasion, when a Thai mission visited the camp with a Japanese major. Toosey maneuvered them into the ulcer ward, but "the stink was so frightful and the sights so grim" that they left at once. One of the officers retched outside.

One of Toosey's most important initiatives was a war against flies. He recruited Fusilier Harry Howarth to dig latrines twelve feet deep. It was the most important job in the camp, the colonel told Howarth. Then he scrounged scraps of leather, wire, and bamboo from the Japanese and set a platoon to manufacturing flyswatters. Every man, apart from the very sick, was ordered to kill fifty flies a day. This command was rigidly enforced, according to Howarth: each man gave his fifty flies to his platoon commander, who passed them on to the company commander and on up to the camp administration.

> Allied to this, the camp was inspected every morning by the Colonel on his official rounds. Morale began to rise, deaths began to fall, we began to feel like soldiers again. Food began to get better due to the efforts of the Colonel who appeared to be greatly respected by the Japanese sergeant who was the camp commandant. Within two months deaths were extremely rare, and flies had almost become non-existent.

In spite of all the measures instituted by Toosey and Moon, however, the situation remained desperate, with supplies of food and drugs still negligible. In July, though, as the number of men at Tamarkan swelled, Toosey found a savior. On a trip to Kanchanaburi to collect rations he met Boon Pong, a Thai merchant who was already supplying Tamarkan with some of its food. Boon Pong told Toosey that if he wrote a letter giving his army number, rank, and name, and the amount of cash and medicines that were needed, he might be able to help. Toosey responded by telling Boon Pong that there were 1,730 sick in the camp, twenty-eight had died in a month, they had no money, and the men did not receive any pay. A few days later he received a mysterious package including a letter written in perfect English, a decent sum in cash, and a very useful supply of medicine.

Toosey had inadvertently made contact with the secret "V Organisation," which supplied money and drugs to several camps along the length of the railway. Future messages to Boon Pong were sent with the ration truck, and after the first few visits Toosey trusted Cpl. D. R. Locke to smuggle the medicine and banknotes back into Tamarkan. Up to November, the value of the smuggled goods, usually hidden in wads of native tobacco, was 42,105 ticals (about £3,500). They helped save hundreds of lives. There was a small hatch in the wall of Moon's room, next to the quartermaster's store. As the baskets of tobacco arrived, a Korean checking them with the quartermaster, some were rifled, the goods pushed through the hatch to Moon.

Dealing with the Thai underground was nerve-racking, as Toosey admitted. If the Japanese learned of any contact with the Thais, savage punishments inevitably followed—a beating at best, death at worst. It was equally dangerous for Boon Pong himself, whose whole family was involved: his wife, brother, and two daughters. Thanks to the risks taken by him and Toosey's men, though, the rations at Tamarkan improved, and by October the death rate had fallen to one a week (six men had died on one *day* in June). The patients certainly appreciated the results: the "hush-hush" money made it possible for Capt. Simpson, who now ran the canteen, to soar to new heights, said Capt. Blackater. Sausage rolls, Cornish pasties, meatballs, steaks, and roasted chickens all appeared on the bill of fare at "Simpson's," while in the afternoon cakes, "jam" tarts, and shortbread were hawked through the huts by canteen servers. There were also dry-goods canteens that provided soap, limes in season, bananas, notebooks and pencils, Thai cheroots, and many other commodities. A small profit was made on everything, and it all went back into the men's messing, the purchase of medicine for the hospital, and, above all, subsidizing the excellent diet center for the sick run by an officer who was in the catering trade in civil life, of which Blackater said,

> Tamarkan was not a bed of luxury, but the effect on morale in providing a penniless sick man with a bun at four o'clock in the afternoon, when he was hot, tired and in pain, was very great indeed. And Toosey's team of welfare officers were provided with sufficient funds to give their wards a titbit every second day, apart from the provision of extra eggs and tinned milk for the very sick, at the ward MO's discretion.

Blackater supplied Simpson's from the duck and pig farm which he had set up after Toosey recalled that he had been a poultry farmer, and which Toosey had persuaded Saito to sanction. It was the happiest period of Blackater's life as a prisoner, and he experienced the sense of humor and compassion that existed among the men and helped to raise their spirits. Wherever Blackater and his assistant L.Cpl. Gathercole went, a murmur of quacking followed them. Two of the ten pigs were tame and were named Lucille and Algernon.

> The farm became the focal point of the camp. After work a visit to the farm was the thing. Rows of men would lean on the top bar of the pig pen and gaze at the satiated creatures inside. . . . We were a small community on our own. We built a little kitchen, big enough to hold us all [eventually there were three other farmworkers] and there we brewed delectable stews of vegetable peel and kitchen swill for the livestock, infinitely richer than our own diet. Simpson's was our chief customer for drakes. I would take them to the canteen by way of the hospital as it amused men who had not been off their backs for six, eight or ten months to see the colourful birds in our arms. They liked to touch them, something from a world they had almost forgotten existed. We used to arrange with the MOs to take people down on stretchers to see the farm. We would dump the stretchers in a pen and soon the ducks would be all around it.

By now the camp was fully licked into shape. The fit men played sports—soccer, softball, volleyball, and badminton. There were concerts, lectures, and discussions. Chess and bridge tournaments and arts and crafts were inaugurated as therapy for the convalescent. At an exhibition in September, paintings, engravings, woodcuts, and models were displayed. Toosey presented the prizes—most of which went to the Dutch—at a special ceremony. News from the secret radio bolstered morale. The huts had been well built. Gravel paths led to the cookhouses and latrines, and there were roads rather than the paths of other camps.

When a compulsory memorial service was held at Tamarkan on November 14, 1943, attended by 1,143 men, there had been a total of 202 deaths, a remarkably small number by comparison with some camps farther up the railway line toward Burma. It was a significant achievement for Toosey's style of leadership. Soon afterward, most of the sick were moved to the hospital camps at Chungkai and Nong Pladuk. Toosey and Boyle left 318 men at Tamarkan when they moved to Nong Pladuk on December 11. Three days later an advance party of men who had been working in Burma arrived, and Tamarkan reverted to being a prison camp.

Many of the men returning from the miseries of Burma were Australian, usually reluctant to show any admiration or respect for the English, especially their stuffy officers. (Toosey was an exception—a "fucking gentleman" to the few Australians who had been with him over the previous months.) But after the squalor of Burma they found a camp with kitchens, canteens, gardens, duck and cattle yards, pig pens, playing fields, and concert parties, as well as military police and hut guards. Among their number was the war correspondent Rohan Rivett.

> Tamarkan was so much better than the jungle camps that for some time we were very content. In a single day we received more greens in the ration than we had seen in the jungle in the past six months. Vegetables in profusion poured into this camp. We did actually see some meat, fish or pieces of egg in our evening stew. But best of all was the canteen. We could get bananas for a cent each, and quantities of duck eggs—fried, boiled or omelettes for ten cents. In those palmy early days when our cooked foods canteen was functioning we could even buy a roast duck now and then. On my birthday, a fortnight after arrival, with eight of my cobbers I had a discussion with four roast ducklings, stuffed with onions and herbs—a discussion more profitable in our pellagra-ridden condition than the finest of the Socratic Dialogues.

Sgt. Stan Arneil, a fellow Australian, found the camp like a home away from home. His ulcers were dressed, there had been a "wonderful" vegetable stew, thick with celery and pumpkin, and he had bought two pints of brown sugar, two pints of peanuts, and four eggs for $1.50. "Such prices are incredible after the prices up country. We are lying on our beds now awaiting lunch and looking forward to our special diets. Fancy special diets for beri-beri!"

Men still died every day, legs still had to be amputated, but the worst of Tamarkan—and for its new occupants the hell of building the railway—was now over. Those who returned south from the Burmese and Thai camps to the north did light work—constructing huts, building a Japanese HQ, and unloading food barges. They were allowed to swim in the river for half an hour daily and there were regular concerts. The men at Tamarkan, by railway standards, led a quiet life, until the American bombers arrived a year later.

The film bent history. It was not commandos but American and British bombers that destroyed the bridges on the River Kwai. The raids began on November 29, 1944, when twenty-one Liberators of the USAF 7th Bomb Group scored at least one direct hit, but the steel bridge remained standing. Two more unsuccessful raids followed on December 13 and January 23. A few days later, eight planes of the 9th Squadron succeeded in destroying two sections of the wooden bridge, but the steel bridge again withstood the bombardment. Capt. Richard Sharp had left Chungkai that day and was welcomed to Tamarkan by the USAF:

> The spectacle was thrilling, huge shining Liberators coming in at what seemed no more than 200 ft to drop their load, soar over the roofs of the huts with all guns blaring and crackling, and fly round to come in again, and yet again. But much too close for comfort. The Tamarkan people had suffered casualties in earlier raids, so by the time some bombs were dropped in the camp, we were all well away in the far corner. But the raid was disappointing; for apart from putting the fear of God into us, they achieved little, and the bridge had to wait a few days for a neat little raid.

That "neat little raid" came on February 13. The bombers, four Liberators with four one-thousand-pound bombs, destroyed one of the concrete piers and two spans of the steel bridge, and scored direct hits on the wooden bridge. Louis Baume, who was in a camp in Kanchanaburi, noted the attack in his diary:

> Today the American Air Force came over to bomb the bridges at Tamarkan; the planes fairly plastered them for over three hours, coming in extremely low across the river and dropping very heavy stuff. Unfortunately our guards opened up with light machine guns and one of the planes sprayed the camp with cannon fire in retaliation.

The Japanese immediately began to repair the bridges, and in the meantime used barges to carry loads across the river. Within six weeks the wooden bridge had been repaired (using Japanese labor, not the prisoners') and was being used by diesel cars and loaded wagons pushed by hand, not by locomotives.

The bombers retaliated with yet another attack on April 3. USAF Lt. Col. William A. Henderson recalled this dangerous mission when the war was over: "We were alerted in the afternoon of 2 April for a 00.30 briefing and a 02.30 take-off. When the target map curtain was parted and the 14.50 hour duration mission at a bombing altitude of 6000 feet was revealed, a murmur of impending extraordinary danger went up from the crews." Baume again watched the attack from a ringside seat at Kanchanaburi. The repairs to the wooden bridge had just been completed and the first train had moved across when in the afternoon "the Yanks came over and knocked the bridge for six."

Once again the Japanese set about repairing the two bridges, and once again the bombers (this time the RAF) returned, to make the final attack on Tamarkan on June 24. Baume, as usual, saw the assault:

> The RAF has been over again on one of its spectacular low level attacks on the bridges this afternoon. Shells exploded low over us as the planes dived in from all angles—shrapnel, bullets and bombs seemed to fill the air. The RAF adopt very different tactics from the Americans: they do not rely so much on mass-bombing from a high altitude but come in individually to press home the attack. We much prefer the high stuff in one way. . . . It was a terrifying experience this afternoon for throughout the raid we were forbidden to take shelter.

Another witness was Capt. John Barratt. He had been taken ill with a suspected twisted bowel at Chungkai and transferred to Tamarkan for an operation, which was conducted by oil lamp under a mosquito net using a penknife as a scalpel. Barratt was sedated by injecting distilled rice wine into his spine; his wound was sewn up with the bootlaces of a dead soldier. He came to the next morning with incisions in his stomach and side, a board at his back, a mosquito net as a pillow and another under his knees to keep them bent. He soon recovered sufficiently to move about the camp, though, and watched the four British Liberator bombers from 159 Squadron as each in turn came down within a hundred feet of the main bridge, bombed it, and circled for more. "We were so proud and delighted that we moved up the slit trenches towards the bridge and watched everything," he said. The attack destroyed three spans of the steel bridge and breached the wooden bridge in two places. When the bombers returned in July they were dropping propaganda leaflets rather than bombs. The Japanese surrendered in August. The bridges on the River Kwai were destroyed. The story of Tamarkan had reached its conclusion.

The Bridge on the River Kwai has been so successful across the world that Tamarkan, alongside the river itself, is now known as the camp where a British colonel was so determined to build a bridge that he opposed its destruction by his own side. That, as this chapter has shown, is a libel on Philip Toosey. Those who served with him, as well as Gen. Percival, have tried to put the record straight. As a result of their efforts there is a brief notice in the credits that the film is fiction, not fact. But the memorable images of David Lean's powerful film and Pierre Boulle's equally powerful novel have overpowered the truth. Many features of the film are wrong: men at Tamarkan didn't whistle "Colonel Bogey" (that was at Nong Pladuk, where it was played daily by a cornet player as work parties under Lt. Harold Payne marched past the guardroom); Toosey wasn't a regular officer; there were no Americans at Tamarkan; there was no successful escape; Toosey was never put in the punishment hut; there was no infiltrating officer whose job was to blow up the bridge. But, as Stephen Alexander discovered, it was useless to explain that the Tamarkan bridges were never blown up by commandos, that no pretty little girls came tripping through the jungle, that the Japanese engineers required muscle, not expertise, from their prisoners, and that a leader as boneheaded as Alec Guinness's Col. Nicholson would soon have been pounding peanuts in the cookhouse while someone more pragmatic took over. Toosey, who had made the best of a very bad job, and who saved even more lives at Tamarkan when it became a hospital camp than he did when building the bridge, was thus inevitably tarred with the Nicholson brush. "It was a most undeserved association for a man of much enterprise and courage," said Alexander.

Sixty years on from the end of the Second World War it is difficult to comprehend the scale of Toosey's achievement at Tamarkan. Only those over seventy have any real experience of war as it was fought before the age of smart bombs and laser-guided missiles. But those who served with Toosey are in no doubt. They admit that his success involved a degree of collaboration with the enemy, but none accuses him of being "Jap-happy." Those who worked at Tamarkan knew that the real issue was not building the bridge but how many prisoners would die in the process. There was only one way to persuade the Japanese to improve rations, provide medical supplies, allow regular holidays, and reduce the brutality of the guards: the prisoners had to convince them that the work progressed better if such concessions were made.

For the prisoners, the alternative to anarchy, in the vacuum created by the absence of Japanese camp staff, was to set up their own organization, including a system of justice. Toosey became a legend as the man who could "handle the Nips." He was lucky in some ways, said Ian Watt. The bridges over the Kwai were such a big job that the camp there was more permanent, and had better facilities, than most of the others. It was also in the "egg belt," whereas farther up-country overwork and lack of food were often so extreme as to defeat the efforts of even the best leaders.

Still, Toosey fully earned his reputation. His general strategy of taking over as much responsibility as possible (often much more than the Japanese knew) was gradually put into practice by the most successful British, Australian, and Dutch commanders in other camps. Even more convincingly, in 1945, when the Japanese saw defeat ahead, and finally concentrated all their officer prisoners in one camp, the vast majority of the three thousand or so Allied officers collected there agitated until various senior commanding officers were successively removed, and Col. Toosey was put in charge. He remained in command until the end of the war in August 1945, when to general consternation all kinds of ancient military characters precipitately emerged from the woodwork to reclaim the privileges of seniority. As Watt concluded:

> What it comes to is that in the very special circumstances of the Japanese prisoner-of-war camps, Col. Toosey was almost universally recognized for what he was—a hero; a hero of the only kind that our world today can afford: a man, that is, who understood the unprecedentedly difficult conditions for survival, and who faced up to the implications with exactly the same resolve and imagination as if it had been a question of winning a great victory.

INTERLUDE

Boon Pong

Boon Pong Sirivejjabhandu, who became a legend to the prisoners working on the Burma–Thailand railway, was a captain in the Free Siam Army and the underground agent in Thailand of the remarkable underground V Organisation that had been founded in Bangkok. Its members smuggled money, food, and medicines to the sick and starving men in the prison camps. As his obituary in *The Times* recorded in February 1982, Boon Pong risked his life countless times to help camps from Nong Pladuk to Takanun. He cashed camp commanders' checks, delivered secret medical supplies for camp hospitals, supplied batteries for the secret radios, and advanced cash against personal valuables such as watches, rings, and cigarette cases. The valuables were "scrupulously and amazingly" redeemed after the war.

The V Organisation was set up in September 1942 by an elderly British businessman, Ken Gairdner, who was married to a Thai woman and had retired to Bangkok. When he heard that prisoners were being transported to Thailand to build the railway, Gairdner contacted another civilian internee in Bangkok, Peter Heath, a twenty-seven-year-old junior in the Borneo Company shipping department, and invited him to help raise funds. Gairdner's organization became an important conduit for relaying military intelligence from the prisoners to Allied governments and the Red Cross. Heath and Mr. R. D. Hempson, who had worked at the Anglo-Thai Corporation and whom Heath recruited to help V, set up their own organization which involved French, Dutch, and Swiss nationals and a network of Chinese, Thai, and Eurasian assistants. One key accomplice was Betty Millett, who was married to a French diplomat in Bangkok. She contacted Chinese pharmacies in the city to supply the medicines and also bought items on the black market.

A Chinese messenger from Gairdner first contacted the British surreptitiously in Ban Pong when he handed a note signed "V" to an RASC lance corporal, R. G. Payton, who had worked in Bangkok before the war. Payton, who drove a ration lorry detail between Ban Pong and Nong Pladuk, passed the note, which asked for details of the prisoners' conditions, to Maj. R. S. "Paddy" Sykes, the British commander at Ban Pong. At first Sykes was worried that the note was a plant by the Kempetai, but after a discussion with three of his captains—Ewart Escritt, K. A. Bailey, and P. E. Briggs—all agreed that the risk should be taken. Sykes's drivers passed notes to up-country camps and brought back the replies, allowing Sykes to provide V with intelligence on Japanese troop movements and accurate accounts of the harrowing conditions on the railway during the 1943 "Speedo" period. The reports were passed to Walter Siegenthaler, the Swiss consul in Bangkok.

The diaries and recollections written by the officers who worked on the railway contain many admiring references to the courage of Boon Pong. His premises in Kanchanaburi were searched at least twice by the Kempetai, but they could never prove anything against him. At Chungkai, Lt. Col. "Cary" Owtram regularly obtained five thousand Thai dollars a month for nearly two years from Boon Pong which he "banked" in a hollow upright bamboo pole in his quarters. At Tarsao, Lt. Col. "Knocker" Knights estimated that the camp received the equivalent of £2,400 in cash and medical supplies. Their value in the saving of life and the amelioration of suffering was "inestimable," he said. According to John Coast, the prices of this staunch pro-British friend were always the lowest and his profit the slightest. He hid duck eggs, tobacco, canned pilchards, sulfa drugs, copies of the Bangkok *Chronicle,* and banknotes in his vegetables and delivered them to most of the river camps. He arrived at Wampo one day with ten thousand eggs, bribed each guard with a dozen, and arranged to sell the rest to the prisoners at five cents each. That day every prisoner stuffed himself with eggs. According to his own account, medical officer Capt. Stanley Pavillard started with a twelve-egg omelette, went on to six scrambled eggs, ate three poached eggs for tea, and had another three boiled eggs before going to bed. He was not the only prisoner to suffer a restless night.

The official report on the V Organisation, written by Philip Toosey in 1945, paid tribute to Sykes as the initiator and organizer of the scheme in Thailand. His conduct, fearlessness, and clear-sighted policy were the foundations of its undoubted success, the report said. When Sykes was killed during an Allied air raid, his work was carried on by Maj. R.A.N. Davidson.

When rumors reached Britain in 1947 that Boon Pong had fallen on hard times, three camp commanders—Toosey, Knights, and Lt. Col. Harold Lilly—launched an appeal among former Thailand prisoners of war. He had delivered £40,000 and large quantities of medical supplies, and saved thousands of lives, they said. The appeal raised £35,000 and enabled Boon Pong to start the Boonpong Bus Company, which flourished.

The British awarded OBEs to Heath, Hempson, and Mme Millet. Maj. Davidson was awarded the MBE. Boon Pong's bravery was rewarded with the George Cross.

Chapter 5

"SPEEDO"

As Philip Toosey and his men labored on the bridges across the River Kwai, preliminary work had started on clearing the jungle and building embankments, viaducts, bridges, and cuttings to the north. By that stage, the Allied forces were already beginning to turn the tide: the Japanese were suffering shipping losses, the situation in New Guinea was critical, and there was the threat of an Allied counterattack in Burma. As a result, the railway had to be built faster. So the "Speedo" period began in February 1943. The Japanese were determined to develop an efficient supply line to their troops in Burma in order to facilitate an advance on India, and the prisoners were the means to build it. "As the cry of 'Speedo, Speedo' went up from the engineers, waving their metre-sticks like the Egyptians their whips," said Lt. John Durnford, "so the working parties dwindled in numbers through sickness and death. . . . Another day from dawn to sunset, another metre, another kilometre, another life lost, so that they call it now 'The Railway of Death,' reckoning a life expended for every sleeper laid."

At Wampo, forty miles north of Tamarkan, the Japanese made phenomenal progress. When Bdr. Hugh Clarke arrived with an Australian party in early 1943, he was reminded of the pyramids at his first sight of the embankment. He found the British diseased and dejected, which was scarcely surprising. They had been working day and night shifts and had finished the job—laying a three-hundred-yard track by cutting and by viaduct across a limestone cliff face that rose high above the River Kwai—in just over two weeks. More than three thousand men had been pressed into action. The heat and the glare of sunlight reflected from the bare rocks caused many of them to collapse. Some made shoes of jungle leaves and tree bark to reduce the pain of walking on scorched rock, but only the strong could carry on, said the British medical officer Capt. Stanley Pavillard. They worked blindly in a jerky, mechanical fashion, as if hypnotized or dazed, aware only of the harsh sunlight boring mercilessly through their eyeballs. The Japanese showed their twisted sense of humor by firing dynamite charges without warning signals and watching the men run for shelter. Eventually, said Pavillard, the men's brains became scrambled: "Then they would lie there, chest heaving, heart throbbing, face grey and steaming with perspiration. I got these cases into hospital as quickly as I could, but they were suffering very severely from shock and often died quite soon afterwards."

One officer at Wampo was Capt. Richard Sharp, a Cambridge-educated Scotsman:

> Here the perpetual fetch and carry of the earth and rubble-filled baskets as the men dig down into the cutting and strew the waste rolling down the slope. There the constant clink of steel on stone, as the pairs of hammermen (one holding, one hitting) chisel out their metre-deep holes ready to take the blast charges. And on both sides of the river, timbers are prepared for the viaduct; on this the officers' party bore the holes, and carry the huge beams to their assembly point, while on the other, Chinese coolies trim the logs with adzes, bore them, and have elephants to drag them down to the water's edge, from where they are floated—so heavy that they half sink—across to the bridge side. There is no let up in the work. To a Jap, none was working so hard that he could not work harder, and "Speedo—hurriupoo" was their unchanging yell.
>
> Work by day, work by night. Day shifts, night shifts, no shifts at all. When they tried to bring in the shift system, 3 shifts of 8 hours was suggested, approved, and lasted 2 days. 8 hours was not enough work for a man. Then two 12-hour shifts, and then the system broke down, and things became a scramble. But on 16 April, the viaduct was completed; and in the end, in the heat that was poured off the rock face, the troops were set to metalling the south cutting. Starting at the foot, they picked up a stone out of the heaps that had earlier been sent tumbling down, clambered up the 150-ft slope, dumped their load and came down, to go round and up again in a continuous ant-like motion.

Even the prisoners could not deny the "stupendous" achievement of the Japanese engineers and their three thousand "pre-dynastic slaves." When John Coast first passed Wampo there was nothing there. Three weeks later there was a vast bridge with steam engines limping slowly over it. It was characteristically Japanese, he said, not only because it was a crazy wooden bridge that nevertheless functioned, but because no other nation on earth in 1943 would have bashed, bullied, sweated, and slaved prisoners to such fantastic lengths for such an object.

The railway arrived at Tarsao, thirty-six miles north of Tamarkan, on May 1, 1943. The British medical officer Capt. Cyril "Pop" Vardy was amazed when he went to see it two days later. Where there had been virgin jungle three weeks before, there was now a huge clearing with several sidings and the main line, a huge store for firewood, a water pump, a signal box, a level crossing, and the beginning of a station. While he stood on the track, wondering what it all meant and where it would lead, suddenly in the distance he heard a train's whistle, and shortly afterward the first steam engine drew up in Tarsao "station," pulling two empty trucks and one guard's van. On the front of the engine were packed several Japanese officials, fully arrayed in dress uniforms and wearing swords. "It struck me as being rather funny—an undreamed-of modern enterprise winning through against terrific odds and being carried out by officials who still cling to uniforms, jack-boots, spurs and swords—and all in the midst of a tropical teak forest and bamboo jungle."

Then, on May 22, a "remorseless invader" swept down on Thailand and Burma: the monsoon. In Burma it rained relentlessly for seventy-two hours without a break. A wall of water seemed to shut out the surrounding world, said the captured war correspondent Rohan Rivett. He continued:

> In its fury, it battered on the atap roofs of native houses and coolie huts and roared torrent-like down the deep gutters of village streets; it lashed the bamboo clumps until each leaf streamed with moisture; in the space of hours it converted tiny dry watercourses into foaming spates; it stirred to savage life the sluggish, moribund creeks which had been wandering aimlessly along; within the first day and then with ever-mounting zeal, it widened the muddy rivers until they began to spread prodigiously and climb their jungle-fringed banks; dominating and assertive, it intruded on every conversation and even on the privacy of your thoughts; it brought change of habit to every living thing that plodded, scurried, flew, crawled or wriggled in the trees, in the rivers, on the earth or under it—not least along the narrow red scar running through the jungles where tens of

> thousands toiled, seeking to wrest a new highway for man from territory which had belonged to nature since time began.

The monsoon, which lasted for four and a half months, and the evil-smelling mud that it created, sapped morale. The men worked in the rain, ate in the rain, and felt the rain as it seeped through their leaky tents at night. They were never dry. Sixty years later it was the mud that was the abiding memory of Lewis Altman. It made the camps as slippery as ice rinks: a journey to the cookhouse or latrine, particularly at night, often entailed the men falling into pools of water and returning to their tents with two inches of mud on their boots and an inch of it adhered to the seats of their shorts. After two days the road around the camps was a morass, often rutted and banked up with several feet of glutinous mud; every successive day of rain made it worse. "Wet clothes stayed wet—how could you dry them?" said John Coast, who was at Takanun. "Before you left your tent in the morning you groped in the gloom to pile all your kit under a ground sheet or gas-cape in a dry spot. When you returned, half your bed would inevitably be soaking wet."

Adding to the miseries of "Speedo," the monsoon, and the mud were the hazards of working in dense, mountainous jungle. Above all, there were the insects. One of the men who suffered this "curse of the jungle" was Signaller Ronald Searle (who later created the "girls of St. Trinian's" cartoons):

> They ate us alive. Mosquitoes and foul fat flies were a horror, and their bites were often fatal. At night after work, tired as we were, we were kept awake by the swarms of bed-bugs that wandered over us, sucking our blood and nauseating us with their smell when we crushed them. Day and night the lice burrowing under our skin kept us scratching. Sometimes giant centipedes wriggled into our hair when we finally got to sleep and stuck their million poisonous feet into our filthy scalps as we tried to brush them off, setting our heads ablaze. I think there were moments when any one of us would have preferred to brave the mountain lions rumoured to be out there somewhere, than face another bug.

Beyond Tarsao, thousands of prisoners from Singapore were now set to work building the rest of the railway to the north. Among them were the 2,780 British and 2,220 Australians of D Force, under Brig. C. A. McEachern, AIF, and the 3,270 British, Dutch, American, and Australian prisoners of H Force, under Lt. Col. H. S. Humphries, with Lt. Col. R. F. Oakes, AIF, as his second in command. One battalion of D Force had worked at Wampo before moving to Konyu 3 Camp. They were joined in June by a party under Oakes and worked on the Konyu cutting, which became notorious as "Hellfire Pass," situated dizzyingly high on a rocky mountainside above the river. The pass was part of a two-and-a-half-mile horseshoe-shaped section of the railway that necessitated the building of seven bridges and five cuttings. It was in two sections, one about five hundred yards long and twenty-five feet deep and the other about eighty yards long and eighty feet deep. By the end of the first week the men had hit solid rock. They worked with shovels, eight-pound hammers, and steel drills. The hammer and tap men had to drill into the rock: one man held the drill and twisted it after each blow; the other swung the hammer; water was poured into the holes to make drilling easier. Dirt and crushed rock were extracted from the holes using a thick-gauge wire flattened at one end to make a spoon. The wires were also used to flog the workers. The men found the heat and glare almost unendurable; many had no boots and the rocks were so hot that they blistered their feet.

As dawn broke each day, the prisoners were stood to attention, and when the signal was given they faced east and chanted as best they could the "soldier's prayer" that was set down in the "Imperial Message" of the Emperor Meiji in 1883:

A soldier must honour loyalty as his most important virtue
A soldier must be impeccably polite
A soldier must be courageous
A soldier must treasure his principles
A soldier must be frugal

Then, as Searle reported, they set off for hours of rock-breaking:

> We would drill holes for the charges millimetre by millimetre with a sledgehammer and steel bar, a job that could take a whole day with hands that were swollen and numb. After blasting the rock face and breaking up the lumps that were so heavy to move, we were formed into an endless human chain. Then basketful by basketful, we hauled the tons of rubble to the edge of the cutting and tipped it into the valley below. This routine was perhaps the most soul-destroying of all our tasks. The never-ending trudging back and forth, which at the height of the "Speedo" could continue for as long as sixteen hours, often meant that we started walking before dawn and with one break for rice and water continued until long after dark.

The Japanese blasted the rock with dynamite twice during each shift, the fuses lit by prisoners with cigarettes provided by the engineers. Teams of men then cleared the shattered rocks while the drillers made more holes for the next blast. When rail-laying parties reached the cutting in June, the equipment was augmented by an air compressor. A dozen Cambodian jack-hammer operators were also introduced, as were elephants. There were now more prisoners at Konyu 3, and the progress accelerated. Most men were working up to eighteen hours a day for the next six weeks. At night the cutting was lit by bamboo fires, containers filled with diesel fuel, oil, burlap wicks, and carbide lamps. Hugh Clarke thought that the scene from the top of the cutting resembled Dante's Inferno—the burning fires at intervals of about twenty feet, the shadows of Japanese moving around with their sticks, beating the men.

An equally grueling project was going on a little farther up the line at Hintok, where a bridge 440 yards long and thirty yards high was being constructed of green timber fastened with wooden wedges, spikes, bamboo ties, rattan or cane rope, and wooden dowels. It fell down at least once during the building process and was known as the "Pack of Cards" bridge.

After sixteen months of captivity, the men at Hellfire Pass and Pack of Cards bridge were emaciated and starving. Many were also suffering from dysentery, malaria, or tropical sores. But the sick were forced to work, and all the men were flogged on by the guards. The engineers' commander, Lt. Hirota, ordered sick men out of the hospital, threw stones at the prisoners, and beat them with sticks. Exhausted workers who fell out of working parties were beaten. Men with inflamed and swollen feet were used to haul logs and clear rocks. To meet the targets set for working parties, men were carried piggy-back to the parade ground or tottered there on sticks. Those who could not stand were carried to the lines and ordered to work with hammers or axes from a sitting position. Maj. G.E.G. Garrett described how sick men who could not stand properly were beaten to their feet, and how he, too, was beaten when he tried to intervene. The men were driven by engineers armed with bamboos—"just as cattle were driven"—to work two and a half miles away from camp. Many collapsed but managed to straggle back to camp, some not returning before midnight. The cruelty extended to officers, too. Lt. Barbour was collecting a four-gallon can of boiling water for the kitchen when he was stopped by Harimoto, the Korean medical orderly at Hintok:

> I was clad in sarong and cotton singlet. The Korean was in a state of frenzied anger, and struck me on both sides of the face with all his

> strength so that I was completely dazed. I was still forced to stand to attention and to my horror Harimoto picked up the still bubbling can of boiling water and flung the entire contents into my face with the obviously deliberate intent to seriously injure. I am in no doubt that Harimoto knew that the water was boiling as he saw me remove it from the fire, that the handle of the container was hot and the bubbling of the water plainly visible. I know that he aimed at my face. His eyes were glaring straight at mine as he picked up the can. As he swung the can I instinctively jumped and turned my back, but could not avoid the boiling stream, and the whole four gallons poured over my head, shoulders, and buttocks. Completely unnerved, I rushed towards Maj. Spencer's tent when the Commandant Kurikuni intercepted me, stood me to attention, and further reproved me, during which time the boiling water was searing into my flesh and seeping between my legs and arms. I was eventually got away to receive medical attention. Numerous blisters formed all over my back, buttocks, etc., and these eventually coalesced into one huge blistered area. I was sick and in pain for over a month. I still carry some of the scars resulting from this unpleasant experience.

One particularly vicious guard at Konyu, nicknamed "Musso" because of his resemblance to the Italian dictator, was the subject of several stories cited in an official report by Lt. Col. Humphries. When one prisoner collapsed unconscious, Musso beat him with a bamboo rod, pushed the rod into his mouth, then prodded his genitals. Lt. G. Mansfield reported what happened next:

> An hour later the same IJA guard dragged the still unconscious body down to the end of the trolley line, and indicated to me that I was to place the man under the railway line, and empty the next load over him. This, of course, I refused to do, and was immediately beaten about the face. I was again ordered to dispose of the body and again refused, and this time I was struck on the head with a 4 lb sledgehammer and a crowbar. The next trolley now arrived, and the guard ordered all men back to the face of the cutting, and then personally threw the unconscious body under the end of the track, and tried to dump the trolley of spoil himself. This he could not do, whereupon he ordered me to assist him and upon refusing I was again struck on the face a number of times. The wretched man now regained partial consciousness and grasped the projecting nails, and attempted to raise himself. Immediately the guard saw this, he seized a shovel and struck the unfortunate man on his head with all the force he

> could muster. This completely knocked the man out again, with the result that he slid and rolled down the side amongst the loose rubble and rock, a distance of about 150 feet into the valley below. Eventually the man was returned to hospital and the matter reported to the camp commandant. [The prisoner died two days later.]

Musso struck Lt. Allan Collins of the Royal Norfolks with an axe handle and a crowbar, and then whipped him with a fuse wire. A Royal Norfolks captain, H. P. Pilkington, who could use only one arm because of a war wound, was asked by Musso if he was an officer:

> He seized my arm and examined the scar, and without further provocation struck me with his fist and shouted, "One arm—no good." He then left, returning later, and attacked me again. I treated him with indifference, infuriating him to such an extent that he struck me repeatedly about the head until I was bleeding, and my right eardrum was smashed. He concluded by seizing a shovel and striking me over my wounded shoulder. Two hours later when I sought permission for an obvious cholera case to be returned to camp, I was again assaulted and he continued to attack me without provocation at intervals throughout that night. At 07.15 hours in the morning, preparatory to blowing charges, I ordered my men into a small trench for safety. Although it was completely full when "Musso" arrived, he forced his way into the trench by burning my legs with a paraffin flare which he was carrying.

On other occasions, Musso stood on a man's face and forced it into the ground to test that he was unconscious and assaulted three prisoners with bamboos and a pick handle. He then forced them to stand in the blazing sun holding a section of light rail above their heads and beat them when they faltered.

But the Japanese could be as brutal with their own men as they were with the prisoners. At Takanun, Capt. A. K. Butterworth was with a group who were taken to a jungle clearing beside the railway and made to stand in a circle around a group of Japanese troops who were being treated as if they were guests at an important ceremony. Then, two Japanese with their hands tied behind their backs were led in, made to kneel, their necks cleared of their shirt collars, and then beheaded as the Japanese onlookers clapped and laughed. The executed men had been surveyors. Their crime had been to get their calculations wrong when clearing the jungle for the tracks, so that their two sections did not coincide.

It will never be known exactly how many men were lost during the building of both projects, but the Hellfire Pass Memorial suggests that sixty-eight prisoners were beaten to death during the blasting of the cutting alone. Thirty-one men were also reputedly killed in falls from the bridge, and twenty-nine beaten to death.

The senior medical officer at Hintok Mountain camp was the Melbourne surgeon Lt. Col. E. E. Dunlop, commanding officer of the "Dunlop Force" of 878 Australians who had left Java for Singapore in January 1943 and traveled from there to Thailand the same month. Dunlop, who had played rugby for Australia before the war, was universally known as "Weary," stood six feet four inches, and became one of the legendary medical officers in Thailand. He had willingly ceded command to McEachern so that he could concentrate on the sick. After the war he described how, during the "grimmer" months of "Speedo," sick men were deliberately persecuted by the guards. Men with horribly festering feet were forced to work on sharp rocks or in thorny jungle hauling logs. Disabling ulcers were struck or kicked. Men who collapsed were savagely handled. Sufferers from dysentery and diarrhea were forced to foul themselves while working. Dunlop earned lasting affection by his spirited defense of these sick men. On one occasion the guards tied his arms behind a tree, a Japanese officer faced him with his rifle and bayonet and asked if he had any last words. "If I had, I wouldn't tell it to thugs like you," Dunlop replied. He kept a diary throughout his captivity which recorded the sufferings of the men.

> 19 March: Tomorrow 600 men are required for the railway. All work on benjos [latrines], anti-malaria and "improve water" schemes must cease; worst of all, light duty and no duty men and all men without boots to go just the same. This is the next thing to murder. Obviously the Ns have a great reserve of manpower here and at Singapore and they are showing every intention of just breaking men on this job, with not the faintest consideration for either life or health. This can only be regarded as a cold-blooded, merciless crime against mankind, obviously premeditated.
>
> 10 May: Late in the day 29 of the sick returned, terribly exhausted after a hell of a day. They were lorried about two kilometres out and then had to roll 500-lb oil drums, three to four per drum, some kilometres to the compressor party. They were warned that if they rolled off the mountain track they would have to get them up again. Finally they walked home four kilometres over the hills. These were sick men, most

> of them covered with huge sores and many weakened by fever and various illnesses. This is the most horrible thing I have seen done as yet, apart from their executions. The most primitive of races would scarcely treat sick and starving dogs in this fashion.
>
> 7 June: Today notable for the beginning of severe, acute dermatitis of the feet. The feet become red raw with tinea, injury and secondary infection; they swell grossly with redness, weeping and loss of skin. The poor wretches stand either in mud or water or on rocks all day and the feet never get dry. Those suffering the miseries of ever-present diarrhoea and dysentery, of course, are forever getting up in the mud and slush at night and that makes things worse. The plight of these men is pitiful. They take hours to walk four to five kilometres in from work and just about cry with the pain of walking and standing on raw, bleeding feet. The Nipponese, of course, just bash them for being late to work or too slow. The wet season work immeasurably increased the misery of the men and doubles and trebles the labour of the day. Our neighbouring camp of 500-odd men, who are living in squalor, short rations and misery, had already reached a hospital figure of 250 today when the Nipponese paraded all sick in engineers' lines and drove them out to work in the pouring rain and muck to the tune of 100 men, plus one medical orderly allowed. These Englishmen are frail stuff in most parts, skin and bone already and many will soon die.

A week later Dunlop noted that only 341 of 1,085 men had satisfactory boots. Between January and October 1943, more than five thousand patients were admitted to the hospitals at the camps at Konyu, Hintok River, Hintok Mountain, and Kinsaiyok, nearly two thousand with malaria and eight hundred with dysentery.

As if "Speedo" and the monsoon were not enough for the men to endure, cholera broke out among the native laborers and then the prisoners. At Konyu the first case occurred on June 16, at Hintok three days later. The camp where Richard Sharp was working, near Takanun, escaped the epidemic, but the work went on at "Speedo" pace as the men cut through a rock face and built bridges and culverts. The rice rations dwindled and the sick received only a third of what the fit were given. Most men wore sand shoes or worked barefoot. The number of sick increased rapidly, but work had to go on. "You are soldiers," the men were told. "You must die at your posts." Sharp evoked the despair in the camp:

> In that one month, we struck the depth, feeling lost and forlorn, suspicious of our neighbour, receiving no aid from below, and little food from

> anywhere. We had brought with us seven days' rations, and were promised more. Fourteen days passed before we did get any more, and then it was cattle on the hoof (very welcome, but we could only kill one in three days, and the meat kept for only two of them) and nothing else. By rights we should then have been feeding on rice and dried potatoes, but Peter T. was firmly thrifty with his stores, and made everything last till eventually more stuff did arrive. The rations we had brought were rice, dried potatoes, dried meat (cured in our main camp, and already crawling), dried fish, about the size of a large haddock, 4 to one meal for 120, 8 pumpkins, our only fresh vegetable, a few lbs of small beans, a small quantity of tea, and a still less quantity of salt, sugar, oil and pepper. Out of that, three meals a day. Breakfast, pap rice, a thin rice soup; tiffin, dry boiled rice, with a morsel of fish, and the fish water poured over; supper, dry boiled rice, with a stew of potatoes, and a shred of pumpkin, and of meat if you were lucky. Every third day a fried rissole, flavoured with fish or sugar.
>
> We had, on occasion, to go out, walk for miles to bring in a load of banana flowers, bamboo shoots and wild spinach, which grew sparsely. The wild bananas were useless, skin and seeds with no flesh. And every day it rained, and most of each day: two days after we arrived, the river rose, and the road we had come was under water, while the men to get to and from the work had to swim or wade across the bridge, chest-high in water. The cattle, after they came, liked it as little as we did, and it was on killing days usually a race between the butcher and the beast, the butcher trying to kill the brute before it died on his hands. Not that that made any difference—carrion or not, we ate it.

Using the underground V Organisation, the camp commanders and medical officers tried to alert the Red Cross and the Vatican to their plight. One letter sent to Bangkok in July on behalf of "The British and Dutch prisoners of war in Thailand" by Paddy Sykes said that at a camp near Tonchan men stricken with cholera were placed on rice-bag stretchers and left to lie on the ground in leaking tents. At an Australian camp at Tonchan in July there had been two hundred cases of cholera among one thousand men; eighty-five had died and been buried in communal graves. At another camp four hundred men were without a medical officer: if any claimed they were sick, they were taken out by a guard, made to run up and down, beaten, and sent out to the railway. Morale was at an all-time low. Some men had gone insane while others were so weak that they were mere skeletons with hardly sufficient strength to go to the latrines—which in some cases were within fifteen feet of the cookhouse. By September, fifteen thousand of the forty thousand prisoners in Thailand were "sick," and that figure excluded those with dysentery and beri-beri who were still working.

Louis Baume recorded the conditions at Kinsaiyok, one of the worst camps. His diary is a vivid *cri de coeur* written with all the raw emotion, anger, and desolation he was experiencing during "Speedo":

> I have been working on the stone cutting, by far the worst job now, an absolute hell under swinish Nips. The tasks on the earth cutting and the stone cutting have been doubled to two cubic metres per man! It's well nigh impossible. The working conditions are almost unbearable—hacking away at the rock in the full glaze of the midday sun or digging up the thick red clay and mud in teeming rain: bare-footed, with feet cut and bleeding from the broken rock or sharp bamboo thorns, hatless and naked except for a brief "jap-happy." Most of our clothes are worn out and rotten and only a few of us have hats, shorts or footwear. And all the time the blasted, bloody Nips screaming and shouting, bellowing, beating, bashing, kurrahing, kicking and hurling stones, sticks and insults, forever urging, forcing and bullying us to work faster, faster and faster. And at the end of the long day's work we stumble back to camp in the dark, along a rutted road knee-deep in thick black jungle mud. And after a poor and insufficient supper eaten in the pitch dark or, at the most, by the dim light of a flickering coconut-oil lamp filling the foul air with its thick black smoke, we lie down to sleep on the bamboo slats of our filthy hut, crawling with bed-bugs, lice and maggots. It is a restless sleep for even then we are carried back to the green and dripping jungle to carry fantastic loads of eternal bamboo or baskets of earth while all the yellow devils of Hell stand around with sticks in their hands, shouting and kurrahing us on to work faster, faster, faster. And in the morning it all starts over again. There is no end to all this—except one—it just seems to go on and on.

Although Richard Sharp and his fellow prisoners were spared cholera, they had no idea how they managed to avoid the disease, because the native laborers—Tamils, Malays, Chinese, "a jumble of miserable humanity," all carriers of cholera—were passing through their camp on their way to the railway at Konkuita. Sharp observed them journeying with their goods upon their heads or their shoulders, often with their wives and small children, going wherever they were ordered by the dominant race, whom they hated but dared not disobey:

> Defy their masters, and they were starved into submission. Be submissive, and they were driven like cattle to work, cursed, beaten, cudgelled, and in

> the end, were tumbled into the common pit that was dug for them. It was small wonder they lived without hope, and hopelessly laid themselves down to die. "Master," said one, "may I come into your tent, so that I may die?" Out of every four that went up the river, only one came back.

Elsewhere, cholera struck with deadly force. Within nine days after June 16, when 266 British prisoners joined Lt. Col. Oakes, seventy-two men died and there were four hundred fifty in the makeshift hospital at Konyu 2. The stream used for water at Konyu ran through another camp stricken with cholera, a "coolie" camp, and a watering place for elephants. The Japanese refused to build a bridge across the stream to the cholera compound, so it had to be crossed in contaminated boats. One cook washing potatoes in the stream absentmindedly chewed a piece and was dead by the evening. Sometimes as many as ten bodies were cremated at one burning, but the Japanese eventually stopped cremations—the labor involved in gathering wood was deemed too heavy—and the dead were buried in mass graves. By July 4, 91 had died, 110 had cholera, there were 118 suspected cases, and only 120 men were able to work, out of a camp of 750. Rats and lice were everywhere. In mid-August, 1,290 of the 1,727 prisoners in the Hintok area were hospitalized.

But the most pitiable victims of cholera were the native laborers. One headman lost 146 of the 160 workers he brought from Malaya to the railway within two months. Many ran away, but they were shot if captured. Louis Baume observed how they were treated at Kinsaiyok:

> A Nip stands at the bottom of the embankment with a stout bamboo in his hand and hits the natives on the back each time they pass, men and women alike. When one of them drops dead, his body is thrown on to the earth embankment to help build it up quickly. "Cholera Lane," along which we have to pass to get to the viaduct, is where a lot of the native families live. It consists of a row of old tents—just one canvas, no sides—and in these the Tamils with their wives and children live, suffer and die. Behind, buried a few inches below the soil, are the bodies of all those who have already perished. The place is reeking with filth and disease and the air smells of excrement and rotting flesh; the whole area near here is contaminated with dirt and vomit.

Capt. Charles Johnson was the senior officer of an officers' party sent on a dangerous mission to help an Australian doctor dealing with dying native laborers at a camp near Takanun. He could not promise that any of them would survive, he said, and warned them not to touch the bodies. In five days they carried out and burned 120 corpses, using long poles to maneuver them to the floor and then dragging them to the fire party with ropes tied around the legs and shoulders. The camp was then burned to the ground.

Burials were often denied to the native laborers, but they became routine among the prisoners. There were seven in one day at Kinsaiyok in June, Louis Baume noted. Sometimes the Australian padre attended, but often the deceased were buried by the men just as they were or wrapped in a piece of bamboo matting; blankets and clothing were too precious and needed for those who were still alive. If they had died of cholera, their bodies were first burned on a bamboo pyre and the ashes and bones then collected and put in an old tin or handkerchief. Initially a small hole was dug for each, but eventually several would be buried in one grave. Those who had died for other reasons at least had their own graves. In spite of the conditions in which they had died, the men tried to bury them with some dignity:

> An officer and two or three men, dressed up in borrowed clothes, approach the cemetery and on reaching the graveside lower the flag-draped body onto the ground. As the ropes are passed underneath, the officer reads from the burial service: "I am the resurrection and the life, saith the Lord: he that believeth in me, though he were dead, yet shall he live: and whosoever liveth and believeth in me shall never die." And as the body is lowered into the grave, or the biscuit tin placed in its hole, the officer reads: "Forasmuch as it hath pleased Almighty God of his great mercy to take unto himself the soul of our dear brother here departed, we therefore commit his body to the ground; earth to earth, ashes to ashes, dust to dust. . . ." And the handful of earth thrown in rattles to the bottom of the grave. After the Lord's Prayer, spoken by all, someone might recite a few remembered lines of Laurence Binyon:
>
> *They shall grow not old, as we that are left grow old:*
> *Age shall not weary them nor the years condemn.*
> *At the going down of the sun and in the morning*
> *We will remember them.*
>
> Or else a verse of Rupert Brooke's poem, "The Soldier":
>
> *If I should die, think only this of me:*
> *That there's some corner of a foreign field*
> *That is forever England. There shall be*

> *In that rich earth a richer dust concealed;*
> *A dust whom England bore, shaped, made aware,*
> *Gave, once, her flowers to love, her ways to roam,*
> *A body of England's breathing English air,*
> *Washed by the rivers, blest by suns of home.*

> Each one salutes and leaves; there is another burial in 5 minutes' time. The grave-diggers shovel in the earth; it is wet and heavy and has to be trampled down or else the grave will sink and fill with water. "Earth to earth, ashes to ashes, dust to dust."

A scathing report on the treatment of H Force, who worked along the twenty-mile stretch of the railway between Tonchan and Hintok, was written by Lt. Col. Humphries after the railway was completed. He indicted the "incompetence and inefficiency" of the Japanese for a great deal of the hardship suffered by his men. Their officers were incapable of regulating the conduct of their subordinates who had been entrusted with supervising the prisoners, he said. They were therefore able to give full play to the high degree of "vindictiveness and sadism" which seemed to be an inherent part of the Japanese temperament. He named Lt. Yamakowa, the commissariat officer of H Force, as a war criminal who seemed to delight in the spectacle of starving, emaciated, and oppressed white men. He was especially scathing about the state of the hospitals:

> Hospital accommodation in the camps consisted throughout of primitive improvisations of split bamboo, inner fabric of tents etc. The Japanese, whilst acknowledging the necessity for hospital facilities, did nothing to assist in the provision of same, and the conditions under which these soldiers suffered through the various stages of their diseases, and under which many of them unfortunately died, are indescribable in a report of this nature. They can best be described as filthy charnel houses, and but for the untiring efforts of the Medical Officers and orderlies, the death toll, heavy as it was, must have been doubled or even trebled. Japanese guards were heard to say that they hoped the sick would die and thus save Japanese rice.

Among the men of D Force, the death rate was estimated at 18 percent, although in some battalions it reached 50 percent. The toll on H Force was greater, reaching 885 (27 percent). But not even this terrible statistic could compare with the situation in the camps near the Burmese border, where the conditions were the grimmest on the whole railway.

INTERLUDE

Smokey Joe's

Lt. Col. "Knocker" Knights, the British commander at Tarsao, had been lobbying the Japanese to set up some place for the men to meet after the day's work. He wanted to establish a canteen administered by the prisoners so that any profits could be credited to the hospital fund. The Japanese insisted that they should control the canteen and contract its running to a Thai merchant.

> The contract was awarded to an elderly Thai lady who we designated "Nam Cham Pee Wee," it was the nearest we could get to her real name. She was quite an extraordinary character, liable to quick outbursts of temper, but generally conforming to the typical Thai cheerful nature, continually chewing betel nut, her teeth were quite black through it, and expectorating expertly at frequent intervals. She had no romantic appeal, which was probably just as well seeing that she had to live in close proximity to about 3000 POWs

whose association with the female sex had been non-existent for the past two years.

In spite of a rough exterior, Nam Cham Pee Wee had a kind heart, and a sincere sympathy for the unfortunate sick POWs, a sympathy which she gave tangible expression to by frequently handing me sums of money to help them, insisting on my keeping these presents secret, because if the Japanese knew, they would punish her. The fact that these presents were part of the canteen profit did not, in my opinion, reflect on the spirit in which the gifts were made.

"Smokey Joe's," as many of us knew the canteen, soon assumed the importance and atmosphere of the local pub, naturally with certain qualifications. It did not sell intoxicating liquor, the furnishing was extremely crude, consisting of table and seats constructed from bamboo poles, the former being very uneven such that one had to be extremely careful to ensure that anything placed on them would not be upset, and the latter most uncomfortable and decidedly hard on one's bottom. The place was dimly illuminated by oil lamps which smoked continuously (hence the name "Smokey Joe's"), creating an atmosphere reminiscent of a London fog.

In spite of these defects, "Smokey Joe's" to us was like an oasis in the desert, and it became customary to invite one's friends to dine there on the extremely well cooked, by Thai natives, dishes of "Flied eggs and lice," as the natives described it, or other tasty Eastern concoctions the composition of which should not be enquired into too closely, finishing off with black coffee, a welcome change from the watery tea supplied with camp meals. We felt, in these circumstances, that we had reached a stage higher in the social ladder, even if we were still far from the top.

Chapter 6

SONKURAI

Valley of the Shadow of Death

The seven thousand men of F Force—thirty-four hundred British and thirty-six hundred Australians—were destined to endure the greatest ordeal of the Burma–Thailand railway. They were cruelly deceived from the start. In Singapore, they were told they were not going on a working party, so it did not matter if they were unfit or ill. They were informed they would have a better chance of recovery with better food in a pleasant, hilly country with good recreation facilities. The climate would be like Singapore's but cold at night, so warm clothes should be taken (by now most of the prisoners wore only shorts and most had no hats). There would be no marching, except for short distances; transport would be provided for baggage and for those men unfit to march. They were to take all tools and cooking gear and a generator for electric light, and a military band was to accompany them. Blankets, clothing, and mosquito nets would be issued at the new camps. Those reassurances led to some one thousand of the British (but only 150 of the Australians, who were more suspicious of their hosts' intentions) being unfit to march or work. (The Australians even staged races to select their contingent.)

"The Japanese told us we were going to a health resort," said Noel Duckworth, one of the five padres with the force. He continued:

> We were delighted. They told us to take pianos and gramophone records. They would supply the gramophones. We were overjoyed and

> we took them. Dwindling rations and a heavy toll of sickness were beginning to play on our fraying nerves and emaciated bodies. It all seemed like a bolt from the tedium of life behind barbed wire in Changi. They said, "Send the sick. It will do them good." And we believed them, and so we took them all.

There was a "schoolgirlish" atmosphere as the officers discussed the trip, as if they were going on holiday, reported Capt. Harry Silman, one of the British medical officers.

Under Lt. Col. Stanley Harris (with Brig. Charles Kappe commanding the Australian contingent), the first five of thirteen parties of F Force departed from Singapore on April 18, 1943, leaving only 8,200 prisoners at Changi. The Australians marched out singing "Waltzing Matilda," accompanied by bagpipes. It was at Ban Pong, at the end of the grueling five-day rail journey from Singapore, that they realized they had been duped. George Polain, one of the Australian padres, arrived with the third train and saw the men subjected to "cruel, savage" treatment from several Korean guards: they were herded and beaten through throngs of Thais, who were amazed to see white soldiers treated in such a humiliating manner. Three weeks earlier, Sgt. Stan Arneil, AIF, had been lying on the grass at Changi listening to a recording of *La Traviata:* "I love this place," he had written. Now, writing his diary on the train, he was looking forward to going to a mysterious land. "This is adventure, this is romance, come on adventure. You can't stop me from liking it." The adventure quickly turned sour. "God protect us," he wrote at Ban Pong. "We are in a bad way, weak, filthy, exhausted." Next day he sold his sweater, shirts, sheets, and blankets for twenty dollars.

There were no lorries to transport the men to their work camp, as they had been promised in Singapore. They were going to march, the guards told them, for 185 miles. "They just laughed," said Duckworth, "and in that spiteful, derisive, scornful laugh which only a prisoner of war in Japanese hands can understand, we knew that here was another piece of Japanese bushido—deceit!" About fifteen truckloads carrying the men's medical supplies and hospital equipment, two heavy electric lighting sets and miles of electrical wire, their tools, flashlights, cooking gear, and kit that could not be carried had to be abandoned. They were told that it would be sent on later. A grand piano was sold to a local café. As the men laid out their kit for inspection, the guards helped themselves to anything they fancied and searched their pockets. The men started discarding what they could not carry and sold boots and clothing to the local Thais to buy food, a decision that was later to have fatal consequences. Looting was rife: men stole from one another and looted kit that had been left behind by earlier marching parties. One Japanese officer ran a brothel which some men used at a dollar a time; but after Ban Pong it was going to be more than two years before their thoughts again returned to sex. One of the guards used a heavy steel golf club to hit the men: a major's head was cut open and many others were severely injured.

They soon started the forced march along elephant tracks, through dense, mountainous jungle, all by night, to the northernmost camps in Thailand. Apart from the sick, most of the rest had suffered from diphtheria, dysentery, and/or beri-beri at Changi, and they had not eaten proper meals for more than a year. Nobody was truly "fit." Anxious about what lay ahead, the men were still carrying loads that were too heavy, they were physically soft after eighteen months of captivity, and the "rest periods" on the march, disturbed by fatigues, meals, washing, medical formalities, and lack of shelter, were hardly restful. The fitter men helped the sick with arms around their shoulders; the sickest were carried on improvised stretchers. The march took seventeen days, and for some who fell behind, even longer. Even trained infantry in good physical condition would have found it arduous, said Harris, himself a notable sportsman who had represented South Africa at tennis and England at rugby, and had boxed in the Olympic Games. Those who were "fit" not only had to help carry the unfit, but were burdened with the three- and six-gallon water containers and medical gear. Lt. Col. Charles Wilkinson watched as men whose boots had fallen to pieces continued in bare feet.

> At times in the darkness they could only see the man immediately in front by his enamel plate or mug fixed on his pack. Sometimes white pieces of cloth or towels were hung over people's shoulders so that we could see them and so keep close together. Often they slipped in the ruts and went sprawling in the mud, and trekked for miles over the ankles in wet and mud.

As the men marched, the rain made the jungle stink of rot. Steam and mist hung low over the ground and in the undergrowth. They were often up to their knees in mud that sucked away their boots. They had to wade through streams that had overflowed, and were sometimes up to their waists in water. Clouds of midges or sand flies got in the men's eyes, ears, noses, and mouths. Thousands of them would bite simultaneously. To have their arms free to battle with these insects, men threw away their kit, but their limbs were easy prey, and everyone seemed to be smacking and scratching all night long. Not all of the assailants were so tiny: giant horseflies the size of bumble bees attacked the men, too. They didn't know of their presence until they felt their bite, like a prick from a very blunt needle. Idris "Taffy" Barwick, an RASC driver, recorded their misery:

> All that could be heard now was the weary steps we took, the jangle of the tins, the laboured breathing and occasionally a half-suppressed groan. Men were now suffering in silence, each with their own particular aches and pains. Each with their own thoughts and each so terribly exhausted. I only knew that my whole body seemed to be on fire. My head, like a drum, seemed to be rolling about uncontrollably. My eyes seemed raw and were kept open with the utmost difficulty. My shoulders were skinned raw from the chafing shoulder straps of my pack, which was worsened by the loss of flesh. Each day brought an increase in the protrusion of my bones, the gnawing pain in my stomach, my knees ready to give way at every step and my feet like lumps of raw beef.

Sheer grit saw the men through, according to Maj. Noel Johnston, in command of the Australians who arrived on Train 5. Men were reluctant to be left behind and separated from their comrades, so the fitter men helped the medical officer at the rear of the column to assist those who were struggling. Yet, however weary his men were, they did not forget Mother's Day. As dawn rose, word came down the line and they started to pick tiny white jungle flowers and draped them over their packs.

Harry Silman had "the world's worst job" of assisting the sick, lame, and weary, supporting them, carrying stretchers, helping with their kit as well as his own. By the fifth night he was losing weight and suffering from diarrhea and strained Achilles tendons:

> My mental and physical condition can be imagined as I struggled on through a tropical storm, through water, swirling and rushing waist-high on two occasions. One of my shoes was torn off, so I discarded the other one and completed the journey barefooted. Every step was agony. I had never realised before what it meant to go through a night of mental and physical torture.

Maj. Cyril Wild, who had been the British interpreter at the surrender in Singapore, was now attached to F Force HQ as staff officer and senior interpreter. He saw the men toiling through the pitch blackness and torrential rain, sometimes knee-deep in water, sometimes staggering off bridges in the dark. Sprains and bruises were common, and fractures of arms and legs occurred. Thai bandits armed with knives followed the tail of the column in some areas, ready to strip the equipment of any man who fell behind. Some of the twenty men who disappeared on the march probably met their deaths at the hands of these bandits.

At the staging camps, which were merely roadside clearings in the jungle, there was no overhead cover and it was impossible for the men to rest properly. Food generally consisted of rice and onion stew, with hot water to drink. It was a diet that was insufficient to maintain health and was entirely inadequate to support the physical strain of the march. The staging camps were in the charge of truculent Japanese NCOs who demanded large fatigue parties when the men should have been resting. Night after night they forcibly drove the sick onto the road with blows to continue the march, in spite of the protests of their officers. At the Tarsao staging camp, Wild took fifty sick Australians, whom a Japanese corporal had insisted should carry on marching, for inspection by the Japanese medical officer, who agreed that thirty-seven were unfit to march. But the corporal ignored a written order and insisted that all but ten of the men should continue that night. At the time scheduled for parade, Maj. Bruce Hunt, a senior Australian medical officer, fell in the thirty-seven "officially" sick men in two batches—of twenty-seven and ten—and he and Wild stood in front of them:

> The corporal approached with a large bamboo in his hand and spoke menacingly to Maj. Wild who answered in placatory fashion. The corporal's only reply was to hit Maj. Wild in the face. Another guard followed suit and as Maj. Wild staggered back the corporal thrust at the major's genitalia with his bamboo. I was left standing before the patients and was immediately set upon by three guards. One tripped me, while two others pushed me to the ground. The three men set about me with bamboos, causing extensive bruising of the skull, hands and arms and a fractured metacarpal bone. After I was disposed of, the corporal then made the majority of the 27 foot-sufferers march with the rest of the troops.

Three were carried back after a few hundred yards. The rest were helped or carried by their comrades to the next staging camp. Similar arguments about how many sick men could be left behind occurred at every stop, but every night seriously sick men, with blistered and ulcerated feet, dysentery, beriberi or malaria, were driven out of the staging camps, often with stones, to join the march.

At Konkoita, one of the last staging camps, each of the marching parties was forced to camp for one or more days within a few yards of huts filled with hundreds of cholera-stricken native laborers, on ground covered with infected feces, where the air was black with flies. British officers asked for the loan of spades to remove this filth. "Use your hands," the Japanese replied contemptuously. Stanley Harris, who had traveled in Train 7 and was unaware of the chaos that had met the first six trains, protested to Lt. Col. Banno, the elderly Japanese commandant of F Force. He warned him of the inevitable consequences of a cholera outbreak and demanded that all forward movement should be stopped or that Konkoita should be bypassed. But nothing was done and the march continued—again with fatal consequences. Banno took Harris forward with him in a lorry, but two stages on he ordered all the officers of the rear HQ to dismount with the medical stores to start a wayside hospital for the marchers. The result was that the senior British medical officer, Lt. Col. Huston, and his medical stores were miles behind the men's camps during the critical first six weeks. The stores, indeed, never arrived—the road was destroyed by the monsoon.

On arrival at their destination, near the Thai-Burmese border, the men were distributed among five camps. By the end of May, there were about eighteen hundred Australians at No. 1 Camp at Lower Sonkurai; about sixteen hundred British at No. 2 Camp at Sonkurai; 393 Australians at No. 3 Camp at Upper Sonkurai; another seven hundred at No. 4 Camp at Konkoita; and seven hundred British at No. 5 Camp at Changaraya. The headquarters was soon moved from Lower Nikhe to Nikhe, with about two hundred of each nationality. About 1,350 men had yet to arrive.

No. 2 Camp was fifteen miles from a main road (over the border in Burma) and about sixty miles from the coast; Three Pagodas Pass was twelve miles to the north. There were three ranges of mountains, each about five thousand feet high, between the camp and the coast to the west, and the surrounding country was thick jungle. Surrounded by sloping hills covered with eighty-foot-high trees, the camp was in a clearing on the banks of the River Huai Rho Ki. It was almost always in the shade and was such a melancholy place during the monsoon that it quickly earned the name Death Valley. That was to become an apt description. Two of the camp's three huts were dilapidated and unroofed, and alive with maggots and thousands of flies. The Korean guards and British officers were in the only hut with a roof. Most of the natives who had been working on the site had died. At one end was a pile of cholera victims; the stench was indescribable from the many bodies, most partly decomposed, lying all over the ground. Company quartermaster Sgt. John Franks thought that they had died where they stood and been left to rot. No attempt had been made to cremate the bodies, so the cholera germs were still active and presented a serious hazard. The monsoon had started, but it was two weeks before the men's huts were roofed, so they slept in wet clothes and wet bedding. It generally rained twenty-four hours a day. Maj. David Price, adjutant to Lt. Col. Tim Pope, the officer commanding the camp, did not see the sun from May 19 until the middle of August, when the sky cleared for about two hours.

The parties were given two days to clear the site. They burned the bodies and a mass of rubbish. They cut bamboo to build huts, organized the pyre for cremation, and established a kitchen. John Franks took charge of cooking and feeding. The huts for sleeping were two hundred feet long, each with a center gangway about four feet wide and a platform on each side, two feet from the ground. The platforms provided everybody with sleeping space of six feet by two feet. By June, when L.Cpl. John Stewart Ullman, one of only three prisoners with F Force who spoke fluent Japanese, arrived, there were eight huts, and a cookhouse had been built by the river. But the huts were falling apart, the roofs were leaking and there weren't enough men in the camp to repair them.

When the guards demanded working parties, the men of F Force had their first experience of the Japanese railway engineers. They were the most "evil" breed of men the prisoners had so far encountered, said John Franks. They had complete authority over the normal guards and were utterly ruthless in their determination to complete the railway. Capt. Peter Coates was asked for just two hundred fifty men, but with dysentery and exhaustion rife, many of the contingent he mustered were unfit for work. Their job was to build a thirty-mile stretch of the railway, through hilly and flooded jungle, immediately south of Three Pagodas Pass. Their day started in darkness at 6 A.M. as they filled their mess tins with water and brewed old tea leaves. Breakfast was a watery rice, which they called "pap," sometimes with a few brown beans. Roll call was at 7 A.M., two hours before the working parties set off, when the men in rags, all dirty and many barefooted, stood hunched in the drizzle to be counted. After the "fit" men had been chosen, they trudged as much as eight miles through deep mud to the line.

Their first tasks were building a road and embankments for the rails, digging cuttings and approaches, and then constructing a high-level, heavy timber bridge across the gorge of the river. The work involved clearing jungle, cutting down trees, adzing timber, driving piles, loading elephants, carting earth, and moving rocks. Leveling of the track involved carrying all materials by hand in flat baskets or on stretchers. Building methods were primitive: the three-span wooden trestle bridge was held together by iron spikes driven in with heavy hammers; there were no nuts and bolts.

The men worked until long after dark, continually pestered by leeches, scorpions, snakes, and flies. At the short midday break, which should have been an hour but was sometimes only a few minutes, they ate some cold boiled rice and a few beans. Then they were driven on again with blows from fists, rifle butts, sticks, and wire whips. Men were constantly shouted at—"*Kora!*" ("Here you!"), "*Bakaero!*" ("Fool!")—and forced to work at bayonet point in the intense heat and pouring rain until they literally dropped where they stood. If a man died at work, he had to be carried back to camp to be counted at roll call before he could be cremated or buried. If they were thought to be slacking, the men were made to stand holding heavy rocks above their heads; if they dropped them, they were beaten.

The same ordeal was suffered by the Australians at Lower Sonkurai. To get to work they first had to cross a high, eighty-yard bridge over a track of slippery logs, and were then herded off to their jobs about two miles away through deep mud or across sharp gravel. They were then divided into teams of three or four, one man to pickaxe the cutting face of the rock, one to shovel, and two to carry away the shale, rock, or soaking clay in bamboo baskets for a distance of seventy-five yards through yellow, oozing clay on a bed of gravel. One of the greatest trials, the return journey at the end of the day, was eloquently described in the official Australian report on F Force by Charles Kappe:

> Exhausted from work, feet cut and sore, clothes wet and cold, they set out to pick or feel their way in the dark through two miles of mud, including a balancing task across three bridges. Arriving at camp at about 22.15 hours, they would line up to sterilise their mess gear and then draw their evening meal of rice and jungle leaf–flavoured water. The more fortunate would cluster around a fire and then grope their way down to the river to wash off the day's mud and sweat. Another sick parade and dressings completed, the men were able, usually by 23.00 hours, to don a damp shirt (if such an article was still in their possession), roll themselves in a blanket, probably damp, and lie down under a rotted dripping tent.

Unsurprisingly, the workforce was collapsing from the start. The grueling work demanded by the Japanese engineers, added to the strain of the march, the state of the camps, and the stop at Konkoita, where some had become infected with cholera, meant that the men immediately succumbed to disease. Cholera had been diagnosed at Lower Sonkurai on May 15, before the men had even started work, but the Australians were fortunate to have an outstanding medical officer in Maj. Bruce Hunt, who was assisted by Capt. Lloyd Cahill, Capt. John Taylor, and Capt. C. Juttner. Hunt was a big, physically powerful man, who on the march to Sonkurai had carried not only his own gear but the kit of stragglers and the medical supplies, even though at forty-four he was twice the age of most of the men. A few thought he was "unbelievably conceited," but most considered him astute, tough, and efficient. He also had the stamina and endurance that were now required of him, and a "messianic dimension." Where there was pessimism and fear, he strove to give hope and pride. Throughout the months at Lower Sonkurai, he stood up for his patients even though he was regularly beaten and slapped, and constantly harassed.

On May 18, Hunt and Cahill inoculated 1,400 men with vaccine they had accumulated at Konkoita, and work was started on building "Cholera Hill," a hospital made of tents and marquees supported by bamboo, adjoining the camp. There were two waves of cholera at Lower Sonkurai. In the first, five of the twenty cases died within seven days. The second wave began in the camp itself. It was raining incessantly, and the ground between the latrines and the nearest hut was contaminated by the feces and vomit of men who had been unable to reach the latrines. After the long march the men were listless, downcast, and oblivious to personal hygiene. The disease was spread by men treading their boots in the mess, by the flies, and by the men's failure to clean mess tins or cover their food. Hunt, determined to stop the spread of the disease, called a conference of officers. Lt. Bob Kelsey observed him as he spoke, his face lit by the flickering flames of a hut fire:

> Gentlemen, things are grim. I have diagnosed a disease of which I have had no experience. It does not occur in Australia but I have read of it in textbooks and I am sure it is cholera. I have conferred with the Japanese camp command and have learnt that they are, with good reason, terrified of the disease. They understand that without vaccination their prisoners could all die and they would lose their workforce and much "face." A supply of cholera vaccine has been requested from their main headquarters. In the meantime, work on the railway will temporarily cease. Fires will be kept alight at intervals in every hut. Before you use your eating utensils you will pass them through the flames and you will see that your men do the same. Water must be boiled for at least seven minutes. No water will be drunk direct from the creek. Tomorrow we will clear the surface filth from the camp area and it will be burnt or sterilised in the fires we will light over it. If a fly alights on the rice you are about to eat, the grains it lands on must be spooned out and burnt for, I assure you, if one contracts cholera one dies in great distress.

Under Hunt's direction, new latrines, sealed tightly with wooden lids, were built. Each morning, all excreta on the ground were cleared. Trestles were made to hold the rice containers. Every grain of rice which fell to the ground was picked up to stop flies from feeding on it. As each man lined up for his rice, his mess tin was plunged into a caldron of boiling water. By the beginning of June, the effectiveness of Hunt's program was evident in the sharp decline in the number of new cases. The last case was diagnosed on June 29. According to Hunt, there were 209 definite cases of cholera at the camp, of whom 101 died. As we shall see, this was a much better record than was achieved in other camps.

Lt. Fukuda, the Japanese commander at Lower Sonkurai, had allowed three days' rest so that the men could work on the camp, but his promise was broken on the third day, May 29, when the engineers ordered 750 men to work. The senior officers decided to register a strong protest, and Hunt drafted a letter to Banno which was also signed by Maj. Johnston, the Australian commander at Lower Sonkurai, and Maj. C. P. Tracey and Maj. R. H. Anderson, the commanders of 1 and 2 battalions respectively. The situation at Lower Sonkurai was extremely grave and becoming worse every hour, they wrote. Altogether eight hundred of the two thousand men had become ill or were required to nurse the sick. They demanded an indefinite cessation of work until the epidemic was under control so that roofs and drains could be built and the men could rest and recover. The letter also asked for drugs and medicines, extra food, blankets, tents, and water containers. It was translated into Japanese and sent to Banno, with a copy sent to Harris, who had been making similar protests from Nikhe.

One immediate result was that Fukuda resisted the engineers and canceled work for a day. Meanwhile, the letter persuaded Banno to visit Lower Sonkurai with the British Lt. Col. Francis Dillon on June 1. Banno almost immediately ordered work to stop, and the letter probably persuaded the Japanese commanders to relent and draft plans for the evacuation of the sick to a hospital at Tanbaya in Burma. However, those plans were not implemented for three months, which was far too late for many.

Meanwhile, cholera continued to rage throughout F Force. At No. 2 Camp, Taffy Barwick went to see the MO and was sent to the sick bay:

> I inquired about the treatment and was told there wasn't any. If I had cholera it was just too bad. The men were in an awful mess and sickening to look at. Their eyes seemed to sink deep into their sockets and became dark all around. Their faces became drawn with pain and weakness and most of them were still dirty with the dirt from the work parties, as

> they hadn't washed for days. Their hair was dishevelled and matted and their bodies covered in the bile and mess that had been vomited over them, either by themselves or the men who laid beside them. They suffered from uncontrollable and unrestrained attacks of the most violent vomiting, which was also accompanied by "hair raising" screaming and groaning during the awful pain and strain of retching. Also they would probably be lying in their own excreta, being so weak and helpless and with severe cramps in the upper leg muscles, they had been unable to move when the awful purging took place. These poor men were unrecognisable. As I entered the sick bay, one called to me in a weak croaky voice, "Taff, have you got some water?" I emptied some into his mug and looked hard at him and realised it was Dyke, one of the men who had helped to carry my kit when I collapsed on the first stage of the march, but what a change in the man in so short a time. He was dying and knew it, poor fellow.

So many men at No. 2 Camp were sick by the beginning of June—when John Stewart Ullman arrived only three hundred out of sixteen hundred men were fit for work—that Harris petitioned Banno to evacuate three thousand sick men to Ban Pong. He was turned down, but Banno conceded some days of rest so that Tim Pope could carry out improvements to hygiene and sanitation. In this period Japanese medical officers tested the men by inserting glass rods up their backsides and decided that 175 were cholera carriers. For Peter Coates, what followed was the most "inhuman act" he had ever witnessed. On June 5 the Japanese ordered that all the cholera carriers were to be moved to an isolation camp, that diarrhea patients were to be collected in one hut, all fever cases in another, and all fit men in a third. The order was made at 5 P.M. and was to be carried out at once. Coates described what happened that night:

> All available fit men were turned out to carry and pitch tents for the new camp. It had been raining hard and the ground was in an appalling state. Eventually tents were put over a half completed hut, fires lit inside and food sent over for the new inmates. Meanwhile Lt. Col. Pope had been trying to persuade the Japanese to permit us to move the sick men and hospital patients the following morning. Three separate appeals were made and on each occasion they were refused. On the last occasion Col. Pope was informed that in the IJA orders were never questioned and were carried out regardless of any other consideration. It was clearly stated to the NCO i/c camp that to carry out this order meant moving men who were dangerously ill but this made no difference. By 0200

> hours all but 27 walking wounded and 4 stretcher cases were moved across. The remainder and the move of the diarrhoea cases were completed between 0700 hours and 1000 hours. Accommodation for the isolation camp was 500 yards away near the hospital hut where the coolies had cremated their dead and was beyond description. The ground was a quagmire and strewn with bodies, the roof of the hut leaked badly and the men had nothing to lie or sit on other than their own kit which in many cases did not even include a blanket or groundsheet.

Lt. James Bradley was the only officer in the isolation camp. "We were put out there so we wouldn't pass it on to the others and we would probably die there," he said. "No food was issued to us because we weren't working. We were fed by the workers who shared their rations with us." Over the next two days the isolation patients were transferred into tents and the hospital patients moved again. Pope, now sick with dysentery, relinquished his command to Lt. Col. Alan Hingston.

In the midst of this carnage at No. 2 Camp, the building of the timber rail bridge over the River Kwai, 120 feet long and 20 feet wide, had begun, with both day and night shifts working up to their waists in swiftly flowing cold water. It was slave labor, said Padre Duckworth: "Exhausted, starved and benumbed in spirit, we toiled because if we did not we and our sick would starve. As it was the sick had half rations because the Japanese said, 'No work, no food.' " After one protest, which Duckworth made with Pat Wolfe, one of the medical officers, both men were beaten and thrown into a pit, where they survived on water alone for several days until they were released.

Military men are notably dry and unemotional, but there is real passion evident in Harris's report on F Force. The work was very heavy, he wrote, beyond the endurance of fully fit men and far beyond the capacity of starved and debilitated men:

> Obviously obeying instructions from their officers, the engineers in charge of parties drove the men savagely with blows from fists, boots, sticks and wire whips. Protests by our officers out on the work site often resulted in their being hit too. Visible resentment or objection were treated as mutinous and savagely punished. It is necessary to emphasise that most of this continual beating was not disciplinary but was used to drive men as beasts to efforts beyond their strength.

It was difficult for the padres to lift the men's spirits. Writing on June 27, when nine hundred men were sick, the Methodist padre John Foster Haigh noted that there was no cheery conversation, no ribald songs, no laughter:

> Long faces and embittered men live here. The going is hard. The life bitter. No church exists. Services are held in the different huts and I have four today. Our task is Herculean for I am sure one of the great things we have to do is to infuse these men with new hope—to lead them out of the slough of despair into the green pastures of confidence. It is not easy. But when I think of all that these men have gone through and all the loved ones at home waiting for their return I feel no effort is too great if by means of it these men recover their fighting spirit.

Haigh died of chronic beri-beri three months later.

The Australian padre at Lower Sonkurai, George Polain, described how trying it was to conduct a service in a hut containing three hundred men, with the nauseous stench of ulcer cases all around and often half a dozen dysentery cases squatting on their bamboo pans around him during prayers and scripture readings.

At one point, Lt. Fukuda complained indignantly to Bruce Hunt that the patients who had recovered from cholera were not working. When Hunt replied that the men were half starved and would not be fit for months he was called a liar. He paraded some twenty-odd "human scarecrows" before Fukuda to prove his point. They had obviously not been eating their 300-gram ration of rice, Fukuda retorted.

Food was an obsession of all the prisoners, and they quickly overcame any fastidiousness. When Capt. Bill Bishop arrived and first saw the "nauseating mess" of his supper, he tried to separate the rat droppings from the rice. "You one of the new lot?" somebody asked him. He nodded. "I thought so. When you've been here a week or two you'll eat the stuff, rat droppings, the lot, and go to look for some more." The Japanese quartermaster issued bags and boxes of potatoes or meat with a lofty disregard for their fitness for consumption. The potatoes were soaked during transport and storage and many were fit only for the refuse pit, according to the medical officers. The preserved meat, coarse-fibered, possibly buffalo without the bone, partially salted or pickled, arrived in boxes, usually swarming with blowfly maggots, and was frequently in such an advanced state of decomposition that it dripped a gray-green liquid, according to F Force's nutrition officer, Capt. Thomas Wilson. The men simply washed away the maggots and then cooked it. Cases of prawns sent from Bangkok arrived as putrefied shells, eaten out by maggots, but they were boiled thoroughly and made into "prawn soup," which at least added some flavor to the rice.

At No. 2 Camp John Franks assumed responsibility for feeding the men. Apart from the breakfast of pap, the men took a ration of cooked rice to work and returned to a stew of whatever vegetables Franks could find, usually beans or onions. For men working up to twelve hours a day, the daily ration was 10 to 14 ounces of rice. The shortage of food was so serious by mid-June that the Japanese ordered that there would be only two meals a day, except for working parties. After negotiation they agreed that there would be three, but the ration was cut by half. The camp, moreover, was isolated—the railway in Thailand was built only to Tarsao, seventy-five miles to the south; in Burma it had been completed for only ninety kilometers to the south. From rail-head to road-head was about seventy miles and from the road-head to No. 2 Camp about twelve miles. The only trader in the vicinity of the camps at Nikhe had a poor selection of foodstuffs which he sold at high prices. Fit men earned a quarter of a tical per day; palm sugar cost 40 ticals and coconut oil 35 ticals for four-gallon tins, and canned herrings were up to 3 ticals for a 15-ounce tin. Meanwhile, the camp hospitals had the first claim on any more nutritious foods. In any case, by mid-June long stretches of the road used to get rations from Nikhe to Sonkurai were underwater and impassable.

So the men had to look after themselves. Near Sonkurai a large area of ground was covered with a species of wild gourd similar to a loofah, and its leaves made a pleasant green vegetable, but the staples remained rice and onions, supplemented very occasionally by beans, potatoes, dried meat, and whitebait. A party of fifty men was sent sixteen miles to Changaraya with four bullock carts to collect rations. The men had to pull the carts themselves because the bullocks were exhausted and the road deeply potholed. When they returned, they looked like the mud-men of New Guinea. More expeditions followed: eighty barefooted men from Lower Sonkurai were set to pull carts on the ten-mile return journey to Nikhe. They set off at 8 A.M. and returned at 3 A.M. the next day with ten bags of rice and two each of salt and beans.

Cattle were slaughtered if they looked as if they were about to die. Adversity, said Harry Weiss at Lower Sonkurai, made animals of some of the men. He was writing after six convalescents had wandered down to a Thai corral in broad daylight and killed a yak. They were caught and all six had to do without meat for a few days. A sergeant was caught going through the workers' mess when he had already eaten in the hospital. Some men killed cattle for private profit, selling pieces of fresh meat for fifty cents each. The Australians stopped this illicit trading and brought the business under camp control, with some meat going to the kitchens and the rest sold to the men at a reasonable rate. "This allows the men to get a bit of meat for private cooking and yet does not allow one man to make enormous profits," Lt. Norman White, AIF, wrote in his diary. "Any profit from camp sales is now to be used to buy tobacco and cigs for issue to troops." To supplement their diet, the men hunted snakes, collected bamboo shoots and grubs, and tried to trap rats and monkeys, but feeding off the jungle was a full-time job.

During the sixteen-day period to July 21, the sick men's daily rations were estimated at 1,420 calories, made up of 340 calories from onions, beans, potatoes, whitebait, dried meat, and oil, and the rest from rice. This is less than the amount needed for basal metabolism and maintenance of body weight even in full health. However, the rations were supplemented by deductions from the pay of fitter men, camp funds being used to buy tinned fish, milk, and sugar, although never in large quantities. Once a man became sick he either died of disease or was gradually starved to death, said a report to Stanley Harris from Lower Sonkurai on July 31. "No sick man could lose a single day's feeding without the direst consequences. With malaria or the flux of dysentery upon them, eating was difficult and sometimes impossible. Thus died many prisoners." Rations for fit men were higher, but still well below normal requirements for the sort of work they were doing.

Several factors combined to exacerbate the horror at No. 2 Camp. The commandant, Banno, who was sixty in 1943, a "doddering old donkey" carried around in a sedan chair, was occasionally moved to tears by the plight of the prisoners. But he was too weak to resist twenty-three-year-old 2nd Lt. Abe, the engineer supervising the construction of the bridge. Abe was "brutal and completely insensible to any decency," said Charles Kappe, and an "unmitigated brutal bastard," according to a British officer who dealt with him. But, of course, the Japanese were equally brutal elsewhere on the railway. What made the situation so bad for F Force was that neither Harris nor Kappe was as effective as other Allied commanders in dealing with their captors. They failed to eke out concessions, so the men became progressively more exhausted and increasing numbers fell sick. When the monsoon broke, the road to the south was cut off and the road to the north had not been waterproofed, so the men's rations could not get through from Harris's HQ at Nikhe.

The total number of deaths from cholera at No. 2 Camp during the thirty-seven days after May 21 was 219 out of the 315 admitted. Victims would be taken into the hospital in the morning and by evening be almost unrecognizable; most were dead within twenty-four hours. Men from the Manchester Regiment who had received only half their prophylactic injections at Changi were the first to suffer. The "hospital" was a normal hut with sixteen to a bay (a twelve-foot by sixteen-foot bamboo platform).

The medical officer Harry Silman described the scene at the cholera center in his diary on June 3:

> It looks like a scene from a film, completely unreal. There is a long, dark atap hut, with over a hundred thin skeleton-like beings, writhing on the long platform, vomiting and passing motions where they lie. Groans and cries are the only noises to break the silence. Two or three orderlies with masks over their mouths were giving intravenous injections of saline, using Heath Robinson contraptions. About nine corpses lay covered with blankets and groundsheets, and a little distance away, the smoke of the pyre where the corpses are burning could be seen.

John Stewart Ullman, the camp interpreter, saw the patients groaning and twisting in agony, their faces white and sunken:

> At the onset came the "rice-water" stools, followed by vomiting and cramps. Liquids leached out of the body. The chances of survival were one in five. We had no drugs, not even saline solutions to combat dehydration. The patient was carried to the isolation ward, a hut on the hill. At the entrance corpses were stacked like logs waiting to be carried to the funeral pyre that burned night and day. Once inside he was deposited on a bamboo platform viscous with excrement and vomit. The air was laden with the stench of rot and death. All around him men were dying. Few lasted more than a couple of days. The corporal in charge of the cremating party felt the first cramps early morning. By evening his body was in the flames.

John Franks never forgot the look on the sick men's faces:

> A deathly pallor descended and their eyes bulged from their sockets. They didn't have the stamina to fight back and the doctors were denied the drugs that could have saved them. With no proper medical equipment, we improvised, boiling river water and mixing it with salt to make a saline solution and then using bamboo holders as it was fed into the veins of the victims. In the evening I would watch the bodies being carried to the corner of the camp where they were cremated. There was no ceremony or word of comfort—death had become commonplace.

The ingenuity of the medical officers nevertheless saved many lives. Bedpans were made from large bamboos; cannulas for intravenous saline injections, from bamboo tips. Bamboo was also used for stretchers, buckets, and water containers; shirtsleeves and trouser legs were cut up for bandages and dressings. Bruce Hunt at Lower Sonkurai forced a high intake of fluid—

water, rice-water, tea, and nutrine—on his patients, and wherever possible administered intravenous saline, a mixture of stream water and common table salt which was warmed to blood temperature. Cyril Wild estimated that about seven hundred lives were saved by this method.

However wretched their condition, the men still had compassion. With so few medical officers, Hunt appealed for volunteers to man the cholera wards after thirty-five men had succumbed to the disease in a single day. When the working parties returned to camp after dark—soaked to the skin and exhausted after toiling for twelve hours—he explained the situation and the risks. He gave up taking names when he had seventy-five on his list. He also devised a system of using officers, usually of company commander status, as wardmasters, each with a staff of two NCOs or clerks to help keep records and control messing. It did the officers a world of good, he said, giving them a job in which they were working solely in the interests of the troops. They threw themselves wholeheartedly into the work and spent virtually twenty-four hours a day in the wards.

Other diseases—tropical ulcers, dengue fever (which causes swelling of the joints), dysentery, and beri-beri—though less fatal, added to the misery during the cholera epidemic. On June 1, at the peak of the cholera outbreak, there were 788 patients in the hospital at Lower Sonkurai, but on July 13, with the worst of that disease over, 1,453 were hospitalized. On that date, of the five thousand men north of Nikhe only seven hundred were working on the railway, and half of those could not manage heavy work. With no soap, the men used sand to clean themselves, which aggravated skin complaints. Almost every man suffered from scabies, which made the victims want to scratch. Some tore the skin from the affected parts of their bodies as they tried to ease the constant irritation. The condition of tropical ulcers worsened. Some doctors scraped the ulcer with the sharpened edge of a teaspoon, but there was no anesthetic, and the patient would scream as two friends held him down to stop him from flinching. Live maggots were often bound into an ulcer to eat the dead flesh and clean the sore. As gangrene set in, amputations were commonplace. Stan Arneil observed one in which the patient lay on a bamboo stretcher under a shelter of atap leaves and had an arm removed: "The open latrines were 20 yards away and two orderlies had to keep waving branches to shoo the flies away."

So many men were dying that the bamboo funeral pyres were stoked constantly to keep them burning. The bodies awaiting cremation were sprinkled with lime and covered at night. There was no religious ceremony: "We would just slam them on," said Capt. James Mudie, who was in charge of the cremation party at No. 2 Camp after June. "The awful thing was that you knew some of them; one day it was the adjutant of my unit."

One of the patients who had been ordered to bed in the officers' tent with dengue fever as soon as he arrived was Charles Wilkinson. He soon contracted malaria, too. Then his feet, legs, scrotum, and the small of his back swelled. His scrotum was the size of a football. By the end of May he had been bedridden for two weeks and was also suffering from beri-beri. He kept a diary that shows the extent of the men's sickness as well as the compassion they showed toward their equally ill comrades:

> 26 May: There are cholera wards, malaria wards, dysentery and diarrhoea wards and those for general complaints. The doctors and nurses are run off their feet day and night. Some nights 20 men would die with cholera. There is a huge fire permanently burning to burn the bodies, after which their ashes are buried 20 to 50 at a time. Since coming to this camp 160 men have died from cholera within a period of roughly three weeks. Our food has been fairly good. A small amount of fresh meat has been available about every two days. We also get dried fish every few days but our main food is rice with stew made of beans and stock when there has been a killing. At first we bought a few bananas from the natives but this is now impossible as they are segregated during the cholera scare and contact with them is not allowed. The monsoons have started and so we get a lot of rain. This makes the place all muddy and unpleasant. The doc [Harry Silman], who is my partner and sleeps next to me, also looks after me and gets all my meals, did a good deal last night. He sold a few of our odds and ends to a Nip soldier for a good quantity of brown sugar, cheroots and a little spaghetti. The sugar . . . is especially good on the burnt rice sort of porridge we get sometimes at breakfast. [According to Silman's diary, he sold a wallet, a watch and a cigarette case to the guards, and Wilkinson a fountain pen.]
>
> 15 June: Ration situation is serious. The Nip in charge laid down that fit men who were working get three meals per day but that sick men only get one meal a day. We have wangled it so that everyone gets two meals a day. Actually without the Nips knowing we've managed some rice and gippo [soup or stew] at tiffin the last two days. We have one or two yaks left and so have had a taste of meat out of the stew, sometimes less and sometimes none—it's just luck. Scrotum and legs more swollen than ever today.
>
> 21 June: Total deaths in camp to date 212. Last night we had an ex-

ceptionally nice Church service in our billet seated around the log fire. Padre Foster Haigh conducted and preached a good sermon. Padre Duckworth assisted and said all the prayers. We sang three hymns.

30 June: I have been put on a special diet. I have almost no rice and each evening for the past four days I have received 7 ozs of lightly cooked yak's liver. It is grand to eat and I hope I shall continue to get it. Food has been good recently. Stew has been better and we've had whitebait once and dried fish a few times. I have had three more vitamin B inoculations. On Sunday night we had our evening service in billet—Foster Haigh conducted, Duckworth preached.

Within only four to five weeks, there had been a marked change in the men at No. 2 Camp. Morale was sapped by the constant rain, the stench from the overflowing latrines, the growing number of sick (who now included men with plate-sized tropical ulcers that rotted their bones), the piles of bodies awaiting the funeral pyres, and the beatings at work. David Price reported that men had ceased caring to such an extent that they were defecating indiscriminately around the camp. Spirits would soar at a new rumor of an early return to civilization only to fall still lower as weeks went by and there were no signs of a move. Said Thomas Wilson: "It was a vivid illustration of hope deferred making the heart sick. A yielding to hopelessness and despair—in common parlance 'dropping one's bundle'—came to be a final factor in many deaths." That sense of despair was vividly conveyed in the diary of Sgt. William MacDonald "Tam" Innes-Ker:

God, what a place this is. . . . Sanitation foul—open shit pits with shit not only inside but all around as well, where dozens of fellows couldn't make it. Everyone has festering sores, which are covered in flies. We have no more bandages and little antiseptic. Rain and ankle-deep mud for weeks. No-one has any socks left and many no boots. We are not allowed to bathe in the river and of course all drinking water must be boiled. We have to carry it 200–300 yards up a slippery slope. To feed 1200 men we have 20 buckets, so feed in relays. Some get breakfast at 5.30 a.m. and some at 11! Ditto for supper. Rations are now reduced as trucks cannot get through to us either way from Burma or Thailand.

The consequences for the men were noted in a report by Capt. Peter Coates and Regt. Sgt. Maj. Peter Neild:

They have lost what spirit they had. Their reaction to orders is very slow indeed and they go about with a vacant look and lost expression on

> their faces. They get no holiday unless they are in hospital. They have breakfast in the dark and very often supper as well. They have no form of light at night and no reading matter. They have little or no money and can buy very little when they have—very inferior tobacco only. When they are working they are treated little better than animals and certainly it can hardly be wondered at if they are losing their individuality and in many cases their self-respect. The officers have no opportunity to put these matters right as they are never with their men except when they are working or when they are sick.

The numbers of men demanded by Lt. Abe for his working parties meant that sick men always had to be included. On most days chances were taken and fewer workers were produced than had been demanded, but the bluff was sometimes called and guards went into the huts to pull out those who they thought looked fit. Assessing the men by sight was deeply misguided, however. Those with awful-looking tropical ulcers were let off while those suffering from less visible but much more debilitating illnesses such as beriberi, dysentery, and malaria were press-ganged into action. Sometimes the medical officers were able to intervene, catching the least eligible at the doors and substituting men who were less mortally sick, such as those with ulcers. These choices naturally put a huge strain on the doctors. Generally there were twice as many "unfit" as "fit" men in the working parties.

The plight of the prisoners of Sonkurai prompted one of the most audacious escapes that occurred in the Far East during the war. It was made by ten prisoners, led by Lt. Col. Mike "Wilkie" Wilkinson, who believed that the inhuman conditions in the railway camps should be brought to the notice of the outside world. The others were Lt. James Bradley, Capt. Bill Anker, Lt. Jack Feathers, Lt. J. F. "Robbie" Robinson, Lt. Ian Moffat, Lt. Guy Machado, Lt. T.P.D. Jones, Cpl. Brown, and Nur Mahommed, an Indian fisherman. As a patient in isolation, Bradley had, under cover of the noise of the men's axes chopping timber, cut a path through the jungle to give the escapers a good start. Stanley Chown, Bill Anker's batman, had stolen food—rice, soya beans, and fish—from the Japanese stores for the escape party, and a medical officer had given them drugs. All the escapers joined the party on the understanding that if any became a casualty they would be left behind. They estimated that they were about fifty miles from Ye on the Burmese coast, and hoped to reach there in three weeks, using a rough map of the Burmese coast drawn on a silk handkerchief. Their only equipment was a prismatic compass made back at Changi and set into the false bottom of Bradley's water bottle, along with an axe, three sheath knives, and a few personal possessions. They set off at dawn on July 5, each with a pack with blanket, groundsheet, and rations—which allowed for four ounces of rice a day with a few tins of fish. In total they had seventy pounds of rice, some dried fish, mosquito cream, water-purifying tablets, candles, blankets, matches, mugs, and billycans.

They ran into hill country, and the jungle soon became so dense that they were lucky if they covered five hundred yards a day. On July 25 they were down to the last of their rice, and three days later they shared a small tin of pilchards between them. Then they sustained their first casualties: Brown, suffering from gangrenous tropical ulcers, simply walked off, never to return or be found; he was followed by Feathers and Wilkinson. Next to fall were Robinson, suffering from septicemia and dysentery, and Jones, who lost consciousness. The survivors left Jones with a full water bottle, knowing that he would never be seen alive again. Bradley continues the story:

> On 14 August we reached the wide and slow-moving River Ye, the point for which we had been aiming. It was good to be out of the dense jungle and to see the sky for the first time. We decided to use our last strength to cut bamboo for a raft, a task which took three days, with our slow, laboured movements. We are all by now down to half our normal weight. Ian Moffat's legs were in a terrible state with maggot-filled tropical ulcers from his thighs to his ankles. On completion of the raft, lashed together with strips of blanket, we set off down river. Our progress was short-lived however as the river turned sharply west and we saw in front of us a narrow gorge with tremendous rapids. The raft was totally smashed and we lost everything.
>
> We managed to reach the bank and met the first human beings we had seen since leaving Sonkurai, two Burmese hunters who took us to their hut and gave us food, our first for three weeks. At this point our troubles really began. The following day, 18 August, we met the headman of Karni kampong [settlement] and over the next few days were displayed to the curious but kindly local villagers. However we never trusted the headman of Karni, whom we suspected of having sold us to the Japanese for a large reward.

Their suspicions were justified. After being free for forty days, they were arrested by Japanese troops, who were accompanied by Burmese police, and taken by boat to the Japanese HQ at Ye, where their captors at first refused to believe they could have crossed the mountainous jungle: they presumed they had landed by parachute. After prolonged interrogation, they were sentenced to death, but were saved by an eloquent appeal to Banno by Cyril Wild, who persuaded him to commute the death sentence by telling him of the disgrace that he would bring on the Emperor if he sanctioned the execution of such brave men.

Bradley, Anker, Moffat, and Machado, the only prisoners to survive an escape attempt in Thailand during the war, were transported to Singapore and sentenced to solitary confinement at Outram Road jail. After two months Bradley was unable to stand after being forced to sit at attention during the day. Nur Mahommed was separated from the others but also ended up in Outram Road.

When the escape was discovered by Banno, who was visiting No. 2 Camp, he told the commander, Alan Hingston, that he would have to shoot him. Banno eventually relented, but all officers were punished and deprived of food for forty-eight hours. The escape also hastened the removal of Hingston, who was disliked by the Japanese. His replacement was Lt. Col. Francis Dillon, who arrived with the rest of F Force HQ when it relocated from Nikhe to Sonkurai on August 2. Dillon, known as "Dillo" or "Andy" to his friends, was to become a legend among the prisoners. An Ulsterman, he had served in the Indian Army and had won the Military Cross in action on the North-West Frontier. He had landed in Singapore only days before the surrender, was ordered to escape, but was picked up by the Japanese when he was within sight of Ceylon. He was to become the effective commander of the whole of F Force, and was able to boost morale while simultaneously imposing strict discipline. At the same time the gentlemanly Lt. Wakabayashi, who became known as "Rockabye Archie," took over from Banno. He was the only Japanese officer who showed the "slightest glimmerings" of humanity, said Harris.

Dillon had been forewarned about the state of No. 2 Camp. In June he had asked Don Wall, an Australian private who drove for the Japanese, to prepare an intelligence report on the camps along the route to Burma and to try to find out why so many British were dying. Wall had reported back on the disgraceful state of No. 2 Camp—he had found feces over a wide area of ground. Dillon decided to pay Hingston a visit. Entering the first hut, he had asked for the hut leader and learned there was nobody in charge as all the officers were ill in the next hut. To Dillon, this absence of leadership explained why No. 2 Camp suffered the highest number of deaths of all the camps. (When F Force records were assessed in April 1944, there had been 678 deaths from all causes at No. 2 Camp, compared with 156 at Lower Sonkurai. Bruce Hunt had been rebuffed by the senior British medical officer at

No. 2 Camp when he had offered help.) In spite of this foreknowledge, Dillon was still shaken by the state of the men's morale and the state of the camp itself in August. When he arrived there were eight hundred men in the hospital, which was a shambles. Cyril Wild was equally shocked when he visited a big hut housing seven hundred sick men:

> There were no walls and a stream of water was running down the earthen gangway. . . . They were lying two deep along each side of the hut on the split bamboo platform. Their bodies were touching each other down the whole length of the hut. They were all very thin and practically naked. In the middle of the hut were about a hundred and fifty men suffering from tropical ulcers. These commonly stripped the whole of a man's flesh from the knee to the ankle. There was an almost overwhelming smell of putrefaction. The only dressings available were banana leaves tied round with puttees and the only medicine was hot water. Emerging from their crowded huts or leaky shelters in the pouring rain, even the fitter men appeared gaunt and starving, clad in rags or merely loincloths, most of them bootless and with cut and swollen feet. In addition, some 50 or 60 sick men from "hospital," leaning on sticks or squatting in the mud, would be paraded to complete the quota and would become the subject of a desperate argument between their officers and the Japanese engineers. Sometimes all of these, sometimes only a part, would be taken out to work, and would leave the camp hobbling on sticks and half-carried by their comrades. Many of the men had not seen their camp in daylight for many weeks and had had no opportunity of washing themselves or their clothes.

Dillon was unstintingly courageous in his dealings with the Japanese—he wore a hearing aid for the rest of his life as a result of one beating—but he stood firm against his own men, too. He had shown his mettle at Nikhe back in May when he found that all semblance of discipline and solidarity had disappeared among the men left behind on the march. He told them they were the scum of the earth: "Dogs!" he exclaimed. "You complain of being treated like dogs by your own officers but never have men in such dire need of mutual support let each other down as you have. I know that these yellow curs are partly responsible for your attitude but are we going to let these bastards think that the white man even in defeat behaves like an animal?" The men were almost cheering him by the time he finished, according to John Stewart Ullman. He showed that same fortitude when he went to reveille at 5 A.M. on the morning after his arrival at No. 2 Camp. The men were mostly a "ghastly sight." By the light of some bamboo bonfires, and in pouring rain, he met many dispirited, ill, despairing creatures. Only 80 percent of the men were on parade by seven-thirty. They received another savaging:

> This is a hell of a bad camp and you have had a bad time. But there is no reason why the camp should stay as bad as this and there is no reason why a great deal of your trouble should not be removed. In the first place, tomorrow morning reveille will be at 7.00 instead of 5.00. At 7 o'clock your breakfast rice will be in the hut ready. I expect you to get up, eat your breakfast rice, do your bits and pieces, wash and be on parade at 8 o'clock. I will do my utmost to get your conditions, both in and out of the camp, improved, but I expect you to play your part and when you are told to turn out at a certain time, to be there at that time. Any man who is sick coming in from work will report sick in the evening before he turns in. The doctor will be available in your hut.

Dillon was in luck that morning. When the Japanese ordered him to bring out more men, he snapped back that there weren't any more because the Japanese had made them unfit: "No more are coming on parade today." The guard was so taken aback that he accepted Dillon's word and went off with the working party. But as the men left there was a buzz, "something between a cry of amazement and a cheer," and Dillon felt that he had taken the first step toward improving No. 2 Camp. He also attended to small details: the bugler was to blow British instead of Japanese calls from now on; sing-songs were held during the first dry spell; the British organized themselves much better for roll call so that the Japanese could check the camp in two or three minutes, and thereby avoided the recounting and face-slapping of the previous three months.

One of the sick men was Ken Stevens, who developed ulcerated sores on his legs and arms on the march from Ban Pong. He went straight into the hospital and stayed there for eighteen days, then displayed early symptoms of cholera, but he starved himself for five days and recovered. However, he was a "bag of bones." By June 15 he was back in the diarrhea center. He was a close friend of Tam Innes-Ker, who cared for him during his illness. Many men tried to make captivity endurable by dreaming of what they would do after the war. At first Innes-Ker and Stevens thought of starting a smallholding raising hens, calves, pigs, and bees, which might net them £200 a year. Then they made plans to open a small cake shop in London or Norfolk. Innes-Ker thought he would take a course in cake-making. When he had recovered somewhat, Stevens went around the camp gathering recipes from men who had been in the catering trade, which were written down in Innes-

Ker's diary. He suspected that his friend was too ill to survive, but their dream kept Stevens thinking about the future, and he was certainly consoled, as his own diary reveals:

> 27 June: Starved myself for two days, feeling rotten but it secured the necessary end and I reduced from 20 times a day to about single figures. Tommy Judson, another carer in the hospital spoilt me thoroughly with people drawing my food for me, extra yak stew daily (from mysterious Manchester Regt individuals) and even with rissoles fried in oil! The latter complete and absolute heaven. Tam and I have now abandoned "Primrose Farm" and intend opening a bakery near Norwich and Yarmouth with a cake shop in the former and a curry-puff stall in the latter in the summer. Tam already knows of a bakery we might be able to buy and we are both most impatient about it all. In my bay here is a very nice CMP L.Cpl. Hadley who is a master-baker and he has been most helpful and encouraging.

On July 10 Innes-Ker noted: "Ken is better but terribly emaciated—a living skeleton. I do hope he comes through but I fear for him if he gets dysentery again." The next week, Stevens was still ill, but optimistic:

> 18 July: At the end of last week I had myself moved down to 18 Bay to get away from being near the Diarrhoea Hospital (who had moved up to my end—seeing 8 men die in the first 36 hours rather shook me) . . . Tommy bought some oil so have had rice rissoles every night—very satisfying. Early in the week some canteen stuff was sold and I got one-tenth of a pint of gula malacca—complete Heaven once more. Tam and I have brought our bakery scheme to an advanced stage. Thursday, Padre Duckworth celebrated. I partook—felt that it would bring me nearer my darling. . . . Roll-calls of 2-3 hours' duration continue twice daily—an awful bore. I continue to be hideously spoilt by everyone.
>
> 25 July: I am much better but appallingly weak—can't get up from the knees-bend without a support. But the food has improved, the last three nights have had 5 new potatoes each—completely satisfying—and some dhal in the gippo which greatly improves it.

Four days later Innes-Ker wrote: "What a bloody place this is—in the last ten days I've seen three of my good pals die and now I greatly fear Ken Stevens will never pull through this show. He has lost the use of his legs now and it really is only a matter of time before he will be too weak for anything.

If only we could get some eggs and sugar or even oils." There *was* some extra food for Stevens, but it didn't come immediately, and was not nearly enough.

> 11 August: On Thursday I was put on an extra diet—beans and extra stew—as my legs have given way and I need help to and from the latrine. Had a very bad day on Thursday when I felt I might be "for it" but got two MG 693s [Mag Sulph pills] on Friday. Wednesday evening dear old Kerr-Smith passed away after a long period of unconsciousness and Friday morning reveille found Ken Scovell dead—both of them for some reason just gave up, but it has worried me, especially as I have been having palpitations! An "extra diet" on Friday night (to which I don't think I was really entitled) was some very diluted but completely heavenly hot, sweet milk!!

That was the last entry in Ken Stevens's diary. The last page continues with a note by Tam Innes-Ker reporting that Stevens died after relapsing into a coma. He drifted away quietly with a smile on his face and was in no pain.

> Ken's passing has been felt deeply by all the Volunteers and others who knew him. They all had watched the magnificent fight he had put up from the terrible ulcers he arrived with to the last final struggle against exhaustion, for that is what he really died of. God, when are we going to get food and medical supplies in the quantities required—otherwise I can see—anyone can see who looks through the hospital—that another 2/300 men must die.

Innes-Ker was right. From his sickbed Wilkinson kept a tally of the mounting toll of the dead. (It might not have been totally accurate; Harris reported 562 dead on 25 August and 620 at the end of August.)

> 15 June—187
> 18 June—205
> 21 June—212
> 30 June—220
> 11 July—249
> 30 July—342
> 6 August—432
> 23 August—525
> 28 August—603

Dillon was a hard man, a regular officer, but he was obviously moved by the plight of the patients. On his first day in charge he had found desperately sick men packed in a double row on each platform on either side of the gangway in the huts. Many, he wrote later, had the look of death upon them, although in some ways morale was higher among the patients than the workers: "Whatever their ills, they felt at least they were safe from the slavery on the bridge. I am quite sure many died happy to be released from the horrors about them. I was amazed at the almost casual acceptance of death on the part of the majority . . . many of them died with a smile, gladly, without any great bother for themselves or anybody else." There was not enough wood for cremation, so the dead were buried, six to ten to a grave six feet deep. The corpses were rolled up in matting, bound with ropes, and carried by four men to the cemetery—none was heavy to lift—where they were unrolled out of the matting, which was taken back for another load. Often the feet of the dead man stuck out at one end of the matting and his head from the other, a horrid sight, admitted Dillon, but there was no other means of carrying corpses: blankets and clothing were too precious to be used. Rings and trinkets were removed, eventually taken back to Singapore and returned to the men's families.

Padre Duckworth said that the spirit of the jungle hovered over No. 2 Camp. The men constantly asked him, "How long now, Padre? What's the news?" but amid their suffering, utterly cut off from civilization, the prisoners had one consolation—news from a radio set operated by Capt. James Mudie. Mudie had worked with the British Malaya Broadcasting Company before the war and had operated a domestic-type radio set in Changi, but he had decided to make a smaller set ready for any potential working party away from Singapore. He fashioned it from a hollowed-out 6-volt battery and components salvaged from a Japanese balloon transmitter, and managed to smuggle it all the way to Sonkurai.

As he was initially in charge of the cremation party at No. 2 Camp, Mudie, along with a corporal and a signalman, was isolated from the main camp in a tent in the cholera area, an eerie place shrouded in mist until noon where the only sound was the cry of baboons. The Japanese were so terrified of cholera that they hardly ever visited the burial area, so Mudie was able to tune in his radio, listening with one ear for the rattle of rifles and bayonets signaling that sentries were on the prowl and with the other for the tune of "Hearts of Oak" and the words "This is the BBC." It was powered by 6-volt batteries taken from Japanese lorries (flat ones were put in the good batteries' place). Concealment was helped by the Japanese insistence on Tokyo time, which meant that it was dark when the BBC service to the Far East began each evening. When the BBC failed, Mudie turned to All India Radio or the Australian service. He delivered the news to Harris or Wild the next morning when he went to the main camp with his roll call. But one day he was careless: he left the set in his hut while he was delivering the news to the main camp. A sudden, rare search was called by the guards. The camp bugler blew the officers' mess call, the prearranged signal for a search. This was heard by Pte. Paddy Carberry, Mudie's batman, who threw the set down a borehole in the nick of time.

> The search was a near disaster. The Japs found enough incriminating evidence but Cyril Wild persuaded the camp commander that the battery, wire and pliers were part of the hospital equipment and were used to set up lights for emergency night operations. Fortunately they believed him—and the hospital was even allowed to keep the "equipment." There is little doubt that the guards were suspicious. The camp CO had probably been asked to carry out a search after the discovery of a set in a camp down the line [probably at Kanchanburi, where two men were beaten to death after its discovery]. The recovery of our set was a messy business—we took it out, washed it out in the river and we were in business again fairly soon. It survived to perform subsequently in Changi.

The suffering of the seven hundred Australians under Lt. Col. S.A.F. Pond at Takanun, some forty-five miles south of Sonkurai, equaled that of the main F Force. In a letter to Banno in August, Pond said that there were 356 men heavily sick, 58 with cholera, and 185 ought to be evacuated and hospitalized since they would be unable to work for at least two months. He estimated that he had only 112 "fit" men. The sense of despair at Takanun was captured by Capt. Adrian Curlewis:

> God, how weary I am of squalor, mankind and illness. I live in a tattered tent with nine officers who are too ill to work, who talk of nothing but their illnesses (my breakfast in the dark as they lie in bed is accompanied by boasts of the number of their visits to the latrines at night). My day is amongst foul-mouthed animals who have lost all self-respect and decency, who rob their mates, who cry to me for help on all occasions and then let me down by lying. Razors have been sold for food, brushes and combs gone, soap almost unobtainable, clothes in rags and dirty, tempers on edge and hope gone.
>
> His diary entries were interspersed with verse:

When your stomach turns to water and your feet begin to rot
When your outer skin is frozen but your blood is bloody hot

When your limbs begin to swell
And your ulcers burn like hell
Then you can say, but only then
You've joined the F Force, Thailand men

When malaria has hit you or Thai typhus comes to town
When dread cholera stalks behind you and the rod test bends you down
When the sandflies bite your ears
Or a "basho" Nip appears
Then you can say, but only then
You've joined the F Force, Thailand men.

Back at No. 2 Camp, conditions began to improve under Wakabayashi and Dillon, even though it had been decided to close three of the F Force camps and regroup Australians and British together there and in No. 3 Camp at Upper Sonkurai so that each camp could provide about eight hundred working men. Another motive, according to Australian accounts, was that the higher morale and standards of hygiene and fitness among the Australians would help to improve conditions at the British No. 2 Camp, which—as far as the Australians were concerned—was in a deplorable state. In spite of protests from Harris, seventeen hundred sick prisoners were hauled out of bed and marched through rain, knee-deep in mud, carrying their kit, and cooking and medical gear, to either No. 2 Camp or No. 3 Camp. The more seriously incapacitated, also numbering about seventeen hundred, were left where they were for the time being; they were eventually moved to the hospital in Tanbaya in Burma.

Dillon succeeded in instilling new spirit into the men. They improved their meals by catching any stray buffalo that chanced to join the small herd that the Japanese had bought for rations, bringing them back to camp, and dispatching them the same night, before the Japanese knew anything about it. They swindled two men from working parties and used them to cut wood into small logs and to lay wooden tracks around the camp so that they could move about dry instead of sloshing through mud. From the moment the tracks were finished, according to Dillon, there was no more trouble about casual defecation outside latrines. If any man kept alive in the men's hearts the belief that they would one day recover their liberty and dignity as British and Australian citizens, it was Dillon, said the Canadian corporal Hamish Tod. He constantly nagged and lobbied the Japanese, but Harris was still officially the commander of F Force, and on August 18 he sent another letter to the Japanese. Sickness and death rates were accelerating day by day, he said. The main reason was not disease but overwork, ill-treatment, malnutrition, and lack of drugs. Wakabayashi had helped to improve sanitation, hygiene, and cooking facilities, but 120 men had died since Harris had arrived from Nikhe, the 1,400 sick were weakening, more men fell ill every day, and there were now only 150 fit men, with 250 others who should have been excused duty on account of illness making up the daily working parties of four hundred. "I must therefore implore you to take suitable measures immediately to prevent this situation developing into an overwhelming tragedy." Within three weeks, the first party of sick left for the hospital at Tanbaya.

The weather was improving, Wakabayashi was controlling the brutal Abe, and elephants had arrived carrying food and soap, but the ordeal at Sonkurai was not yet over. On August 20 the engineers ordered that unless the number of men in working parties was doubled, all prisoners, sick or fit, would be turned out into the jungle to fend for themselves when the monsoon was in full flood, making room for coolies who could do the work. A few days later Wakabayashi created an opportunity for Harris, Dillon, and Wild to approach the engineers' colonel directly, and he was eventually persuaded that the prisoners could retain two thirds of their accommodations, with the rest given over to native labor. (The British grimly estimated that they could spare the other third because of the inevitable deaths that would occur among them.) But the Japanese insisted that the men had to be prepared to work through the night—the railway was only two miles to the north and the line had to reach Sonkurai by September 16. On September 14, reveille for the Australians under Kappe was at 6:30 A.M., and the men remained out until 2:30 A.M. the next day. They were woken again at 6:30 A.M. and worked until 2 A.M. The next day they worked from 5:30 A.M. until 10 P.M. They were automatons rather than human beings, said Kappe, and it was only the thought that the end was in sight that sustained them through days of "sheer torture," when three quarters of a mile of track were being laid every day. Their work on the railway was completed on September 18, and the next day they were given their first holiday since they had left Changi five months earlier. Their reward was paltry—a few cigarettes, a bag and a half of sugar, 140 tins of milk, and 86 tins of margarine for several hundred men.

For the Australian Peter Rushforth, one of the most dramatic and heart-rending episodes of his F Force experience occurred when the work at Sonkurai was nearly finished:

> Quite late at night the silence was broken by a distant rhythmic beating sound, then quite quickly out of the darkness came flaring lights, men

> carrying primitive looking torches and then before us was a scene of frenzied activity. Sleepers were laid, rails placed into position and hundreds of men, naked to the waist, their torsos glistening with sweat, worked in unison. Many were Asian working as slave labour with the European POWs. Over the chanting as workers drove spikes into the sleepers, guards yelled and gave orders, then as quickly as these men had appeared out of the darkness they disappeared out of sight and the sounds of machinery, hammering, chanting and guards yelling faded into the night.

Very few men had watched a railway pass by their front door at night and a train pass by in the morning, said L.Cpl. Cliff Bayliss, AIF, at No. 2 Camp. Most of the camp were woken up and turned out to watch the spectacle.

Under so cruel a regime, sentimentality was fatal, and the men became hardened. Even though the pressure had relaxed, there were 149 deaths at No. 2 Camp in October. Some resorted to thieving from their friends to get a little extra food or tobacco; no article was safe if it had any salable value among the natives. Others resorted to malingering; some refused to obey orders. In a speech to hospital wards at No. 2 Camp, Bruce Hunt warned the men that any who transgressed for selfish ends would be sent out to work irrespective of the state of their health. The welfare of decent sick men was paramount and could not be jeopardized. John Stewart Ullman witnessed the inhumanity of man to man:

> Sometimes a small group formed up and "hunted" as a pack, generally men from the same regiment. It was not so much the moral aspect of stealing that was to be deplored but the incalculable harm that it did to a man who had half or the whole of his worldly possessions taken away from him—the loss of a blanket or a pair of boots might very well be the eventual cause of death of their erstwhile possessor. Curiously many men could not see anything reprehensible in stealing common property such as food or drugs. Most of the stuff stolen was sold to the natives for tobacco and food. Another scandalous feature was the way in which certain NCOs in charge of huts were amenable to a bribe in return for which they did not detail that particular man for the working parties. This would mean that a sick man without the means of bribing his way out went on the road to work while his wealthier and fitter comrade stayed in camp.

But in such conditions how were thieves or corrupt NCOs to be disciplined? Dillon was unwilling to hand men over to the Japanese for punishment, but found that some regular officers could not exercise control without the panoply of sergeant majors, daily orderly room, and guardroom of peacetime. Many temporary officers, especially volunteers, had no idea how to handle the troops. The men, moreover, were either so ill or so exhausted by the time they returned to camp that punishment drill or cutting rations was out of the question. Unlike a few other officers in F Force, Dillon did not resort to corporal punishment, either. Instead he held summary trials. A regular sergeant whose duty was to deliver dead men's clothes to a store where they were cleaned and reissued to the sick converted some of them to his own use. He was demoted to private. A corporal who stole all of a sick man's salable possessions, including a watch and tobacco, was also drummed down to private, while the private who had worked with him was given a severe dressing-down.

At Tanbaya, Bruce Hunt, who had been installed as the hospital camp's commander, was less fastidious. Black marketeers were beaten and thieves made to run the gauntlet. Some of the wardmasters were squeamish about inflicting punishment, so Hunt himself laid into them with his fists and a stick. "It is the only way to deal with these chaps, although it is probably against King's Regulations," said Harry Silman. Ullman found that the pressure to survive blunted the finer points of ethics. Communication dwindled to a rough terseness. Humor, such as it was, became coarse and callous, said Bill Bishop: "Each man, while he had the will to do so, concentrated on the strongest of all human instincts, the struggle to keep himself alive. There was no time or energy for anything else, no room even for pity." Some officers, he said, feigned illness to avoid working parties. The cremation parties started stripping the dead and selling their clothes to the coolies. Even the Japanese were surprised by some of the men's behavior. Once Ullman had to accompany a Japanese colonel on an inspection tour:

> He offered me a cigarette. Neither of us had the means to light it but on our left we could see smoke rising from behind a hill. We arrived at the funeral pyre, always a gruesome sight. A score of bodies were burning. Flesh bubbled and limbs writhed. I bent down, with one hand protecting my face from the heat, and with the other picked out a burning twig. I held it out to the colonel. He backed away. "Is that so?" he said. "Is that the way you light your cigarette from the fire that's consuming your friends?" I replied that life was terrible here and it was better to face it as it was. I used a Japanese expression, shikata ga nai koto, a nothing-to-be-done thing; an inevitability before which it's better to bend. The colonel looked at me and lit his cigarette from mine.
>
> I thought of the morning, a few days before, when, observing the

> man who slept next to me and thinking he wouldn't last the day, I asked him to let me have his toothbrush. As soon as his body was taken out of the hut, his belongings would be looted. And I needed a toothbrush. Mine had been stolen. He said, "Take what you need." He knew that he had only a few hours left. I placed my hand on his shoulder and said adieu silently—and then opened his pack and took the toothbrush.

Some men simply lost the will to live. One was a friend of Ullman. All his kit, apart from his haversack, was stolen on the march to Sonkurai. He was weak when he arrived and did not bother to wash or shave. His friends got him an easy job boiling water all day, but he was eventually sent out to work on the railway and his health and morale declined fast. His friends bribed a guard so that he stayed in the camp for a few days, but once again what was left of his kit was stolen. All he owned in the world were a grubby singlet, a shirt in shreds, and a few rags around his middle. He was sick of life and despairing:

> He hadn't washed for two months and however much we talked to him nothing and no one managed to change his attitude. He declined and was moved to a hospital hut. The downward slide continued. His friends brought him such extreme rarities as tinned milk, fish and soap. But he was so little interested in the business of living that he gave them away. He died very quietly of disgust and hopelessness two and a half months after his arrival in Sonkurai.

On September 3, the fourth anniversary of the outbreak of the Second World War, there had been no deaths at No. 2 Camp for twenty-four hours; it was the first full day without a death since May 25. With the better weather, the conditions for the working parties improved, and there was an unexpected issue of fifty cigarettes each, a tin of milk for every five men, and a tin of margarine for every ten men. By mid-September the canteen was stocked with gula, oil, tobacco, and peanuts, as well as eggs, brought to the camp by elephants. The first train passed through the camp on the twentieth, the very same day that the monsoon began to peter out. Thereafter, there were regular supplies of food, and the worst of Sonkurai was over.

However, the death toll among those evacuated to Tanbaya the month before had already risen to more than 350. Nevertheless, the move to Tanbaya undoubtedly saved many men's lives. After the fetid closeness of the jungle, said Lt. Robin Fletcher, the air seemed almost fresh, and a great load of oppression seemed to have been lifted. The camp was on the plains of

Burma at the foot of mountains. There were lovely views and the air was bracing. Without the constant threat of working parties and the consequent despair and listless fatalism, there was a new aura of freedom and a new spirit of help and cooperation. The men could sleep in peace knowing that the Japanese would not come through the huts demanding more men leave their sickbeds to work.

The Australian officers seemed to Tam Innes-Ker to have "a lot more push and go" than the British, and one of the main reasons for the revival of morale was Hunt's inspirational leadership. Robin Fletcher was one of Hunt's juniors at the hospital camp:

> When a patient arrived, broken in body and mind, often with three weeks' dirt as his only covering apart from some filthy pieces of sacking, weary of life and only wanting to turn his face to the wall and die in peace, he found himself washed, shaved and fed, and for the first time for months he saw around him people who could spare the time and energy from their own struggle for existence to help him too to live. Parties from the working camps were to arrive at all hours of the day and night (chiefly of the night) for the next ten days. No previous notice of their coming would be given, so we had to have a sentry permanently stationed to blow a whistle when a train appeared to be stopping. The condition of these parties beggars all description. They had left Sonkurai already at death's door, clad in the same noisome rags they had lain in for months. The 80-kilometre journey to Tanbaya had taken as long as 48 hours, during which time they had had no shelter and very little food. They had been packed as many as 54 to a truck. No wonder that on arrival there were corpses among their number. Washed and shaved [for the majority it was their first shave for three months] the seeds for a rebirth of self-respect had been sown.

The staff helped to revive the men's faith in human nature. Orderlies with flaming bamboo torches helped them off the trains. Medical officers sorted them into different categories and arranged their accommodations. On one occasion they gave up their own meal to feed a party that arrived with no warning. In the lives of the Fepows, as Fletcher wrote, "it could truly be said that greater love had no man than that he should give up his meal for another." As they arrived they were addressed by Hunt in unsentimental terms. He promised speedy, drastic retribution for malefactors, castigated idlers and "bludgers," and told them to be men and soldiers. There was a good reason for Hunt's warning. In spite of his harsh, sometimes personal, treatment of miscreants, the chief cause of friction at Tanbaya remained the black market.

Although the men were short of clothing, some were always to be found eager to sell their own (or preferably a fellow patient's) to the locals for a few eggs or cheroots.

There were soon fifteen hundred patients at Tanbaya, but Hunt had only meager medical stores; and although there was some meat and a supply of fresh vegetables, rations were still short. The same was true of cooking utensils, but the cookhouse was kept busy from dawn until 11 P.M. A special effort, however, was made on Christmas Day, when the officers dined on watermelon with white sugar, sweet rice porridge, fried eggs and bacon, brains, liver, pomelos, and coffee with sweetened milk. Carols were sung in the wards on Christmas Eve, and Padre Duckworth, who had accompanied the parties to Tanbaya, conducted a service by the light of blazing bonfires. Concerts were started again, and ended with the men singing or humming "Australia," "Land of Hope and Glory," and finally "God Save the King," after which Duckworth would shout: "Are we downhearted?" The thunderous reply invariably was "No." As he left the ward, "Ducky" would roar in stentorian tones, "To Hell with the Nips," and the Japanese who had come to watch would grin. To the men of F Force, Duckworth was a hero, a "cherubic ball of energy with his lung power wholly intact," according to Fletcher. On one occasion Fletcher heard him conducting choir practice at the kitchen a good half-mile away, and on his return was able to repeat to the padre much of what he had said. For Duckworth, such a task—chatting with a sick man—was a pleasure, not a duty.

When the surviving patients were sent back to Singapore in 1944, a total of seven hundred fifty men had died at Tanbaya. (One in two of the British patients from Sonkurai and Changaraya died, compared with about one in four of the Australians.)

Meanwhile, with their section of the railway completed, F Force had left the five main camps in November, moving first to Kanchanaburi and later onward to Singapore and Changi, traveling in the same terrible conditions as their first journey by rail to Ban Pong. Philip Toosey met many of them at Tamarkan and "cosseted" them before they continued. "They were in an appalling condition," he said. "I remember unpacking one lorry full of these poor wretches in the middle of the night—when they usually arrived. They were packed in standing up so that they couldn't fall down, but some were dead when we unloaded them." Kanchanaburi was a grand fattening paddock, said Capt. Roy Mills, an Australian medical officer. Eggs were twelve for a dollar, bananas less than a cent each, peanuts twenty cents a pint, and paw-paws, pomelos and tobacco were all available at decent prices. "It is grand to see the hollow-cheeked lads filling out and losing that starving, hungry look they have so long had." The men stayed in the hospital for a week or two, where they were fed with some pork stews and plenty of vegetables, before moving on to Singapore.

Lt. Wakabayashi, a man who had already displayed his decency at Sonkurai, confirmed the fact in an incident on the journey to Singapore. At Ban Pong the men were allowed to collect their gear from where it had been dumped on the outward journey. Wakabayashi told them that he knew there were radios among dumps but said he would take no further action if they were all handed over. The prisoners did as he suggested. After a short examination of his haul, Wakabayashi selected one, but he was told it needed repair. "Never mind," he said, "Captain Mudie will soon fix it for me."

Seven thousand men had set out with F Force. When the survivors returned to Kanchanaburi at the end of November, about twenty-five hundred had died, two thousand were ill, and fifteen hundred were fit only for light camp duties, which left no more than a thousand men fit for hard labor. When they had left Changi in April 1942, they were almost totally free of malaria. One in four of the 3,122 who returned to Changi were carrying the malaria parasite. Some had suffered as many as sixteen attacks during their eight months in Thailand. Over the next seven weeks there were 2,942 separate attacks of malaria among them. As has been said, the Australian camps fared much better than the British in combating disease, and this was as true for malaria as it was for cholera. Stanley Harris attributed this to several factors in No. 2 Camp: overcrowding in unroofed huts, poor rations, the absence of a canteen until August, and sleeping in wet clothes. Sick men were forced to work up to their waists in water and to lift excessive weights. At No. 2 Camp there were no drugs, antiseptics, or dressings for the sick. There was also no permanent IJA officer, only a sergeant, who was constantly overruled by the engineer officer (the despised Lt. Abe), who prevented improvements to the camp.

The Australians saw the survival rate differently. Their officers and men were members of a single volunteer force, the AIF, with a common emblem and outlook, said Charles Kappe in his report to "Black Jack" Galleghan. The average standard of the Australians was incomparably higher than the British collection of regulars, territorials, militiamen, conscripts, and local volunteers, many thrown together at Sonkurai for the first time. The Australians had a higher standard of fitness and completed the march north before the main monsoon broke. There was not the slightest doubt, he wrote in a joint report with Adrian Curlewis, that the lower death rate among his countrymen was due to a more determined will to live, a higher sense of discipline, a particularly high appreciation of maintaining good sanitation, and a more natural adaptability to harsh conditions.

Kappe's analysis was supported by Bruce Hunt, who also attributed the Australians' higher survival rate to the selection of whole units or sections of units for F Force. Unit spirit had helped morale and assisted the officers in controlling the men, he said, whereas the British had simply selected the required number of men without bothering about units. Among the Australians there was also a closer bond between officers and men—and the tougher the conditions, the tighter that bond became.

The Australians' diaries support Kappe's and Hunt's analyses. Lt. Norman White was among the Australians who were moved to No. 2 Camp in August 1943:

> This is just one hell of a camp and up to our arrival was occupied wholly by Pommies [British]. The whole area is filthy, the officers and men have a dirty, downtrodden appearance and not a thing done about decent hygiene and cleaning the place up a bit. If anything out of the ordinary happens or goes wrong, the officers just throw up their hands, sit down and do nothing about it except to talk about how bad things are. They have had 399 deaths here so far and no wonder. They are only now getting over the shock of our arrival and the few days since. We now have our part of the camp cleaned up fairly well and have established water boiling and sterilising points—things that were never thought of before. We have built our own kitchen and will go into action here in a day or so and our officers have built an officers' kitchen. The Pommy officers are impossible and even if one decides to get off his back and give a hand he is usually so damn useless in this type of work that he'd be better staying down.

A month later, Stan Arneil was worried about the Englishmen under his care. They practically walked to the cremation pyre, he wrote. They stopped eating, lay down, and refused to live. Instead of hanging on to life with both hands they started to criticize their meals. Arneil, in contrast, said, "Breakfast is almost revolting but most of us regard it as a legitimate ticket home and religiously poke it down. I must get home." The British would not try to help themselves by getting under the eaves when it rained to have a wash, said Pte. Bill Anderson. Another Australian, Lt. Bob Kelsey, asked a skeletal soldier from the Manchester Regiment why No. 2 Camp, with seven medical officers, a good supply of water, and the benefit of vaccination before leaving Changi, had lost so many men. They died of broken hearts, the man replied:

> They were a city crowd with useless officers uninterested in their men. Where we at Lower Sonkurai soon learned to weave bamboo strips to form baskets to carry rice to several messing points, the men in Sonkurai 2 had only one messing point at the cookhouse—necessitating a reveille some two hours before it was necessary. It did not occur to them to have fires in their huts to make life more bearable, to dry their clothes and sterilise their dixies [mess tins], as well as providing some light.

Some of the charges made by the Australians were undoubtedly unfair, rooted in the longstanding love-hate relationship between Aussies and Poms. Adrian Curlewis wrote of the "utter failure" of certain senior Australian officers, too. A minority of Australian officers also took the line of least resistance, according to Sgt. Erwin "Curly" Heckendorf, who said that many men resented the officers' higher pay and readiness to accept privileges. When the men first arrived at Lower Sonkurai, the officers took the one small section of a hut that was roofed. When another hut was roofed, they kicked the men out and moved in. But the statistics tell a story: among the Australians, three officers died while there were 1,065 deaths among the other ranks. Stan Arneil contrasted the rations that the officers drew—a quart of gula malacca and sugar each, tins of milk, and as much soap, tobacco, and oil as they wanted—with the pints of sugar for 250 men and the pint of gula and oil for each hospital patient. It was "wicked," he wrote: "Surely these officers do not expect to be respected when they finally discard the uniform."

Yet the decision to switch Dillon to No. 2 Camp in August had been an obvious acknowledgment that standards among the British were not good enough. That fact was conceded by Stanley Harris himself in his report on F Force, when he wrote that Dillon had "restored" courage and self-respect to hundreds of broken, dispirited men and given lasting inspiration to the officers under his command. His strict discipline, said Harris, had won the admiration of all ranks, notably the Australians, as had his ceaseless efforts on their behalf. He also singled out the remarkable endurance of Bruce Hunt, whose determination, drive, and medical ability saved hundreds of lives.

When the Australians at last returned to Singapore, Galleghan and a great throng of prisoners were waiting for them on the road outside Changi. The men had been on the train for almost a week and appeared as wraiths, slow-moving skeletons emaciated beyond belief compared to those who had remained at Changi. They were clumsy, did not call out to their fellow Australians, were leaning on sticks or on each other and holding one another up. Many had dreadful sores and peeling skin. Nearly all were infected with malaria or suffering from beri-beri. "We saw them as they were, bits of rags on bits of skeleton men," said Capt. Leslie Greener, AIF. But they held to the code of behavior that had sustained them at Sonkurai, lined up and marched in time. Some could not stand and were laid down by their mates with touching care at the end of the line. "Where are the rest?" asked Galleghan, to be told that a third of his 2/30th Battalion were dead. As he walked along the parade, he cried, the tears running down onto his collar.

Stan Arneil arrived at 1 A.M. on December 21, observing Changi prisoners who were healthy, clean, clothed in good shorts, and booted. He made his diary entry the next day: "We arrived here last night and were bedded down in new huts at 4 a.m. We have at last fallen into a prisoners' paradise."

Tam Innes-Ker weighed 105 pounds when he arrived back at Changi, clad in half a towel and one gym shoe:

> Were we glad to get here! Most of us are hospital cases. . . . On Christmas Day I had a sharp relapse of malaria and unfortunately couldn't interest myself greatly in the food which was very good, all reserves of tinned stuff being turned out for the benefit of the returned "martyrs" as we are regarded by those who have stayed in Changi's sheltered area. True, they all look very fit indeed, full weight and strong, as compared to the tattered skeletons from Burma and Siam. I've met old pals who have showered me with gifts of clothes, tobacco and the odd dollar . . . I'm going to do my damnedest to stay put for the duration—no more work parties if I can help it.

The men at Changi had been hoarding scraps of food for Christmas—salt, red-palm oil, and extra rice, even some gula malacca. They gave their Christmas dinner to the remnants of F Force. It was Changi's finest hour, said David Griffin, who had remained behind when F Force had left. But the men who had returned were so ill that they did not realize what a sacrifice had been made for them. The average loss of weight was seventy to eighty-nine pounds per man; eight in ten had to be admitted to the hospital immediately; many had to lie on bare boards or concrete floors because of lack of space.

Of those who returned to Singapore, 95 percent were heavily infected with malaria, 80 percent were suffering from general debility, and half required hospital treatment for an extended period, chiefly because of dysentery, beri-beri, chronic malaria, skin disease, or malnutrition, according to Cyril Wild in his report on F Force. When two Japanese medical officers who wanted men to work on aerodrome construction examined the three thousand survivors, they could find only 125 who were fit for light duty.

By April 1944, 44 percent of the men who had left with F Force a year earlier were dead, nearly half from cholera or dysentery. Among officers, however, the death rates were under 1 percent for the Australians and under 2.5 percent for the British. The death toll was highest at No. 2 Camp: 1,175 of the 1,602 who arrived had died by April 1944.

	AUSTRALIAN	BRITISH	TOTAL
Left Changi	3,662	3,400	7,062
Died by April 1944 (or unknown fate)	1,060	2,036	3,096
Percentage	28.9	60	44

As Cyril Wild reported, the experience of F Force occurred not in the comparative security of a POW camp but in the remoteness of the Thai jungle and at the hands of a "callous and vindictive" enemy. Wild's report was used at a joint British-Australian war-crimes trial in 1946. Banno was sentenced to three years' imprisonment, Abe to death, commuted to fifteen years' imprisonment, and Fukuda to death, commuted to life imprisonment.

INTERLUDE

Ave Maria

It was 1944, somewhere near the Three Pagoda Pass on the Burma-Thailand border. The British and Dutch prisoners had marched from sunrise to sunset for two days. Fred Seiker was one of them.

> We had not drunk a sip of water all day. Our bodies were dried out, our throats were hoarse, our tongues felt like leather strips in our mouths. We were giddy from exhaustion and most of us suffered stomach cramp. The familiar gibbon calls could no longer be heard. It meant there was no fresh water for miles around. We made camp at dusk in a clearing close to a muddy pool, alive with insects. Several thrust their faces into the murky water, drinking greedily. Moves to stop them were met with violent objections. Most likely we would bury some of them later. The Japs grinned! Fires were lit for boiling the pool water and cooking the maggot-infested rice. A portion of this and a small piece of

dried fish was our meal for the day, washed down with boiled brown pool water.

Our bodies ached and our minds were numb as we crouched around the fires, which were kept burning to keep wild animals at bay. No one spoke. What was there to talk about? Each man was cocooned within his own thoughts. They were a comfort, your own thoughts. The night was black now. The jungle canopy had closed in over us. I realised that further marching the following day would decimate our numbers. Was that the plan perhaps? A chill ran down my spine. For the first time in my life I knew total misery. I felt alone and very frightened.

Then I became aware of a voice mingling with the many sounds of the night jungle. At first softly, haltingly, then louder, more certain, singing "Ave Maria" in a clear tenor voice. The jungle sounds around us subsided one by one as if the night creatures were also listening. The voice was now singing jubilantly and triumphantly. It was a moment of awe and wonder. The voice filled our hearts and minds as it rose into the silent blackness above us. I knew then that this magic moment would sustain me in whatever situation I would find myself in the future. Faces lifted, tears glistening in the fire's glow. Men struggled to their feet, some helped by their comrades. It seemed an impulsive gesture of defiance, as if to say, "We cannot be beaten." Were they feeling the same as I did? Were they also ashamed of their earlier misgivings?

I believed they were. A glow of pride rose within me. A pride of belonging. Also a feeling of victory. Victory of the human spirit over adversity. Both Japanese soldiers eyed us with bewilderment and suspicion, rifles at the ready. Their eyes darted around the group of quiet men. Men with haggard faces, damp rags hanging from their bones. We were no threat to their wellbeing, yet their eyes showed fear. Fear of something they could not understand. I felt pity for them, then.

As the voice softly remingled with the returning jungle sounds, the Japanese soldier suddenly snapped, shouting "kurra, kurra," threatening everyone in sight with the glistening, menacing bayonet. As he approached me I smiled. It sent him into a rage. After all, how do you fight a smile? The rifle butt thudded into my body, sending me crashing to the ground. I looked up into his face, now grinning, fury spent, the ridiculously large bayonet aimed at my throat! After a short while the Jap ambled away, kicking the ground as he went, mumbling to himself.

My mates hauled me back on to my feet. Their eyes tearful with suppressed anger. I realised then that my chest was throbbing with pain. "No sense of humour, these bastards," someone murmured. I smiled. How right he was.

Chapter 7

THE RAILWAY OPENS

The two ends of the Burma–Thailand railway were united at Konkuita on October 25, 1943 in deep forest about twenty-five miles southwest of the border and 163 miles from Nong Pladuk. Maj. Gen. Ishida Hideguma presided at the opening ceremony at which Lt. Col. Sasaki, commanding officer of the 5 Railway Regiment from Thanbyuzayat, and Lt. Col. Imai, commanding officer of the 9 Railway Regiment from Kanchanaburi, drove specially made gunmetal dog spikes into an ebony sleeper—missing at their first attempt. To wild shouts of "*Banzai*" from the Japanese troops, they then stepped forward and formally reported completion of the railway. A military band performed, as a locomotive decked with two Japanese flags approached from the Thai side.

The fittest prisoners were sent up the line, given special clothing, and filmed laying the last rails. Once the filming was over, the clothes were removed, but the photographs appeared in Japanese newspapers to show how fit and happy the prisoners were. Their reward was one tical each. Every up-country prisoner was given a large tin of Japanese fish and two small tins of sliced pilchards. The men were ordered to hold a thanksgiving service at the cemetery nearby, at the foot of the huge wooden cross. It was an "insulting mockery," said Lt. John Coast. The men made wreaths from orchids and other flowers, three of which were presented to the Japanese so that they could lay them in position. After a hymn and a few prayers, Col. Yanagida, the Imperial Japanese Army commander of 2 Group, spoke to the men in uninterpreted Japanese from a vast scroll. "From the restless way some of the Nip officers kept looking at the cemetery they obviously knew the thoughts in every British mind there," said Coast. The men were then marched back to camp and again addressed by Yanagida:

> You prisoners of 2 Group started to build this railway in Chungkai. You then went on to Wampo, where you blasted your way through rocks and made a great bridge. You then came further up with me to Takanun where you completed the sector allotted to you in a satisfactory manner. For one month it was difficult to get vegetable rations in our camp, owing to the bad road, and the ration was reduced. Some of you were sick, and some of you died. But you must acknowledge that you have always been fairly and justly treated by the Imperial Japanese Army. It is now your stern duty to improve your health in order to be able to carry out any further tasks which may be allotted to our group.

The men were given some rubber boots, and a few received cheap cotton shorts. That evening there was a combined Japanese-British show, but there were few British performers. The Koreans got roaring drunk, but the British escaped to their huts as soon as they could. According to Coast, they then examined and criticized the characteristics of the Japanese until far into the night, concentrating especially on the claim that they had been "fairly and justly" treated.

At Tamarkan, midway between the camp and the bridge on the River Kwai, British prisoners built a memorial (which still remains) to those who had died on the railway. On March 21, 1944, Brig. A. L. Varley and a selected group of officers and men were marched to the memorial to witness the opening service, which was filmed by newsreel photographers. The memorial had been decorated as if for a harvest festival: the cenotaph and oblation stone were covered with fruit and vegetables, a supreme irony to the men there who had seen so many comrades die for lack of basic foodstuffs. After the speeches, Varley read out a statement emphasizing that the conditions under which the men had worked would be investigated after the war. The ceremony was an insult to God and man, remembered the war correspondent Rohan Rivett, a gesture required to meet the demands of saving face. The only real point of interest was that on the memorial the Japanese admitted that seventy thousand fellow Asiatics, whom they were supposedly "redeeming from Anglo-Saxon bondage," had perished.

The 61,800 prisoners and 270,000 "coolies" had laid the track at a rate of 970 yards a day. The toll on human life was terrible: an estimated 12,399 prisoners, including 6,318 British, 2,646 Australians, 2,490 Dutch, 132 Americans, and hundreds of unknowns, as well as at least 73,000 native workers, died during the building of the railway. Among the prisoners, the death rate was on average about 20 percent, but it reached more than 45 percent within eight months among H and F Forces. One in three of the Australians who lost their lives in captivity died on the Burma–Thailand railway.

It is questionable whether the Japanese benefited as they believed they would. From 1944 on, the railway was under regular bombardment by the British and Americans. The initial goal of transporting of three thousand tons a day, mainly of ammunition, ordnance, petrol, clothing, and provisions, was never met. The best estimates are that between 450 and 500 tons were transported each day. Thousands of troops and casualties were also transported—but mainly away from the battlefield rather than toward it. Once the war was over in 1945, most of the railway was soon reclaimed by the jungle.

After the war, as Lt. Ian Watt wrote later, silence descended on the railway. Robbers furtively stole the telegraph wire; termites ate away the wooden ties of the line and the timbers of the bridges; the monsoon rains washed away parts of the embankment; and sensing that all was normal, the wild elephants that the prisoners had never seen once again emerged from the jungle and leaned against whatever telegraph poles inconvenienced their passage.

The British army dismantled two and a half miles of the railway at the Burma-Thailand border, and 185 miles were handed over to the Thai government. The Thailand State Railway dismantled the rest of the line from the border to Namtok (near the wartime camp of Tarsao). The wooden bridge built by Toosey and his men was also dismantled. Locomotive C5631, which had been at the opening ceremony, was repatriated after the war and displayed in the grounds of the Yasukuni Shrine in Tokyo. Another locomotive is displayed at Tamarkan. The spans of the bridge over the River Kwai were rebuilt by a Japanese company as part of the war reparations. Now a tourist attraction, it is crossed daily by trains on the line from Nong Pladuk to Namtok, which also travel, very slowly, over the Wampo Viaduct. It is a short drive from Namtok to the Hellfire Pass Memorial, built by Australians and Thais and opened in 1997, where the misery and terror meted out to the prisoners in 1943 can be vividly revisited. Young Japanese visitors sometimes break down in tears.

PART TWO

Chapter 8

SURVIVAL

Years after the war was over, one of L.Cpl. John Brown's most vivid memories of his years in captivity was of his first day at the hospital camp at Chungkai after being evacuated from the Burma–Thailand railway. He heard somebody singing and was so surprised by the emotion in the man's voice that he turned around to stare. Then he realized why he was so surprised—the man was happy and carefree. Where Brown had worked on the railway, nobody had sung or laughed:

> The experience had changed us all to a degree that no other experience could and yet I find myself marvelling that we have not been irremediably coarsened. We have returned and we have taken our part in British life almost as if nothing had happened. We are not the striking oddities that we expected to be. It appears that the human spirit is no less resilient than the human body. Few would have believed—certainly not the pre-war army authorities—that men fed and housed as we were could have done heavy, slavedriven work throughout the heat of a tropical day or could have survived so many illnesses lacking as we did the most elementary medical supplies.

For nearly sixteen hundred days—more than four years—the prisoners of the Japanese were overcrowded, underfed, overworked, treated as "beasts of burden," and beaten like "slaves," as they wrote so often in their diaries. They labored in the copper and zinc mines of Japan and Taiwan, as well as on airfields, roads, and railways in Burma and Thailand, the Spice Islands, and the Philippines. If they were "fit," they were fed three meals a day—rice for breakfast, rice for lunch, and rice for dinner, with a few vegetables and a sliver of fish if they were lucky. They were crowded together in squalid bamboo huts like pigs in a litter. They suffered from all the tropical diseases, especially cholera, malaria, dysentery, beri-beri, and ulcers. Most were emaciated and starving skeletons clad only in a sort of G-string or "Jap-happy." The surprise is not that so many died—25 percent, compared with 4 percent in Germany—but that so many survived. "It wasn't as bad as you think and worse than you can ever imagine," said the Australian chief petty officer Ray Parkin. Parkin wrote *Out of the Smoke,* one of his three books on his experiences with the Japanese, on toilet paper during captivity. He became a close friend of Weary Dunlop and one of the most notable chroniclers of the prisoners' suffering in Thailand and Japan.

Those who survived did so by summoning up the deepest resources of the human spirit. After being beaten by the Kempetai when secret radios were discovered at Kanchanaburi, Lt. Eric Lomax was almost blind and pathetically thin, but he had a fixation about learning to read and write again after being tortured at Kanchanaburi. In jail at Outram Road, he laboriously copied out simple words from a child's spelling book that had been found in Changi. He survived and years later wrote the prize-winning *The Railway Man* about his experiences.

Some of the prisoners had much better chances of survival: the cooks and clerks, doctors and drivers, for obvious reasons; men with skills or crafts—cobblers, for instance—that made them indispensable; those who remained in Singapore throughout captivity; those who were at the southern end of the Burma–Thailand railway, where there was a constant supply of fresh eggs; and the officers (most officers did not do the menial work of the men, and as they were better paid, they could afford to buy food). Older men could not take the physical hardships, said Lt. Robert Reid, while younger men cracked up because they had less experience of what life had to offer than those who had wives or sweethearts to live for. Those from India and Malaya possessed resistance to tropical diseases. What mattered most, however, was the will to live.

The survivors had to overcome self-pity, animal hunger, squalor, and oppression. They also had to combat boredom. For many, as 2nd Lt. David Piper found in an officers' camp in Taiwan, captivity was not a perpetual regime of suffering. There was, as he put it, the "sheer going-on-ness" of life in prison camps, the way in which under almost any conditions human beings indomitably establish the comfort of routine. But hunger aroused animal instincts—selfishness, hatred, envy, jealousy, greed, self-indulgence, laziness—and some men lived by the law of the jungle: the weak were trampled underfoot, the sick ignored or resented, the dead forgotten. L.Cpl. John Stewart Ullman described life in such an alien environment:

> When starved and worked to death in jungle camps, thoughts of home and freedom only served to widen the gap between the reality and the hope. Only the present counted, not the past or the future. Everything and every circumstance around us was utterly new and unexpected. We had been prepared for none of it. Not for our extraordinary habitat, the rain forest; not for our closeness to another people and its culture, the Japanese; and certainly not for the breakdown of our own group structure. With its societal skin flayed, human nature became visible as never before. Greed, cowardice and vanity, perseverance, altruism and generosity, in brief the wide panoply of virtue and vice, were there to be observed in the open, without pretence, with no place to hide.

Allied to the will to live, a sense of common humanity—which embraced comradeship, compassion, and courage, as well as self-sacrifice, pride, and fortitude—was the greatest savior of lives. These were qualities that the Japanese did not understand but nevertheless admired.

One constant theme of captivity was a sense of helplessness. When was it all going to end? What was happening to mothers and fathers, wives and children? The occasional arrival of letters brought good and heartbreaking news in equal measure. At Chungkai in May 1943, Lt. George Henry "David" Boddington described in his diary letters in which men's wives or sweethearts announced they were leaving them for someone else.

Capt. Cyril "Pop" Vardy, one of the most popular doctors, wrote that he had forgotten how to think as a normal human being:

> I feel sure this constant glumness, hopelessness of outlook will have a permanent effect as the days pass after a few regular chores such as shaving in the morning, repairs to fastly diminishing wardrobe, bath at night in a bucket—concern over meals three times a day—only one meal (midday) being at all palatable—a few hours' uncomfortable sleep—some work and hours of gloomy thought. 7-10.30 p.m. each evening is the low mark—no proper lamps—cannot read (eyes getting a bit funny)—turn in 10.30 to toss about until 2 a.m. thinking, thinking, thinking. On top of all this my birthday is upon me—42—finished and

> I cannot remember anything, except misery, disappointments, unhappiness—disillusions—friends, love, peace, home, comfort all seem to have flown out of life's window. Along is coming 1945 and I left Australia in 1941. When will it all end? I pray, pray, but I sometimes feel as if I have lost touch with God—makes me utterly miserable—so I try again to pray but cannot concentrate and then sometimes weep in the darkness at the hopelessness of it all—and the thought of never getting out strikes terror into me. So I ask forgiveness and try to take comfort.

By 1944 that helplessness was exacerbated by the fear of dying not at the hands of the Japanese but from the American and British bombers that were flying overhead. "Who is our friend? Must we POWs fear both sides?" asked Rabbi Chaim Nussbaum. Fear and insecurity dominated Changi, he wrote. The men viewed themselves as though they were proceeding through a long tunnel, the end of which grew darker until it was finally sealed off completely—the moment when the end was reached.

The squalor of most camps was another dispiriting factor in the men's lives. There was the daily battle against lice and bedbugs. The latrines were often disgusting, seething with maggots, with long queues for a free seat. Those who suffered from dysentery frequently could not contain themselves and soiled the ground. Some men at Capt. Atholl Duncan's camp in Japan didn't even bother to find the latrines but fouled the passageways in the prison blocks. He was disgusted that their sanitary habits had degenerated into those of an untrained dog. There were rats everywhere. They chewed through mosquito nets and nibbled at feet as men slept. David Boddington was awoken one night by rats clawing at his feet. They ran over sleeping men's faces. At Chungkai one major could hear the rats squealing as they chased each other along the bamboo poles every night. An extra-loud squeal meant they had been snared by a snake. "I often feel them run into my net at night and their droppings give evidence of their presence on top of my net. They make a habit of raiding stores of peanuts and pomelos and bringing them or bits of them inside a haversack or pack to eat. When I clean out my pack I nearly always find a few pomelo pips and outside skin of peanuts. Jolly Fellows!" Rats coursed about Weary Dunlop's bed, tugging at his hair and gnawing his clothing. At Kinsaiyok ten thousand rats were killed and incinerated within six weeks because the Japanese thought they were carriers of bubonic plague. Flies were another hazard. With a team of twenty men and his homemade swatters, Lt. Col. Philip Toosey saw to it that up to thirty thousand were killed each day.

Surviving in these desperate conditions obsessed the Australian doctor Capt. Rowley Richards. After the war he wrote a book about how he and his comrades managed it. He had revised his theories as captivity progressed. At first he thought survival depended on the regiment as a fighting force—discipline, camp hygiene, adequate rations, physical fitness, a proper balance between work and recreation comprising sports and concerts. But in the jungle survival became basic—fighting the heat, cold, rain, filth, disease, despair. And all he had in his medical armory were hygiene, rest, and boosting the men's hopes. So, did survival of the group depend on the will of the individual to live, on small groups of friends battling against the odds through camaraderie? Was conventional morality now out of order? Ought the scroungers, bludgers, parasites, wheeler-dealers, and thieves to escape censure since they were trying only to survive? The answers were easy, he eventually concluded: many factors played a part—sheer luck, determination, camaraderie (for the British) and mateship (for the Australians), improvisation, adjustment of moral values, positive thinking, and attitude.

All the men had perforce to adjust to their conditions. Capt. Stanley Pavillard and his fellow officers adapted to captivity by redirecting their whole outlook. Life became a game of make-believe, and they acquired the knack of turning their attention away from discomfort and deprivation. This psychological technique (and a sense of humor) saved morale and lives. Pavillard explained:

> As a doctor I had many opportunities of studying the mental reactions of my fellow prisoners, and all too often I saw men failing to adapt themselves to this make-believe game, this mental camouflage of reality, and then in consequence becoming morose and gloomy and in the end invariably dying. On the other hand, those who did master the knack became quite happy; a fact which may be hard to believe but is none the less true. Few of us could have survived on any other basis.

Some were kept alive by their hatred of the "Nips." Weary Dunlop recorded his emotion at Hintok Mountain in May 1943 after performing an unsuccessful operation:

> These days, in which I see men being progressively broken into emaciated, pitiful wrecks, bloated with beri-beri, terribly reduced with pellagra, dysentery and malaria, and covered with disgusting sores, a searing hate arises in me whenever I see a Nip. Disgusting, deplorable, hateful troop of men—apes. It is a bitter lesson to all of us not to surrender to

> these beasts while there is still life in one's body. It is squalor and degradation of body and mind. I could never go through it again.

For most, the survival factor became, as John Brown put it, a combination of fatalism and determination:

> We had ceased to think of ourselves as having any control over our own lives. We recognised that we were now just so many units of manpower in the hands of the Japanese to be used by them as they thought fit. Our food and our living conditions, our very lives indeed, depended on them. We were no longer able to shape our own destinies, escape, which we often considered, being entirely out of the question.
>
> Yet at the same time most of us cherished and fostered a determination to get home. Perhaps it wasn't consciously done apart from that first day after capture when, happy to find we had not all been shot on the spot, we said that, come what may, we were going home some day. Perhaps it was simply that we refused to think in terms of not going home. We took our survival and ultimate freedom for granted and related all our experience as prisoners of war to that fact.
>
> It is difficult to express just what was in our minds. To some it was a burning faith which provided them with strength to keep going when it seemed that they no longer had the physical strength and such men repeated daily as a kind of cabalistic formula, especially when conditions were particularly trying, the phrase "I will get home." For others this determination meant the conscious exertion of the will to carry the body and mind beyond the normal limits of endurance. I discovered later that it was this conscious exercise of the will that had carried men through the almost unspeakable horrors of the jungle and had brought them back to health when it had seemed inevitable, to friends and doctors alike, that they would die. I saw later that, given this determination to live on the part of the patient, doctors could effect, with the limited resources and supply at their command, almost unbelievable cures but that if the will to live was not there they were powerless to save the patient, no matter how hard they might try. It was this sense of fatalism which made us now take everything that came without surprise. We knew our place in the Japanese scheme of things and we knew now that we could expect no consideration.

Such determination brought out the best in most of the men, who shared their sorrows as they shared their food and gave succor to the sick. It was a common sight on the way back to camp after the day's labor to see a tired man with three or four picks on his shoulder while two others were half-carrying another man who was too exhausted to walk. The old idea of "every man for himself" disappeared. Instead, the prisoners felt they were all in this together: if they could help the next man along, without prejudicing their own chance of survival, they did. There were selfish, greedy men among both officers and enlisted men in every camp, but it was the strength of comradeship that enabled men to keep going under almost intolerable mental and physical stress. The depth of the bonds between the soldiers was impossible to explain to those who weren't there, said the Australian sergeant Stan Arneil:

> Difficult to understand death, for example. In Australia one dies in a sterile hospital bed. If the doctors are quick enough they might have the relatives there, but many times the patient is dead before the next of kin get there. In Thailand when a man died, he died in an aura of love and brotherhood which is not available now possibly anywhere in the world. You died with your head in the lap of a mate, with somebody holding your hand, with somebody with a hand on your forehead saying a little prayer, and people actually sorry to see you die. That's a bond which you just cannot obtain now. Many of the people who were there became closer to their friends than to their families.

If they were to survive, the men had to help one another, and so they banded together in what were known as "kongsis," usually small groups of four, five, or six who agreed to assist one another. The strength of the strongest increased the chances of survival of the weakest, and men became their brothers' keepers. "Everywhere one looked," said U.S. Marine Howard Robert Charles, "men were caring for one another, washing faeces and vomit from bamboo beds, taking drinking water to someone, bathing a man's forehead with a damp cloth, doing whatever could be done to bring comfort and hope." Early on at Jaarmarkt Camp at Surabaya in Java, L.Cpl. James Home and his RAF friends assessed their possessions. Home had a watch, lighter, signet ring, a small blanket, and a spoon. One of his mates had a fountain pen, a wallet, a ring, and a watch, all of which could be traded. Another friend had lost all his belongings—they had been stolen with his haversack—but four of them decided on a contract: all for one and one for all. The same spirit inspired the men at the Kinkaseki copper mine in Taiwan. Their worksheets were marked, and "diligent" workers were rewarded with two extra rice balls. Meanwhile, the rations of the sick were cut by half. A majority voted to break up the rice balls, put them in a communal bucket, and serve equal rations to everyone. Some men objected, arguing that they had earned the extra rations, but the selfless majority triumphed.

The kongsis enabled the men to share their emotions, tell stories, and share dreams. There were a dozen men in Sgt. A. E. Mills's kongsi. They met in the quartermaster's hut after dark and pretended they were civilized as they sat together in their "Jap-happies":

> There we squatted, at the end of the day's work, almost naked, puffing away at the raw Siamese tobacco and sipping our tea. All you could see in the blackness was a little circle of pulsing cigarette-ends like glow-worms in the dark. There were about a dozen of us, and we talked about everything under the sun. One man was an architect, one was a scientist and one a professor of English. The rest of us were civil servants and rubber-planters and businessmen; but there were several who had considerable knowledge outside their own jobs. One of the businessmen talked all one evening about music; another time somebody explained psychoanalysis, and one night we had a talk on Greek literature. The great thing was that our minds had something to chew on and for an hour or two we were able to forget about the Japs and rice and shovelling stones.

Survivors told moving stories of the compassion inspired by comradeship. When AB Allan Gee arrived at Tamarkan, he was met by his fellow Australian, Seaman George "Slim" Hendrick:

> To my delight Slim was waiting to greet me. He was rotten with dysentery and fever. Diarrhoea was running down his legs and he was blown up with beri-beri. He was standing there with this big smile. He said, "I've got your wardrobe here, your urn for boiling water and a bamboo container for washing. And I've got you a new pair of pants made out of a piece of canvas. But the best news is I've got you an egg!" That was the great affection we shared as prisoners of war, and it never left us. We have always said that if you didn't have a mate on the railway you died, and Slim was my mate. I owe him my life. I loved Slim.

Maude Hendrick (Slim's wife) added:

> Allan was in a bad way, almost blind by then. My husband told me he would wait for Allan each day when he came off the railway and wash all the dirt off him. George was the one who really looked after him. [She holds up a sketch made by Jack Chalker.] You can see by Allan's

face that he was in pain. George is looking at Allan with a smile that seems to be saying, "Come on, you'll be all right. I'm going to take care of you." Allan looks as if he was feeling that he couldn't go on any more. It's a wonderful sketch and says more than words can ever say.

When the airman James "Freddie" Chandler went into St. Vincentius Hospital, Java, with other patients in 1944, the current residents went without meat so that the new arrivals received a good portion:

> The following day the last of the dirt was removed when we were all shaved and my head was as clean and shiny as though there had never been hair on it. It was wonderful to feel clean again and also to eat bread. I was most anxious to regain the use of my limbs and voice, but until such time as I could, everything was done for me. My bread was cut up, my nails cut, and I was dressed and undressed and washed and shaved.

In Zentsuji, Japan, Australian captain David Hutchinson-Smith's birthday was royally celebrated in 1943. He was first given a cup of hot, strong coffee and a Camel cigarette, which his fellow prisoners had hoarded for the occasion.

> Then the birthday cards started to roll in and last, but by no means least, a crowd gathered round and I was presented with a bound souvenir volume of the Christmas and New Year festivities. The pages were of drawing block paper, the binding a piece of red Kanaka lap-lap and the paste made of rice. The book was beautifully illustrated in colour and was encased in a khaki cover on which had been embroidered the Australian Rising Sun badge. Much of the work had been done by my room-mates, who had worked assiduously on it every time I happened to be out of the room. It had taken them three months to complete. As the day was a Sunday, doughnuts were served at tea and I was delighted, although reluctant to accept, a gift of a dozen doughnuts, contributed willingly by hungry men. If this was not a pretty stiff test of friendship, I do not know what is.
>
> Many trite things have been said and much unconvincing matter has been written using the old worn-out clichés about comradeship and *esprit de corps,* but if any moral lesson was to be learned from the experience of a prison camp, I think it was to be found in spontaneous and planned Christian acts such as these. Any man would indeed be an unregenerate cynic or a faithless automaton if he were to remain unmoved by such expressions of loyalty and affection.

Another group of Australians saved Capt. Reginald Burton when he collapsed and could not stand. A Japanese sentry kicked him in the ribs as he lay prostrate on the track back to camp. Then:

> There suddenly appeared a bedraggled little group in shabby bush hats. I had another moment of clarity and recognised them. There was good old Bert Savile. And with him John Norbury, Spike Grieve, and Peter Playfair. They trudged up to me and stopped. One of them, I'm not sure which, turned to the Nip sentry and said menacingly: "Bugger off!" Perhaps the quartet looked dangerously villainous even to an armed sentry. He departed. The four turned their attention to me: "Come on, Reg, you'll be okay with us." They lifted my rice sack, quickly and efficiently redistributed their loads, and then gently lifted me. So with my burden of rice I was carried back to Tonchan. Here I was put to bed, laid low by the ravages of malaria. I believe I had been very near death, in collapse as well as from the Jap who might well have shot me for failing to obey an order. I'd also, in those brief sunset moments, had a vision of beauty which transcended the filth and ugliness of my circumstances. And then that filth and ugliness was defeated by the compassion and help of the four tough Australians, or four good Samaritans would be the best description. Perhaps, as there was still such goodness in the world, there was also some hope of survival.

The Australian spirit of mateship was well captured in a poem written by Cpl. Duncan Butler:

I've travelled down some lonely roads,
Both crooked tracks and straight,
An' I've learned life's noblest creed
Summed up in one word . . . "Mate."
Someone who'll take you as you are,
Regardless of your state,
An' stand as firm as Ayers Rock
Because 'e is your mate.
Me mind goes back to '43,
To slavery an' 'ate,
When man's one chance to stay alive
Depended on 'is mate.
With bamboo for a billy-can
An' bamboo for a plate,

A bamboo paradise for bugs
Was bed for me and mate.
You'd slip an' slither through the mud
An' curse your rotten fate;
But then you'd 'ear a quiet word:
"Don't drop your bundle, mate."
An' though it's all so long ago,
This truth I 'ave to state:
A man don't know what "lonely" means
'Til 'e 'as lost 'is mate.

The Australians, who had been fighting in Malaya longer than most of the British, considered that they were better equipped to survive than the "Poms," many of whom had either landed in Singapore only days before the surrender or had been fighting for mere weeks before they were captured. All their lives, the Australians had all benefited from rich food, sunshine, and exercise. They were used to the outdoor life, were more resilient, protected one another, stole for one another, and lied for one another. Why was it, one Australian asked a British major, that with five hundred Australians and five hundred British, the Australians suffered eighty deaths but the British four hundred when they were on the same rations and did the same work in the same conditions?

> "Well," he said, "you Australians are well fed." "Christ, no," I said, "I was brought up in poverty." "No," he said, "you got meat at least once a day even if it was only scrag end. You got vegetables. You got good bread, you got a bit of butter on the table, all that sort of thing." "Well," I said, "you don't look too bad. You're a pretty muscular sort of bastard." "Yes," he said, "I'm county family, old boy. Everything of the best. But my men got up in the morning and had half a cup of black tea without sugar; that was their breakfast. White bread and margarine for lunch. Black tea again with no sugar. At worst, well, they might get a vegetable soup. My men are real men, but they just haven't got the background," he said. "You can't starve them in the womb then in infancy, boyhood and young manhood and expect them to stand up to those conditions as well as your people do. Don't sling off at my mob; they're a wonderful set of men." "Yeah," I said, "they're all going to die, though."

Philip Toosey did not agree. The British men who stood up best to the conditions, he said, were the former slum dwellers of Glasgow, Liverpool, and

London. They were stunted men who had had to fight for the whole of their lives. In Java, Acting Lt. Col. Laurens van der Post noted their bowed legs and "Rowlandson" bodies and faces, the consequence of their severe neglect by the British ruling classes before the war. Yet, to Van der Post, their spirit was cheerful and invincible. He had never yet known a crisis, however brutal, he wrote, in which they had lost their nerve:

> Appeals to their pride and honour had never been in vain. Always they had responded instinctively in a measure as great if not greater than officers born, bred, well-nourished from childhood, schooled and trained for precisely this sort of trial. Their need of honour, or a life of self-respect too, was as important as their need of food. They were all slowly dying from lack of food at the time, but there was no hint of impending death in their conversation or sign of defeat in their emaciated faces. Instead there was only an extraordinary and intense kind of gaiety that to me was far more moving than any signs of depression, melancholy or defeat could possibly have been.

The Norfolk farmers who had lived in the "lap of luxury" on the land did not have the "steel fibre" of the Cockneys, the Glaswegians, and the Argylls. According to Toosey, "By God, they were tough." Statistically, it was best to be in your late twenties or early thirties, compact and in good shape, a non-smoker, to come from a small town, a farm, or a mining community, and to be used to hard physical labor. It was also highly advantageous not to be overly fastidious.

Gunner Russell Braddon adopted his own "inflexible" philosophy for survival: he determined that he would eat *everything*—thus, cats, dogs, frogs, snakes, bad fish, bad meat, blown tinned food, snails, grubs, fungus, crude vegetable oil, green leaves from almost anything that grew, roots, and rubber nuts all went down the same "remorseless" route. He decided never to complain about any food he received, because that might unnerve someone who had just steeled himself to swallow it. Similarly, he would not tolerate the company of anyone, however much he liked him, who complained:

> One could have no time for the man who pointed out to you that your rice was full of weevils—one pretended that the weevils were not there and ate them, being grateful for the calorific content they might yield. I determined that, so long as trees grew leaves, or the earth grass, I would eat of these products in an effort to stave off the vitamin deficiency diseases which were already rampaging through me. It was significant in those days that the ornamental bushes which grew round the jail were

> quickly stripped of every leaf that grew on their branches. Finally, I determined that I would seek help from my friends as seldom as possible and expect it never.
>
> I would make my own decisions unaided and abide by them. I would steal whenever and wherever possible. I would keep my mind active by reading whatever I could lay hand to and by talking to whomever could endure me. There being no room for optimism in Thailand—there being in fact no such thing as optimism in Thailand—some such insulating philosophy against the physically and mentally corrosive circumstances in which we existed was essential. Mine, which I found effective enough, was simply that "It didn't matter—nothing matters." The deaths of my friends, the ugly diseases that beset us, the constant reduction of rations that already seemed impossibly small, the bestiality of guards—against all these things, whenever they seemed likely to impinge upon my mind, I flung up the conscious barrier of "It doesn't matter—nothing matters."
>
> It was a kind of narcotic, a self-induced drug, and no doubt—like all drugs and narcotics taken habitually—damaging. The fact remains that starting in Thailand, and continuing on right through my captivity, and stopping I'm not sure where, I withdrew into the ostrich-like burrow where "nothing mattered," and there, mentally secure, I remained.

Survivors needed to be able to eat anything; those who could not force themselves to do so often died. "They needed the fortitude and discipline to make themselves wade through accumulated human filth to the latrines, and the wit and care to cleanse themselves afterwards, as thoroughly as possible, in a world that was suddenly devoid of soap, hot water, razors, and other routine paraphernalia of our civilisation."

Remarkably, the men's compassion extended occasionally to the Japanese. On the Spice Island of Ambon in 1944, a shipload of wounded Japanese arrived at the dockside for transfer to a nearby empty ship and were expected to get themselves from one to the other. The British prisoners stood by and watched, then suddenly, although they were starving and being humiliated and kept in squalor by the Japanese, they could no longer stand the sight of the pathetic injured men. They went on board and carried those who could not walk to the new ship, much to the incredulous surprise of the Japanese. To the medical officer Flt. Lt. Dick Philps, their action exemplified the "boundless compassion" of the men, compassion probably heightened by the suffering they had been through: "There was absolutely no thought of revenge in their minds. One of the men put it to me quite simply: 'We just couldn't stand and let the poor buggers drag themselves across on their stomachs.' "

The men acted in many different individual and collective ways to keep up their spirits. At the risk of beatings or even beheading, some kept diaries, sketched, or painted, so that their experiences were recorded for posterity (as they have been in this book). Ronald Searle's mission was to emerge from the camps with a "significant" pictorial record that would reveal to the world what had happened. Photos of loved ones—wives, mothers, sisters, and sweethearts—were treasured and helped hundreds of men to carry on living. They gave nicknames to the guards—Mad Mongol, Pig's Vomit, Rubberhips, The Undertaker, Mickey Mouse, The Bull, Twinkle Toes, Black Adder, Glamour Boy, Poxy Paws, Mussolini, Napoleon, Frankenstein, Hot Shit Harry, The Blue Arse Fly, Black Panther, Pock Face, Quack Quack, Pig Boy, King Kong—which perhaps helped lighten the perilous situation in which they found themselves. They dreamed of home or food or what they would do after the war. "Oh! I long for the familiar things of home—the curtains and rugs and pictures and vases with cared-for flowers in them," MO Ernest Norquist wrote in Cabanatuan, a camp in the Philippines.

> There is even the smell of home that I want to know again. It is an amalgam of cooking, cleaning, woodwork, and human odours that mingle not unpleasantly there. I want to hear the sounds of home—the water running in the kitchen sink; the sound of familiar footsteps, the sound of beloved voices. All these and more I want to hear.

They built imaginary houses and argued for hours about bricklaying, carpentry, plastering, plumbing, plans, and designs, or laid out gardens and planted them.

At Konyu, 2nd Lt. J. S. Milford lay awake and dreamed of his menus for an ideal day:

> Breakfast, Force [cereal] with milk and sugar, kidneys and bacon and fried bread, toast and butter and jam and coffee; lunch, roast pork with apple sauce and roast potatoes, plain suet roll with golden syrup; and in the evening, cold chicken and ham followed by a fruit pie, preferably gooseberry, and cream crackers and butter.

They suddenly remembered the simple pleasures of ordinary life which they had taken for granted. For the Australian journalist Ken Attiwill, who had been in England since 1929 and was captured in Java, it was a long list:

> Things like striking a match, choosing what you will eat, sleeping on a bed in a room by yourself, having hair on your head to brush, reading in bed

> and turning out the light when you want to sleep, taking a bath in a bathroom all by yourself, writing a letter, going into shops and buying things, reading newspapers, listening to radio—or turning it off—telephoning, wearing shoes inside the house, choosing your own daily routine . . . and a host of other things which are all little in themselves, but combined, make up the tremendous, exciting adventure of living in this delightful world.

It was a huge lift to morale to sabotage the projects on which they labored, or to outwit the Japanese. The same stories are recounted so often in the diaries and recollections that they cannot all be apocryphal. When a Japanese admiral visited Kuching (in Borneo), he found fault with every aspect of the camp—there were too many prisoners, but the cookhouse and the latrines were too good for prisoners of war. Major Suga, the camp commandant, had lost face; his camp had been severely criticized. L.Cpl. George Pringle tells the story:

> The Admiral signalled to Suga the visit was over and instructing his driver to start the motor car, the doughty couple seated themselves and prepared to be driven in state through the groups of prisoners who, attracted by the circus, were extremely grateful for anything breaking the monotony of their day. Solemnly the motor car proceeded down the main camp road giving everyone the opportunity to bow and salute. The salutes were returned in great style by the Admiral. Suddenly the car came to a halt and we could see a heated altercation going on between the Admiral, Suga and the driver, the driver obviously coming off worst. Out stepped the driver and lifting the bonnet of the car made an examination of the engine. Puzzled, he reported to the Admiral and, to our huge delight, received a heavy gloved fist full in his face. He was then made to stand to attention. A Korean guard was called and instructed to beat up the unfortunate driver. He did a real good job, much to our satisfaction. Stunned and bleeding he resumed his seat at the wheel. A group of prisoners were called and ordered to push the car towards the main Japanese lines. Suga very crestfallen and the Admiral in a towering temper, preserving as much dignity as possible under the circumstances, occupying the passengers' seats. How fortunate for us all they did not hear the shout of laughter speeding them on their ridiculous way. Even the Korean had a smile on his face. A most satisfactory morning. Later in the day, Freddie, our self-confessed thief, reported to our camp master: "Got any use for about four gallons of petrol, Sir?" During the visit Freddie had taken full advantage of the absence of the car occupants and had quietly siphoned off their petrol!

Singing was a huge source of solace and defiance, and helped the prisoners to confound the Japanese. After working all day in Singapore, they marched back to camp with the snap of a Guards brigade, said Stan Arneil, roaring in the moonlight the marching songs they had been singing in Australia three years before. Daily they grew thinner and more ragged, but still they sang. At Hellfire Pass they sang "They'll Be Dropping Thousand-Pounders When They Come." The guards would ask them to sing the "kai yai yippee song," but when a gang of Australians were ordered to perform for a Japanese film documentary, they refused to sing. Two retakes later and the guards were furious. Col. George Ramsay, AIF, hit on a solution which he explained to the men. The adjutant, Capt. Hence, told the guards that the men were ready. Ramsay explained what happened next:

> This time, when the sign for a marching song was given, the movie makers got it. They got it with full force, with great feeling, with everything the diggers could put into it. Right through the gate, on to the road, even after the filming had stopped, they were still singing!
>
> The Japs were delighted. One came over to Captain Hence and expressed his admiration for the fine cooperation given by the Australians at last. While he asked why the prisoners looked so gay and cheerful this time, Captain Hence waved to the officer in charge of the work party, indicating that the men should stop repeating over and over the refrain of that moving classical Australian marching song,
>
> *Fuck'm all, fuck'm all, fuck'm all,*
> *Fuck the short, fuck the fat, fuck the tall,*
> *Fuck all the commotion*
> *This side of the ocean,*
> *We'll fuck'm*
> *We'll fuck'm all mates, fuck'm all—*

As so often happened, however, the Japanese had the last word. They left after the filming in the camp had been completed, certain of some fine footage. Three days later Col. Ramsay was called over to the camp office. In a torrent of abuse he was told to line up every Australian officer in the camp. But the beating that followed was worth it for the tweaking of the guards' noses, said Ramsay.

After the national anthem was banned, "Land of Hope and Glory" became the anthem for the British. It was sung even during the worst days of the "Speedo" period in the Thai jungle, strong and defiant, after a shift of thirteen hours. At Kinkaseki in Taiwan the prisoners, as a concession at Christmas, were allowed to sing any song except the national anthem for half an hour before roll call. Everybody stood for the last song after they had sung "Pack Up Your Troubles" and "Tipperary" and roared out "Land of Hope and Glory, God who made the mighty, make thee mightier yet!" The British commander, Maj. J. F. Crossley, told the Japanese it was a hymn of praise sung with Christmas carols. Whenever the men at Kinkaseki were allowed to sing, they sang the song that later became the official anthem of the Far East Prisoners of War Association.

For Signalman Arthur Titherington, "Land of Hope and Glory" remains a poignant anthem:

> It still brings tears to my eyes and a distinct stirring inside me whenever I hear it. . . . To recall the sound, many years later, of a few hundred starved and exhausted men raising their spirits by singing that song as we walked out of the mine is indescribable. Our rendering of such a nationalistic tune had a dual purpose, of course. It was not only to raise our spirits, but was also an act of defiance, one of the few we could make, and I don't think even selective beatings would have stopped us. In many ways the words were rather ironic—"Britons never shall be slaves"—because we all knew that was exactly what we were. Nevertheless, each one of us, despite the necessity of hope, had the feeling that what we were enduring could go on for ever, or until the day we died. But we sang with all our might, and we meant every word of it.

The best night Russell Braddon remembered in Thailand was when the "Poms" suddenly started singing in clear, young voices: "There's a long, long trail a-winding, into the land of my dreams," followed, when that had finished and every man in the camp was listening, by, "When they sound the last all-clear / How happy, my darling, I'll be." "The next hutful of Pommies joined in, and the next with those, and the worst of Thailand was over," said Braddon.

A few prisoners also had the kind of experience that sends shivers down the spine. Capt. A. K. Butterworth went into a coma at Takanun with Japanese yellow fever. When he came around briefly two weeks later, he heard the doctor standing by his bed saying that the rest of his companions were dead. Butterworth was now blind, being able to distinguish only light from dark. An orderly asked about his chances of survival. Butterworth was in crisis, said the doctor, but he was young. If he survived the night, he should make it:

Hearing this probably saved my life. I knew I must stay awake but in my weakened condition this was not easy, my eyes kept closing, all I wanted to do was drift off—it was all too much of an effort. I was about to give way when suddenly I had a strong feeling that my mother was standing beside me: she was smiling and encouraging me to fight and not to give up. The awareness of her presence was so acute that I became wide awake. There was no longer a desire for sleep, and it was not until I could distinguish the light of dawn that I fell into a deep, restful sleep from which I awoke feeling refreshed and much better. I remembered the feeling I had had about my mother and thought it must have been my imagination playing tricks. It was not until I was released from camp that I learnt she had died of a heart attack on that same night. The doctor was delighted with my progress but confessed he had not expected to find me alive in the morning. "It's a bloody miracle—I doubt if there has ever been a case of anyone recovering from Weil's disease without medication."

Chapter 9

BOOKS

One solace in captivity was provided by literature; books were treasured. They were read and reread by their owners, lent to camp libraries, and used by the "universities" that flourished in many camps. On his voyage from Thailand to Japan, Chief Petty Officer Ray Parkin described how tattered books changed hands, sometimes being read by a dozen prisoners at a time, each man passing on the detached page as he finished it. "Thus twelve men would be in the grip of the same emotion at the same time." Using a lamp made out of an old tin, coconut oil, and a bit of string for a wick, men in the thick of the Thai jungle at Brankasi read aloud to one another from *The Canterbury Tales* and *The Pickwick Papers,* with the reader lying on his belly and with his head so close to the flame that it almost singed his hair. "If, as we hoped, we survived the war, we would have to enter the real, everyday, competitive world and there was no reason to suspect preferential treatment just because we had been POWs of the Japs," said Lt. Jim Richardson. "The mental discipline of writing, thinking and reading helped to keep burning the vital flame of intellectual curiosity and drive. To keep our minds active was imperative."

"Universities" were set up by the British and Australians soon after they arrived at Changi. The British university had faculties of modern languages (French, German, Italian, Spanish), English language and literature, history, geography, mathematics, economics, and theology (with departments for both Church of England and Free Church students). Each faculty had four to five lecturers, offering six to eight lectures a week as well as tutorials. A notice on the university read:

> Many officers and men whose studies were interrupted by the war will wish to continue them, either as preparation to entering a university proper or as preparation for a post-war career. The lecturers chosen for the university staff will be freed from any military duties which might interfere with their duties as lecturers. A lecturer's duty includes study and the preparation of lectures as well as the delivery of them. Candidates who have been admitted as students will be free to attend the lectures and tutorial classes at the times laid down.

Among the founders of the university had been Lt. Guthrie Moir (who had been at Peterhouse, Cambridge), Lt. Henry Fowler, and Lt. Ian Watt (who had been one of the brightest young men at Cambridge and had won a scholarship to the Sorbonne). Another Peterhouse graduate, 2nd Lt. Stephen Alexander, attended their English literature lectures, which were given in a small mosque. They may have been held in an overcrowded prison camp, but they were as elevated as any at Cambridge:

> We learned from Ian that literary works are not things to be enjoyed unthinkingly, but dissected and related not only to their own social background but to ours, too. Would Wordsworth have been so trusting of nature if instead of reclining above Tintern Abbey, he had been caught in the monsoon in the Malayan jungle? . . . Auden, rather, should be our guru; had he not seen through the delusions of physical beauty no less acutely than through those of capitalism and, of course, patriotism? And was there not a class feeling in the more traditional kind of war poetry that invalidated it as art?

Every unit organized talks and lectures on general and technical subjects to keep the men's minds active. Both Gen. Percival and Maj. Gen. Beckwith-Smith gave lectures on the fighting in France in 1940. The officers' eyes were opened. To Maj. E. W. "Jim" Swanton, who became the *Daily Telegraph* and BBC cricket correspondent after the war, there was a "surprising" thirst for learning among men he had seen before only as other ranks: "You go round and see a flock of gunners listening to a lecture on the modern history of Europe or a Shakespeare play reading." For the Australians, "Black Jack" Galleghan told the Japanese that a supply of books would prevent disaffection and reduce thoughts of escape. He thereby won permission to send a convoy of lorries into Singapore, where twenty thousand volumes were collected. Classes were set up in agriculture, business training, and general education, followed by mathematics, languages, law, engineering, medicine, and science. Alec Downer (later, as Sir Alec, a member of the Australian parliament) even started lessons in diction because he couldn't bear the Australian accent. The classes were thronged with expectant audiences equipped with paper and pencils to take notes on an arresting dictum on political economy or the prevalence of lice in poultry. There were eighty to ninety teachers for the nineteen hundred students of business principles and 120 for the 2,300 who enrolled for elementary English, arithmetic, and geography. Four hundred Australians learned to read and write at Changi.

When Stephen Alexander was reunited with Lt. John Durnford at Tamuang after helping to build the bridge on the River Kwai, they joined with Ian Watt and Guthrie Moir to resume the literary explorations they had started at the University of Changi. Tamuang had an efficient, well-run central library in part of a hut to which the men had given books so that they could be enjoyed by fellow prisoners. Among its volumes were Boswell's *Johnson, Eothen, The Knapsack, The Golden Treasury,* two volumes of *Letters to Malaya* (and a third in manuscript), and a tract of St. John's gospel. Ian Watt had the *Faber Book of English Verse,* Legouis and Cazamien's *History of English Literature,* some Dante, a selection of Yeats, an *Oxford Book of English Verse,* and an issue of John Lehmann's *Modern Writing*. It was "Bloomsbury on Kwai," said Alexander, and he and his friends engaged in debates worthy of an Oxbridge common room.

Durnford was a poet; nearly a good poet, thought Alexander. The following is one of his efforts:

PSALM 137

Be sure of this, no sufferings matched your own;
Egypt and Babylon fell long ago,
Be comforted you do not weep alone.
Complacent and indifferent worlds shall know
Sorrow like Israel's and a wilderness
(Such as those other children wandered in);
Whose sun destroyed the flesh made to caress,
And fevers sucked the blood beneath the skin;
Where if a yard was costly, lives were cheap,
And fear of company and want of rest
Made grown-up men cry as they turned to sleep

For the remoteness of another breast,
When by the bitter waters of disgrace
Sat down to weep another "chosen race."

E. W. Swanton's treasured 1939 *Wisden Cricketers' Almanack* was thumbed by thousands of men in twelve different camps and was in such demand that at one point it was lent out only for periods of six hours. As camp welfare officer at Changi, Swanton formed a library of several thousand books brought back by men on working parties in the European area of Singapore. The Changi libraries had five thousand subscribers for six thousand books. When men were sent away to Thailand they were allowed two books each, and consequently modest libraries were set up along the length of the railway. When they moved camp, some men retained one book to exchange in the next. The books survived primarily because they were rebound time and time again with gas-cape covers. The Australian bookbinders used boiled rice for paste and unraveled fire hoses and shirttails for thread. The twenty bookbinders at the officers' camp at Kanchanaburi rebound fifteen hundred books in a period of six months.

In Thailand, once the railway was built, and in Java too, the men had time on their hands. "Quite unexpected people" were anxious to discuss the problems of the times and sort out their ideas, said Swanton. There was a "spontaneous hunger" for education. As a result, a great many informal universities were established, all of which were crucial in helping men to survive. At Laurens van der Post's Java camp, where the men did not have to labor as they did elsewhere, a vast prison organization for re-education—a sort of prison kindergarten, school, high school, technical college, and university rolled into one—was created. A British officer, Maj. Pat Lancaster, taught two Australians to read and write. Airman "Don" Gregory coached people for their bachelor and master of arts degrees. There were active schools of drama and music and an extensive faculty of arts and crafts, said Van der Post:

> The whole of this side of our life in prison was one of my special responsibilities. But the person on whom this, for us, vast and creative prison edifice was well and truly founded was a remarkable scholar of French, a sensitive Welshman of great quality and imagination called Gunner Rees, MA. The arts and crafts faculty of this university, which attracted almost as many Dutch, Menadonese, Ambonese and Chinese prisoners to it as British, was very dear to Rees and it owed a great deal to him. At the same time he helped me more than I can say to make our prison

> schoolmasters, professors and artists aware of the fact that one of their main functions was to keep alive in our men their sense of continuity. The greatest psychological danger threatening men in the conditions of imprisonment we had to endure was the feeling that imprisonment was a complete break with their past and totally unconnected with their future lives. This danger we overcame in such a triumphant manner that with exceptions which I could count on the fingers of one hand, imprisonment for our men was transformed from an arid waste of time and life into one of the most meaningful experiences they had ever known.

At Chungkai anybody who wanted to learn was welcome. A thirst for knowledge was the only qualification for admission. Gunner Ernest Gordon resumed his study of law, but also broadened his horizons: he read Plato's *Republic* and Aristotle's *Nicomachean Ethics* in the original, lent to him by an Oxford classicist. Soon he was teaching moral philosophy to two groups of his own. A group would gather around a teacher in a given subject and there they would have a seminar. As rapidly as students learned, they would put their knowledge at the service of fellow POWs by acting as leaders of other seminars. Gordon explained:

> The taught became teachers in a chain reaction. Courses were offered in history, philosophy, economics, mathematics, several of the natural sciences, and at least nine languages, including Latin, Greek, Russian and Sanskrit. The faculty was handicapped by a shortage of textbooks, but they were not deterred. They wrote their own, from memory, as they went along. Language instructors compiled their own grammars on odd scraps of paper. A library was formed. It was a peripatetic library; it had no home, no lending system. Men made known the books they had and arranged by word of mouth to pass them on to others. As the library grew, the presence in camp of a surprising number of books was brought to light. Men had clung to any books that fell into their hands—for practical reasons. They were useful for barter. The pages were prized for rolling cigarettes, for writing letters home, or for use as toilet paper. Now the situation was reversed. Books were again valued for the information they contained.

Some form of concentrated study became essential at Zentsuji in Japan in 1944 to distract the men's minds from the cold and constant hunger. There were classes in French, Italian, and shorthand, but it was one teaching the law and accounting that merited the prisoners' description of their tuition as Zentsuji University. At the termination of the lectures a regular examination was held and students either "passed" or "failed" according to the high standard set by the examiners. One student from Sydney, who had left Australia just before he was due to sit his final law examinations, passed. When the war was over, his pass at Zentsuji was recognized by his institute on production of the affidavits of his lecturers and the examination papers. This seems to be the only instance of a professional qualification being granted as the result of study carried out in a Japanese prison camp.

Chapter 10

FOOD

When it came to the crunch, it could seem as if the only essential quality of the men in the prison camps was "animal hunger," said 2nd Lt. David Piper, who was a prisoner in Malaya and Taiwan. Across the Far East, wherever the prisoners were held, the diet was the same—rice, rice, and more rice—and there was never enough. The daily food ration of an enlisted man in the American army was 2,013 grams. The combat ration was much higher. The Japanese set the ration for a prisoner doing hard labor at 790 grams—but they usually received less. As their diet was composed almost entirely of carbohydrates, the prisoners were deprived of essential proteins, as well as components that make food more palatable: sugar, salt, and fat. At Honshu in Japan, Chief Petty Officer Ray Parkin and his fellow Australian prisoners working in the Ohama coal mine received only three teacups of rice a day: 560 grams for mine workers, 720 for surface workers, 520 for camp workers, and 420 for the sick. Often only a fraction of the promised vegetables and meat was supplied. Lt. Col. "Weary" Dunlop also noted the difference between the prisoners' entitlement and what they received at Konyu in March 1943: the meat entitlement was 3,212 kilograms, and they received 300; rather than 18,000 kilograms of vegetables, they were given 4,500.

Unsurprisingly, food became a daily obsession. The men were always thinking about food and listening to conversations about it. They went to bed thinking about it and woke up thinking about it, said L.Cpl. George Pringle, who was in Borneo:

> Food. Food all the time. A few of the men have adopted a most peculiar habit when eating their meals. Carefully collecting a few empty tins they strain the water from their ration of stew, place this in one tin and this is "Consomme." The leaves are placed into another tin and this is the "Savoury." The rice ration is the "Main Course" and if by good fortune a few chillies or a spoonful of curry powder has been purloined, then the meal becomes a feast. Invariably some old piece of cloth becomes the "Napkin" and the meal is eaten by taking a small portion from each tin. Somehow this gives the impression of "Having Dined." Most of us, the less refined, gobble our food as quickly as possible, belch loudly and thank our lucky stars we were able to eat it without being called away either by a dysentery patient needing cleansing or an irate Korean desperate to beat the daylights out of someone. Anyone.

The men stole for food, traded for food, fought for food, dreamed of food, abased themselves for food. Finding a lump of pig fat in the stew gave as much pleasure as going to a dinner party. A few dessert spoons of sugar, on the rare occasions when it was supplied, made them feel like new men. At Sandakan in Borneo they resorted to using axle grease from their handcarts as cooking fat. At Zentsuji in Japan, officers raked the pig food for edible tidbits. When powdered groundnut was issued to some men on H Force for use as fertilizer, they decided to eat it instead.

The chefs eventually learned how to cook rice, but it was not the rice that mother cooked, baked and flaked with milk and sugar. It was glued rice, half-stewed rice, stone-cold rice, old rice, unfit even for dogs, the sort you throw to hogs, as Capt. W. Store wrote in a poem at Mergui in Burma in 1942:

> *We got broken rice, outspoken rice*
> *That argued with your plate,*
> *Unpolished rice, abolished rice*
> *Some few years out of date.*
> *We got burned rice, that wasn't rice*
> *That tasted just like cinders*
> *And brittle rice, sharp little rice*
> *Like bits of festered tinders.*
> *We got boiled rice, quite spoiled rice*
> *And kerosene-drum-oiled rice*

That no one could call rice.
We got baked rice and caked rice
That weevils made their bed in.
We got bad rice, sad rice
That filled you with its sorrow.
We got podgy rice, stodgy rice
That meant no latrines tomorrow.
We got limed rice, grimed rice
And ought-to-have-been-crimed rice,
Disrupted rice, corrupted rice
Undischarged, bankrupted rice.
We got sloshed rice and squashed rice
But never any washed rice,
Half-caste rice, half-mast rice
And lots of jungle-grassed rice.
We brewed rice, we chewed rice,
The lucky ones they spewed rice . . .
We starved on, but we lived on
In spite of everlasting rice.

But unless the men ate their "everlasting" rice, and whatever else was offered to them, they fell ill; and if the sick didn't eat, they died. Some Americans chewed a mouthful of rice a hundred times before they swallowed it, or ate it one grain at a time. The medical officers insisted that they eat no matter how unappetizing the meal seemed. The route home, Lt. Col. Albert Coates, the Australian medical officer, told the men, was inscribed in the bottom of their dixies: "Every time it is filled with rice, eat it. If you vomit it up again, eat some more. Even if it comes up again, some good will remain. If you get a bad egg, eat it, no matter how bad it may appear. An egg is only bad when the stomach will not hold it." When some rice—"the blessed food of Nippon"—was thrown away at a camp in Taiwan, the prisoners quickly learned that they had insulted their captors. They were lined up, stripped to the waist, and harangued about the "divine food," rice sent by the gods so that Japan would never starve. "You will learn to love the rice, relishing and worshipping each grain," they were told. "It will save your lives, if you wish." The commandant was right, of course, but his words were repeated sarcastically time and again by the prisoners.

All the normal revulsions of Westerners were forgotten in the search for food. The men ate cats, dogs, rats, snakes, bats, lizards, iguanas, snails, frogs, insects, and slugs, even vultures. It was all "tucker," and not only to the Australians. Regt. Sgt. Maj. John "Macca" McQuade described how he and his friends in Burma once dragged a dead and festering cow which they had found in the jungle into the cookhouse. "It was green, and so pulsating with maggots you'd swear it was still alive. I thought we'd have to throw it away, but the cook said, 'No way, it may be green but it's meat.' We boiled it for hours until the maggots floated to the surface, then we ate it with rice."

The men were so hungry that they ate whatever they could steal, hunt, or trap. On one occasion, a single emaciated dog was shared among two thousand men. They had developed such a craving for even a hint of greasiness in their food that it was a red-letter day, said LAC Don Peacock. At Sakata in Japan, the dogs were deep frozen in the snow, but as it melted the men saw paws or a little nose pointing out at them. The dogs went in the pot. They tasted rather like veal, said George Pringle, but left him feeling like a cannibal.

Monkeys were easy to catch in Thailand. Men fixed a large piece of bamboo to the ground with a small hole in the top and put some rice or fruit inside. After the monkey had put its hand in the hole to grab the food, it was unable to withdraw it. The monkey sat there forlornly until a prisoner dispatched it with a tap on the head. Pringle described the horror of the Kuching camp commandant, Yamamoto, when the prisoners decided that Georgina, their pet monkey, was the only solution to their hunger. Georgina was dying but was still, unlike the prisoners, well fleshed. The men decided that she had to die, and she was converted into a thick, juicy meat stew:

> Is it callous of me to suggest that I much prefer Georgina as thick stew than as a real live monkey? We all expect trouble from Yamamoto when he learns of the death of Georgina and her fate.
>
> "What happened?"
>
> "We killed her."
>
> "Why?"
>
> "To eat her."
>
> "You eat monkey?"
>
> "Yes."
>
> A long silence.
>
> "Bloody hell."

According to Pringle, cats made excellent eating, but snakes were the most palatable bushmeat: they tasted like gritty chicken or—to Lt. John Coast—fried whiting. At Changi, Ronald Searle and his fellow prisoners earmarked three kittens for their Christmas supper in 1944 and fattened them up. Gently fried, they made a memorable meal and tasted like baby rabbit, but sweeter and more delicate. Snails were edible when cooked with hot chilies or curry, but rats were eaten only when the men were very hungry. In Burma a fat, uncooked rat cost thirty cents, or fifty cents if curried; a mouse was twenty-five cents. At Kuching in Borneo, Capt. H.A.D. Yates was surprised at how far a chicken would go.

> When one of our previous birds died it was raffled and the lucky syndicate got two or three good meals out of it. The only waste was the feathers (used as pipe cleaners), the gall bladder and the appendix. Everything else went into the pot and the bones provided one or two good soups, after which they still had a value and were roast hard, ground down and eaten.

Sparrows were a delicacy at Changi. Three men in Sgt. Edward Burrey's hut rigged up a trap and caught thirty. They were cleaned, boiled, and fried, and tasted delicious.

On their midday breaks or the march back to camp at night, the men collected edible green leaves, roots, and mushrooms for the evening stew cooked over wood fires. Sgt. Peter Hartley described the evening ritual at his camp in Sumatra:

> Dozens of little cans would be suspended over wood fires, containing the accumulated foragings of two or three men, while their owners squatted round stirring and fanning the flames like witches round a cauldron: weird brews of rat and jungle-weed soup or, if they had been lucky, monkey or snake, flavoured with half-rotten leeks salvaged from the rubbish heaps outside the Jap cookhouse. Nothing was ever wasted; nothing which was fish, fowl, flesh, or vegetable was considered too loathsome to eat—as long as it was not poisonous. A handful of strong red chillies could disguise the taste of most things.

The cookhouses also used their ingenuity to improve the food for the working men. Capt. C. F. Blackater listed some of the extras produced from the Japanese ration, supplemented from camp funds, for five hundred men:

- Hash. Boiled vegetables: add half-day's ration of liquid from the meat stews, 1 bucket uncooked rice; boil together = ¾ pint per man.
- Pea Soup. Save up ration of shell and dried peas, boil overnight, add liquid from boiled meat, add spring onions = ½ pint per man.

- Bread. 50% ground rice to 50% boiled rice, 2lbs tapioca flour, 1 pint white sugar, 10 pints yeast (camp made), 1 pinch salt. Bake. This could be fried and served in that way, or, on occasion, fried and decorated with a little scrambled egg.
- Scotch Eggs. Prepare batter of boiled rice, make into balls putting half hardboiled egg in centre, fry.
- Apple Pie. Pastry of tapioca flour. Roll thin and line tray. Spread bananas mixed with sugar and cloves, rate 1 banana per man. Cover with second layer of pastry, bake and serve in slices.
- Tamarkan Pie. A cup made of pulped rice filled with meat and vegetables, a little paste lid on top, baked.

It should be added that the "doovers" thus produced were only a titbit, they were very small, but they were such a welcome break amid the everlasting rice and stew.

In Japan, whale blubber was rendered down and the oil mixed with rice. The remainder, which the whalemen called "fritters" and which they used as fuel under their cooking pots, was called "crackling" by the prisoners and put out on trays with the cry: "Crackling! Come and get it! If you've got the guts." There would be a thunderous rush down the wooden corridors. Men would soon be squabbling like seagulls over it—seldom without a fight, said Ray Parkin.

The comradeship and compassion in the camps were vividly demonstrated in the men's decision on what to do with leftovers—the few crumbs of rice left after each man had received his ration. Initially, it was first come, first served, but the same two or three greedy men took the lot while the rest politely waited, exerting acute self-control, and watched them in anguished silence, according to Gunner Russell Braddon.

Then one day the three pigs fought. And one of them, in his desperation, hurled himself head foremost into the tub, where he snuffled the rice up, his legs twitching with greed in the air above. Thus to acknowledge, so unashamedly, that we had been reduced to the status of animals was too much. There was a roar from all sides and a decision was made, there and then, whereby to deal with all future surpluses. We would all, it was decided, have numbers. We would take it in turn to receive an extra ration. The extra ration was known as a "leggi" [*leggi* being Malay for "more"]: the number you had was your "leggi" number. Thus does any society develop the rules by which its communal life is

> made both possible and tolerable. "Leggis" were an institution that remained with us through all the days that were to follow until the war ended in 1945. They are a striking example of civilised man's ability to resist even the animal gnawings of starvation in the interests of the communal effort. It cannot be too strongly stressed how, in those days, the individual had to subordinate his desires to society rules if that society were to survive. The three things that could, at any time, kill us all off were work, disease and starvation.

As Braddon explained, only a faithful adherence to the rules could ensure that the tiny amount of food would keep everyone alive, that the limited water would slake thirst, keep the men clean, and wash their eating utensils. All such things were managed. "The prisoner of war life of those four years was an object lesson in living together." The men's skills and ingenuity helped too. "Butter" was made from peanuts. They adopted the native method which consisted of a mortar made of a hollowed-out teak log and a pestle of similar wood which looked like a large club and was about three times as heavy. It was hard work, particularly in the men's unfit condition, said Lt. Col. Cary Owtram:

> There were three processes in reducing the nuts to butter; the first process was to reduce them to a rough squashy mass, after which one handed them on to the second squad who reduced them by similar means to a finer form of porridge, stopping when there were no lumps left and when the oil in the nuts caused the mass to look like putty. The final process of refinement to the finished article was done on tables made of the ubiquitous fish-box lids, on which the mass was rolled out still finer with the aid of glass bottles used as rolling pins.

The proceeds were delivered to the canteen and sold daily over the counter in five-cent pats.

At Chungkai and Kanchanaburi, the men built a bakery, constructing the ovens from forty-gallon diesel-oil drums. The cooks made "bread" from ground rice flour. Cakes were made in the Burmese jungle by pounding cooked rice, rice flour, and an egg, using chintagar and wild ginger plants as flavoring.

The Dutch possessed useful knowledge of the local flora and worked on Project Kedley Bean. The precious beans were first soaked. A few of the walking sick were given a crash course in kedley stomping, and spent long hours dancing on the submerged beans until they were battered into submission. They were then stacked on shelves and left to generate a grayish mold. Don Peacock explained:

> After a few days they were pronounced to have transformed themselves into tempe, crawling with vitamins and God knew what else, and ready to eat. And that was not all. Another batch of these versatile beans was ground to a powder, mixed with moderately clean water and left to mature as kedley milk, far richer, they assured us, than anything mere cows could produce. The milk benefited the seriously ill. All of us got a little tempe in turn. And if the beans weren't life-savers, we believed they were, which was almost as good.

When the rations at a camp near Chungkai included fresh pork for the first time, the cooks turned out small sausages and brawn—jellied loaves made from the head of a pig—served on a rotation system, enough each day for fifty men. They were "unforgettable" mornings for John Brown when brawn, sausage, and a few chips were served with the rice.

By 1945, the men were practiced at gleaning food from their surroundings. At Changi there was a factory making soup from the long grass called *lalang,* which helped to combat the vitamin deficiencies of the diet. The lalang was chopped, crushed, and generally mangled until it was reduced to a green slime, which was then fed into a retort, where it fermented. The concoction produced by the soup factory was very rich in vitamin B and many lives were saved by it, according to Capt. Reginald Burton. However, it was not pleasant to drink.

> Its beneficial results . . . did nothing to endear it to the palate. Its taste was so disgusting—like drinking rotten seaweed and green slime scraped out of a sewer—that we were given the mixture under compulsion. All the vitamin deficiency sufferers had to parade, and after forcing down the lalang mixture under supervision their palates were further offended by the issue of a portion of rice polishings. These looked and tasted like sawdust. It was impossible to swallow the necessary spoonful, so the dose was stirred into water and drunk as a paste. Even then it didn't go down easily. The lalang soup always gave me nausea, but I found the best way to tackle it was to close my eyes and swallow as fast as I could. The means were decidedly unpleasant, but the beri-beri and pellagra were combated.

Guinea grass was also crushed in the factory to make a juice extract which contained vitamin B. A thousand pounds of paspalum was picked each day and the five hundred pints of juice produced from it used to treat the almost universal complaint of scrotal dermatitis—"Changi Balls."

Equally ingenious methods were used to brew alcohol. Bamboo bedposts were filled with water, a handful of rice, and a rotten banana. Within three to four days the prisoners had created alcohol packed with vitamin B. A coconut Christmas "toddy" was brewed at Sandakan in Borneo by boring a hole in the unripened coconut's outer skin, adding molasses or another fermenting agent to the milk, plugging the hole, burying the coconut in the ground, and waiting for it to go off. Some of these blew up while still underground.

Conditions in Thailand improved, if only slightly, for most men once the railway was built, especially if there was a canteen in the camp. Lt. David Boddington had twelve dollars—allowing him forty cents a day until he was next paid—when he arrived at Nakhon Pathom in 1944. He had to decide how to spend it most advantageously and to get maximum value for his money. His daily expenditure bought a raw duck's egg, bananas, peanuts, peanut fudge, and toilet paper. He resisted the jam tarts that were also on offer.

After September 1942, the prisoners in Thailand should have received much more food courtesy of Red Cross parcels, but the parcels were always looted by the guards and often held until the food was rotten or stale. At Nong Pladuk, the guards helped themselves to 100 tins of mackerel, 50 tins of marmalade, 420 pieces of soap, 33,700 cigarettes, three bags of peanuts, 66 kilos of white sugar, and 132 kilos of brown sugar before the parcels reached the prisoners. The remaining contents were meticulously shared among the men or divided by ballot. Among the goods that 2nd Lt. Louis Baume at Nong Pladuk received were six prunes, a fifth of a tin of salmon, pâté, chocolate, a third of a tin of butter, and a tenth of a packet of Kraft cheese. The milk powder went to the hospital. Such extras helped, but as Capt. "Pop" Vardy noted at Nakhon Pathom, the Red Cross ration for 1,080 men was just 38 tins of butter, 119 tins of peas, 4½ four-gallon tins of coffee, 60 kilos of soya beans, 18 hams, and 4¾ thirty-kilo bags of sugar, plus one bar of soap and 57 cigarettes per prisoner. Added to that were biscuits, sardines, jam, peanuts, books, and twenty-six packets of tobacco. It may sound like a huge supply, but it equated to only two or three meals per man.

At Cabanatuan in the Philippines the parcels were delivered on Christmas Day 1943. Each man received one of his own. There were tears as the fit men handed the parcels to those who were too weak to stand. A wasted skeleton could cry because he received a package of goodies from home, said Pte. Andrew D. Carson, one of the American prisoners. The man who handed it to him could cry because he knew the wasted skeleton wouldn't live long enough to enjoy it.

> They were crammed with food, wonderful, wonderful food. Right on top was an eight ounce bar of Hershey's chocolate. I knew it was Hershey's chocolate because it was shaped like Hershey's, looked like Hershey's, and tasted like Hershey's. Hershey's, but in a different wrapper with a Canadian brand name. There was a can of corned beef, a can of fish, large sardines in tomato sauce, a box of prunes and a can of powdered milk with a cutesie brand name, Klim—"Milk" spelled backwards. There was a can of Nescafé, not instant coffee but the first soluble coffee, quarter-sized wafers that you could drop into a cup of hot water, stir like hell and make coffee. There was a can of pork and beans, a can of sweetened condensed milk, and three packs of American cigarettes. Every box was a treasure trove. I remembered the words of one POW who summed it up for all of us. Smiling like the Cheshire cat he told us that he was like a blind dog in a butcher shop, couldn't decide which one to eat first.
>
> I unpacked my box and arranged the items on my blanket, examined each item carefully, then repacked everything. I repeated this two or three times, then I decided. At the evening meal I opened my can of sweetened condensed milk and mixed some of it with my rice. I hadn't been able to eat for days. Burnt out. A bite or two and give the rest away. But this evening, with the sweetened condensed milk mixed with my rice, I ate my ration and could have eaten more. The food parcel may have broken the logjam, may have saved my life. At any rate, for the first time in days I was able to eat my whole ration. Then, after dark, I made a damn fool of myself. I ate like a pig. Spoonful by spoonful I finished the can of sweetened condensed milk. It was sickening sweet and I loved it. I wiped the can clean with my finger and licked the finger, didn't waste a drop. I went to sleep stuffed, bloated, and as far as one can be so in a prison camp, happy.

Carson spent the rest of the night being sick.

The officers consistently had more food than the men. The contrast in their diets is best exemplified by the Christmas Eve menu for their suppers—five courses for the officers, three for the men:

MEN	OFFICERS
Pork, beef, potatoes and veg	Meat gravy soup
—	Fish rissoles
—	Pork and veg

Sweet	Christmas pudding (made of rice, brown sugar, peanuts, ginger and cinnamon)
One orange	Fish savoury
Ten cigarettes	

There were always special meals for Christmas, whatever the conditions. On the first Christmas of captivity, the prisoners at Nong Pladuk were sent food by the local Christian Chinese and Thais. After the Japanese had helped themselves, the gift included two hundred chickens, a hundred kilos of beef, eight hundred eggs, and two hundred kilos of rice, as well as sugar, salt and fruit. There were, however, thirty-two hundred men to feed. They managed a Christmas supper of vegetable stew, a small piece of steak, rice, a creamed rice cake decorated with mock chocolate cream, a doughnut, and sweet tea. By 1944, at Nakhon Pathom, with an unusual cash contribution from the Japanese, no man went hungry on Christmas Day. They had egg for breakfast; pork pie and gravy for lunch; Christmas cake for tea; and steak, gravy, roast potatoes or chips, cabbage, peas and beans, a sweet, and coffee for dinner. A supper of shortbread and tea was also served. The meals were certainly appreciated by Cpl. Foster, an Australian journalist:

> It can truly be said that this was one of the few festive occasions in our POW life that there was an equal sharing of the "Good Things" in the way of food. For the down and out POW it was a really happy Christmas—a day entirely free from the pangs of hunger. Strange to relate patients did not have the capacity to eat as large a helping as anticipated and on this and the following day they had ample proof of prior medical opinion that our internal organs would take considerable adjustment to better fare after the war.

Extra food was also obtained from farming. There were allotments at many camps. At Changi in 1944 and 1945, a thousand men worked in the gardens, and the officers had their own. The main crops were tapioca root, bayam, Ceylon spinach, and brinjals. There were aloo gardens at Chungkai, but the men's work extended to tending ducks and pigs. Several hundred young ducklings were bought from the Thais and kept in elaborate pens and shelters. Pig pens were made by digging moats about four feet deep, with a high bank on the outside to keep the animals from escaping. The runs were roughly thirty yards square with a hut in each. There were about thirty sows and several boars which fed on swill from the camp cookhouse, and several litters of piglets were produced. Rabbits were also popular. At Zentsuji, 929 rabbits yielded about 2,635 pounds of meat and bone that went into the soup pot between spring and autumn 1942. Each prisoner received about four and a quarter pounds of rabbit meat.

When the commandant of Chungkai decided to introduce a herd of cattle, Cary Owtram, the British commander, appointed the Australian herdsmen, knowing that some of them had been ranchers:

> It was a very popular job as they lived outside the camp and led a free existence which suited them down to the ground. From time to time more cattle arrived until we had about 250. Quite a lot of calves were born to add to the interest. The object of the cattle ranching exploit was to provide us with meat, so every week a number of the older animals which showed signs of ailing, plus a few of the younger ones, so long as they were not thought to be "in calf," were driven in to the camp and butchered. The abattoir was pretty crude, but we had no option. We asked the Japanese to shoot the beasts but they said ammunition was too precious! Since they would give us no rifles and ammunition and would not shoot them themselves, we had to kill the poor brutes with a sledgehammer. As a rule this was completely effective with the first blow, it certainly was with the cattle, but with the water buffalo which we still bought to augment the ration, very occasionally it took more than one blow. They had enormously thick skulls and anything less than a well-aimed blow in one particular spot at the base of the skull was useless. One man, a blacksmith by trade and six feet tall, was the regular executioner, and took the greatest care in endeavouring to carry out his unpleasant task as mercifully as possible. It was a case of the buffaloes' lives or ours through starvation, so it had to be the buffaloes'.

Australians were also in charge of the big herd of cattle at Nakhon Pathom. As the luxuriant grass of September withered in the drought of December 1944 and January 1945, the animals were starving, so it was decided to kill them off at the rate of about three a day. But there was only about a hundred pounds of meat on each beast—one ounce per man per day. Such minimal rations were still savored, but many more lives were saved by a much more humble food—the duck egg, which could be bought cheaply in the southern Thailand egg belt. The officers contributed a third of their monthly income to a fund for the hospitals, nearly all of which was spent on eggs. In most of Thailand, eggs were plentiful, and were bought in colossal quantities. On the railway, Capt. John Barnard drew the working men's pay in bulk and purchased goods, allowing men credit up to the amount he had drawn from them:

> Many doctors attribute the small death rate among officers compared with that of the troops solely to the number of eggs eaten by the former. Prices slowly rose year by year, but eggs were always the best food available. Whenever the food situation at any camp became serious, I used to invest 70 per cent of the total pay drawn in eggs, and issue a certain number to each man, whether he liked it or not. We decided that it was far better than handing over the money to them, as they were always out when a canteen barge came along, and I used to get better terms buying in bulk in any case. Also if a man was tempted to buy too many cigarettes, or native cakes—well, he had not got the money, but received most of his pay in a form which might at least keep him alive. Of course, a small amount was available to each man, in cash, or for use by him in the purchase of sugar, etc., but we had few complaints, and any man who did complain, as some of them did, "I want me money in me 'and, Sir, and b—— the eggs," was usually talked to quietly for some time until he saw sense.

One consequence of the men's malnutrition was that they lost interest in sex. Peter Hartley never heard them talking about women or telling smutty stories. A Freudian psychologist would have been hard put to find that sex was a basic instinct, he said. Their basic instinct was self-preservation, and that meant food.

The Dutch ensign and interpreter Cornelius Dirk Punt (who wrote under the pseudonym Cornel Lumière) had attached himself to the Australians. As they sailed from Singapore at the end of the war, he told the captain that it was not worth going ashore in Bali to see the girls. Even the most beautiful Balinese woman was unlikely to stir any Australian. He was greeted by boos, and asked the captain to be the judge:

> "Gentlemen," I started, "nothing can illustrate the reason for my comment better than the experience of a group of sturdy and aggressive Australians, once the pride of their country and, no doubt, the terror of many a mother, moving along a Burmese jungle track. Two Japs, bayonets fixed, escorted these fifty-odd walking bags of bones under the hot sun to a railway job. Hunger was written on every face; hunger was shining in every eye. Rations had been short all too long, work was too exhausting every day.

"Wearily, the prisoners walked along without noticing the silvery ripple on the small stream which they just crossed, without noticing in the distance a native figure approaching along the narrow path. It was a young Burmese woman, dressed in a colourful lungyi—the sarong—which by the more primitive in these parts is worn in a fashion similar to the style in Bali. The neckline of this fastidious native girl from lower Burma started at the hips.

"With springtime in her steps the young woman rapidly came nearer, balancing on her head a large woven tray with golden ripe bananas. The Australian prisoners of war, indifferent to their surroundings, too absorbed in their worries, had not yet seen the traffic approaching from the opposite direction.

"The young woman came closer and gradually one might have detected a reaction in the eyes of the marching men. First a few, then all the prisoners noticed that the jungle track was not deserted. When the girl was a few feet away, every man had his eyes on what attracted him most. One digger, too eager to control a comment, summed up the feelings of every man when he exclaimed, 'Look at those bloody bananas.' "

The captain agreed that I had won my bet.

Chapter 11

RELIGION

The most uplifting moments of captivity, often even for those without faith, were the services conducted by the padres, notably at Christmas, when they were given added resonance by their setting in the jungle and by the men's search for solace in their suffering. Capt. Harry Malet celebrated his first Christmas in captivity at Kinsaiyok in 1942. The church was a clearing in the jungle overlooking the river and the altar a large boulder. A five-foot-high bamboo cross was placed behind the altar.

> There must have been about 150 to 200 sitting in rows up the hillside. At 8.30 I went to Holy Communion at which were over 100 Communicants and very beautiful it was. The early sun coming through the morning mist and shining on the river and opposite jungle-clad hills. The early bird songs in the trees around us and the old accustomed monkey calls, "Wah-Wahs" being the most prevalent. A small flight of giant toucans flew over and the wild peacocks called to each other stridently—a really jungle setting for our Christmas Communion, with the 14 little white crosses of our cemetery beside us. At midnight last night I went to Mass—in the RC "Church"—a little clearing in the bamboo jungle on the hillside between the two valleys in which our huts are built. They have a little altar, altar rails and side table—all fronted with ataps. Father Bourke looked very civilised in scarlet cope with gold embroidery over a white cassock. Candles in bamboo sconces were lighted—incense

> made from jungle dammar was duly swung in a censer made from an old jam tin burnished and hung on an old dog chain, but the whole effect was perfect! A huge fire was kept burning which lighted the scene.

A year later 2nd Lt. Stephen Alexander was at Hindato, where on Christmas Eve some of the prisoners processed around the camp singing carols and carrying coconut-oil lamps and torches of pitch.

> The light leaped up into the shadows of the trees, playing on the lianas and dancing in counterpoint to our voices. Alan Lewis took the solo parts in an ethereal baritone. "In the Bleak Midwinter" and "Amid the Winter Snow" of that tropical night we felt an unearthly happiness. Our magi's journey still seemed endless but if it was better to travel hopefully than to arrive, the worse the journey the more vivid was the hope.

The services could not have been more moving if they had been held at Westminster Abbey or the chapel of King's College, Cambridge, the men wrote in their diaries. No Gothic cathedral was needed to give atmosphere to voices raised in praise, said Capt. David Hutchinson-Smith at Zentsuji: all denominations joined in a paean which reduced some of the congregation to "sobbing, choking beings."

Some settings were not so glorious—at Jesselton in Borneo, communion was taken behind the officers' cells, facing a row of earth closets, with a standard lamp for illumination and the cross mounted on a biscuit box. The Roman Catholic padre at Cabanatuan wore his vestments when he said Mass outside the dysentery ward and alongside the latrine—but underneath were bare feet, ragged shorts, and a lot of naked skin. The altar boy, Andrew Carson, was naked apart from a G-string.

Even Britain's Salvation Army worked in captivity. At Chungkai they sang between the huts, clashing tambourines with a fervor that reminded Fusilier Harry Howarth of London's Albert Hall: "The preacher held forth for sinners to repent before it was too late, a sad irony, for most of the sinners were dying. The sinners who were left were attempting by fair means or foul to avoid meeting their Maker."

For the men who sought spiritual solace, church-going had flourished from the start of captivity: the first Easter Sunday was celebrated in a small wooden hut without walls by the Rev. John Chambers. There were seven services, with nearly five hundred men attending a parade service at 8:45 A.M. St. George's Day was also celebrated, with all ranks wearing homemade red and white roses. After Maj. Gen. Beckwith-Smith addressed the battalion on parade, they marched to St. George's Church, previously the mosque of the Hongkong Singapore Artillery but converted by the prisoners into their place of worship. The interior had been decorated with murals, and "It even had a harmonium, brought in a damaged state by a working party and repaired by the Sappers," recalled Lt. Col. H. S. Flower. "The Order of Service included the regimental hymn. After Church, the Battalion marched past the General and was dismissed to dinner—improved by minute portions of corned beef reserved for the day and topped off by a lot of rum all round (saved since 1940 by Quartermaster Purcell)."

Some of the men grumbled that to the officers, church meant compulsory spit-and-polish parades—and they were as heartily disliked as any compulsory church parade in England. L.Cpl. Brown worshipped at St. George's, where the padre was the Rev. E.W.B. Cordingly:

> In the evening when the air was cooler with that soft fragrance of the tropics, we were glad to go of our own free will. If our prayers there, earnest prayers, achieved nothing else they gave us a sense of contact with those at home. The engineers made the Communion Table, altar rails, pulpit, lectern and wardens' staves while the Ordnance Corps fashioned an altar cross out of a brass shell case and inscribed it with the badges of the four units. They also arranged the lighting, made two candles for the altar and repaired a small harmonium to accompany the choir while the Service Corps undertook to provide every week the bread and wine for the Communion. Even in those early days morals ran a poor second to hunger and although it was an isolated case it is noteworthy that someone broke into the padre's bunk one Saturday night and stole the bread which had been prepared for the following day's service.
>
> To Mr. Cordingly his section of the camp was his parish and he carried out his ministrations in that spirit so that his church was filled to overflowing for every voluntary service even during the week and many men either returned to religion or discovered its comfort for the first time in that church. Whatever people at home feared might be happening to us in the summer of 1942 they can scarcely have pictured us as we were on Sunday evenings dressed in our best. After the evening service we paraded round the area, much as we might have done at home after church, and enjoyed the cigarette which we had been carefully hoarding for days. Then hope was renewed and it seemed that the faith which can move mountains might soon bring the war to an end and return us to our loved ones.

Those were the times, said Brown, when the men talked quietly of home, deluded themselves with the fond thought that the war would be over by Christmas, and came nearer to happiness than they ever did in the years that followed. Many were led to seek full membership in the Church. Their wishes were met when the Rev. Cordingly arranged for the Bishop of Singapore, who afterward endured great punishment at the hands of the Japanese, to come to the camp to conduct a confirmation service.

Sgt. Stan Arneil was working with fellow Australians in Singapore, all of whom were stealing food. Stealing was a matter of conscience for Catholics when they went to confession. Father Gerard Bourke, a young priest who had been attached to the Singapore Volunteers, wrestled with their problem but found a solution in common sense: they could steal as much as they liked to keep themselves alive, he told them.

Sinners, however, were the subject of one sermon Capt. Adrian Curlewis attended: "Here we are removed from the vices of ordinary life—greed, gambling, drink, sex," said the padre, "and are we any better for it? No. We have become selfish and jealous and life centres round our own misfortunes." When Harry Howarth went to an open-air service, sinners were again the subject—they had stolen the bread and wine, which were always in short supply. At one Holy Communion in Singapore, Cary Owtram's bread was stodgy dough and the wine a concoction of watered-down black-currant jam. Elsewhere, biscuits were used in place of bread, and tea, sugar water, coffee, and coconut milk all substituted for wine. At Zentsuji the men found a use for raisins condemned as unfit for human consumption. After consulting a British chemist, they made a communion wine that lasted for nearly eighteen months.

There were several different motives for attending church services, as Sgt. Peter Hartley noted in Sumatra. Some men went because they enjoyed singing the hymns, some because they attended church at home and were reminded of civilized values, others because they knew their families would also be praying at home in Britain or Australia. "Whatever the motive, deep down within them they were satisfying a need for spiritual refreshment," said Hartley. By taking their troubles to Christ and coming away fortified in spirit, they were ready to face another week of monotony and hardship.

> Unfortunately, for every "wise man" there were many fools—men who preferred to remain outside the fold; men who tasted the bitter dregs of their cup of sorrow, lonely and forsaken. While the church service was on, they lay on their wooden beds and bewailed their miserable state, only too well aware that the evil days had come and they could "find no

> pleasure in them." These men, if they gave heed to God at all, tended rather to curse and revile Him, instead of worshipping Him. They, who had no place for God in times of peace and prosperity, had even less in times of suffering and need.

Hartley discovered his vocation in Sumatra and took holy orders after the war.

The padres, often nicknamed "sky pilots," "Holy Joes," or "Bible bashers," were caught between the hostility of the Japanese and the indifference of most of the men, but their bravery made them inspirational figures to those of the prisoners whose lives they touched. They never gave up, said George Pringle. Before the prisoners were even settled in a new camp, the padres were designing churches and procuring material for altar coverings and vestments, as well as stones, timber, and bamboo to build the altar itself. At Tandjong Priok on Java, the Australian padre, after the success of his opening service, decided to hold regular Holy Communion services. But he ran into a familiar problem:

> The communion service has again attracted a large attendance of the genuine, the curious and the "not sure" worshippers. The servers are all spruced up and ready to serve or whatever they are supposed to do. Padre Bill has done his best to look as a real Padre should and is about to commence the service. A minor distraction is caused by one of the servers running through the assembled congregation and as he whispers into the ear of Padre Bill. I am acutely conscious that something has gone dramatically wrong. How true. His face flushed a brilliant red and his hair almost standing on end, Padre Bill regretfully announces that the Holy Communion service must be abandoned. Momentarily forgetting his status and his Church he tells us why: "Some bastard has pinched the bloody bread."

One particularly respected padre was Noel Duckworth, one of the heroes of Sonkurai. Thousands of Australians and British would remember Duckworth's name until the day they died, said Russell Braddon. In his "God-box" at Changi he made the men feel that they were merely spectators of all the horrors around them, rather than part of them. He was outspoken, he organized lectures, and early on in Malaya he founded Pudu Jail's black market and formulated outrageous lies about Allied triumphs to boost morale. By the time a secret radio was delivering authentic news, the men were sufficiently toughened to accept it. He created a chapel out of a cell where non-believers were able to sit and think about home or God. On Sundays, as has already been noted, he "blasted" the Japanese in his sermons, "lumping them together as 'The incarnation of evil' and pointing an accusing and fearless finger at them as they stood nearby, self-consciously guarding us."

Similarly inspirational was Padre Alfred Webb, a Presbyterian Welshman. One day, Webb noticed that a young patient at Chungkai was being moved nearer and nearer to the nursing station. That was usually a sinister sign, and Webb asked an orderly what was wrong with the young man. He had just given up, the orderly told him. Whenever the Roman Catholic padre gave him the last rites, however, the patient became distraught by the assumption that he was dying. Webb's pastoral care consisted of common sense and common humanity rather than Bible-thumping. He discovered that the patient was a Manchester United fan, and he appealed around the camp for any recollections of the team. After the Catholic padre's next visit, Webb sat by the young man's bed and asked him about the Cup Final in 1938. The patient was distracted from the horror around him, took heart, and eventually recovered.

Sapper Lionel Morris observed the sorrows of Francis Hollis, the Bishop of Kuching in Borneo, as he trudged wearily from compound to compound, comforting the dying and being abused by the guards, who suspected him of passing information from one camp to the next. Hollis became a respected symbol of hope, and Morris marveled at the example he set and was spellbound by his composure: "Surely he must break soon, I thought." Yet, stooping with beri-beri, ankles swollen, and suffering from acute malnutrition, Hollis followed the coffins and conducted burial services, sometimes as many as twelve a day. He also found texts that spoke directly to his growing congregation.

> One day he delivered an outstanding sermon based on the 91st Psalm. I listened with rapt attention as he began to find the place in his tattered Bible, and began to read in a forthright, steady voice:
>
> > *Surely he shall deliver thee from the snare of the fowler, and from the noisome pestilence [i.e., the guards].*
> > *Thou shalt not be afraid for the terror by night; nor the arrow that flieth by day.*
> > *Nor for the pestilence that wasteth at noonday [i.e., dysentery].*
> > *A thousand shall fall at thy side, and ten thousand at thy right hand; but it shall not come nigh thee.*
>
> I am perfectly sure, each man took to himself this message as a personal reassurance, that eventually in the fullness of time, all would be

> well. Marauding guards sometimes interrupted the Bishop and demanded their usual quota of homage or recognition, then uncomprehending they, and we, just stood motionless waiting for the next move. Often the Bishop was forcibly expelled from our midst, and beaten in sight of the perimeter wire, but mostly the sentries became bored and even embarrassed by the sheer humility of the event.

There was no religious freedom, and the church and the chaplain were always suspected, according to the Methodist padre, Christopher Ross. It was a crushing blow when Ross was told that the men were not to sing in their huts or at services. They were also forbidden to pray for Allied victory or for England.

> Our services were curtailed and all preaching or speaking had to cease. Protest had no effect so we suffered. . . . [The] Japanese made a systematic search of the whole camp and in our hut I seemed to be the main object. My books, papers, sermon and class notes, hymn sheets, hymn books, book of offices, and Bible were taken from me. My heart was sad. What could I do for the six thousand men in the camp if I had no Bible? I went to see the Nip officer and was told that when their interpreter had censored my papers and books, I would have them returned. That was a polite way of telling me that I had seen the last of my precious belongings.
>
> The officers and men were very kind to me at that time and instead of the church breaking it seemed to gather a spiritual strength, before unknown. Here was real persecution. Then—wonder of wonders—my ordination Bible and book of offices appeared in my bunk, and were none the worse for the ordeal. God had answered my prayers; the evidence was before my eyes and in my hands. I wept for sheer joy. The British Camp Adjutant had gained access to the Japanese store-room and recovered them at great personal risk. That was his way of serving the Church; to me it was God's answer to my prayer.

The padres had to make do and mend as best they could. Ross's "church" had eight different sites and was moved bodily by fifty to sixty volunteers. When he arrived in Thailand as the only padre at Nong Pladuk, whose strength varied between two thousand and five thousand, he trained Christians as lay preachers so that they could conduct simple services, including burials, in camps where there was no padre. According to his own account, a quarter of a million Holy Communions were given during captivity to communicants of all faiths—Anglican, Plymouth Brethren, and Baptists as well as Methodists.

"Persecution made good Christians," he said. Small groups, guarded by a lookout, met for Bible study, prayer, and instruction. More than three hundred men were subsequently received into the Church.

Chaim Nussbaum, who was probably the only rabbi in the Japanese prison camps, celebrated Hanukkah in Java in 1942. It was an act of rebellion after the Dutch authorities at Tjilatjap had ordered the removal of all Jewish symbols for fear of retribution from the Japanese. Hanukkah celebrates the rededication of the Jerusalem Temple in 165 B.C. and the miracle of one day's supply of oil lasting eight days. Nussbaum had the sacred candelabra brought to his barracks and posted friends at the entrance to warn of approaching guards:

> The menorah stands on a table (my bedboard playing a useful role) inside our room to the right of the entrance, but noticeable—to fulfil the entire commandment. Our light was made from coconut oil—a Chanukah gift donated by our chief cook, a devout Protestant. The flame was small and the smoke looked blue. The menorah shone in its own light. We have publicized the miracle of continuity. And our own present miracle.
>
> Ten Jewish boys came. We sang the majestic song "Maoz Tsur" [Rock of Ages]. Slowly, the room filled. Other friends came, stood and stared into the tiny flame as if all truth and explanation were there. They asked questions about the holiday, about Jews. "You have a lot at stake in this war, haven't you?" someone asked, an abruptness in his voice. I looked at him. "Don't *you?*" I asked. He thought for a long while before answering. When he did, his voice was low and soft. "We all do," he said, then buried his face in his hands, turned and left the menorah.

By 1944, when he was at Changi, Nussbaum was holding regular services as well as giving lectures and lessons. He had also started *Habeemah,* a Jewish magazine, whose contributing artists included Ronald Searle. A *shul* (a small hut) had been built by Scottish highlanders and named Ohel Jacob, the Tent of Jacob. Nussbaum thought that it was probably the only synagogue built in any Second World War prison camp.

Given the squalor of their conditions, even the padres' faith was tested to the limit. Peter Hartley was often despondent, especially when one of the most faithful members of his congregation told him that he had lost his faith. Hartley did not know how to answer and gazed hopelessly upward, playing for time, first searching the ceiling in the vain hope that the answer would be scrawled in "mystic script on the whitewash":

But this was not whitewashed ceiling that met my gaze, nor was it an empty sky. It was a gloriously painted sunset. A huge vermilion disc was sinking majestically behind a range of mountains. From the highest peak a lazy stream of volcanic smoke rose perpendicularly, and was lost in the deep purple glow above. Even as I uttered the words "Look at that" my heart leaped with joy, for surely there was the answer, written boldly enough for all to see. There was the effulgence of God's glory. There was the symbol of a power far greater than man. The Japanese might have conquered the land; they might have control over the life and death of thousands of prisoners, but they could not control the unseen force symbolized by that smoking volcano nor, though they worshipped its rising, could they order the course of the sun. As the picture faded we began to walk round the compound. We both felt elated—elated because a great burden had been lifted from our tired shoulders. We realised how near we had been to losing the one thing that really mattered, the one possession which the Japs could never confiscate, and together we began to count our blessings, to realise that we still had a lot for which to thank God.

Chapter 12

JUNGLE MEDICINE

The "hospital" at Tarsao where Capt. "Pop" Vardy was medical officer was a bamboo hut in the Thai jungle with a platform on which the sick patients were crowded shoulder to shoulder. There were no mattresses, no sheets, no pillows, no blankets. The "kitchen" was an open wood fire and a flat stone; the dispensary was a wooden box; and the only drugs were some Epsom salts, quinine, Atebrin, and iodine. In November 1942, Vardy recorded in his diary that there were 125 patients. He almost wept when he did his rounds:

> One dysentery has hiccough—had it for 10 days—it is killing him and I have no drugs to try to stop it. The dysentery diet consists of four cups of sweet tea, two cups of diluted milk and one cup of weak Marmite per day—that or boiled rice—take your choice—they nearly all die—diphtherias also. I have seen some extreme examples of inadequate medical treatment—midwifery in the slums of Newcastle or North Shields, but nothing like this—we haven't any bedpans, or wash bowls—and the dysenteries when they soil their trousers lie in it for hours—the stench is terrific—their plight heartbreaking.

A year later at Tarsao, Vardy was overseeing a hospital with 2,400 patients, of whom 135 were suffering from serious malaria or avitaminosis, 200 had large tropical ulcers, 120 had amoebic dysentery, and another 220 chronic diarrhea or bacillary dysentery. Between August and December 1943 there were 241 deaths. The legs of twenty-seven men with tropical ulcers were amputated—seven of those amputees subsequently suffered from mental disorders. Some of the patients were bags of skin and bone with not an ounce of flesh, and with bumps and hollows which Vardy had never dreamed belonged to the human frame. There were eighty patients in Ward 2, with the worst fifty on special diets and thirty-five receiving extra eggs before, almost inevitably, they died. Vardy's tour of the ward took two hours each day. Then he escaped: "But it's always too late—all my spirits have gone and I spend another bloody day."

Vardy's experiences were typical of those of all the medical officers. During captivity, Capt. Stanley Pavillard saw an average of 120 patients each day—but five hundred a day during the "Speedo" period at Konyu. At the Nong Pladuk hospital there were about twenty-five thousand patients between July 1942 and January 1945. On October 27, 1943, the Chungkai hospital admitted its ten thousandth patient in just over a year. Three days later its death toll reached one thousand. Vardy, an English north-countryman, was unusual in that he had some experience of the Far East and had worked in Malaya with the Colonial Medical Service. Lt. Col. Albert Coates, the most senior of the Australian medical officers, saw him as a man of compassion who personified the legacy Britain had left in Malaya. But only a few, if any, of the doctors and surgeons who were prisoners had been trained to deal with the conditions they confronted between 1942 and 1945. The Dutch from the East Indies were used to dealing with tropical diseases—but not when they were exacerbated by starvation, beatings, overcrowding, and overwork in camps with the most primitive arrangements for personal hygiene. So the medical officers had to develop new ways of treating the sick in an environment resembling the Dark Ages.

It was apparent to Lt. Col. "Weary" Dunlop by March 1943, after the "Speedo" period had been inaugurated on the railway, that a medical tragedy was inevitable. The medical officers repeatedly warned the Japanese, but they showed "complete and utter indifference." Medical control of the lives of many thousands of men in the area was invested in a Japanese army corporal with no knowledge of medicine, and sick men were mercilessly forced to work daily and driven with appalling brutality by the Japanese engineers. Whenever visits from higher officers were due, there was ferocious pressure on the sick to join the work parties and increase their numbers:

> On one occasion preceding the visit of a Nipponese general, Lt. Col. Ishi, commanding more than 12,000 POWs [in] No. 4 Group, was

> shown by me some hundreds of emaciated sick, massed 20 per leaking tent. Referring to large numbers of dysentery patients, he was told that IJA had given us no drugs for the treatment of dysentery, not even magnesium sulphate and that the only treatment possible was to give the men no food for a period of a few days. He then asked "How long no food?" to which I replied "Usually 2 or 3 days." His dictum was "No good. In future remember no food one week."

The medical officers were forced to improvise. At Wampo, Pavillard had a cut-throat razor, three pairs of artery forceps, one pair of rusty scissors, a few surgical needles and some catgut—but no knife—when he had to operate on an appendix abscess. He used chloroform as an anesthetic. At Lower Sonkurai, performing the same operation, Capt. Lloyd Cahill had to use the pot in which the breakfast rice was boiled and a few handkerchiefs as towels. A mosquito net was raised over an ambulance stretcher placed on a few sticks of bamboo, and the camp dentist administered the anesthetic. When Cahill asked a Japanese medical officer if he would help, the answer was a "silly grin" and a reply that he would just watch. The patient survived. An impacted wisdom tooth was removed at Cabanatuan with a pair of forceps and a small bone-cutting chisel. The roots were crossed deep in the bone and the doctor had to chip at the jawbone to free the tooth. When he finished, he was ashen and soaked with sweat, and his hands were trembling.

There was an emergency at Konyu in February 1943 when an Australian, Pte. Jones, collapsed with a perforated peptic ulcer—almost always a sentence of death. Dunlop and his two colleagues, Maj. Arthur Moon and Maj. Ewan Corlette, decided to operate, in spite of the difficulties of doing so at night in the jungle. Patients in the dysentery tent were moved into the open; an operating table was fashioned from bamboo; two flashlights and a few candles were borrowed from the guards; and fires were lit to add extra light and warm the tent. Water was sprinkled over the floor to lay the dust. A bamboo mask was made for the anesthetist, a stretcher transformed into an instrument table. Towels and instruments were boiled. The operation went ahead at 2:25 A.M. For Dunlop, it was one of the strangest operations he had ever attended, conducted by the fitful light of weak hurricane lamps, large fires, and the beam of a flashlight, and with an audience of Japanese soldiers. It lasted two hours. The patient was wrapped in blankets with hot-water bottles and left on the table. Dunlop finally left at five-thirty. Jones deteriorated at first, but five days later he was much better.

It was for such actions that the prisoners made sure that the doctors were well looked after. Many doctors became heroes to the men with whom they served. Two months after the end of the war, *Australian Women's Weekly* published an article describing Dunlop as "The King of the River," and Corlette, who had a mustache similar to Al Capone's, as "The Gangster of Kwandi River." Two of the men whose lives they had saved told the women of Australia all about them. Sgt. Don Goldfinch from Adelaide was another of Dunlop's assistants:

> He was a wonderful man. Lots of times I have seen him line up boys going out to work before dawn, and say to the weakest of them, "Could you battle on today son? I'll give you a spell tonight." And these blokes would battle it out for another day just to please old "Weary." They knew that if they didn't the Japs would take some really sick men out of the hospitals and make them work. Weary stood up to the Jap demands for men. Whenever ordered to provide 50 workers from his hospital, he would agree to give only 25, and not budge an inch from that. Often at night he would smuggle 25 worn-out but not sick men into hospital as soon as they returned from work, so that next morning when he had to provide 25 men he could send them out and thus save the sick from going to certain death. Men dying in jungle camps started to want to live again when the magic whisper reached them that "Weary" Dunlop was coming. He organised all camp hygiene and on dozens of occasions I have seen him with his dentists and other doctors digging latrines 12 and 15 feet deep and 20 feet long. He had to do this because the only other men in the camp were those too sick to work.

Pte. Clarrie Slavin didn't believe in storybook heroes until he met Dunlop and Corlette, the "most selfless" men who ever lived. They exposed themselves daily to the cholera compound, where they forced men to drink saline as fast as they could gulp it down. With "utter brutality" they made the infected men endure the agony of intravenous saline injection. If a man could not take the pain any longer and pulled out the needle, they simply thrust it back, added Slavin.

> Whenever word came down that a boy had been hurt on the line, Dunlop would pack his grip and stride off through the rain and mud to succour him. Both he and Corlette took their share of Jap bashings and humiliations, but they never once refused to treat a sick Nip brought to them. A sick man was just a sick man to them. The Pommy troops with us worshipped them. Once in Hintok Camp the Nips put "Weary" in front of the guardhouse and made him stand at attention for 48 hours. He took that without a murmur. Then they made him kneel for a day

> before the guardhouse, and he did that too, grinning at every Nip who passed. The Nips did not know what to do with him. Although he was a huge man, he never resorted to bashing, but abuse from him was worse than a Jap beating. Dunlop and Corlette used to move among worn-out men, encouraging them to eat every scrap they could to keep going. Corlette was tough, too. I have seen Nips stand over him to get more men out of his hospital. The Nips would want fifty and he would offer ten. It used to go like this: Jap Officer: "Fifty men." Corlette: "No, ten men." Then a Jap guard would bash Corlette, and so it continued: "Fifty" bash. "Ten" bash—but in the end the Japs got only ten men.

When another Australian doctor, Maj. Kevin Fagan, collapsed, racked with fever in Singapore in 1944, the men, afraid that he was dying, rallied to help him. He had earned their admiration by his courage, gentleness, and endurance. On marches he had carried men who fell and carried the kit of men who were in danger of falling. He cleaned blisters, set broken bones, and gave first aid. In common with other medical officers, he had also been forced to play God. His worst experience occurred at Konyu during "Speedo" when he had to choose one hundred survivors—from three hundred of the original six hundred Australians in H Force, all of whom had malaria, most dressed only in shorts and without boots—to march the hundred miles north to Konkuita to help with a cutting that was behind schedule:

> I never saw any of those men again. I felt that I had come to the end at that stage because these were the fellows whom I had nursed through difficult times and there was a bond of affection between us. I would have understood if they'd cursed me, turned on their heels and walked away. Instead of that they came and shook hands with me and wished me good luck. And I found it necessary to walk into the jungle and weep for a while. It was the most terrible thing I've had to do. If I hadn't done it, the Japanese would have taken the first 100 they found, and they would all have died. Some of these men had a chance of surviving. None of them should have been asked to do any more. Later on that day the Japanese medical officer came by, a pompous fellow who could speak quite good English. I said to him, "Unless you change your treatment of these prisoners they will all die." He said, "That would be a very good thing; it would save the Japanese army much rice."

At the time of Fagan's own collapse, there was an "endless pilgrimage" of men with tins of food, money, oil, soap, and clothes to his room. According to

Gunner Russell Braddon, Fagan's progress was followed more closely than the BBC news. When he was up and walking again, the camp gazed proudly upon him.

But of all the doctors who worked in Thailand and Burma—including Albert Coates, Bruce Hunt, Arthur Moon, Ewan Corlette, Kevin Fagan, Lloyd Cahill, Henri Hekking, Jacob Markowitz, Stanley Pavillard, and "Pop" Vardy—it was "Weary" Dunlop who became the legend, initially because of the article in *Women's Weekly* and later, according to unkind critics, because he became a "professional POW." This legend was burnished when his diaries were published in 1986. Dunlop spent the rest of his life fighting the cause of the Fepows and was given a state funeral in Melbourne when he died in 1993.

At the outbreak of war in 1939, Dunlop was a qualified surgeon working at St. Mary's Paddington in London. He joined the 2nd AIF and was captured in Java in 1942, when he made two critical choices, according to his biographer Sue Ebury, who worked with him on his diaries: he refused to escape from the advancing Japanese, and he did not promote himself to colonel, thereby ensuring that he would stay with his hospital and his men.

Admiration and respect for Dunlop were universal, but so was genuine love. The men would do anything for him, claimed his lifelong friend Ray Parkin. He added that "Weary" shouldered his own burdens so that they did not worry others and then heedlessly piled on his own shoulders the worries of anybody who asked him for help:

> I am sure it is his presence which holds this body of men from moral decay in bitter circumstances which they can only meet with emotion rather than reason. He is a big man . . . and a most skilful surgeon: a simple, profoundly altruistic man, with a gentle, disarming smile. This selflessness, this smile, command more from the men than an army of officers each waving a manual of military law.

The British war artist Jack Chalker, whose drawings recorded for posterity the conditions in which Dunlop worked, considered him a great man:

> He was one of the most courageous men I have ever met in my life. The Japanese didn't like you being tall, and they used to make him kneel to beat him up and things like that. But he would go to them again and again and again deliberately throughout all those years to try and get better conditions for us, or to stop their brutality, knowing very well that he was going to get beaten up anyway. For somebody to do that continu-

> ously, on our behalf, for three years with the utmost courage, deserves about ten VCs. It's not a sort of sudden bit of fighting, this is very real deliberate courage. And he was very badly knocked about, he had ulcers, he suffered from dysentery, just as we did. The big ulcers are extremely painful and I've seen him go up to the commandant to complain, and he would even quote Shakespeare to the guards to interrupt their beatings! Or something from the classics in Greek or whatever it was. And that puzzled them because they didn't understand it. To have the presence of mind to do this under those circumstances was very, very brave and very controlled. He was like a human dynamo.

Necessity was the mother of invention, but the Japanese expected miracles of improvisation. Dunlop described some of his experiences of jungle medicine in an article for the *British Medical Journal* in 1946. Cotton or silk unraveled from parachute cords were used in place of catgut for stitches, but the most useful thread substitute was made from the peritoneums of pigs and cattle, produced by a Dutch chemist, Capt. van Boxtel. The peritoneum was trimmed into six-meter ribbons, which were twisted and dried. Sterilization was effected at 54.4°C for half an hour, after which the strips were put in ether for a day and then in 90 percent alcohol and iodine. Pocketknives as well as razors were used to make incisions. Bamboo was used to make beds, brooms, brushes, baskets, containers, water pipes, tubing, and splints. Timber was obtained by felling trees and splitting the trunks with wooden wedges. Where solder could not be extracted from sardine tins, watertight tinsmithing was accomplished by ingenious folding. Sources of hydrochloric acid included the human stomach. Flux was readily manufactured if sulfuric acid could be stolen from car batteries. Leather was prepared from buffalo or cow hide, and thread or string from unraveling webbing equipment or kit bags.

Patients had to be enrolled to help equip the jungle hospitals. At Chungkai there was an appeal for tins and containers, solder, flux, nails, wire, screws, sponge rubber, scraps of clothing, stocking tops and old socks, string, webbing, leather, rubber tubing, glass bottles of all sorts, glass tubing for transfusions, canvas, elastic, rubber bands, braces, wax, mah-jongg pieces, and any tools that could be spared. It was stressed that "nothing is too old, nothing is too small." Articles made at Tarsao and Chungkai after such appeals included urinals, bedpans, commodes, surgical beds and pulleys, feeding cups, washbasins, irrigators, sterilizers, small charcoal stoves, disinfectors, stretchers and stretcher beds, backrests, leg rests, oil lamps, brooms, brushes, trays, tables, orthopedic appliances, splints, surgical instruments, and even artificial limbs and eyes (from the mah-jongg pieces). The artificial limbs made at Nakhon Pathom under the direction of Maj. F. A. Woods, AIF, were designed from crude timber, leather cured from hide, thread from unraveled packs, iron from stretchers, and oddments of sponge rubber, elastic suspenders, and so on.

Lt. Col. Albert Coates and Capt. Jacob Markowitz earned reputations for using amputation to save the lives of men with tropical ulcers. Coates was forty-seven when he surrendered in Sumatra in March 1942 after being ordered to escape from Singapore. He could have been evacuated again but opted to stay with his men. As a young man he had been at Gallipoli and in France during the First World War. Back home in Melbourne he had become a surgeon and professor of anatomy at the city's university. He was an inspirational leader and a character, frequently chomping cheroots during operations. He would be knighted after the war. The loquacious Markowitz was "a tiny Colossus." He had been Associate Professor of Physiology at the University of Toronto, where he had worked with the discoverers of insulin and had devised a method of transfusing blood in dogs. A rare Jew among the prisoners, he shocked the padres at lunch one day in Chungkai by deciding to say grace before their meal of rice and kangkung (a green vegetable): "Jesus Christ, the same yesterday, today and for ever."

By August 1943, at Coates's 55 Kilo camp in Burma, there were five hundred patients with ulcers, some so bad that their shin bones were exposed. As the bones rotted, flies laid eggs in them and maggots would start to feed on the marrow. Coates used a uterine curette (normally employed to scrape wombs) to pare away the pus and cut out the rotten flesh. He then applied rice poultices and in a few cases liquid iodine. But some thirty of the men so treated died in agony after prolonged suffering. Eight or nine men were dying every day, so Coates decided to try amputation for the worst cases. Lt. W. W. Tilney, the camp adjutant, watched the first operation. Coates, suffering from typhus, was hardly able to stand. The theater was a bamboo shelter with a leaf roof and a bamboo table, and the surgeon had no gloves or medical uniform of any kind.

> I have seen some very brave men—men had to have incisions in the ulcers to take away the rotten flesh and they have lain down and held on while the Colonel got on with the job of cutting away bad flesh. They knew it was for the best. Tears would run down their cheeks; they would curse and bite their hands and hold onto their mates like grim death but never shout while the Colonel was working on them. It was worth it for the relief they got. They often told me they suffered hell,

> and many a brave man after all he went through to live recovered from the amputation and I have seen them working and then get dysentery and fever and die. Many and many a case was like that. Others had sent for me and asked if I would speak to the Colonel and get him to take their legs off as the pain of the ulcers was driving them insane and they were frightened to die.
>
> The courage of these men was astounding; their confidence in Colonel Coates absolute. He would say, as he bent over a hopelessly eaten-away leg, "It's no good, laddie. I think we'll take it off for you and give you a chance. When would you like it done?" "Right away, sir, and let's get it over." Within the hour, the injection would have been given, the patient, smoking one of the colonel's own cheroots, would have witnessed the removal of his leg, and would be carried back to his bed. As one man said, as he surveyed the stump, "Gosh, that feels good. It's the first time in months that I haven't felt my ulcer."

The skills and ingenuity of the men around Coates, whose only medical instruments were a scalpel and a pair of forceps, helped him overcome some of the handicaps of working in the conditions—as he described them—experienced by doctors in the day of Nelson and Wellington. His saw was borrowed from the kitchen. It was field surgery without any modern frills, he said, but it was the best work of his life as a surgeon. Between July and November 1943, Coates carried out 115 amputations of limbs and snipped off hundreds of fingers and toes. About 10 percent died after the operation and 50 percent of the rest within two months. Without the amputations, the death rate would certainly have been much higher. The men whom Coates denied amputation despite their pleading were restored with deformed scars, which were grafted when they returned to Australia; they suffered no subsequent disability.

Where Coates summoned up the ghosts of Nelson and Wellington, Markowitz, when he described his amputations for the *British Medical Journal,* thought of Florence Nightingale and the Crimean War. Cary Owtram observed "Marco" at work at Chungkai in August 1943 in circumstances similar to those experienced by Coates. The patient's thigh was about half as thick as his knee joint and there were two enormous ulcers on the leg, one affecting about three quarters of the shin. The flesh had been eaten away to such a degree that the tibia was exposed for about ten inches. The other ulcer had spread over the whole of the inside of the patient's foot, exposing several square inches of the ankle bone. Several medical orderlies stood by to assist the anesthetist and the surgeon—all of them clad only in shorts, with sweatbands around their foreheads to prevent perspiration from dripping on to the patient. Owtram described the operation:

> Markowitz made his incision on the thigh, all the while supplying a running commentary for the benefit and interest of a small crowd of onlookers. There was practically no flesh to deal with, but he clipped or tied the various arteries as he came to them and then sawed through the bone. There was no proper saw but the British camp carpenter had supplied his tenon saw and this had been well boiled before use. By way of antiseptic appliances there were a couple of much chipped enamel bowls of hot water into which permanganate of potash had been put. Swabs and bandages were bits of gauze bandage or other material, stained brown by repeated use on previous occasions. Whenever a gust of wind blew, little eddies of dust flew through the air while flies and bluebottles in their hundreds buzzed incessantly round and were flicked off when they settled on the scene of operation. In well under a quarter of an hour, the operation was concluded and the patient carried back on a stretcher to his bed of blanket or sacks spread over the bamboo "spring mattress."

At first, Markowitz and his medical colleagues had been reluctant to operate, fearing that their patients would die in the primitive conditions. But they soon found that deaths from the operations themselves were negligible. The patients were always asked for their consent, the surgical officer was consulted, and the commanding officer of the hospital then petitioned for his approval. He normally concurred. Of the first one hundred patients in November 1943, thirty-two had died, but only one from the surgery itself. The other dead men had passed away through malnutrition, pneumonia, or avitaminosis. When Dunlop arrived at Chungkai in January 1944 he was astonished to see so many men standing by the road on one leg.

A few doctors refused to amputate. Stanley Pavillard preferred a treatment for ulcers that had been developed during the Spanish Civil War, when shattered limbs had been encased in plaster of Paris and left to stew in their own pus. When the plaster was removed, the fractures were joined and the wounds healed. In Thailand, Pavillard cleaned the ulcers, applied some of the scarce iodine or sulfonamide antiseptics used to dress ulcers, and applied Elastoplast, which he covered with bandages made from old sheets or bark from banana trees. Unless the ulcers had been enormous, they vanished completely after about three weeks.

The doctor who became as much of a hero to the Americans on the railway as Dunlop and Coates were to the Australians was the forty-year-old Dutchman Capt. Henri Hekking. Born in Java to a white Dutch family, Hekking took his medical degree at Leiden in the Netherlands. After graduation he learned tropical medicine at Batavia (now Jakarta) and then worked for four years on the island of Celebes (now Sulawesi). He was captured on Timor and ended up in Burma, where the British and Australian doctors treated him with disdain because of both his nationality and his junior rank. When Capt. Arch L. Fitzsimmons, the senior American at Kilo 40 in Burma, asked for a medical officer (and traded his and James Lattimore's watches with the Japanese to secure one), he got the neglected Hekking.

In Burma, what Hekking had learned at his grandmother's knee was as crucial as what he had been taught at Leiden and Celebes. He had always remembered that when he caught malaria as a child he was sent to his grandmother, who treated villagers successfully with herbs from the forest. He was also an early pioneer of psychosomatic medicine: he made the men argue and box with each other to keep them stimulated. He used ground charcoal as a remedy for dysentery and clay to absorb the mucus; beef tallow and acetylsalicylic acid were employed against athlete's foot. His methods seemed "crazy" to the Americans, but they worked. He did not perform amputations (in spite of his proximity in the Burmese jungle to Coates, who was wielding his saw in the same period), but his treatments were often just as painful. The American Marine Howard Robert Charles witnessed Hekking's treatment of Glen Self's ulcer. The doctor was going to scrape the pus out with a tablespoon sharpened on a sandstone and then make a cage for the open wound to keep out the flies, let in the air, and keep Self from bumping the wound. He tested Self's heart with a stethoscope to make sure it was strong enough; felt the edge of the spoon to make sure it was sharp enough; struck a match, and held the spoon to the flame. When the spoon cooled, he asked Self to lie back and motioned to four men to take his arms and legs. Charles described what happened next:

> He scraped lightly at first, removing the pus and loose surface material. He then told Albert Rogers from New South Wales to squeeze Glen's leg as hard as he could on both sides of the ulcer. Once the doctor started to probe deeper with the spoon, Glen let out a long, agonizing scream. Then, mercifully, he passed out. Doc worked in silence, stripping away the rotted flesh, scraping the blackened bone. One of the men walked out of the shack to vomit. Looking at the bone, Doc saw more than a tropical ulcer: a part of the bone had been chipped, and soon the infected part of that would have to be removed. He would

> need a surgical tool that resembled a chisel to take it. It took a long time to finish removing the pus. He scraped the bone, but none of this was a substitute for removing the piece of infected bone. That was still to come. He used strips of bamboo split with a pocket knife to make the cagelike contraption to protect the open cavity. The four men used a stretcher made of bamboo poles and rice sacks to carry Glen, still unconscious, back to a shelf in the officers' quarters. He would be in pain and would run a temperature for several days. Doc wanted to be near him to offer as much encouragement as possible.

Hekking received no thanks from the British medical officer, Dr. Wiggins, according to Charles. Wiggins scowled and said that he had planned to amputate the leg. Why hadn't Hekking used a rice poultice instead of his "birdcage"? But poultices were breeding grounds for bacteria, objected Hekking. Wiggins pointed out that bacteria could equally be airbone and fly straight into the wound. Hekking was saved by the Japanese Dr. Sagara, who was so impressed by Hekking's work that he refused to allow Wiggins to perform the amputation on Self. It was after this quarrel that Wiggins released Hekking to Fitzsimmons and the Americans.

The Americans admired Hekking because, like "Weary" Dunlop, he stood up for the sick men. When the camp commandant insisted that only 10 percent could be kept back from work for sickness, Hekking responded that they did not fall sick by quota. A standing order was introduced: Hekking got one lash on his back with a bamboo pole for each man he declared sick above the 10 percent quota. But he did not relent, even though his back was soon so black and blue that he could not lie on it. He constantly surprised the Americans, both by his methods and by their evident success. On visits to abandoned villages with the guards, he utilized the knowledge gleaned from his grandmother and collected the husks from around the stones where the Burmese ground their rice, knowing that they were rich in vitamin B. Back at the camp, he told the disbelieving British cook he wanted to use the husks to make cakes. He showed him how to mix the husks with the cooked rice, kneading it into dough and then into small balls which were dropped into boiling oil. There was one tasteless cake for each prisoner, but they ate them because they were at least a change from the usual diet. Hekking stood by them to see that they took their medicine.

He used ipecacuanha and other weeds, boiling the roots and making the men drink the "vile" concoctions. "It's good for you," he would tell them—and it was. It was questionable whether the drinks contained any medicinal ingredients, but they were a placebo. When he at last found a pomelo tree, with fruit like grapefruit, Hekking scraped the fungus from the skin and diluted it in water to make a paste. It was a powerful antibiotic which worked miracles on scratches and cuts (it was essentially a form of penicillin).

One day the men saw Hekking racing to the kitchen. A buffalo was being butchered and the men were about to dump the blood on the ground. Howard Charles was among the spectators:

> Before anyone could stop him, he grabbed the tub and emptied the contents into one of the kitchen cauldrons. "That's a rice cauldron you're puttin' that in!" an Australian yelled. Doc ignored him. "Why are you doing that?" I asked. He was poking wood beneath the kettle, stoking the fire. He didn't look up. "It's protein. Our bodies starve for protein." "But you expect us to eat that?" "Of course. You will eat what you must to live. In Java, cooked blood is a delicacy." "Java is a mighty strange country," I said. I watched, ready to vomit, as the blood boiled and turned black. Finally, as Doc stirred it around with a pole, it hardened and became grainy. He dipped some of it out with a spoon, blew on it to cool it, then tasted, smacking his lips. A pleased look appeared on his face. "M-m-m-m," he said. "Very good! Here, you try it." Other prisoners were gathering around, some more repulsed than others. The cooked blood was tough enough to chew. If it was good for us, and I had no reason to doubt that it was, I was determined to chew it and ingest it. It tasted a bit like burned rubber with only a bare hint of beef liver. "Not bad," I lied, smacking my lips, trying to hold a straight face. "Excellent," I said, swallowing it. Doc's face beamed. "See? I tell you so!"

Hekking often "deceived" the Americans in an attempt to stiffen their determination to survive, notably when he called them together for a talk. Howard Charles was again in the audience:

> "Boys, I must tell you something," Doc began. Leaves rustled in the trees. Someone cleared his throat. The talking dwindled to silence. "You will be going home one day very soon, now," Doc said. "I must warn you, since I will not be with you to tell you what to eat or how to take care of yourselves once you are home. It will not be the same with you as with other people. You cannot eat like other people. Your stomachs, they are not big, you see? How you say—they have shrunk. So you must take it easy on food. When you get home, do not eat two eggs for breakfast every morning, as I know many of you did in the past. Two eggs are very bad for you. One egg, that is fine. You eat only one egg a day. And do not eat just beef. Eat fish and chicken, because they are better for you."

The critical word from Hekking was "when": there was no "if" about the men getting home. The men took it for granted that Hekking had a private line to the news because there was not the slightest doubt in his voice or manner. His chat had the desired effect: it lifted the men from their miserable surroundings and they started talking about home and what they would do when they reached America. Howard Charles described the effect:

> Why not start a ranch in Texas? With a bull and some heifers? Or some hens? Perhaps a milk cow? Or two? It was going to be fun. They laughed while rain roared in the trees, belting in sheets along the flimsy atap roof, soaking those who were attempting to sleep on the shelves. They laughed as they stood in mud and slosh; intoxicated with hope, confidence radiating from one to the other, the momentum of strength building—all borne out of believing in something they could neither see nor hear nor touch nor prove. And I found myself sharing the great insanity, enveloped with the heady feeling we were going to make it.

After the war Hekking went to reunions of the prisoners where he resisted their suggestion that he had invented psychosomatic medicine. It was hocus-pocus, learned from his grandmother, his *oma,* he said. There was only the jungle, no pharmacy, no medicine, nothing. "We have each other, we have this thing we share. And we have the jungle and things which *Oma* knew." Irrespective of whether Hekking invented psychosomatic medicine, his methods were effective: his patients reputedly had the lowest death rate on the railway.

By 1944, with the Burma–Thailand railway built, the Japanese acknowledged that hospitals were required to treat the thousands of sick, debilitated, and emaciated prisoners. The two biggest in Thailand were at Chungkai and Nakhon Pathom, and it was at Nakhon Pathom in 1944 that Coates, Dunlop, Markowitz, and Vardy found themselves working together to try to save British, Dutch, and Australian patients. Coates was the senior medical officer and exhibited outstanding powers of organization and administration, according to the citation for the OBE he was awarded in 1946, which praised his "initiative, resource and enthusiasm." With two years' experience behind them, the doctors, surgeons, scientists, and crafsmen at Nakhon Pathom practiced jungle medicine against the odds and at its finest. The first thousand patients arrived in March 1944. There were fifty new bamboo huts with wooden sleeping platforms, a big building for an office and clinic, and—a previously unknown luxury—an operating theater with a concrete floor. But initially there was no equipment. Within three months, however, as incoming doctors brought their odds and ends of old or improvised instruments, and a plumber, carpenter, and tinsmith got to work, the hospital was working at full capacity, with three doctors and ten medical orderlies allowed per thousand patients. The average daily number of sick men was five thousand, but the hospital eventually had ten thousand beds.

A Dutch biologist, Dr. A. J. Kostermans, and Pte. Chapman, a British prisoner who had a Ph.D. in chemistry, soon provided thirty-five different products. Alcohol for antiseptics was made with a strain of fungus that broke down rice starch into sugar: a hundred gallons of it were produced. Extracts from grass—250 gallons a day were produced—cured 70 percent of cases of scrotal dermatitis. Oil of cloves was manufactured to make cement for the dentists. Ink was made from the tannin of leaves and iron rust; five gallons of tannic solution for enema fluid were delivered daily to the dysentery wards. Citronella oil was extracted from lemon grass and used to flavor the food; salt was purified for saline solutions; and rough paper was produced from the fibers of water plants.

Bicycles, muscle exercisers, and walking bars and pulleys were constructed by the physiotherapy department. Between August and October 1944 the orthopedic workshop made forty-six pairs of crutches and eighty-one artificial limbs. Hundreds of pairs of spectacles were repaired. The demand for dark glasses to protect against the sun was solved by making frames from empty tins and doubling the number of lenses by cutting them in half and using blue cellophane between broken microscope slides. Maj. A. R. Hazelton, the Australian who ran the eye clinic, constructed an ophthalmoscope using an oil lamp burning coconut oil, parts of a razor, a metal concave mirror, and some lenses.

Such ingenuity helped the doctors and surgeons to treat the sick men. By September 1944, there had been 219 major operations and more than 400 blood transfusions. The pathology department had examined 860 stools and taken 1,600 blood slides a month. The dental center treated 1,100 cases a month and the eye clinic 380. Under the Australian Maj. Syd Krantz, who ran the operating clinic, there were nearly a thousand operations in eighteen months at Nakhon Pathom. "Weary" Dunlop, now managing the hospital's surgical wing, treated more than a thousand patients—operating and grafting ulcers—and also administered the physiotherapy department.

Coates performed an operation on an American officer, John Stiver, who had a suspected brain tumor. The tumor had caused a loaf-sized lump on Stiver's head, his speech was becoming difficult to understand, and he was partially paralyzed. A circular saw about two inches in diameter was made to cut his skull and was fitted to a treadle machine. Silver clips were made out of bits of spoons. Ampoules of novocaine from American Red Cross parcels were used for the anesthetic. Dental forceps were used instead of "bone nibblers." The tumor was located and proved to be irremovable, but the "decompression" of the brain during the operation allowed the patient's symptoms to subside. Stiver survived and was eventually flown home to the United States, where he received further surgical treatment at the New York Naval Hospital. His mother sent details of the American operation to Coates and expressed her thanks to him, but Stiver died not long afterward.

The resourcefulness of the doctors and men at Nakhon Pathom and Chungkai was by no means unique. Similar solutions to the problems of jungle medicine were found during captivity throughout the Far East. Some were very simple: the solution to "Java Balls" in Borneo was to hang them out to dry. The sight of fifty or sixty men lying stark naked holding up their scrotums to dry in the scorching sun was one no artist could ever paint, said L.Cpl. George Pringle. Any artist would have had similar difficulty with the solution to Java Balls on the Spice Island of Haruku after the doctor there received a supply of coconut oil and sulfur powder. One prisoner who experienced the treatment was the British airman Pte. Tony Cowling:

> After supper we were paraded naked under the light of the moon in two columns with our elbows at our sides and hands outstretched, in front of us, palms up. Now medical orderlies walked in front of each column. One poured a little coconut oil into one palm while the other shook out some sulphur powder in the other palm. Thus equipped the two ranks then clapped their hands together and applied the resulting mixture to their scrotum and crotch. Now to make sure that all scabies were attacked, the distribution process was repeated to the men in the rear rank only. After mixing the oil and sulphur powder they applied the mixture to the buttocks of the man in the front row. About turn, repeat the process, and everybody is parasite-free. A most unconventional parade, but effective.

The method favored by Hekking of using placebos was practiced elsewhere. On Haruku, sodium bicarbonate tablets were broken up and prescribed as M and B 693, while sterilized water was injected into the arms of sick men. Both made the men believe they had a fighting chance and helped survival. At Fukuoka, pneumonia was treated by placing a big wooden-framed heat cradle containing four forty-watt bulbs over the patient's chest.

Fukuoka was also the scene of a remarkable operation on a young American prisoner named Vaughan who broke his back after being trapped when a mine collapsed. His condition seemed hopeless, but Dr. Thomas H. Hewlett, the senior American medical officer, disagreed with the Japanese surgeon:

> Vaughan was a very reasonable young man with an intense desire to live. It was explained to him that if the planned treatment worked he would suffer extreme muscle spasm and pain. We had no morphine or similar drug to give him any relief. He agreed to follow our plan and the pain it entailed. A hinged traction table was constructed and placed in the small isolation building and Vaughan was placed in traction. It was hoped that by using the isolation building we could muffle the sound of his screams from the other prisoners. However, I am sure that those who were quartered in the area of the isolation building can recall the nightly screams of this man as he endured the treatment. Eight weeks after his torture was begun we walked him into the camp commander's office. Hewlett's success convinced Lt. Uri that the American doctors knew their business. He ordered the mine surgeon to come to camp and see our results. Unfortunately Vaughan committed suicide in the first year after his recovery from Japan.

When Maj. Gen. T. O. Thompson toured the prison camps at the end of the war for the Repatriated Allied Prisoners of War and Internees (RAPWI) organization, he was impressed by the "extra high morale" of the former prisoners. One reason for this was the radio sets that had kept the men aware of the progress of the Allies. Another was their amazing speed of recovery as soon as they were given proper food. But the third reason was undoubtedly the most important—"the amazing work done by medical personnel in every camp." As the consulting surgeon to the British Army wrote, when introducing Markowitz's *British Medical Journal* paper on amputations, the surgery was "drastic and heroic." Thousands of prisoners owed their survival to that heroic and dedicated work of the doctors, surgeons, orderlies, craftsmen, and scientists who refined jungle medicine to a high art.

Chapter 13

SMOKING *GONE WITH THE WIND*

For smokers, cigarettes were one of the great consolations of prison life. Even when they were starving, some men sold their rice for a fix of nicotine. As a result, cigarettes and tobacco became a means of barter for both smokers and non-smokers. In Japan, for example, salt was scarce. Surface workers at the mines kept a kerosene can of salt water boiling and topped up. At the end of the day it was allowed to boil dry and the residue was scraped into the men's dixies. Half a pint of salt bought thirty cigarettes—and cigarettes had become better currency than money. When Flt. Lt. F. C. Jackson ran out of tobacco at Kuching in Borneo, he traded on the black market and bought all his future rations from a friend for a canteen of cutlery which would be supplied after the war. But for the smoker the biggest problem was finding paper. So they resorted to using whatever they could, including, as Rohan Rivett wrote, precious books:

> In the jungle it was common to hear: "Ten pages of *David Copperfield* for five cents" or "Smoke *Gone with the Wind*—fine quality paper." In spite of certain protests by some of the padres, prayer books and Bibles, their sheets being rice paper, have been the most popular smoking material. Overheard: "Have you seen a copy of *Merchant of Venice?*" "No, it's the only Shakespeare play I haven't smoked."

A copy of *Gone with the Wind* bought for ten dollars was a shrewd investment when the thousand-plus pages were sold individually. One soldier at Kuching sold his copy of *Pride and Prejudice* at three sheets for ten cents and expected to make five dollars from his original investment of sixpence in Jane Austen. Smokers were at their wits' end for "rolls," he wrote in his diary. One man decided to "smoke" his *Belisarius,* but saved his copy of Macaulay's essays, which was on finer paper. Ronald Searle smoked the spare corners of many of his drawings and half of *The Pickwick Papers.* The result was foul and acrid but satisfied his craving.

One padre said he didn't object to the use of Bibles but asked the men to read each page before they smoked it. This strange form of Bible study led to men learning about sections of the book they hadn't known existed, and had certainly not read—Micah, Nahum, Habakkuk, Zephaniah. When Bibles and other books ran out, smokers used whatever they could find—toilet paper, message pads, laundry slips, writing paper, newspaper, wallpaper. The cigarettes were lit from tinderboxes, rope ends kept burning, the cookhouse fire, or by "bumming a light" (and taking a free puff in the process).

There were many names for tobacco—Sikh's Beard, Hag's Bush, and Wog's Armpit were the most common among the British. The Americans had others—Mountain Madness, Monkey Fur, Granny's Armpit, and, for really fine stuff, Maiden's Bush. If the tobacco was from the small supply given by the Japanese, the smokers were often in for a shock. It could have a disastrous effect, as L.Cpl. George Pringle observed:

> This weed is a cruel killer. Unsuspectingly drawing the smoke into his lungs the first reaction of the victim is to give a high-class performance of a man intent on destroying himself by first of all throwing out his eyeballs, secondly by ceasing to breathe altogether, and thirdly by turning a brilliant scarlet colour and falling in a dead faint, to be revived only by the careful application of first aid to the drowning. We have all suffered, but are, by now, fully aware of the effects of this Japanese torture and have devised a method of lessening its deadly effect.
>
> The tobacco must be washed, not once, but twelve times, and then rinsed for at least two hours in running water. The tobacco must then be dried in the tropical sun and washed again for a further seven times, repeating the washing and rinsing processes and leaving for a further three hours drying. Only then can it be smoked, and only by those who have been accustomed to the strongest of our home tobaccos. Some have tried to smoke this weed in a wrapping of bamboo leaf and have become lifelong non-smokers. Several substitutes have been tried with varying

> success. The leaf of the tarong, or egg plant, being the most satisfactory, but one must be desperate for a smoke before indulging in this mixture.

At Changi in 1944 the only smokes on sale were small cigars which were chopped up and rolled into cigarettes with newspaper. Capt. Harry Jessup preferred to use his own methods, however, and experimented with a "tobacco" derived from the dried leaves of the Malayan cherry tree, papaya leaves and chopped-up cigars soaked in a thick syrup of sugar and water. The mixture was put into a homemade press for a day and then dried for three or four days in a cool place. At Sandakan, pipe tobacco was made by compressing alternate layers of oily Javanese tobacco leaves and dried foliage from a papaya tree, or leaves from a tea or coffee bush, between two boards. When the ingredients were desiccated and formed a solid slab, plugs were cut off and smoked in pipes mostly made from corn cob or bamboo. On Haruku, leftover leaves from cigars were soaked until soft, beaten flat, cut into shreds and, still moist, put into an airtight tin with a small piece of banana skin to add moisture. Pipes were carved from teak, with the mouthpieces created from the Bakelite of old car batteries.

At Tamuang a cigarette factory was started, mostly staffed by sick men who could manage the light work. The paper, thin and inferior in quality, was mostly supplied from the POW offices. The men became skilled and the production was of a high order, according to Lt. Col. A. E. Knights, the senior British officer. At Nakhon Pathom, an average of six thousand cigarettes and eight hundred cheroots were made every day when the raw materials were available. The Japanese took a quota and the rest were sold to the men at one or two cents per cigarette.

The consolation afforded by a cigarette was described by John Brown when he was at Chungkai:

> Smoking is always a pleasure but when at the end of a hard day's labour in the heat of a tropical sun one has bathed in a cool river, forgetting for the moment the dangers of cholera, and has eaten a filling if not satisfying meal of rice, and then lights a cigarette, the pleasure becomes joy. And apart from that there was no joy in life. That evening smoke brought complete relaxation and it can be argued that it was that relaxation—induced by a narcotic if you like—which enabled men to keep going. Smoking certainly took the edge off hunger when rations fell—as they often did—for although the Nips were quick to cut down rations when the numbers in a camp dropped they were not so quick to increase them when the numbers were increased by a sudden influx.

When the Japanese allowed some native tobacco into a Sumatran camp, its effect on raising the men's morale was "almost unbelievable," according to Sgt. Peter Hartley, as was the demoralizing effect when the supply ran out:

> A large bonfire had been lit, on the pretext of keeping wild beasts and mosquitoes at bay, and round this the prisoners gathered, smoking their tobacco and singing songs. That it was not the bonfire or the singing that raised our spirits was amply demonstrated a few days later when the tobacco supply was exhausted. We all went straight to bed without troubling to light the fire!

Tobacco even provoked a poem, "The Fifth Horseman," which was written by Charles Brown in the Philippines:

To the wounded went his magic leaves,
And the dying blessed his name.
Hunger vanished in his golden dust,
And it will always be the same.
Where the Beast lets loose his fury,
And his Four Horsemen rage the land,
This Fifth one, called Tobacco, rides
To soothe the stricken man.

Chapter 14

KING RAT

The "King Rat" of James Clavell's novel and the Hollywood film was not an invention of the author's imagination. If the men were to survive, they had to live by their wits. Thieves, racketeers, and black marketeers flourished in all the prison camps of the Far East, often at the expense of their fellow prisoners. Good men stole, too—but usually from the Japanese. Whatever the job and wherever it was, they had one means of asserting themselves—they stole with all the cunning of the professional burglar and the incorrigible enthusiasm of the kleptomaniac, said Gunner Russell Braddon:

> Although it was universally accepted that in this pastime the Australians were without peers (probably, the Pommies maintained, because of our dubious background of convict settlements and bushrangers), the British troops were nevertheless just as diligent and frequently achieved spectacular successes. Thus, though it was the Australians who stole the most food, it was the Pommies who first stole drugs; though it was the Australians who smuggled into Pudu a wireless set, it was the Pommies who brought home some emetine; though it was the Australians who brought in the first weapons—broken bayonets—it was the Pommies who, with typical British abandon, went the whole hog and blithely lined up for the usual search at the gaol gates with hand grenades resting comfortably in the curly hair under their various hats.

But Clavell's King Rat was based on an American prisoner, and it was a few Americans who acted like the Mafia and behaved most ruthlessly toward their comrades. According to U.S. Marine Pte. John W. Wisecup, who had been in Thailand, King Rat—Cpl. King—was a composite of three men who never left Singapore and were together in a hut at Changi in 1944 and 1945.

The most detailed record of the activities of the king rats, apart from Clavell's "fictional" account of Changi, has been written about Fukuoka 17 camp at Omuta in Japan, where three Americans, according to British 2nd Lt. Geoffrey Pharaoh Adams, made the camp a "miserable and desperate" place and were a disgrace to their units and their country. They were known as "The Democrats" or "The Mafia," and all three were remarkable for their immaculate clothes, their well-fed appearance, and their "ruthless talent for self-preservation." One was the camp messing officer, a naval lieutenant known as "Sukoshi Dono," who lived in his "galley" day and night. His accomplices were two sergeants who also had their own private quarters. They mixed only with three American doctors and a warrant officer who "looked after" the possessions of men who had died and held them until the end of the war. The truth, said Adams, was that the three men had callously and calculatedly ingratiated themselves with their captors for their own advantage and were prepared to send a comrade to the wall to further their own ends. They constituted a separate enemy within the camp.

Adams first met the senior American NCO, Sgt. Benito, one of Sukoshi Dono's two accomplices, when Benito entered his office, saluted, and sat down. He revealed that the Americans were divided into Republicans and Democrats. The senior American officer, Capt. Achille Carlyle Tisdelle, was the only U.S. officer who was thin. He was a Republican.

> "Those poor guys who step off to the mine at all hours of day and night—they're Republicans. All thin guys are Republicans. They don't eat. We do." He paused to let the message sink in. "Well?" The penny dropped then with a clang. Benito, "The One" as he called himself, the senior American NCO in the camp, was inviting us to join the racket. If we agreed we should live well. We should be free of the endless chores, the miserable rations, the frequent punishments, the nerve-racking battle of wits with the medics, the guards. . . . We should eat. "And if we don't?" I asked. Benito shrugged. "It's up to you guys but remember Capt. Tisdelle." Another long pause. "We decided to starve the bastard to death, that's all. Not the Nips, *we* decided."

Adams refused to play but survived to tell his story.

Over the next months in 1945 the British and Australians were to discover the extent of Benito's power. The men's ration of cigarettes was ten every ten days, but the supply was controlled by Benito's sergeant and Poms and Aussies were lucky to get seven each. That left about 3,600 for the Democrats to smoke themselves or use for trading. Illicitly obtained food became capital. The Democrats lent food to hungry men and so had them in their power. If they refused to repay their loan, they were beaten up but the debt remained. Smokers craving tobacco sold their rations for cigarettes—half a cigarette for the morning or evening meal. Lt. Charles Burris, an Oklahoman pilot, witnessed five men commit "suicide" for cigarettes: "They traded their meals for half a cigarette and knew they weren't going to live a week by doing that. They'd still do it. When they were giving the death rattle, they'd still be begging for a cigarette." Some lived on the hunger and stupidity of others, said Pte. Roy Whitecross. The Fukuoka Mafia created misery. They encouraged fellow prisoners, desperate for food or nicotine, to gamble for rice, the contents of Red Cross parcels, or cigarettes. Some incurred such big debts that they were getting only one meal a day—with the result that the Americans introduced a system whereby men who owed more than three meals had to sign up and list their creditors. The creditors had to waive interest and were issued IOUs for the rice, postdated so that a bankrupt did not miss more than one meal in ten days. Officers saw the bankrupts through the serving lines so that they could not be strong-armed on the way. They were then supervised as they ate every grain of their rice.

Roy Whitecross recorded that it was common to hear men calling, "Rice now, for rice and soup tomorrow." This meant that someone was eating only his soup for the present meal so that he could trade his rice with someone who could not see further than his present hunger, and who would promise to pay it back tomorrow, plus soup as interest. He was therefore trading his entire next day's meal.

> Food was bought and sold for money. Cigarettes also were bought and sold for either money or food, as well as miscellaneous articles such as clothing, cigarette cases, dixies. Later, when money was forbidden in camp, all these transactions were carried on with cigarettes as the medium of exchange. If cigarettes were short, a packet might be sold for soup tomorrow night, rice on the morning of the third day of next shift, and another soup the following day. Without pencil and paper, the complicated details of several trading transactions had to be carried in the head, so it is easy to understand how some men got hopelessly muddled and ran up debts which could never be repaid.

> It amused us at first that these men could be officially declared bankrupt. This method protected other prisoners against an unscrupulous fellow who would contract deals which he had no intention of repaying, and also protected any man who might starve himself to death in attempting to repay his debts which continued to mount because of his uncontrollable desire for more food. If anyone traded with a declared bankrupt, he did so at his own risk. The bankrupts were not allowed to sell any more of their food, but a proportion of their meals, perhaps one meal a day or every second day, would be collected by an appointed "receiver," who would pay off one of the bankrupt's creditors. This was a serious matter, living on only two-thirds of a ration that was already down to starvation size.

Another merciless American king rat at Fukuoka 17 was Ted Lewin, a civilian who had owned a night club and brothel in Manila and who had ended up as a prisoner rather than an internee. Lewin had traded in rice on the journey from Manila to Japan on the hellship *Oryoku Maru,* during which hundreds died. When the men arrived in Japan only one of them could be called fat—Lewin. He never worked: when he was named for a work party, he waved a thousand-yen note. He had morphine when Tom Hewlett, the senior medical officer, had none and was dealing daily with men brought in from the mine in agony. But Hewlett was one of the few men to beat Lewin. When told by Lewin that he would have to pay for morphine, Hewlett replied that he could keep his morphine but, for as long as the war lasted, neither he nor his friends would receive any medical treatment. Lewin returned with five vials.

The rackets run by the British and Australians were more conventional and less ruthless. They traded, stole from the Japanese, and used the black market. As the prices of fish and eggs in Thailand rose beyond what the men could afford from their meager pay, they started selling "surplus" kit to the Thais. In reality, of course, no kit was surplus, but the money they received from selling shorts, shirts, and blankets was used to buy extra food. By the end of 1943, when many men were seriously ill after their experience on the Burma–Thailand railway, and in 1944 and 1945, as the long days of captivity wore on, they started to sell articles of sentimental value. The choices they had to make were significant. Many smokers chose cigarettes before food, but salt—which could be put in rice so that more of it could be eaten—was always a good investment. Watches, signet rings, cigarette cases, and flasks were sold over the fence by the racketeers, who made good profits but ran great risks and were punished by the Japanese if caught.

In Singapore in 1944, officers whose pay had been delayed traded on the black market. A good Rolex would fetch $150, a ring as much as $60, and flasks up to $30. For officers, most of the dealing was done through two or three of their number; other ranks used the British military police, who went on patrol for the Japanese supposedly to stop the prisoners from trading with the Thais. Some of the decisions were heartbreaking. On November 15, 1944, Capt. "Pop" Vardy was forced to make a trade:

> New low level. Ill again—bowels just cannot take the grass soup. I had no money, haven't been paid since September and I have been compelled to sell my signet ring. Mater gave it to me on my 21st birthday—21 years and a bit ago—I just couldn't get on further without money. Got 75/- for the ring. I can now buy eggs (four daily) and I hope to get bowels settled again. You understand mother? Times are hard and I have felt miserable ever since selling it. I wish I was out of this. Hopeless and just bloody awful.

Toward the end of the war at Changi, Capt. Reginald Burton's craving for a more varied diet was so great that he sold the last of his possessions. Then an Australian dentist removed with a pair of pliers a molar's gold crown. The gold was sold for $200, with 10 percent deducted by the seller. The money bought ten pounds of tapioca root and sweet potatoes, which augmented his diet for about a week. "It was not really worth it," Burton wrote later. "The tooth gave me trouble ever after and eventually had to be pulled out—and the war was over within a few weeks."

The rackets were legion. Using a mapping pen and a magnifying glass, an American sergeant inscribed "Rolex Oyster" on a Marks & Spencer watch, added a coronet beneath the words, and managed to find a Japanese buyer. The proceeds kept the men in Reginald Burton's hut in extra food for quite a time. Using a fine saw, prisoners cut schoolroom chalk into circular discs. Again using a magnifying glass for accuracy, a line was incised across one side and on the other was cut the inscription "M and B 693." The pills were sold to the Japanese as sulfonamide, a cure for the venereal disease which they got from the brothels that traveled with them as well as from local women. The Japanese also bought "flints" for their lighters that were made by sawing the spikes off barbed wire and making them into tiny cylindrical objects.

The racketeers became more important as the Japanese enforced their order against communication with the Thais and Chinese. They needed capital in Thai dollars, as well as a spiv's bargaining ability and courage. They bought whatever fellow prisoners had to sell, slipped out of the camp at night, met the Thais at one of the kampongs, and sold goods at a profit, thereby amassing fortunes. But since they could spend only a small proportion on extra food, some acted with a residual compassion and used what was left to help their fellow prisoners by building up credits on their banks back home.

According to John Brown, the prisoners learned all about currency transactions the hard way. The racketeer's method was to cash checks and advance dollars against IOUs. They charged exorbitant rates—men often being prepared to sign checks at the rate of one pound sterling for one Thai dollar:

> Thus the racketeers were on a good thing considering that the Thai dollar was monetarily worth about sixpence. It was, however, impossible to measure the value of dollars in that way. A cheque for ten pounds meant ten Thai dollars which in return meant extra food and another chance of life. And for that chance men were prepared to pay almost any price. Better to spend one's bank balance in this way and return with the chance of building another than die leaving good money to someone else. The racketeers did very well in this way and some of them returned with cheques and IOUs to the value of thousands of pounds in their possession.

One of Fusilier Harry Howarth's friends, Fusilier Cecil Mackay, was a typical example of the men who survived by the use of graft. He first impressed Howarth by proposing that they go to the local kampong. He told Howarth to take ten cents and order an omelette from a female seller. While Howarth blocked her view, Mackay seized a hen, broke its neck and stuffed the bird inside his shirt. Then they did the same trick again, and that night had their first good meal for weeks. Night after night, Mackay would disappear into the forest and reappear in camp with a four-gallon can, shouting, "Cecil, coffee, come and get it: hot, sweet coffee—five cents a cup." The men were astonished as it did indeed taste like coffee. Eventually he decided to let Howarth and some others in on his secret:

> We entered another smaller clearing in which was a trench fire and two 4-gallon empty petrol cans. A large hot plate straddled the trench at one end and everything had obviously been well used. "Now," he said, "the fire is placed under the hot plate and I scatter dry rice on the plate when it is hot, and this gives me the 'coffee.' When hot water is poured over the roasted rice it tastes just like coffee, add sugar and you have hot, sweet coffee." Several days after that, the night air was rent by the sound and cries of coffee vendors peddling their wares. By that time Cecil was manufacturing "damson" jam. He had discovered a tamarind tree in the middle of the jungle—he kept its position secret, of course, until he had denuded it of all its fruit—and he was the only man selling

> "damson" jam within a 3000-mile range. Cecil Mackay was, I think, the classic example of the triumph of the human spirit over extreme adversity, it was impossible for the Axis powers to win the war: they didn't have any Cecil Mackays.

Mackay was typical of many prison entrepreneurs, as Howarth noted, in his aim to make money and always possess money. But although he wanted his comrades to think of him as ruthless, he was in fact a generous man, prepared to help anyone. However, he did not want them to know it, in case it was interpreted as weakness.

Howarth himself learned from Mackay. At Tamarkan, when rations were at starvation level, he realized he had to earn money. His naïveté showed through, though, and he was outwitted and disillusioned as he learned firsthand about the greed of the dishonest grafters. He went through the sick huts asking for items that the men wanted to sell, saying he would take a 10 percent commission:

> I approached the two men who drove this truck offering them a 10 per cent discount on all sales on all articles they took out, and then I found out why so many valuables were still in Tamarkan. These two men had sewn up the camp: all valuables sold had to pass through them and if they weren't assured of a 90 per cent commission, they refused to handle them. Men died of malnutrition and gangrene because bastards like this stood by and helped them to their graves. These were the vultures of the prison camps. I returned to all the men I had collected valuables from and returned them, informing them of the ethical values of two of their so-called mates. Their obvious disappointment was even greater than my own.

Howarth was more sophisticated by the time he returned to River Valley in Singapore. The men discovered bales of fine-quality paper when they were working at a warehouse. Howarth smuggled out fifty sheets in his water bottle and sold them at fifty cents a sheet to the Chinese through the camp fence. When he discovered the paper was being used to forge Japanese five- and ten-dollar bills he raised his price to a dollar a sheet.

The secret of survival for the black marketeers was to be artful and crafty, a "bastard," according to one anonymous Fepow. Sixty years later, he was still ashamed of his own behavior. During three and a half years of captivity, through grafting and thieving, he spent only one day without cigarettes and two days without money. What he bought in camp he sold at a 300 percent profit outside, believing he was entitled to a return for the risks he took by leaving the camp at night. He gave money, food, and even on occasion blood to his friends. "I wish I could have helped more men and I don't feel proud of not giving away all my money," he said. "It would have been different if we had known the date of our freedom. I couldn't give to everyone." He is still undergoing operations resulting from captivity: "That is my punishment."

The black marketeers started their work in Singapore, where they exploited the hunger of men desperate for any food other than rice. It was also easy to get in and out of the colony's camps. Bully beef could be bought in Singapore for fifty cents a tin, and then sold to hungry men in the camps for eight dollars. Within a few weeks the black market was firmly established. Lt. Robin Fletcher watched it grow. The prince of the black marketeers initially made the journey himself over the wire, Fletcher said. But the 800 percent profit he made on his first few trips enabled him to hire minions to do the risky work for him. Within weeks he was sending out a thousand dollars a night in the hands of his agents.

> He has set up a regular shop and to this come all the great ones of the land, their sense of shame bowing before their imperious greed. Of his profits at this period none can tell. But we find him giving dollars for sterling cheques at the recognised pre-war rate, and at the same time, feeding the sick and undernourished of his battalion free of charge, while supplying his officers' mess on a post-war credit basis. He himself the while is never known to touch rice or draw any of the meals provided through the normal channels.

This entrepreneur with a feel for the welfare state and a dash of Robin Hood no doubt flourished after the war.

Another racketeer was "Joe" at the River Valley Road camp in Singapore in 1942. He began captivity with one hundred Singaporean dollars. He bought watches, gold rings, and jewelry, and meanwhile sold about a hundred packs of Cork cigarettes a day, making a profit of about fifteen dollars. He could thus afford to eat a tin of bully beef each day and bread spread with margarine. Such racketeers were the sleek and fat "nabobs" of the black market, observed Lt. John Durnford at Chungkai. They sat at dusk in bamboo armchairs, holding court over bowls of black coffee heavy with sugar.

Stealing was rife—even from fellow prisoners, even from men on their sickbeds. If prisoners could not afford to buy on the black market, they were sometimes left with little alternative. During one period at Chungkai, there were nine or ten cases of stolen blankets every day. Complaints of theft crop up constantly in prison diaries. Even commanding officers were victims: Lt.

Compassion and comradeship: The idea of "Every man for himself" disappeared in captivity. If the prisoners could help the next man along, they did. Sketch by Jack Chalker. *(Australian War Memorial)*

Singapore, Selarang, 1942: 16,000 men were crowded into barracks built for about 800 when the Allied commanders initially refused to sign a no-escape pledge.

December 1942: the "severe shock" of the journey from Singapore to Ban Pong, when as many as thirty-one men were herded into steel cattle trucks for the 900-mile journey to Thailand. Drawing by Stanley Gimson. *(Imperial War Museum)*

The bamboo huts at Tamarkan, with atap-palm roofs and sides, lashed together with a kind of raffia. Each hut housed three hundred men, who slept on bamboo slats. *(Australian War Memorial)*

As clothing wore out, the men resorted to the "Jap-happy," a length of cotton material with tape around the waist, pulled up between the legs and tucked into the waistband. *(Australian War Memorial)*

RIGHT: At work on the bridge across a gorge at Sonkurai. The wooden trestles were held together by iron spikes driven in by heavy hammers. No nuts or bolts were used. *(Australian War Memorial)*

BELOW: Leo Rawlings's sketch of men at work on the construction of the bridge over the River Kwai. *(Imperial War Museum)*

LEFT: "Hellfire Pass," Thailand, where men worked with sledgehammers and steel bars for up to eighteen hours a day for six weeks. Sketch by Ronald Searle, who was there. *(Imperial War Museum)*

BELOW: This bridge (photographed in October 1945), approximately half a mile south of Hintok Station, was one of six trestle bridges built to carry the Burma–Thailand railway between Hellfire Pass and Hintok. *(Australian War Memorial)*

A deathly pallor descended on cholera victims; their eyes bulged from their sockets, and their faces became drawn with pain and weakness. Sketch by Ronald Searle. *(Imperial War Museum)*

The funeral pyres were stoked constantly to keep them burning. There was no religious ceremony: "We would just slam them on," said Capt. James Mudie. Sketch by Charles Thrale. *(Imperial War Museum)*

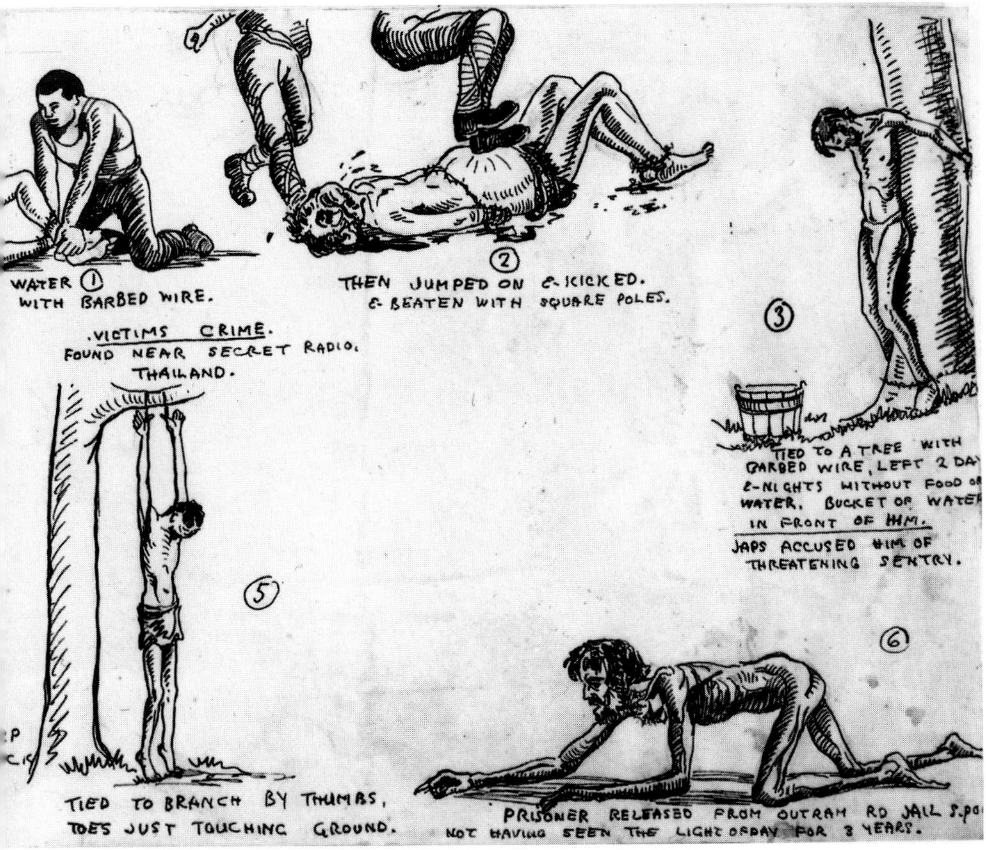

ABOVE: Nowhere in the world was sadism practiced with greater efficiency than in the Japanese army, said Lt. Col. Philip Toosey. Leo Rawlings's sketch shows some of the atrocities committed against the prisoners. *(Imperial War Museum)*

LEFT: Grim-faced men look on helplessly from the rollcall as a prisoner who has been given a "beating up" by a guard is carried away. He had failed to "number" in Japanese. Sketch by Ronald Searle. *(Imperial War Museum)*

Sgt. Okada at Tamarkan, where the bridges on the River Kwai were built. He was supposedly a medical orderly, but he was known as Dr. Death. *(Imperial War Museum)*

The camp commandant, Capt. Noguchi, unknowingly carried the prisoners' secret radio into the camp at Kanchanaburi in his luggage, where it had been secreted by the men. The penalty for operating a radio was death. *(Imperial War Museum)*

The face of the Kempetai, Japan's Gestapo, by Ronald Searle. *(Imperial War Museum)*

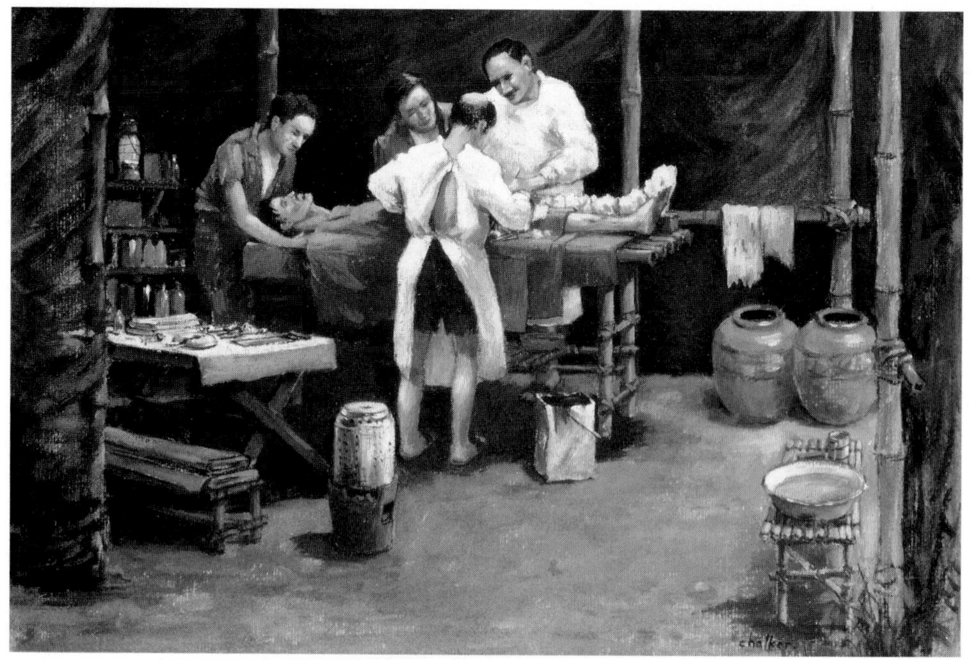

Jungle medicine in a bamboo hut lined with mosquito netting: Jack Chalker made this drawing as a tribute to two legendary doctors. "Weary" Dunlop (with moustache) and Jacob Markowitz never actually operated together, but they were loved by all their patients. *(Australian War Memorial)*

Ingenuity: the alcohol distillery at Nakhon Pathom, where 100 gallons of alcohol for antiseptics was made with a strain of fungus that broke down rice starch into sugar. Drawing by Jack Chalker. *(Australian War Memorial)*

ABOVE: Shows and concerts lifted the men's spirits. The most ambitious were staged at Chungkai, where the theatre was cut into a natural bank side, with seating for up to two thousand. Sketch by Stanley Gimson. *(Imperial War Museum)*

LEFT: Chungkai's biggest success was Leo Britt's production of *Wonder Bar.* As this program cover shows, the set was a scene in the Alps, with snowcapped mountains beautifully painted on the backcloth. *(Imperial War Museum)*

One way in which the men hid their diaries was in old jars and tins that they sealed and buried, often in graves. They dug them up after the war (in this case, eighteen months after they had been hidden). *(Imperial War Museum)*

Parts of a microscope hidden by doctors in the bottom of a water bottle at Nakhon Pathom. *(Imperial War Museum)*

Survivors of the Japanese "hellship" *Rakuyo Maru* are helped aboard the submarine USS *Sealion,* which had sunk them as they were being transported to Japan. *(Popperfoto)*

The spectacle of American and RAF bombers attacking the bridge on the River Kwai thrilled the prisoners. This May 1945 raid was by the RAF, who made the final low-level attacks in June. *(Australian War Memorial)*

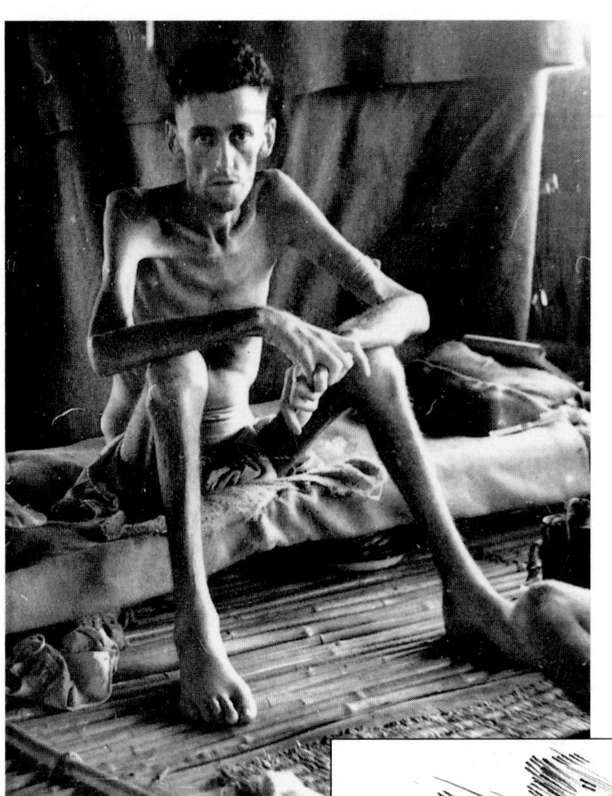

LEFT: August 1945, Thailand: an emaciated British prisoner at the hospital camp at Nakhon Pathom. If the Japanese had not surrendered on August 15, he would have died within two days. *(Imperial War Museum)*

BELOW: August 28, 1945, Changi: When the Liberators dropped leaflets over the camp, even the hospital patients tottered out to look up at the sky. "We all began to cry," said Ronald Searle, who drew this sketch. *(Imperial War Museum)*

LEFT: One of the Changi wards after the Japanese surrender. *(Popperfoto)*

BELOW: September 1945, Japan: Throughout their captivity the men had been obliged to bow to their captors. They knew the war was over when the Japanese started bowing to them. *(Corbis)*

The joy of liberation: When they knew the war was over, the men sang "God Bless America," "Happy Days Are Here Again," and Britain's national anthem, which had been forbidden. *(Corbis)*

Col. Cary Owtram's valise was ransacked at Chungkai. "The troops' morals have gone to blazes and they steal anything they can lay their hands on," he wrote in his diary. He had lost two pairs of shorts, three shirts, and two towels, as well as boots, shoes, a blanket and sheet, soap, some tinned food, and two pairs of trousers. All he now possessed was what he stood up in and a blanket, mosquito net, his camp bed, and an attaché case. Another victim was 2nd Lt. J. S. Milford, who lost his pillow, cushion, Red Cross hat, fifteen tins of food, and all his books and clothing:

> Praise be, my sadly battered and rusty little typewriter is still there. Worth on a long view, all the rest. I must get to work on it tomorrow with a piece of cloth and some of my precious pig fat! Left, too, are a shirt, a pair of trousers and my mosquito net in a very sorry state; the looters seem to have cut the cord, to get to the contents more quickly and to have emptied the whole thing out into the mud where it must have lain for several days until someone went to the trouble of stuffing some of the contents back in to it again. What a pleasant instance of the honesty and consideration of our own troops for their fellows.

Some stealing, though, was for the common good. When Capt. Stanley Pavillard discovered that a cargo of drugs captured from the British had been unloaded for the night in the rice store at Wampo and was on its way to Japanese soldiers at the front, he decided to steal them. Lt. Col. Harold Lilly, the British camp commander, vetoed the plan: it was impractical, and if caught the men would certainly be executed, he said. "Pav" ignored his superior officer, knowing they would soon be short of supplies. He recruited four men and they raided the rice store that night. Each pannier had to be taken from the store, which was opposite the Japanese railway commandant's hut, and carried to Pavillard's hospital room twenty-five yards away. By 2 A.M. they had finished. The next morning, it was with a sigh of relief that he watched the Japanese guards and the prisoners carrying the remaining panniers out of the camp.

> When they had gone I told Lt. Col. Lilly what I had done, and explained that we now had a year's supply of medicines. The old man replied, "I had a notion you would do it, Pav; as a matter of fact I haven't slept a bloody wink all night." I arranged that the loot should be left buried for several days in case of unexpected and delayed repercussions, and that it should be shared out equally between "D," "B" and "F" Battalions if all went well. When I got back to England in October 1945 I submitted a

report to the War Office, describing this episode and suggesting that the bravery and devotion of the men concerned should receive official recognition. None was given, and for the record their names are as follows:

- No. 5707 CQMS Metcalfe, J. M., FMSVF
- No. 7830 Private Wadsworth, K. T., FMSVF
- No. 7396 Sergeant Cassidy, T. P., FMSVF
- No. 13610 Lance Corporal Miles, E. T., FMSVF

I have no doubt that the knowledge that they had put a fast one across the Japanese and had saved the lives of any number of their comrades was then, and still remains, worth more to them than any medal.

But much of the stealing was simply criminal. At Changi, medical orderlies charged dying men for a tin of condensed milk and robbed patients of their money and belongings. Hospital blankets were stolen from the sick and sold over the wire to the Thais. At Chungkai, gangs stole on an organized basis. Nothing was sacred, said Lt. John Coast: rings and watches were stolen from dying men; drugs began to disappear; it wasn't safe to leave washing hanging for more than ten minutes. When a racketeer who had looted corpses died, five hundred Thai dollars were found in his pack: he had been too stingy to save himself with the cash. Looting corpses was the most ghoulish trade. L.Cpl. George Pringle witnessed two fellow prisoners in the act:

> These two had, just a few hours ago, assisted at the burial of one of their comrades who had finally given up the unequal struggle to survive. They had noticed as the burial blanket, which acted as the shroud for all dead POWs, was withdrawn from the body, a gold ring still adorned one of its pitiful fingers. A gold ring meant trade with the Japanese who never refused to buy or trade for gold. And this trade offered a further period of survival for those who had gold to sell. Survival was uppermost in the minds of these two men and had turned their thoughts to the gold ring buried with their companion. They were unable to rest on their return from the burial party and planned to revisit at dead of night, when the sentries were least alert, the last resting place of their dead companion.
>
> Slowly and carefully the two proceeded, always listening intently for any sound of an approaching sentry. The mission on which they are bound is highly dangerous. A mission which the British POW might find just possible to condone, but which, were they to be discovered by the Japanese, would mean their own violent death. The grave they seek

> is not very deep and the earth covering the body is lightly packed. Burial parties lack the necessary strength to dig deep graves and the earth which covers the body is always hurriedly returned. Quickly the two set about the task of removing sufficient earth to enable them to reach the body. But they have frequent stops to rest and breathe, for their breathing is loud and laboured and can easily be heard on this still and eerie night. "I've got him, quick give a hand," I overhear.
>
> A macabre struggle follows before an arm of the body is finally extracted and the gold ring quickly slipped from its finger. Hurriedly the men return the partially exhumed body and replace the scattered earth until the grave again looks undisturbed. The following morning at the working party on Kuching aerodrome they make their sale and receive in return a supply of coconut oil and a few eggs. This will guarantee them a few more days' survival.

One British POW for whom stealing became a passion and a fine art early on in Singapore—from the Japanese rather than fellow prisoners—was L.Cpl. J. S. Cosford. Whatever job the men had to do, their first consideration was what they could "pong" that would be useful, he recalled. When sent to the cold-storage store in Singapore to fetch meat and potatoes for the Japanese, they would distract the guard while they loaded an extra side of meat or sack of potatoes. They worked this trick on several occasions but thought that the game was up one day when the guard checked the sides of meat on the journey back to camp. He counted them several times, and looked very puzzled until suddenly an expression of comprehension came across his face. Grinning broadly, he said that he understood what was going on, and explained in half Japanese, half English, that he had no objection to this sort of thing, provided the men shared with him on a fifty-fifty basis. He made it plain that if they were caught, he would know nothing about it. And, of course, some men were caught: a party returning from Singapore was stripped to their loincloths and thoroughly searched. They were about to be allowed to proceed when a guard noticed a trickle of salt coming from under one man's loincloth. The guard's haul was cigars, sugar, and salt worth $3,000. But George Pringle still pitied the Japanese prime minister Tojo: he had thousands of criminals pitting their wits against his army and almost invariably winning.

While the British did their share, though, the Australians, as has been said, were in a different league. At Zentsuji, Capt. David Hutchinson-Smith reckoned they twisted the Japanese around their little fingers. Their rackets made Chicago mobsters appear like beginners. The cigarette racket was extraordinary and revealed the stupidity of their captors, Hutchinson-Smith said. When prisoners were searched on first being interned, any tobacco or cigarettes were confiscated. There was no canteen where they could be purchased, nor any other legitimate source of supply, yet almost every one of the twelve hundred prisoners and internees smoked openly day and night. It did not dawn on the Japanese for almost five months that they must have been smoking the guards' own cigarettes. They would probably not have discovered it even then had the "scroungers" not taken so many that at last there were insufficient cigarettes left in the main store for the monthly issue to the guards. The Japanese built a special cage which was under armed guard for the safekeeping of their tobacco, but the wooden bars were conveniently placed so that prisoners, by operating on the guards' blind side, could put an arm through. Still the men smoked, although the penalty for stealing was death.

Such was the routine of the little community that worked hard, slept hard, and stole hard. Anything Japanese, valuable and portable, even if screwed down, was fair game, either for food or for disposal in the harbor.

The Australians had been brought up during the "White Australia" period, which restricted immigration to Western Europeans. The vast majority consequently considered themselves superior to the Japanese. This was the main reason, according to Bdr. Hugh Clarke, why their attitude toward their captors was arrogant and defiant—and why they sabotaged anything they touched and stole anything they could, earning frequent reminders from the guards of their convict ancestry. The plugs of 44-gallon drums of aircraft spirit were partly unscrewed to allow the precious liquid to trickle out. Copra (dried coconut kernels) loaded for transport to Japan was drenched with seawater, or "otherwise baptised," to induce spontaneous combustion. Tools and equipment regularly disappeared.

One Japanese commander was given an early lesson in the Australian ancestral inheritance after he warned the prisoners, as they entered Thailand, that the locals were notorious thieves. "My men are worse than that," the Australian colonel responded. Frans Dumoulin, a Dutch medical officer, was soon convinced that the colonel was right. At Ban Pong his group was agreeably surprised to find a thriving trade in vegetables, bananas, and duck eggs. Dumoulin could not understand how one of his Australian fellow travelers was busily trading and had bought vegetables.

> The mystery was soon solved. Upon turning around I found my only remaining shirt missing from my pack, having been bartered with the Thai merchant! Complaining to the Aussie's commander about this

> theft, which trespassed an unwritten inter-prisoner gentleman's agreement on Java allowing stealing only from the enemy, I found him totally unimpressed, reminding me, "You should not be surprised. I warned you on the way up here about the stealing habits of quite a few of my men. Many of these blokes have been recruited from prisons at home, where they have been offered a general pardon for the rest of their time in return for their volunteering for military service overseas, so what do you expect?"

Thieves who were caught were punished by a variety of methods. At Nakhon Pathom in December 1944, thirty-one racketeers were under guard. Courts-martial were frequent. At Chungkai two men found receiving stolen property were sent to the group commander, who sentenced one of them to seven days' detention and the other to twenty days in the Japanese cells, known to the men as the "no-good house." The sentences had to be approved by the Japanese. Other offenses that merited similar treatment included the selling of quinine and drugs to the Thais. One prisoner received twenty-one days for stealing the only microscope at Chungkai and taking it out of the prison to sell. It was a "desperate" act, said J. S. Cosford, himself at one stage a military policeman, and the man got off lightly: "That microscope was the only means we had of detecting malaria. Eventually it was recovered at great risk by MPs and others who broke camp at night to comb the neighbouring kampongs." There were five cells in the no-good house at Chungkai, each three and a half feet wide, six feet long, about six feet high, and made of tightly woven bamboos. There was no water for washing and no bedding, and a hole scraped in the corner served as a latrine. Sometimes there was only one meal a day, but it came from a POW cookhouse and a little stew or fish was often hidden under the rice. On release, the offenders were detained in the preventive detention barracks, allowed on working parties but guarded by military police at the end of the day.

The military police had few powers of punishment and often resorted to "school" methods—they made offenders parade around the camp and do chores with big placards around their necks advertising their offenses. Cigarettes could always be withheld as a punishment, but that usually simply forced the man to steal them from somebody else. Corporal punishment with a leather belt on bare buttocks was no deterrent, and the men recoiled from making offenders run the gauntlet. It was easy to knock a thief down in righteous anger when he was caught red-handed, but to stand around and belt the thief after the event smacked too much of the Japanese. The harshest Allied-imposed punishment for persistent thieving was usually half rations.

In Omuta, though, the Americans went one step further when Lt. Little of the U.S. Navy handed a man over to the Japanese for stealing twelve buns, which most of the prisoners thought was going too far; especially as, after days of torture, the man died.

One racketeer called "Snowy," however, got a cheering comeuppance after the war. He had sold Russell Braddon water, obtaining an IOU for either ten cents or a pound on their return to Australia for every mugful. Braddon eventually owed Snowy £112:

> When two years later I got back to Australia, one of the first letters I received was a demand for £112. I wrote Snowy a polite note saying that I should be enchanted to pay him, every penny of it, so long as he would meet me in Sydney where we might both be photographed by the press—I giving him a cheque for £112, he handing me a receipt for £112—money paid for water received. I thought that as a tale of comradeship in arms, it would read well in the dailies. Surprisingly, I received no answer.

Chapter 15

LETTERS

For all the prisoners, the greatest torment was *not knowing*—not knowing when the misery would end, not knowing how the war was going, not knowing when the next letter from their loved ones would arrive. Letters from home arrived sporadically and up to a year after they had been dispatched. Most prisoners of the Japanese were lucky if three of the few cards they sent home, in which they were allowed to write only brief remarks approved by the Japanese, ever arrived. Most similarly received only three letters from home during their three and a half years of imprisonment—though those at Changi and Zentsuji were more fortunate. Lt. Ken Tomkinson at Changi was one of the lucky men—he received 130 of the five hundred letters written to him by his family.

Grown men wept unrestrainedly when letters arrived. Lt. John Coast recorded sitting on the floor of his tent with tears in his eyes, once again remembering that somewhere on the same earth people existed who cared what happened to him. After mail arrived at Kuching, the silence continued for hours as each man sat alone with his card and his thoughts. They scrutinized one another's cards, hoping that they could read something the recipient had overlooked. For a few brief hours the men were at home among their loved ones and the surroundings they so sorely missed, said L.Cpl. George Pringle. A letter from his stepmother saved Sgt. Peter Hartley's life: it described his family's relief at hearing that he was alive and urged him to return safely to them. Hartley remembered:

> As I read on I began to understand the anxiety, the mental torture, and the awful worry that my family were suffering for me—to realise, as though for the first time, how much I was loved and how terribly I was missed. I could not let them down now. I could not, must not add to their suffering. Somehow I would get back to them. I would fight desperately and go on fighting rather than betray the hope and love of my family. The other letters, written at different times by various members of my family, were much in the same strain, and served to strengthen my resolve. Eventually I used them for cigarette papers, but the first letter I kept and read over and over again until I knew its contents by heart. This was the letter which had saved my life. A letter which had arrived at a time when I was ready to die; now I had a new purpose, greater even than the natural instinct for self-preservation, greater even than myself.

Capt. Adrian Curlewis, who had survived Sonkurai, must have taken the same comfort from the heartfelt letters he received from his mother, which contained news of his wife Betty and his two young children, Ian and Philippa. One was sent on May 31, 1943, and arrived more than eighteen months later, on November 19, 1944:

> *My Darling Boy*
>
> *Oh, the hardness of going on day by day without you! How are you at this moment, I wonder. Cold, wet, comfortable? Or not? We are cold and wet ourselves for a wonder. The long, long drought broke and it has rained in an unprecedented manner for nearly three weeks. There is water now in the dams to last for five years. Today it is cold as the Mountains.*
>
> *I am changing my last help today and with regret for she was uncommonly nice, so I had to advertise for someone to mind me. I wondered whether I'd get a reply at all—you don't if you just advertise for a cook at £2 a week. Next day the 'phone began to ring at seven—It went on like that the entire day and half the next; 80 applicants. It is really cruel, the scarcity of flats or rooms. Finally I made a selection and a young evacuated woman with a husband who fought in last war came today. A dietician she is—like the last—nuts, lettuce and so on, and vitamins from A to Z, so if you find me thin as my rake you will understand.*
>
> *The new ration books are due this week—with the food and clothes coupons. It is stated that 600 million pounds for clothes in England have been saved in the year, and really we have never had a real shortage of either.*
>
> *Everyone asks after you and comforts me by saying that the Japanese are*

behaving well to their prisoners, having come to realise that we are doing the same.

Darling, I don't know what to write to you. Just babble it has to be. Philippa grows lovelier and sweeter. Ian is looking well again. If only my H could have seen his report this quarter. Best he has ever had. Be well, my beloved son.

Ever and ever
Your mother

When letters arrived the men pooled them and shared the news from home. At Chungkai they were published in newsletters. In 1944 Lt. David Boddington said:

> It's astonishing what a wide field the letters cover and for that reason they are intensely interesting. We know the price of whisky, beer and tobacco a year ago, the sports results of a year ago, the allowances paid to wives, the registration of women, the Beveridge Report and the social changes that are taking place in England. And we all look forward to every batch of mail that arrives for though there may be none for us we share in the general distribution of news.

"Prisoners' Post" was a regular, typed, four-page foolscap newsletter issued every two weeks by B Company at Chungkai. The first, published on August 9, 1944, included a cartoon by Signaller Ronald Searle. How the men must have relished the news from home which told them that smoking in England was now expensive and that cheap pipe tobacco cost two shillings four-and-a-half pence an ounce. Sweets were rationed to three ounces a week. Women were earning "fancy" wages, with some unmarried girls paying more than thirty pounds a year in income tax. Corporation workers' and policemen's exemption from service had been raised to thirty-five years. Americans were playing baseball at Everton's football ground. Why Worry had won the Oaks, and Dewsbury the Rugby League Cup. Rachmaninoff was dead, Laurence Olivier was in the Royal Navy, and Clark Gable was a gunner in the U.S. Air Corps. Australians learned that men's suits were being produced without trouser cuffs; that vests had only two buttons; that beer was three shillings a bottle in Queensland, but only one shilling seven pence in Victoria; that cigarettes were ten pence for a packet of ten (but both of these items were declared "hard to get at any price"); that tea, sugar, butter, clothing, and petrol were rationed on a coupon system.

One can imagine the mixed feelings of the recipient of the letter which led "Prisoners' Post" in October 1944, headlined "While The Cat Is Away!" It was the story of two wives of POWs who took a day off in London in June 1943 and spent it as follows:

> We met at 3.50 at Piccadilly and walked on to Gunter's where we had tea and just missed being able to order strawberries. Later, we looked in at the Dorchester; then we saw a news film and after that went by bus to the Strand to see *Arsenic and Old Lace.* We both enjoyed this beautifully acted but very fantastic play. We could not get a taxi on coming out so walked to the Savoy where I asked some Canadians if they would allow us to share their taxi. This they did and we arrived at the Berkeley in state. We had a jolly fine supper and then caught a train home. I am sure that this very unusual outing did us both a world of good. It was not too expensive though neither of us could venture to repeat the dose for a very long time to come. London is crowded these days: there are people of all nationalities so that one seems to be a stranger amongst them all.

Maj. Compton Glossop managed to get a secret message to his wife by using Morse code on his postcard to reveal that he was held in Saigon. Until then, the British War Office had been unaware that prisoners were being held there, and had thought Glossop's camp was in Thailand. Glossop made use of the dotted line along which the prisoners were able to name the person they wanted to send an extra message to, converting some of the dots into dashes and extending the tails of certain letters of the four Christian names, thereby separating the dots and dashes into letters. Within half an hour his wife's brother was able to decipher the code—that the dots and dashes spelled out "Saigon FIC" (French Indo-China). The letter, sent on June 1, 1943, arrived in Britain on January 1, 1944.

Some letters inevitably brought heartbreaking news to the men—of the death of a father or mother or the breaking of an engagement, which were all the more sorrowful for being six or nine months late. A friend of Lt. John Durnford groaned aloud as he read a letter that still smelled of perfume. He stumbled out of the hut, taking with him the photograph of a beautiful girl which had been by his bed. When he returned an hour later without the photograph, it was clear what had happened:

> Fighting back the tears, he said, "Well, that's that, John. She's going to marry some damned diplomat in Paris. Nice of her to let me know after

> all this time, wasn't it?" The letter was six months old. There was nothing I could say to him. It would have been impossible to share his loneliness, his intolerable sorrow, the knowledge that there was no one to look forward to at the end of it. For even beyond his strength or faith, a man is kept going by the love for which he waits and by which he lives.

Durnford himself received a "Dear John" letter on his journey home in 1945.

A friend of George Pringle became depressed and died after receiving just one letter. Pringle and his other mates could do nothing to help him:

> My friend Jack, from Birmingham, is dying. I have noticed the weary process for some time, from the issue of our first and only mail from home. Now Jack is dead. Dead of a broken heart. His much awaited mail from home had advised him of a faithless wife. His hearse is a stretcher carried by four of his more fit friends. His coffin is his blanket. The blanket will be retrieved for future use. Nothing can be wasted. There is a wreath of cannas and balsam. Beautiful flowers that Jack had often admired.
>
> A small procession of men are allowed by the Japanese to follow the cortège and a party of British soldiers at work disregard the orders of a Japanese guard and pause in their work to present a last salute. It is mid-day. The heat is terrific and the procession moves slowly down the road, past the Japanese sentry box. The sentry does not salute. Past the green fields and all living free things. All things Jack had hoped to see again. But today cannot. Jack is dead. Jack is free. He has returned to freedom.

An even more poignant story is of the man who received a letter from his girlfriend telling him that she had decided to marry his father. She added insult to injury by signing the letter, "Mother."

Chapter 16

ENTERTAINMENT

The most popular and cheering diversions from the misery and monotony of captivity were the concerts and plays that were presented wherever there were prison camps. At Changi the Australian concert party was formed within a month of the surrender of Singapore on March 11, 1942, and gave its first performance, a simple variety show of old songs and sketches, eight days later. The Japanese then gave permission for a permanent concert party of thirty, who spent the rest of their captivity staging shows. Most of the scripts and music were written in the camp, and the wardrobe was mostly made from Australian nurses' clothes and the men's kit, sewn together using a purloined sewing machine. The men scoured the camp for musical instruments, and smuggled in two pianos and a drum kit. Strings for violins and banjos were fashioned from signal wire. A large garage was converted into a concert hall. The revues became so popular that a quota system was developed so that each prisoner could see each of the shows—a new production every fortnight. There was also a British symphony orchestra of thirty which gave a concert every Sunday evening and played during ceremonial parades. At one time five different concert parties were operating, mostly producing variety shows and revues.

The East Anglian Division converted one of the old NAAFI (Navy, Army and Air Force Institutes) common rooms into the "New Windmill Theatre" (a windmill was the insignia of the East Anglians), which could hold three hundred men. The first play to be proposed, *The Island,* about the love of a commanding officer for a junior officer's wife, was dropped after one commanding officer said that it would be bad for discipline and lead to contempt for officers. Maj. Gen. Beckwith-Smith opted instead for *The Dover Road,* which opened at the New Windmill on July 11. The production played for a month to packed houses, and parties from other areas were allowed through the wire to see it. The first Australian audience was initially disconcerting, said Lt. Col. Francis Dillon: "The majority of them had never seen a stage play and they sat in pin-drop silence the whole way through the first act; but as the curtain fell there was a roar of applause, loud laughter and pithy comments. From then on they were a normal audience and a very good one."

The production by the Concert Players of Malaya Command HQ in 1943 of George Bernard Shaw's *Arms and the Man* made a deep impression on Capt. J.A.L. Barratt because it spoke to the men's condition before the surrender:

> The Swiss mercenary soldier in the play who escapes up a drainpipe into a girl's bedroom had been under fire for three days and not closed his eyes for 48 hours. I remember him saying, "I can stand two days without showing it much but no man can stand three days without sleep." This was the condition of a number of our forward troops and the play helped me to understand.

Other productions included the Christmas pantomime *Jack and the Beanstalk,* R. C. Sherriff's *Journey's End,* Shaw's *Androcles and the Lion,* Noël Coward's *Hay Fever,* and Walter Greenwood's *Love on the Dole.*

One of the principal singers at the concerts was the Rev. John Foster Haigh, who had sung professionally as John Foster before the war. He took part in a series of symphony concerts at the "Palladium Theatre," which had been the local cinema. They provided a blend of middlebrow and serious classical music to appeal to all musical tastes. Haigh described the repertoire and the talent to be found within Changi in a letter to his wife: the pianist had been a pupil of Myra Hess, one of the most famous concert pianists of the time; Denis East, who led the orchestra, had been a member of the Philharmonic Society; Cyril Wycherley, Haigh's accompanist, had been a cinema organist. There was also a forty-strong male-voice choir. One concert had included compositions by Mozart, Schumann, Elgar, Handel, and Gilbert and Sullivan.

On August 3, 1942, Capt. Adrian Curlewis went to an 18th Indian Division Celebrity Artist concert where three men performed Schubert, Chopin, Kreisler, and Bach by piano, voice, and violin. "I would willingly have donned top hat, white tie and paid a guinea to hear them . . . but we gave them a three-inch platform, palm fronds, some white flowers as decoration and appreciation never heard in Sydney," he recorded in his diary. "Thin brown bodies, clad in shorts reflected by a hospital operating lamp, many bodies without limbs—a night not to be forgotten."

Concerts were also provided from the hundreds of records that had been collected within Changi and were stored with the gramophone in a special hut. On June 12, 1942, Lt. Jim Richardson noted that Lt. Corbin gave a (gramophone) recital of Tchaikovsky, Mozart and Dvořák, including the *New World Symphony*—"the whole composition redolent of forest wildlife, winds and wide open spaces—a lovely virile composition. Makes one really aware of what one is missing by being incarcerated in a POW camp." More was to come:

> 8 Aug: Concert. Lieut. Cliffe, pianist; George Wall, baritone; Denis East, violinist. (All at RCM, London, together)—a marvellous concert. Mendelssohn's Violin Concerto was beautifully rendered. Cliffe played John Ireland's "April," "Perpetual Motion" and the "Old White Donkey," Scherzo in B Flat Minor (Chopin), Prelude—(Rachmaninoff). Violinist (with Cliffe) played Serenade Espanol, Serenade in G from Concerto for Strings—Bach. Waugh sang arias from Samson (Handel), Fairings, Langley Fair, What a Wonderful Place the World Could Be.
>
> 12 Sept: Concert by Lieut. Cliffe—Chopin, Rachmaninoff, etc.—very good. Also male voice choir sang "Green Grow the Rushes O" and "All Through the Night."

When the gramophone needles ran out, the tips of pineapple leaves were used. Some concerts attracted audiences of up to three thousand; others were more exclusive. One man who had a gramophone and a set of classical records lent them out for a pack of cigarettes. It was a fine bargain, according to 2nd Lt. John Milford, who recorded the "remarkable sight" of forty or fifty officers sitting outside in a semicircle around the gramophone, listening in rapt attention to *Finlandia,* the Moonlight Sonata, a Mendelssohn concerto, and arias by Caruso and Gigli.

The prisoners' affection for their records was shown by the example of Flt. Lt. Leslie Audus. When he moved to his radar station on the Malayan mainland in 1941 he took with him an amplifier, turntable, pickup, and speakers, as well as a collection of records. After he was captured in Java, the collection was driven into captivity, but the Dutch provided a gramophone and recitals were given for hundreds of prisoners. When Audus was sent to

Haruku, the records were left behind, but he had scratched his name with a sharp nail on the smooth surface between the label and grooves on every one. When he returned to Batavia in July 1945, he heard a familiar sound—the scratchy strains of the Brahms Piano Concerto in B-flat Major—and was able to claim the record as his. Thirty-six records had survived in total, and Audus still had them in 2004 in their original paper sleeves—a tribute, as he says, to the loving care with which they had been preserved by an emaciated young radar officer.

The most popular shows with the men were the variety concerts, because there were often none too subtle digs at the officers, with lines such as "I've been in the army six weeks now, Sergeant, and I think I can say I know a bit about handling men." At one show there was a satire, still reflecting the disillusion over the surrender of Singapore, which made the brigadiers look down their noses, according to John Milford:

> The scene was the commanding officer's office in an outpost of Empire; he was playing Patience (and cheating!) when a staff officer arrived to tell him that his forces had been outmanoeuvred, outgeneralled and encircled in a war which he had not yet received news of. He expressed proper horror at the casualties (two NAAFI managers and a civilian) and at the total of prisoners (800,000; the last 10,000 had only just come in by rickshaw, and were worn out) but was chiefly perturbed because the local club would have to be closed, and because his captors would compel him to take down his badges of rank, though cheered a little when told that staff red bands would be permitted. All this was so uncomfortably true to certain local occurrences that it was somewhat of a relief when the sketch ended with the three characters joining in a burlesque song and dance. The entire show was without a weak spot, and was greatly enjoyed by all present, with three possible exceptions.

On the Burma–Thailand railway, musical or theatrical events were staged in at least twenty-four camps. But in Thailand it was at Chungkai, a hospital camp, where the most ambitious and sophisticated shows were staged, especially from 1944, when the "Speedo" period was over, the Japanese demanded fewer work parties, and at times there were up to ten thousand men in the camp. The patients needed entertaining to lift their spirits. Lt. Col. Cary Owtram, who commanded the largest camp in Thailand for two years, himself a fine singer who was nicknamed "the singing colonel," became the camp's impresario, presiding over a theater committee of ten until he fell out with his fellow members. He encouraged concerts and planned the site for a theater cut into a natural bankside, with seating for up to two thousand. He paid the orchestra special rates and ensured that they had three hours each day for rehearsals. Owtram was particularly fortunate in having accomplished artists among the prisoners. Two lieutenants, Norman Smith and Eric Cliffe, directed the music. The former, who had been a dance-band leader before the war, became "the Glenn Miller of Chungkai." The latter was a classical musician. Between them, they wrote musical scores from memory for each player on paper "acquired" from the camp office, and rehearsed the musicians endlessly. There was also a professional actor, Cpl. Leo Britt, who had appeared in the London production of the musical *Wonder Bar* and who became a producer and director. The Japanese, who enjoyed the shows as much as the prisoners did, eventually acknowledged Britt's talent and he was excused from menial work so that he could produce the shows. Britt was a controversial and flamboyant character, given to theatrical temperament. He was also a hard taskmaster. The so-called "Bamboo Theatre," a clearing in a thicket near the camp boundary, was used for rehearsals, sometimes as many as four a day. Britt sat on a stand, wearing a pair of clogs, sunglasses, a pink "Jap-happy," and a knitted dark blue skullcap, with Lt. John Coast, his assistant stage manager, beside him.

The roster of performers also included two highly talented female impersonators. Bdr. Arthur Butler had proved a talented tenor on the voyage to Singapore from Scotland; in the camps he transformed himself into Gloria d'Earie. But the undoubted star was Bobby Spong: so talented, according to one account, that the Japanese finally checked his "equipment" to confirm he was a man. Butler and Spong's exotic gowns were made from mosquito nets, wigs from coconut fiber, face powder from tapioca flour, lipstick from betel-nut juice, and jewelry from bits of tin and polished stones. Tragically, Spong died when the ship transporting him to Japan was torpedoed by an Allied submarine.

Several shows and plays were performed in the Thai jungle at Tarsao, including *Cinderella* and *Me and My Girl*. According to Capt. "Pop" Vardy, the camp's opinions on the female impersonators were divided:

> Some of them seem to have taken their "art" too seriously, having shaved their eyebrows off and allowed their hair to pass even the worst soldier's standard. We in the hospital are a bit removed from the main scenes but we hear that one or two "very fierce soldiers" don't like seeing their brother officers with curlers in their hair each morning or their eyebrows shaved and shaded foreheads and mincing ways—most unsoldier-like—I agree but [it's] hardly worth the tempers that would appear to have

> been displayed and certain remarks passed. It is a funny world—it does not seem to matter where or what we are doing, some of us, sooner or later lose our sense of proportion and allow "things"—at which we should just laugh—to develop into terrific issues.

Of course, not all the men were polished performers like Spong. At first most of the entertainments at Chungkai were amateurish, but unrecognized talents soon emerged when the men were given the opportunity to perform. Remarkable ingenuity was shown by the men in creating musical instruments. A set of drums was fashioned from sun-dried water buffalo bladders stretched over empty petrol tins, and a double bass from tea chests and bamboo, with strings made from telephone wire. The camp carpenter, Sgt. Horrocks, made a red-wood neck, strut, scroll, and bridge. Calf hooves were brewed for seven days to make glue that was strong enough. With gifts from the Swiss consul, and ukuleles and mouth organs from the Red Cross and YMCA, the orchestra eventually consisted of nineteen instruments—six violins, two accordions, two guitars, two clarinets, a trumpet, three cornets, two drums, and the double bass. It accompanied plays at the theater and performed concerts.

The theater had an extensive wardrobe, and colored lighting from kerosene pressure lamps borrowed from the Japanese, or lamps lit by coconut oil worked by stage technicians; the actors were attended by dressers and makeup men. Stage hands and set designers worked with bamboo, fish boxes, soot, brick dust, whitewash, and mud to make convincing scenery, which was usually painted on large sheets of the woven fiber matting used by the Japanese to partition their living quarters. Bras for the female impersonators were stuffed with prickly, rough kapok.

The first show seen by the majority of men who passed through Chungkai was *Shooting Stars* in April 1944, a musical comedy written by Leo Britt, with a cast of thirty and a band. Another big success was *Night Must Fall,* but by common agreement the highlight was Britt's production of *Wonder Bar.* John Coast described it as the best all-around show put on at Chungkai:

> The old story was completely changed and re-hashed, and new music by Norman Broad was added to the old hits like "Wonder Bar" and "My Friend Elizabeth." This latter number was sung in French, German and English by three young things who ended in a dance routine of high-kicking that delighted the audience; and seeing those three "girls" capering about on the stage, it was odd to think that in normal times one was an RASC Private, from London; one a Regular Officer; and the

> other a bald-headed Corporal in a Highland Regiment, Johnny Duncan, who had come through cholera, malaria, dysentery, beri-beri and jaundice altogether up country! The second act of *Wonder Bar* was a low-comedy scene between a waiter, Woolley, and a charwoman, Freddie Mills, the latter later becoming the camp's leading actor. But the last act was the best. The set was a most attractive scene laid in the Alps, and you looked through Wonder Bar itself to snow-capped mountains, beautifully painted on the back-cloth and cleverly lit. The whole stage was a blaze of colours, and the music, after five weeks' rehearsal, was first rate. [Coast used pseudonyms: Woolley was Everard Woods; Freddie Mills was Freddie Thompson; Johnny Duncan was probably John "Nellie" Wallace; and Broad was Norman Smith.]

Other members of the audience, such as Capt. Robert Hardie, clearly agreed with Coast's assessment:

> 21.5.44: Leo Britt's "Musical"—*Wonder Bar*—was given last night (when I saw it) and the night before. It was astonishingly good in its way—amazing costumes made out of old mosquito netting, a few pieces of cloth, and some dyes. The setting was also remarkably realistic—the bar, a bedroom—one could hardly believe it was made out of bamboo, a few pieces of wood, and bamboo matting, with some paint (whitewash, some local coloured earths). The actors too were good and the whole thing reflects enormous credit on the company.

Lt. David Boddington was similarly impressed:

> I went to see *Wonder Bar* last night and it astonished me. I have seen worse shows in England and certainly those shows we saw in Singapore couldn't compare with it. How our people did it I do not know. Everything was made by the POWs—furniture, scenery, dresses—and the dresses were marvellous as was the scenery. The show was produced by Leo Britt, a Corporal in the RAOC, who was an actor in civil life. I do not think I shall ever forget last night's performance—after our drab existence here the colours and music made a deep impression on all of us.

The men also enjoyed the concerts, as 2nd Lt. Stephen Alexander recalled:

> As we sat on the mud, keeping the mosquitoes at bay with our "Sikh's Beard" and watching the fruit bats scuttering in and out of the impro-

> vised limelight, the plangent strains of Purcell and Handel would give way to thumping chunks of Grieg, "The New World Symphony," "Leonora" and *The Barber of Seville*. And as for "Finlandia," I could positively see the Russians being swept away and feel, with a catch in the throat and smarting eyes, the snowflakes settling on my sweaty skin.

One senior officer described the dash to the concert hall:

> The moment roll-call was over, we rushed to our outdoor concert hall [which was half a mile away]. The Japanese had already occupied the front-row seats. But there was room for everybody and the men quickly took their places on the ground. Norman Smith, who was wearing fresh khaki shorts and shirt for the occasion, mounted the podium, raised his baton as a signal to begin, and the "heterogeneous" collection of instruments launched into their first piece. The men sat with their hands clasped round their knees, their heads nodding to the rhythm of the music. No orchestra could have asked for a more appreciative audience.

Another member of the audience was Gunner Ernest Gordon:

> Norman had arranged the programme wisely. He had included music for all tastes, ranging from Beethoven's Fifth Symphony to selections from *The Mikado*. From the "abstracted looks" on the listeners' faces, I could tell that their fancies had taken wing, and were soaring far out beyond the bamboo curtain that held us in. Noble memories, long dormant, were stirred once again, helping us on the way to fulfilling the infinite possibilities of the spirit. The night forced itself upon us, and, with the engulfing darkness, too soon, much too soon, the concert was over. At first when the concert ended there was absolute silence, the expectancy of men hoping for more. Then—tumultuous applause. I glanced at my neighbour; his face was shining. "Great! Isn't it great?" he exclaimed. The cheers and the hand-clapping in thunderous echo were proof that this was the unanimous opinion. Even the guards joined in.

Lt. John Durnford doubted that the composers themselves could have imagined such performances:

> The audience a crowd of half-dressed, half-starved human beings, ten thousand miles from far-off Worcestershire or Germany, in a sand-pit under the stars of a tropical night. Standing in listless and uncertain ad-

> miration, sentries at the side of the stage, as mystified as domestic animals, trailed their rifles, gaping at something they could not understand yet to which they were drawn.

At Cabanatuan in the Philippines a Catholic bishop smuggled a tiny piano, a trumpet, a trombone, and a guitar into the camp, and the Americans formed a band, a combo, and a four-piece "symphony orchestra." Every week or ten days an evening program was announced and the prisoners assembled, sitting on the ground. Pte. Andrew Carson recalled the shuffling feet, the rustling of bodies, the quiet conversation:

> There would be the sound of footsteps on the wooden stage, the scraping of a chair. From the audience, absolute silence. The two light bulbs would come on and our four-piece orchestra would be on stage. The piano would begin to tinkle, the guitar and the trumpet and the trombone would join in soft accompaniment, and suddenly in this desolate prisoner-of-war camp, in the midst of the starvation and brutality and death, we would be in Carnegie Hall. Two POW comedians, a comic and a straight man, would perform their same silly slapstick routines, and Paul Brisco, a member of the Fourth Marines, would sing. He had a rich, beautiful voice, had in fact been a cabaret singer before the war. I can still see Paul, clad in no more than a campaign hat and a G-string, belting out "On the Road to Mandalay" with gestures.

Capt. "Pop" Vardy summed up the importance of the shows as well as anyone. "It was absolutely grand," he wrote in his diary after the pantomime *Cinderella* was performed after Christmas in 1943: "The tears ran down our cheeks and for two hours we forgot all our worries and ills."

Chapter 17

SPORTS

Remarkably, considering the prisoners' usual physical state, sports were played throughout the camps. At Chungkai there was a football pitch on which were played out "thrilling encounters" between England and Holland. Football became so popular that most battalions found teams of men who were fit enough to play forty-minute games. A league of about twenty teams was established, and they competed for a shield made by Lt. Harry Collins. Several thousand men would line the ground cheering for their teams. "Touch" rugby was also played regularly. There were occasional tennis tournaments, as well as games of badminton, volleyball, and table tennis. "No one could really complain about the lack of amusements," said Sgt. A.H.B. Alexander. Swimming galas were held in the river, and there were several athletics meetings in which the Japanese and Koreans also participated. It was a matter of "no little surprise and satisfaction" to Lt. Col. Cary Owtram when, even in their comparatively unfit state, the prisoners proved themselves superior to their captors in quite a number of contests, particularly sprinting and jumping: "On one occasion their time for a one and a half mile race round the camp perimeter was nearly a minute better than the time put up by the Koreans over the same course in a separate race."

Cricket was particularly popular. Unsurprisingly, Maj. E. W. "Jim" Swanton, the doyen of cricket journalists after the war, was the main impresario. The first matches were played at Changi, where the rivalry between England

and Australia was revisited. One prisoner had smuggled in a cricket bag with stumps, balls (one of which was new), and bats, and the men decided to stage "Test" matches on rest days. One participant was Swanton himself. Another was Sgt. Geoff Edrich, who had played for Norfolk and who went on to play for Lancashire after the war. The Australians were captained by Capt. Ben Barnett, who had been their Test wicket keeper. There was a typed score sheet, umpires, scorers, and a clay pitch. The three matches were described as the Sydney, Brisbane, and Melbourne Tests, and there were more than a thousand spectators. England won the series, mainly thanks to Edrich, who scored a century in each match.

But the English were not always so successful. Signalman Arthur Titherington played with the 80th Tank Regiment in one memorable match in which the English discovered the caliber of the opposition:

> The Australians won the toss and put us in to bat. We were all out for eleven. They went in to bat and their opening batsmen scored 110 not out. We were devastated. It was not until it was all over that we were introduced to their opening pair, the same pair who had been their wicket keeper and bowler as we scored our magnificent eleven runs—Barnett and A. G. Chipperfield, two of Australia's pre-war Test team.

Night after night, according to Lt. Ian Watt, Swanton would recount the stories of famous Test matches or organize cricket quizzes. At Wampo he organized a jungle Christmas cricket match in 1942. The men prepared a fast wicket of hard baked earth. When a suspicious Japanese guard asked what they were doing, Swanton replied: "Preparing for a religious festival. Cricket is a religion in England." The match went ahead and was notable not only for a century scored in five overs by a young Eurasian who kept hitting the tennis ball clear of the huts, but for a victory of the men over the officers. Cricket was played at Chungkai, Tarsao, Nakhon Pathom—and even in Java, where the hard filling of the ball was replaced by softer material packed tightly into a sort of "soft ball," and baseball bats were used in games between England and Australia.

A match at Nakom Pathom on New Year's Day 1945 earned the distinction of being recorded by Swanton in cricket's bible, *Wisden:*

> The playing area is small, perhaps sixty yards by thirty, and the batsman's crease is right up against the spectators, with the pitch longways on. There are no runs behind the wicket, where many men squat

in the shade of tall trees. The sides are flanked by long huts, with parallel ditches—one into the ditch, two over the hut. In fact all runs by boundaries, 1, 2, 4, or 6. An additional hazard is washing hung on bamboo "lines." Over the bowler's head are more trees, squaring the thing off, and in the distance a thick, high, mud wall—the camp bund—on which stands a bored and sulky Korean sentry. (Over the bund no runs and out, for balls are precious.) In effect, the spectators are the boundaries, many hundreds of them taking every inch of room. The dress is fairly uniform, wooden clogs, and a scanty triangular piece of loin-cloth known (why?) as a "Jap-Happy." Only the swells wear patched and tattered shorts. The mound at long-on is an Australian preserve, their "Hill." The sun beats down, as tropical suns do, on the flat beaten earth which is the wicket. At the bowler's end is a single bamboo stump, at the other five—yes, five—high ones. There is the hum of anticipation that you get on the first morning at Old Trafford or Trent Bridge, though there are no score cards, and no "Three penn'orth of comfort" to be bought from our old friend "Cushions."

The story of the match is very much the story of that fantastic occasion at the Oval in August 1938. Flt. Lt. Cocks, well known to the cricketers of Ashtead, is our Hutton; Lt. Norman Smith, from Halifax, an even squarer, even squatter Leyland. With the regulation bat—it is two and a half inches wide and a foot shorter than normal—they play beautifully down the line of the ball, forcing the length ball past cover, squeezing the leg one square off their toes. There seems little room on the field with the eight Australian fielders poised there, but a tennis ball goes quickly off wood, the gaps are found, and there are delays while it is rescued from the swill basket, or fished out from under the hut. As the runs mount up the barracking gains in volume, and in wit at the expense of the fielders. When at last the English captain declares, the score is acknowledged to be a Thailand record.

With the Australian innings comes sensation. Captain "Fizzer" Pearson, of Sedbergh and Lincolnshire, the English fast bowler, is wearing Boots! No other cricketer has anything on his feet at all, the hot earth, the occasional flint being accepted as part of the game. The moral effect of these boots is tremendous. Captain Pearson bowls with shattering speed and ferocity, and as each lamb arrives for the slaughter the stumps seem more vast, the bat even punier. One last defiant cheer from "the Hill" when their captain, Lt. Col. E. E. Dunlop comes in, another and bigger one from the English when his stumps go flying.

Aside from cricket, horseracing was the Australians' passion. The day of the Melbourne Cup in 1942 was celebrated even in Burma during the building of the railway, with Col. George Ramsay acting as Governor-General and presenting the "cup" to the winning jockey. The jockeys rode piggy-back, and there were stewards and bookies. It was followed by a Cup Ball in a school hall with some of the men dressed as girls, at which Ramsay and his "lady" led the opening waltz as the band played "On the Beautiful Blue Danube." The end of the ball, as a thousand men sang "Auld Lang Syne" and then stood rigidly to attention for the national anthem, was "inspiring and unforgettable," said Ramsay.

The Australian commander also took part in another meeting held in the jungle a few weeks later. The captured war correspondent Rohan Rivett was in the crowd:

> Bits of native sarongs, and odd scraps of material from women's dresses and scarves went to make up jockeys' blouses and caps. A bamboo framework and the linking together of webbing belts produced a totalisator board manipulated by hand, which recorded accurately to the nearest point the current odds on each starter, while hard-working clerks at bamboo tables behind the "windows" dealt with the queues of men anxious to wager their cents on their pals who were running in the race. Bookies' stands with amazing improvised umbrellas, and records sometimes kept on pieces of bamboo, gave us the atmosphere of the ring.
>
> There were "girls" gorgeously dressed from our scanty stock of stage properties—and some of the minxes walked with a roll of the hips that was positively breath-taking. A prize was awarded to Micky Cavanagh as the loveliest "lady." Colonel George Ramsay attended in splendid regalia as the Governor, with the "Governor's Lady" on his arm, while impressive-looking officials bustled about in superb frock coats made from hessian bags—dyed black, with bamboo top-hats and huge rosettes in their buttonholes.
>
> There was a boxing-booth sideshow where boys put the gloves on for a couple of rounds, while vendors with stalls or trays sold peanuts, bits of ginger-root in native sugar, synthetic "coffee" made from burnt rice and other delicacies carefully hoarded for the day from our meagre canteen supplies. In addition, there were taxi men, touts, spruikers, "ladies of joy," professional "urgers" and hangers-on in the best traditions of the racetracks. As these meetings were few and far between—there were only four in three and a half years—betting was terrific and sums equivalent to a month's Japanese pay changed hands over a single race.

"Weary" Dunlop was a "horse" in race meetings at Chungkai. On Christmas Day 1944 there was "a sort of blood match" between "Weary" and Maj. Clive Wallis:

> My odds in the first race, "the Colonel's Sprint," were just fantastic and, as I feared, I flopped. I drew the outside running which was rough and stony. I jumped away to lead and at about half-way hit a rock hard with a bare foot stripping most of the flesh from under a big toe. I rocked in my stride and got my jockey unbalanced just as Good Old Clive Wallis cracked on a tremendous sprint and passed me. I failed to recover the lead and he won by 1–2 feet with the Flying Dutchman, a fine physical specimen, third. (My first and only horseracing defeat.) Clive is a magnificent-looking fellow, aged 31, with a big stubborn jaw, trains like hell, never smokes and is always fit. He is International at rugger, and a fine boxer.
>
> I was determined to win the final race of the day, "The Grand National," a steeplechase event arousing much interest. The first obstacle was a water jump over a large 10-foot drain with a high take-off alighting to a sharply sloping bank. This was followed by a bamboo fence, an atap plain hurdle and a double fence of bamboo. The water jump was approached by a side lane and the course then turned upward towards the crest of a metalled road. I drew the position outside Clive and was faced with losing time on the outside turn into the road, but as it turned out I cleared the water jump with a foot to spare and just ran away from the field, since no one else got clearly over. The Flying Dutchman should have been an easy second but fell at the last fence and Clive came in second after twice losing his jockey. My greatly pleased owner, Lt. Col. Coates, took me along for two impressive restorative "snorts." In the evening we rose to the dignity of a dinner table plus a little more "cup" derived from rice distillate and various sources.

What always intrigued the diminutive Japanese when confronted by the imposing Dunlop, according to the British doctor Flt. Lt. Nowell Peach, was whether the size of his manhood matched his bulk. During an athletics contest in Java their curiosity was finally satisfied. He lost his pants during a hop, skip, and jump—but won with a result of 12.23 meters.

As the Australians celebrated the Melbourne Cup, so one group of British prisoners at Zentsuji marked the annual Oxford-Cambridge rugby match on December 12, 1944. They hoarded rice to make cakes and tidbits for a coffee party and wore light- or dark-blue rosettes. One of the Japanese guards, who had contributed oranges and cigars, revealed that he had been at Cambridge.

Shows, concerts, and games of sport undoubtedly helped to lift morale. According to Swanton, the subject of cricket filled countless hours in pitch-dark huts between sundown and lights-out: "It inspired many a daydream, contrived often in the most gruesome setting, whereby one combated the present by living either in the future or the past."

Chapter 18

INGENUITY

Versatility and ingenuity were key factors in enabling the prisoners to survive. Within every camp there were men with a variety of skills and crafts who were able to pass on their knowledge to their comrades to help them stay alive. Once the worst of the railway-building was over in Thailand, as Capt. Richard Sharp wrote, dumb existence and grudging fortitude were not enough: "Despite the Japs, men were not mere cattle and now creativeness, initiative, enterprise, all long dormant, burst forth. But almost all endeavour was directed to social and useful ends." Practical enterprises predominated—tinsmiths, cobblers, carpenters, cigarette makers—because it was for practical services that payment was made, but ingenuity was also used to maintain some semblance of "respectability" by mending tattered clothing and seeing to haircuts and shaving.

Big camps such as Chungkai and Changi were like small towns, with their own industries and services. Yet, wherever they were in the Far East, and whatever services the men needed—their clothes and shoes mended, cigarettes or rolling paper, soap or candles, shaves and haircuts, an exchange and mart—there were fellow prisoners who could provide them. The men were also always on the prowl for items that could improve their lives: articles of clothing, bottles, tins, and pieces of wire were all treasured. The wire was used for needles or flints. After the war was over, Rolex received one of their watches working perfectly with a bamboo hairspring. Lenses and frames from glasses were collected from the dead and passed on to the living.

A hundred pounds of nails a month were made from lightning-conductor wire. There was no lighting in the huts, so men made small lamps which used string for wicks and burned on coconut oil. The result was bad for the eyes but enabled the men to play chess and bridge, said Lt. David Boddington. There were many small "factories." At Tamuang, for instance, paper was made by mixing bamboo ash with water, adding chemicals, and spreading the resultant "mess," as Lt. Col. "Knocker" Knights described it, thinly over a frame of close wire mesh. The dry mess produced a sheet of paper—although it took many experiments before the first sheet was successfully manufactured. Elsewhere, the main raw material for paper was lalang grass. At Hintok, a water system made from bamboo piped water from a dam several hundred yards to a system of showers and washing points for cooking utensils—and also cooled condensers for a water distillation plant.

At Chungkai there was a barber shop manned by ten or twelve men who gave shaves and cut hair under a stand of mango trees. The senior barber, Sgt. Taylor, had reputedly worked in Hollywood and had been the senior barber at London's Strand Palace Hotel before the war. Each battalion was allocated some free shaves and haircuts, while men earning pay could book ahead. A shave was five cents, a haircut ten. There were tailors and cobblers, the tailor relying largely on the green canvas of tent flaps. There were so many patches on some of the repaired garments that they looked like a jester's wardrobe: Capt. Reginald Burton's shorts boasted thirty-six squares of green patching. Bits of old kit bags were used to patch clothes at Changi, where twenty sewing machines were busy all day.

Coconut fiber with the pith removed was used for toothbrush bristles. Boot polish came from rotten eggs, and soap from wood ash collected from the cookhouses, with tooth powder and milk of magnesia for upset stomachs as by-products. The soap manufacturing process was complex. The wood ash was passed through a series of baths to produce a solution of strong potassium carbonate which was boiled with lime using steam-heated coils, converted to potassium hydroxide, and further concentrated. The used ash was recycled as fertilizer. The concentrated potash solution was used not only for soap but as a degreaser in kitchens and workshops, to make milk of magnesia from seawater, in paper manufacture, and as an anticoagulant for rubber latex. To make soap, the potash solution was steam-heated with palm oil, processed, and run off in molds. The output of the soap factory was prodigious—33,000 pounds of bar soap in the final year of captivity, 320 pounds of shaving soap in eighteen months, and 1,300 pounds of tooth powder in the last nine months, as well as 6,000 sheets of paper.

Cast-off Japanese cotton socks were used for thread. After the cotton was separated, it was starched with rice. Some men did laundry for five cents per article; others did repairs. Shoes and boots were soled with pieces cut from old rubber tires, nailed, sewn, or stuck on with latex collected from the local rubber trees. Lt. John Durnford was the salesman at Chungkai for an organization that sold rawhide sandals. An elderly Australian sergeant known as "Skipper," who had teamed up with a British artillery officer, bought the skins of cattle brought in to feed the camp, stretched them on bamboo frames to cure in the sun, and tanned them with salt and sunlight. The hide was then taken down and cut into soles and sandal thongs. "As in an Indian bazaar, the purchaser's foot was placed on the hide, outlined in pencil, and the 'shape' sewn together in various thicknesses of sole and style, according to the customer's means." There was a jeweler's shop where watches and glasses were repaired. At Nakhon Pathom straw hats were made from the burlap sacks used to transport rice.

It was a source of wonderment to David Boddington how many of the men's needs had been supplied out of practically nothing:

> This life has taught me how little one can manage on and while I realise that these are abnormal times I have learnt much that will be of service later. At the moment I am wearing on my head an old felt hat, round my waist a garment which resembles abbreviated bathing trunks made out of the remnants of an old khaki shirt, and a pair of sandals. It's cool, serviceable and reduces the dhoby [laundry] list to a minimum.

At Nakhon Pathom a "pop shop" was run by the canteen to sell unwanted articles, although British army-issue items were banned in order to stop men from selling their kit. However, many men had private items of kit which they didn't want but which other men needed and were prepared to buy at a reasonable price. 2nd Lt. Robert Reid described how this exchange and mart system worked:

> Supposing I had an enamel mug for sale at $1, I would take it along to the shop and hand it in together with my name, hut number and price required. In exchange they would give me a number and a similar number would be tied on to the mug. Let us suppose that that number was 3985. On the big board outside the canteen on which details of articles for sale were posted daily, the item "one enamel mug $1" would appear under 3985. Every day this list was eagerly scanned by prospective buyers and should a man amongst them require a mug he would go to the counter, ask to see 3985 and if satisfied that he was getting value for his money,

> he would buy it. No. 3985 would immediately be crossed off the list on the sales board. Later in the day I would look at the board to see how my mug was getting on. I would notice that it was crossed off and would know that it was sold. I would, therefore, go to the counter, produce the numbered ticket they had given me previously and would be paid 90 cents—on articles up to the value of $5; above that figure commission was at the rate of 5%. The scheme worked very well. The Japanese kept a close eye on this shop but only in order to make money out of it. Quite 70% of the articles for sale were bought by Japanese and then sold by them to the Thais in the village at about three or four times what they had paid for them at the "pop shop."

Capt. John Barnard created "quite a sensation" at a camp near Hindato in 1944 when he opened his own shop, a central exchange mart to bring sellers with nothing to their names but some spare kit in touch with the several hundred officers in the camp, all with cash but in urgent need of new kit. All items were sold at cost and no profit was made. Barnard took the end bay of a hut, ran up a counter and bamboo hanging rails, and nailed notices on trees around the camp. He was soon running a general store. On the opening day so much stock poured in—towels, razors, bars of soap, hats, penknives, civilian clothing, belts, wallets, mirrors, combs—that he had to make a second counter. He was amazed at what was turned out of kit bags. A man clad only in a few rags would produce a brand-new, snow-white towel. Some of the items Barnard was asked to find for officers included an AA yearbook for someone who wanted to plan his first holiday at home; a technical book on economics; and lead for an automatic pencil. All were found. But sometimes demand exceeded supply and Barnard had to put up notices on the trees asking for items that were much sought after: "Twenty mirrors wanted immediately!"; "Have you two combs? If so why not sell one?"; "Unlimited bootlaces required, must be full length and very strong! Cash waiting."

> "Turnover yesterday exceeded 200 dollars. If you have anything to sell, bring it along now!" The notices meet with a ready response, and I usually obtain what is required, within a few hours. Anyway, it shows that advertising pays even in the centre of a tropical jungle. All this is making quite a lot of work . . . but it is interesting and passes the time. I get a good deal of fun watching the men approaching the shop when they have something to sell. You get one type who walks boldly in and smacks some quite unsaleable article on the counter and says, "Ten dollars, please!" without turning a hair. When you have managed to convince him that it is nearly useless, he replies, "All right, make it fifty cents then!"

> Another type is seen watching the shop from a distance for a day or so, until he musters his courage to enter, and says nervously, "Excuse me, Sir, but do you think you could get me two dollars for these?" holding up a fine pair of home-made woollen socks he has been sleeping on for a year. His face, of course, lights up when you tell him that there should be little difficulty in getting four times that figure, as socks are almost unobtainable.

The main contribution of Barnard's shop to the men's survival was that canteen returns tripled, and the men were buying food that they could not otherwise have afforded.

One of the most remarkable examples of ingenuity occurred in 1944 on the Spice Island of Haruku. The men were working in blinding sunlight to build an airfield from coral, and optical neuritis was causing partial and even complete blindness. (See Chapter 23 for a full account of the horrors of Haruku.) Flt. Lt. Leslie Audus, who had just emerged from the hospital partially blind himself, was urged by Flt. Lt. Dick Philps, one of the medical officers, to start producing yeast to provide the vitamins that were missing from the men's diet. Audus had performed the same function earlier in Jaarmarkt camp at Surabaya on Java. Two Dutch prisoners, Dr. van Papenrecht (who had helped Audus in Jaarmarkt, supplying him with raw materials) and Dr. ten Houten (who had used Audus's methods on Ceram), were asked to join him. Van Papenrecht provided his microscope, hemocytometer, and a supply of reagents for testing for sugar, and allowed Audus and ten Houten to use his "dispensary" for experimenting.

But there was a major problem to be solved. Maize grain had previously been the raw material in the process. But on Haruku no maize was available. Audus's thoughts turned to his preliminary experiments in Surabaya on the use of mold enzymes to produce a nutrient medium from steamed rice. Picking up where he had left off in Java, he soon isolated a mold fungus that was extremely efficient in converting starch into sugar. This mold turned out to be *Rhizopus oryzae,* the species used in the production of *tempeh kedelai.* Audus described how he finally succeeded:

> *Kedelai* is the soya bean which we were sometimes given to eat but long boiling did nothing to make it digestible in the stomach. Dr. Pieters, an Indonesian prisoner arriving with the Amahaiers [Dutch prisoners who had previously been held at Amahai on Ceram], instructed me in the method the natives use to make it digestible by growing a fungus on it producing *tempeh kedelai,* a cheese-like material which was then fried in oil. It is an acquired taste but very nutritious. After we had acquired the

technique we regularly made the product whenever the beans were provided. The prisoners undoubtedly profited from this protein-rich product.

Then followed weeks of crude but intensive tests to determine the growth conditions for the mould on steamed rice and the optimum temperature for the subsequent killing of the mould with release of the effective enzymes. In this, fate and my dormant optimism had played a crucial part since I still had the thermometer I had made in the Jaarmarkt. The optimum temperature for sugar production determined thereby turned out to be 55 degrees C. Thus encouraged we turned our attention to finding the source of the yeast and following that deciding the final method of bulk production and the assembling and construction of equipment for it.

Yeast was easily isolated from the surface skin of a ripe banana by putting a small piece in some rice digest fortified with cane sugar. The fermentation which followed yielded a healthy suspension of yeast cells.

Bulk production started about Christmastime. For the mass production of the essential rice/fungus mixture we simply "stole" the *tempeh kedelai* technique. Wooden trays, with sacking bottoms, were filled with inch-thick layers of steamed rice inoculated with the *tempeh kedelai* fungal spores and sandwiched between layers of large leaves to keep them moist. The fungus was left to grow for 38 to 40 hours, when it had turned the rice layer into a grey, spore-covered "blanket" which could be lifted entire from a tray. A small portion with its spore content was retained, dried and powdered to provide inoculum for subsequent trays. "Blankets" were mashed up with a small quantity of water in a large wooden tub and the resultant "porridge" put in 25-litre earthenware carboys originally containing soya sauce for the guards. To this porridge was added boiling rice-washings to dilute it and bring the temperature up to 60 degrees C. The carboys, closed with sterilised wooden bungs, were incubated for 22 hours in "hot-boxes," old tea chests lined with layers of empty rice sacks, after which up to 80% of the starch had been turned into sugar by the fungal enzymes. The digest, strained through mosquito netting to remove fungal threads and rice cell debris, was diluted with three times its volume of water and sterilised by boiling. After cooling for 22 hours in large steel drums covered with sterile sacks it was inoculated with the yeast culture. The supply of that inoculum had been the province of Dr. ten Houten who had maintained it on a concentrated rice digest fortified with cane sugar.

The final drum fermentation lasted 48 hours and was virtually complete by then, thanks to a massive inoculum. That milky suspension of

> yeast cells was sterilized by heating to 70 degrees C for about 15 minutes in a *wajang* [large iron wok], cooled and issued in 100 ml doses to the hospital patients and, ultimately, to the whole camp. At that time my central retinal scotomata [blind spots] had become so extensive that all microscopic observations and cell counts had to be done by ten Houten. . . . The final yield for the bulk production was 50 to 75 million yeast cells per millilitre. That "medicine" was received with varying degrees of enthusiasm by the prisoners since it was not particularly palatable but, as far as I know, no one rejected it.

When the Japanese discovered his secret activity, Audus was hauled up before Lt. Kurashima, the camp commandant, to explain why rice was being wasted to make alcohol. When Audus explained, tongue in cheek, that sterilization by boiling removed all the alcohol and that the sole aim was to combat avitaminosis, he was excused, on condition that six bottles of the yeast suspension were provided every day for the guards. "This we did for some days until no empty bottles were forthcoming and the Nips had either forgotten their proviso or lost faith in the efficacy of our product," said Audus.

According to Dick Philps, Audus achieved a triumph against seemingly insuperable odds. Almost single-handedly, he saved the eyesight of hundreds of men. No cases of optic neuritis occurred after the men went on the yeast ration. The remarkable story of how Audus, ten Houten, and van Papenrecht created yeast is an inspiring example of how prisoners in Japanese prison camps used their scientific knowledge and ingenuity to triumph over the most squalid and primitive conditions. Audus went on to become a professor of botany at London University after the war.

Chapter 19

THE "CANARIES"

Secret radios, constructed and operated at risk of torture and execution, were a crucial factor in boosting the prisoners' morale. They were operating in camps within the first few weeks of captivity and were an outstanding example of the men's ingenuity. The men in Thailand relied on news broadcasts for their sanity and hope, said one of the operators, Col. John Beckett. After Stalingrad and Tunis they needed desperately to know that the tide of the war had changed. Reliable news from radios also squashed the exaggerated or false "borehole" rumors which were swapped at the latrines. At Ban Pong it was the same ritual every night, said Lt. Eric Lomax: the tense guard around the hut; Sgt. Maj. Lance Thew, the operator, huddled under his blanket; the earnest discussion of the news afterward. "Unfamiliar names on hazily remembered maps: Kharkov, Kursk, the Trobriand Islands. Lines of victory as well as lines of defeat were now connecting us to the world at war." The joy of hearing the news while slaving at the other end of the railway in the Burmese jungle was incalculable, said Rohan Rivett:

> The good news from the world, which seemed incredibly remote to those toiling day long in the dust and heat on cuttings and embankments, came like a great light to pierce our darkness. It brought hope and comfort to weary men, exposed daily to the brutalities and incomprehensive whims of brutal guards; it helped to stiffen morale when we were overwhelmed

> with the hopelessness of our conditions and the calculated inhumanity of our captors.

The radio set in Rivett's camp had been smuggled from Java by LAC Arch Caswell in a bottle from which water flowed normally when it was uncorked. A supply of valves, strapped around his waist inside his belt, had also been smuggled from Java by Don Stuart. It was forbidden to listen to "enemy" broadcasts, but the secret radio enabled the prisoners to follow Montgomery's advance across the Western Desert and the siege of Stalingrad.

When the prisoners had first arrived at Changi, the Japanese had given repeated instructions that all wireless sets were to be handed in. They knew that the camp was receiving news and threatened to cut rations if the order was ignored. Japanese signal trucks with detection apparatus visited the camp but with no success. The source of the news had to be kept secret not only from the Japanese but from fellow prisoners, as idle chatter risked lives. Some prisoners, the Australians found, wanted to boast that they knew who operated the set and who wrote the news bulletin. In the bulletin there was never any mention of radios: the news came from the canary, the nightingale, the dicky bird, the insects, birdsong, the Old Lady, the Box, the dope, or the doovah. When the bulletin bemoaned the lack of "birdseed," there were no batteries to operate the radio.

Capt. James Mudie, who, it will be recalled, later operated the set at Sonkurai, made his first set in Changi. Working secretly, he converted a radio that had been buried for months to work from batteries. A push-bike was pedaled for an hour and a half every day to recharge them. The set was hidden in the eaves and reached through a complicated series of sliding panels in the bathroom ceiling. Mudie and his collaborators converted the duckboard on the bathroom floor so that by reversing it and standing it on end it became a ladder to the secret chamber. When he made another receiver it was erected in the demolished magazine of a six-inch gun battery. He and his collaborators had to crawl down into a dark cavern to get to the set, and they listened to the news among a mass of old six-inch shells and other equipment. They made notes of the news from London and produced a news sheet covering four double-sided pages of foolscap, which was discreetly circulated. About ten bulletins and commentaries were transcribed every day. Each filled two foolscap sheets and was given to the intelligence staff, who at first circulated a typed sheet. As the Japanese grip on Changi increased, however, they reverted to word of mouth instead of paper and developed a cell system to keep identities anonymous.

On August 16, 1942, after sets operated by individual prisoners at Changi had led to the circulation of false rumors, the Australian command entrusted Maj. W. A. Bosley with sole responsibility for their radio and the printing and promulgation of a semi-official daily news bulletin. At first the radio was hidden in an army hatbox underneath a layer of earth and concrete slabs in a urinal or kitchen, but the tropical rain meant that it constantly had to be dried out. They then switched to an electric set that was hidden in a bungalow with plaster walls and ceilings. It was held in a wire cradle, fitted between the rafters by removing roof tiles, and worked by adapting the electrical fixture in the ceiling so that it could be swiveled aside and a screwdriver used to adjust the wavelength and volume.

By April 1943, Bosley's daily bulletin was running to four typewritten sheets, and it became the official publication for the whole camp. (Bosley was assisted by two technicians, L.Sgt. G. F. Noakes and Signaller N. J. Arthur, and by two shorthand-typists, Sgt. F. W. Terry and L.Sgt. A. M. Leahy.) Between 6:30 P.M. and 11 P.M. Bosley would listen in succession to Sydney, the BBC, Chungking, San Francisco, Russia, and Delhi, all the while dictating bulletins. At 11:30 P.M. men from various parts of the camp took delivery of their copy. A system of pickets at various vantage points was set up to warn Bosley of interruptions from the guards. There was a lunchtime reading to men in the hospital or working within the camp and a second reading to those returning from work parties outside the camp. All copies of the bulletin were returned to Bosley at 8 P.M. and immediately burned. The bulletin continued until December, when it was again decided to pass on the news solely by word of mouth: Bosley met two groups at 11:30 A.M. and 12:15 P.M. and read them the bulletins; the rendezvous points were altered daily.

When John Beckett was sent to the Burma–Thailand railway he smuggled the condensers, valves, and resistors for his set to Thailand in tins of bully beef supplied by Harry Cotton, quartermaster of the 2nd Cambridgeshire Regiment. At Chungkai, Beckett met Tom Douglas, a signals lieutenant who had been a BBC engineer and was now making wireless sets in the corner of his bamboo hut using a soldering iron and a fire. He built at least eight sets. When Beckett was moved up country, he left with a radio receiver concealed in a water bottle which could pick up transmissions on the 19- and 25-meter bands. The only other piece of equipment he carried with him was the sawn-off earpiece of a telephone—the radio's speaker—which was usually housed in the toe of a spare boot.

> The arrangements for the operation of our set were very simple and unobtrusive. About 20 torch batteries were required to work the set and were

> placed end to end in a hollow bamboo pillar which appeared to be one of the supports of the hut. The aerial wire was the wire which supported the mosquito net over my bamboo bed. It took only about five minutes to twist wires together and make the set operational while my CO, Col. Mapey, and other officers went outside the hut to watch for sentries. The set had a tendency to emit high-pitched howls from time to time, which was a trifle disconcerting. In daylight there was nothing to see, except my hot-water bottle hanging at the head of the bed. This survived several searches by the Kempetai but we were usually warned of imminent Kempetai searches by the camp guards, who did not love them.

When Beckett returned to Chungkai he handed his set over to the Webber brothers, Max, a captain, and Donald, a lieutenant, both of the Malay Regiment, who operated one of the most successful sets in Thailand. (Both were awarded MBEs at the end of the war.) It was then transported from Chungkai to Tamarkan in the legs of chairs and in bamboo stools, and from Tamarkan to Kanchanaburi in bamboo building poles. On the journey to Tamarkan, under Japanese escort, Max Webber carried a six-month supply of batteries in his army pack. At Chungkai the Webbers' set had been hidden in the quartermaster's store. They had compiled more than seven hundred bulletins while it was operating, which were distributed to other camps using the British drivers who shuttled between them. The news was written on the inside of a cigarette paper after it had been translated into Malay and then transcribed in Tamil script, which could be read by some of the former planters.

At Kuching in Borneo there were three camps—for officers, other ranks, and civilian internees—in close proximity. The news was passed from the men's camp, where the radio was hidden in an empty oil drum under the cookhouse fire, to the civilians, who were separated from the soldiers by a single barbed-wire fence. The civilians then passed the news to the officers. The radio, made by RAF corporal Leonard Beckett, a radar mechanic, was another masterpiece of ingenuity. It was christened "the Old Lady" to maintain security and hidden under the cookhouse fire. The receiver was made from the stolen damper of a Norton motorbike, a coil from a Bakelite soap container, and the variable condenser from a stripped and remodeled biscuit tin. A hearing aid supplied a resistor and valves, a shaving-soap container the high-frequency choke; stolen brass, Bakelite, and wire became a rheostat, while glass and mica purloined from the airfield were used for insulation. Work parties "salvaged" scrap iron, soft Swedish iron, and copper from the docks. Some parts were supplied by Chinese outside the camp who had been contacted at great risk by L.Cpl. George Pringle. They agreed on a deal whereby the parts were exchanged for news. At one stage, Pringle recorded, the news was passed to the women's camp through the intermediary of the Catholic priest who celebrated Mass every morning with the interned nuns and other Catholics. The news was delivered in Latin during the service.

When the electricity supply failed, Beckett built a hand-powered generator, which was christened "Ginnie." The pulley wheel was taken from the aerodrome and a flywheel removed from a Japanese motorbike. (Extra food was allocated to the man who had to turn the gearing mechanism.) It was a tense moment at 8:30 P.M. when the men involved in operating the Kuching radio (including Pringle's comrades Freddie, Alan and Dick) were summoned to the first trial of the generator:

> "Ginnie" could dimly be discerned firmly screwed to a newly erected bench. How had Freddie managed to steal the wood necessary to build it? The illumination, afforded by three tin lids holding a few drops of coconut oil using pieces of rag as wicks, enabled us to see that the two pulley wheels and the lid of the oil drum were in their places and that the piece of Japanese belt that was to do duty as the driving belt was already in place. Alan, looking like some machiavellian monster, was stripped to the waist and standing at the handle which would turn the oil drum lid, this in turn speeding up the smaller pulley wheel and this in its turn forcing "Ginnie" to turn at the required 3000 revs per minute. Dick was standing by with his watch, the only one the Japs had not been able to either steal or buy, ready to give the signal when a radio broadcast could be expected.
>
> We waited with bated breath for this all-important signal, inwardly cursing the slowness of time passing. Suddenly Dick gave Alan a nudge, no words were spoken, and taking a deep breath Alan commenced to turn the oil-drum wheel. I felt, and probably correctly, that history was being made. Rapidly Alan speeded up his mighty efforts, sweat pouring from him in buckets, and "Ginnie" was alive! Len, bent over the knobs of the "Old Lady," gave a thumbs-up signal and then we knew we were back in business. The weeks of waiting, stealing, planning and hard work had not been in vain. All the calculations had been accurately worked out and one of the most audacious enemy-defying schemes ever to be devised was now purring away in absolute triumph.

There were several new "canaries" at Changi after the prisoners returned from building the railway. By now they were adept at hiding them. At one stage the official Australian set was kept in a "dummy" latrine—whenever guards were about, an officer was detailed to sit on it. Another radio was bricked up in a wall cavity in one of the cells. A hole was knocked into the brickwork, the set put inside and connected to a power supply diverted from the cell lighting. A time switch was installed so that the set switched on only at the times of day when BBC news broadcasts took place. The set was then cemented in place. "A four-inch nail was driven through the wall and its tip just touched the diaphragm of a headphone within the wall cavity," said Pte. George Aspinall. "We listened to it with a kind of stethoscope. All you had to do was put the end of a bit of rubber tubing over the head of this nail, and hold it tight with your finger . . . and you could hear the transmission."

Col. George Ramsay, commander of the Australian 2/30th Battalion in Burma, was so impressed by the positive effect of radios on morale that he flouted an order from Brig. Varley, the commander of A Force, to cease the use of Arch Caswell's radio for fear of the torture or death that would be meted out if it were discovered. In one Dutch camp the officer who had operated a secret set had been slowly beaten to death in front of the others. But Ramsay believed that authentic news was the only check to the detrimental effect on morale caused by the "untraceable, wild and unfounded" rumors that were constantly circulating. At a Christmas Eve service he made a speech in code that was understood by the men but not by the Japanese.

> I understand that you have been in the habit of hearing a little bird singing in this camp, but that, coinciding with my arrival to take command here, its song was no longer heard. I am given to understand that this is attributed to me, but I can assure you that is not the case. I do not think my friends would recognise in me one who has any particular influence with our little feathered friends, but I think in this instance I may be able to assist the bird of whom you are so fond to sing once more.
>
> This, however, is dependent upon certain conditions, the first of which is that this bird, which sings with a clear true note, is very timid, and any attempt on the part of any one of you to locate its nest may cause it to cease singing altogether. Any discussion of the tune it sings may also have the same result. The bird I refer to is a nightingale, and must not be confused with the note of another bird which is of Australian origin named the lyre bird. This may not be spelt the same way but it has the same meaning. As you know, it is a mimic and reproduces anything it might hear, whether there is any foundation for it or not. If there is any doubt in your mind at any time as to whether the song you hear is from the nightingale or the lyre bird, any one of your officers—

> who are all keen bird lovers—will be able to set you right. If you observe these conditions rigidly, and do not go on any bird-nesting expeditions, I feel confident that the results will be to everyone's satisfaction.

The danger of discovery and the reason why operators insisted on secure hiding places for sets were brutally demonstrated at Kanchanaburi in August 1943 after a search by Japanese guards uncovered a map, a pair of wireless headphones, and four small wireless sets in various stages of construction. Eleven men suffered the full retribution of the Japanese. They were forced to stand at attention in the blazing tropical sun for twelve hours at a time, some for four successive days. Then they were given iron sledgehammers and made to hit a block of wood, hour after hour. When they collapsed they were brought to their feet and forced to continue. One of the victims was Eric Lomax, who watched the beating given to Maj. Bill Smith:

> A hefty Japanese sergeant moved into position, lifted his pick-handle, and delivered a blow across Smith's back that would have laid out a bull. It knocked him down, but he was trodden on and kicked back into an upright position. The same guard hit him again, hard. All the thugs now set to in earnest. Soon little could be seen but the rise and fall of pick-helves above the heads of the group and there were sickening thuds as blows went home on the squirming, kicking body, periodically pulled back on to its feet only to be knocked down again. Bill Smith cried out repeatedly that he was fifty years of age, appealing for mercy, but to no avail. The group of attackers seemed to move in concert with their crawling, bloodied victim into the darkness beyond the range of the miserable lighting from the guardroom, but the noises of wood on flesh continued to reach us from the dark of the parade ground. They were using pickaxe-shafts, like solid, British Army–issue handles, and perhaps that is indeed what they were. The guards behind us did not move. There was no expectation that we ourselves would move, intervene, run away: merely the slack, contemptuous knowledge that we were trapped.

Then it was Lomax's turn:

> I was called forward. I stood to attention. They stood facing me, breathing heavily. There was a pause. It seemed to drag on for minutes. Then I went down with a blow that shook every bone, and which released a sensation of scorching liquid pain which seared through my entire body. Sudden blows struck me all over. I felt myself plunging downwards into

> an abyss with tremendous flashes of solid light which burned and agonized. I could identify the periodic stamping of boots on the back of my head, crunching my face into the gravel; the crack of bones snapping; my teeth breaking; and my own involuntary attempts to respond to deep vicious kicks and to regain an upright position, only to be thrown to the ground once more.
>
> At one point I realized that my hips were being damaged and I remember looking up and seeing the pick-helves coming down towards my hips, and putting my arms in the way to deflect the blows. This seemed only to focus the clubs on my arms and hands. I remember the actual blow that broke my wrist. It fell right across it, with a terrible pain of delicate bones being crushed. Yet the worst pain came from the pounding on my pelvic bones and the base of my spine. I think they tried to smash my hips. My whole trunk was brutally defined for me, like having my skeleton etched out in pain.

When the beating finished, both of Lomax's forearms were broken, several ribs cracked, one hip damaged, and there was no white skin visible between his shoulders and his knees: it had turned blue-black and was swollen and puffy. The others were in a similar condition.

Another four men—including 2nd Lt. Jack Hawley and Lt. Stanley Armitage—were the next to be arrested. According to an eyewitness account by the interpreter who accompanied them, Armitage was ordered to strip to his shorts and to hold his arms above his head:

> The whole area was dark except for a dim light thrown by two hurricane lamps and a flash lamp. He was then assaulted by the whole mob of Japanese simultaneously, armed with heavy split and round bamboos. After about forty blows on the back, buttocks and thighs he was violently tripped up from the front and thrown on his back. He was then turned over and the beating continued on the ground, usually about three Japanese striking him simultaneously. He was dragged along the ground by the legs across the area which was covered with gravel. Hawley was led out, stripped and treated similarly, the punishment being accompanied by all manner of insults in English shouted by Kanematsu and Komi, who were both present during the whole proceedings and who had obviously been drinking heavily.
>
> Armitage was the first to lose consciousness, but was soon revived by kicks in the back and stomach and buckets of water, which were thrown over him. He was forced to his feet and the punishment continued. He

> fell down repeatedly and had to be held up by the Japanese. Finally he was beaten senseless while lying on the ground, after having been dragged about all over the place on the gravel. Simultaneously Hawley was receiving the same treatment and was dragged across the area and flung into a deep anti-malarial drain with about a foot of mud in the bottom, where he was ordered with kicks and blows to get out; but by this time his legs had become paralysed from the repeated blows and he was unable to move. Finally he was dragged out and the beating continued once more. Apart from a few involuntary grunts when blows fell on his kidneys, Armitage made practically no sound at all. Hawley's last remarks were a wholehearted cursing of the Japanese for their bestiality.

Both men died during the night and their bodies were thrown into the guardroom latrine. The others were delivered to the Kempetai, tortured, and tried. They were sentenced to between five and ten years in Singapore's Outram Road Jail.

Fear of detection naturally increased after word of these beatings spread through the camps. But still the radios operated. By 1945 the set at Laurens van der Post's camp in Java was so small that it could be hidden in a pair of wooden clogs, made slightly bigger and thicker than normal, with the transformer in one, and the receiver in the other's toe, with the earphones in the heel. Another was concealed inside an accordion. At Surabaya, the American "Buck" Buchanan made a radio and hid it inside his tin leg. When he had access to electricity, he took off his leg and plugged it in.

There were some sweet moments for the operators after Japan surrendered when they were at last able to reveal their sets to the Japanese camp commandants. At Kanchanaburi, still maintaining the pretense that they had no radio, the officers asked Capt. Noguchi, the Japanese commandant, for a wireless set to hear the news. He refused, so they asked his permission to procure their own set. It had been secreted in Noguchi's luggage, which he himself had carried into the camp.

Chapter 20

OFFICERS AND GENTLEMEN

Men without officers were dead men, said Lt. Col. Francis Dillon, the savior of No. 2 Camp, Sonkurai. Dillon was a regular officer and a martinet, but he was admired because he led from the front and stood by his men. There is no doubt that the example set by such officers as Dillon and the Australian commander "Black Jack" Galleghan, with their insistence on maintaining discipline even in the hellish conditions of Japanese prison camps, helped raise morale and save lives. Many officers, however, did not conduct themselves in the same way as Dillon and Galleghan, and there were also significant contrasts in the behavior of the British, Australian, and American officers.

The Australians and Americans who started arriving at Changi in September 1942 were shocked by the attitudes and behavior of the British officers. The new arrivals found that they were much more informal and democratic than the British. When Lt. Col. "Weary" Dunlop led his "Java rabble" into Changi he was astonished to see neatly dressed British officers carrying canes, blowing out puffy mustaches, and talking in an "old chappy" way. His reaction was shared by other Australian prisoners: Gunner Russell Braddon, for example, thought that the aim of the British was to preserve the distinction between officers and other ranks through as many tactless and unnecessary orders as could be devised. He found that officers could not freely mix with their friends who were other ranks, nor vice versa. Other ranks were compelled to salute officers whom they had seen cowering in terror at the bottom of a slit trench, as well as those who had done a good job. The men were compulsorily stripped of clothing which—at their own discretion and on their own backs—they had carried to Changi, so that these garments might be distributed to officers who—though they did not work—must, it was deemed, at all times be well dressed. Far from waiting till their men ate and then eating the same food themselves, Braddon observed that officers ate in a separate mess and usually before the men. Officers were allowed to keep poultry; other ranks were not. There was fuel for an officers' club to cook light snacks; for the other ranks there was not.

> One day some British other ranks were charged with a completely trivial breach of regimental discipline and—to our universal astonishment—sentenced to cells and only one meal a day. There being no cells available they were incarcerated in a filthy wooden shed. There being no room in our lives for such nonsense, we tore the shed down, released the prisoners and used the timber for firewood.

When Chief Petty Officer Ray Parkin's Australian party left Changi on January 19, 1943, their commanding officer wrote a bitter parting message to his brigadier: "Two weeks ago my men arrived in a pitiful condition in this camp from Java. You have done nothing to alleviate their needs—tomorrow at 8.30 they leave in the same pitiable condition: bootless and in rags. You have done nothing."

The contrast in the behavior of the British and Australians was noted throughout captivity. The British medical officer Capt. "Pop" Vardy observed at Tarsao during the building of the railway:

> Not only could the Australians rough it better than the British but they were much friendlier. There was a more pleasant spirit about their mess, amongst the officers, amongst the men and between the officers and men. Their CO is friendly—they all chat together, laugh and play the fool—yet he is undoubtedly their CO and if the time calls for it they jump to it (I have seen it time and time again) while in our mess there is a bloody barrier almost everywhere you turn. There is hardly any general conversation—just in little groups. We get secret letters sent round the mess telling us how we should behave towards ORs—Ye Gods, such piffle at times like these and when after all, we are all POWs—no, we are so frightfully frightfully British don't you know, while they (the Aussies) are bloody good fellows.

The Australians often balked at the attitudes of their own officers, but pompous British officers were easier targets. L.Cpl. George Pringle described the day when a fiery British regimental sergeant major stormed into the barrack room and suggested the men should jump out of bed:

> Unknown to the RSM we have Australians in our group. "Get on him Bert." "Blimey mate, does your Mother know you're out?" "How about him Willy?" "Ugly looking bastard ain't he?" And a few more very choice epithets guaranteed to raise the blood pressure of even the mildest of RSMs. This particular RSM cannot be described as mild. Now he is raging mad and threatening dire vengeance. We are in a state of near mutiny and I think he realises the moment is near at hand when even his commanding presence will be at risk. Using words even Arthur would wish to know and our General has yet to hear, the Australians force the RSM to retreat. Peace reigns again.

Younger subalterns were more adept at getting on with the Australians. Lt. Donald Wise, another prisoner who, like Pringle, became a journalist after the war, described the mocking reception he was given when put in charge of an Australian working party—and how he snatched victory from imminent defeat:

> In those days I wore a big moustache and the first time I went on parade there were about fifty or sixty of these Australians lined up with their big hats, and stripped to the waist. I walked on parade. I didn't see anybody move his mouth, but a voice said, "What is it?" and I thought, "They are going to stand me up." Another voice said, "I don't know, never seen one like this before." And then a third voice said, "Jesus, do you reckon it fucks?" I thought, "Well, do I stamp my tiny lieutenant's foot and get angry or do I laugh or what the hell do I do?" This was an impossible situation which I'd never learnt about in officers' school. Finally a voice said, "Looks like a rat peering through a broom." Now all this, I may say, was from men who apparently weren't moving their mouths. They were just talking like ventriloquists. . . . But they were getting the stuff over. When he said, "Looks like a rat peering through a broom," I just fell about laughing; I just roared. Of course it saved the day. If I'd started shaking my little finger at them I think all would have been lost. That was my opening gambit with Australian soldiers and from then on we got on fine.

The Americans were equally shocked by the snobbery of the British officers, though it was the English, the "limeys," whom they singled out, strutting around with swagger sticks, demanding military courtesy and formal salutes, even having their men do pack drill for punishment—all this in a Japanese prison camp. H. Robert Charles was horrified that British officers could wear their rank and "parade and preen" in full uniform as though they still owned Singapore. "We Americans could barely believe our eyes as we watched British soldiers stand to attention and salute their own officers, the officers actually prancing around expecting it," he remembered.

Many Americans interviewed after the war accused the British officers of treating their men like dirt, and thought that they wanted to treat American soldiers the same way. But the Americans refused to play the British game: they would make as if to salute officers and then scratch their heads or pretend to swat a fly; they raided the officers' chicken coops. On one occasion they stole, skinned, cooked, and ate a British dog—a mascot that had been in combat with the RAF at Dunkirk and Crete. When an RAF officer went to complain, the Americans refused to apologize: the British were feeding their dogs instead of Americans, they said. "Americans are cannibals," the British officer said disgustedly.

British other ranks reacted to their officers' self-regard by showing their usual bolshiness, said George Pringle:

> Fail to salute an officer, and before you can say "Jack" your name is in the book and you are charged with the serious crime of "failing to salute an officer." This can mean seven days' "jankers" [punishment cells] with all the resultant loss of privileges—and all this in a prisoner of war camp. One outcome of all this saluting nonsense is Changi now resembles nothing more than a tic-tac man on a day's outing to his local racecourse. Everyone salutes everyone. It is much safer that way. We have great fun. The officers do not approve.

The British insisted on distinctions of rank from the start. Gen. Percival and his staff described themselves as the Malaya Command. As Lt. Robin Fletcher observed, Malaya Command established a "correct distance" between themselves and "lesser mortals" by creating a separate staff area within Changi and descending hierarchies below Command HQ:

> All the old staff wallahs rushed to find themselves new staff appointments. These gentlemen solemnly paraded the streets wearing armbands and emanated an air of great importance. Their new job might be the rather humble one of being Staff Office i/c Dustbins or digging of bore-holes, but they would gather together a large subsidiary staff of

> majors and subalterns, and by keeping these as a buffer between themselves and the sordid trivialities of their job they would keep up the illusion of self-importance and support their self-esteem.

Such attitudes endured among some officers even when they were building the Burma–Thailand railway. When Lt. John Durnford arrived at Tarsao in 1943 he found that it was in danger of becoming an Aldershot in the jungle. Saluting was practiced, as was the blowing of reveille and retreat. There were officers' compounds, officers' huts, officers' messes, dinners, bathing, even—the "final absurdity"—officers' latrines. Not content with isolating themselves by notice boards of the "officers only" variety, many huts were further sheltered by enclosures of palm-thatched walls at their entrances. "Within these, officers took the evening air rather as they might on the veranda of a permanent station mess. No doubt many of these arrangements were good for morale, but under such unconventional surroundings they struck the more cynical of us as slightly comical."

But life could be trying for redundant senior officers. A colonel who had no camp or regiment to command had to decide whether to remain with his own kind or become one of the boys. The former solution required a communal job like cutting wood, manning a pump, pounding peanuts into butter, or digging latrines. 2nd Lt. Stephen Alexander had some sympathy with their plight:

> To go out on working parties or to do the nastier camp jobs with junior officers and other ranks required a flexibility many did not have. Those who could not be included in the communal jobs and were too windy to join general working parties tended to seek niches in which to ensconce themselves or, if the worst came to the worst, nurse some recurrent ailment. The niches would consist of hospital visiting, "keeping records"—a useful catch-all—or a sudden vocation for Christian mission.

Many officers certainly found themselves cushy "niches." At Tonchan, Capt. Stanley Pavillard found one of the "biggest and most shameless Jack Clubs" he had ever had the misfortune to meet: "The place was full of officers who sat around on their fat behinds and did nothing either for the men or for the hygiene and decency of the camp; they played bridge, they ran sly rackets for food and then lit fires to cook little meals for themselves, and they cared damn-all about arriving parties, and least of all about the helpless sick." When Capt. Richard Sharp arrived at Chungkai from the railway in 1944, the hospital stank and skeletons walked with swollen bellies among the ten thousand prisoners. Not all the men were emaciated, however:

> Beside the wrecks left over from the railway, there were those who had never seen the railway, never seen an angry Nip. More or less fit, more or less youthful, by some plea or other, sickness or some secure job, they had avoided the up-country parties, and had stood aside to let older and sicker men go. Now they sat back in comfort, living only for the satisfaction of their own desires. "This place isn't what it used to be. The standard of the canteen stuff's going down terribly—and you can't get near the place nowadays—all these people from up-country, crowding it out and buying it all up. Oh! I know, old boy, you had a toughish time. Pretty foul was it? You know, it was grim down here too. Why during the floods, when there weren't any canteen supplies—we didn't get eggs for three whole days!" But luckily his type was comparatively rare, and most of them had considered Chungkai too near the railway by far, and had got themselves evacuated still further down country. You couldn't, after all, expect self-sacrifice: with self-interest so blatantly ubiquitous.

Many British soldiers shared the resentments of the Australians and Americans. Thomas Evans, a British private with the Singapore Volunteer Corps, had assumed that the men would lead a communal life for their mutual protection and well-being. He was soon disabused:

> Despite all their cant about discipline—that hackneyed caste creed of the British army—no attempt was made by our officers to institute this way of living. Their failure to set any decent sort of example was in tune with the high-handed behaviour of these so-called gentlemen in our civilian clubs before the war, and with the half-truth legend that the Battle of Malaya was lost in the ballrooms and bars of Raffles and Tanglin. Such men must expect to receive from their men the abounding adverse criticism—much of it erroneous and malicious—which is now flung at them.

Some British officers agreed with Evans. According to Capt. Ronald Horner, who had arrived in Singapore only seventeen days before the surrender, it was unpleasant but true that life as a prisoner of war turned formerly decent officers, particularly among the field rank, into "selfish, mean and unscrupulous" beings who would stop at nothing as long as their own ends were satisfied.

The men's diaries contain repeated references to the conduct of officers, most but not all written by young officers in their twenties. Surrender and defeat stung all ranks, and the officers who had led the men to defeat became the target upon which they could vent their sense of shame. The ranks of

British officers had been swollen by surplus officers from the Indian Army who had been separated from their men, and by civilians employed on war work who had been given commissions by the Governor of Singapore. Among the Australians in 8th Division, many officers had been appointed in 1940: they were teachers, bank and insurance clerks, salesmen, and lawyers who had the education to pass military examinations. Some became excellent officers, but when they failed, resentful men tended to see them as the privileged who had never earned their rank.

There was a strong argument for maintaining military discipline in a prison camp holding up to fifty thousand men. The officers had been as shocked as the men by the surrender of Singapore, a defeat as traumatic to the British psyche as the unexpected resistance of the Boers or the Indian Mutiny. They had been abandoned by London and defeated by the despised "Nips." Any sacrifice of the natural order would represent a complete collapse of standards, they believed. Democratization would lead to anarchy.

As Sibylla Jane Flower, the most authoritative scholar of the Burma–Thailand railway, has written, no one who saw the desolation of the Asian laborers' camps doubted that there was an advantage in being part of a predetermined military order—which the Japanese accepted and were prepared to work through. Maintaining discipline was the greatest factor in preserving life, said "Weary" Dunlop. Discipline was never questioned when officers set an example in "unselfish devotion" to duty. The British and Australian commanders—who probably could not have realized that their captivity was to last for so long—also believed that they might be called upon to attack their captors if Allied forces invaded Singapore. The men therefore needed to be kept in readiness.

Yet the evidence of the diaries, albeit written in the heat of the moment, suggests that a significant minority of the officer class, particularly among the British but also among the Australians, failed to meet the high standards demanded by their rank (although Flower believes that the vital role of officers has been subordinated in most published accounts). According to the men, too many officers adopted the attitude, "Fuck you, Jack, I'm all right" (though the diaries, written in the 1940s by gentlemen, usually utilize asterisks). The men also complained about the higher pay given to officers, which meant that they did not suffer to the same extent as the men. At Changi the officers could buy tinned food and cigarettes. "How many times, watching a cricket match, have we worked our way behind the officers' chairs, avidly watching the smoke rise, and pouncing hungrily on the cigarette end flung so carelessly away?" asked John Brown. What was wrong about the behavior of the worst officers was captured in a comment made by Dunlop, an exemplary officer, when some of his fellow Australian officers had refused to contribute a portion of their pay to a fund to help the sick in Java in 1942. There was opposition to the scheme from officers who thought that some troops were not worthy of being given officers' money as they had not been sufficiently grateful for money given to them previously. "This is magnificent—it seems that an officer's duty is something which is only carried out if the troops are worth attention! The idea is that officers retain their money and help the worthy troops independently (buying gratitude)," wrote Dunlop. Two days later, the argument was still raging. Were officers going to contribute or did they want to lead out eventually a regiment of crippled and broken men? asked Capt. Macnamara. Dunlop concluded the meeting by saying he would write to each officer personally, requesting donations at the level recommended:

> I left this melancholy affair in almost the lowest frame of mind imaginable and disgusted at the light in which Australian officers had been shown. Imagine, after a clear statement of the miserable health of the troops and low finances, to head a discussion by officers as to whether they would give the help required. Where is that principle "my horse, my men, myself"? The leadership in this matter is disgusting.

One British officer who was miffed by the deduction of pay for the sick was 2nd Lt. John Milford at Chungkai. Out of his monthly pay of $30, his hospital contribution was now increased from $10 to $15, which meant that a total of $22 vanished after deductions for soap, haircuts, clothing, toothpaste, and other items. "I shall have to dismiss my batman as I cannot possibly afford to pay him 1d a day," he wrote in his diary. His batman fetched food, cleaned his dishes, washed his clothes, and fetched his bathwater.

The British lieutenant colonel "Knocker" Knights agreed that it was a "bit hard" to deduct pay from officers but was a strong proponent of the scheme. When the Japanese discovered what was being done to help the sick, he was ordered to stop, but he persuaded his senior officers to disobey the order, even though they knew the penalties if their disobedience should be discovered. He gave them a deserved pat on the back: "I have often wondered whether this action on the part of officers was sufficiently realised and appreciated. To give up a third of one's pay, especially in those awful circumstances, was no mean sacrifice. To me it has always been an outstanding example of real charity."

There were notorious examples of selfishness among the officers, says Flower, but the Territorials, who had not spent their careers in the army, were generally much more selfless. It was largely because of subscriptions from the officers that Lt. Cols. Philip Toosey at Tamarkan and Cary Owtram at Chungkai were able to finance their hospitals.

British and Australian officers, for all their generosity with money, remained convinced that decent clothes were theirs by right, whereas the men could do without. In Changi in April 1944, Sgt. Stan Arneil noted that many of the men who worked every day were reduced to a single pair of shorts each. Yet when clothing arrived, officers were allowed three pairs of shorts, two pairs of pants, two pairs of boots, one pair of shoes, and four pairs of socks. "Men without socks are unable to be issued until officers who do not need them so much are issued with four pairs," said Arneil. "I give you this as it stands. We are asked to be loyal to our leaders and I do not discuss these things with the troops."

One commendable reason for such commandeering, argued Robin Fletcher, was to spread what clothing there was around and to make stealing and selling more difficult:

> Many officers—those who had never left Changi—were still in possession of almost peace-time wardrobes, and these gentlemen made a furious fuss over having to help their less fortunate brethren. They even proposed that they should be allowed to sell the items they had in excess of the scale laid down. As one whose clothes had been reduced to rags in Thailand while the would-be profiteers had never got off their backsides in Changi, I felt a little bitterly about such a proposal. However, the Powers-that-were refused to countenance such a shameless proceeding and excess clothing was removed without compensation. Even then there were senior officers (one of them a Padre) who approached junior officers whose clothing was below the scale laid down, and tried to "lend" them their excess blankets which were due for confiscation.

Officers such as these were the subject of a parody of Wordsworth's "Upon Westminster Bridge," written in Changi in 1944:

> "The Stars in Their Quarters"
> (With apologies to William Wordsworth)
>
> *Earth has not anything of stranger sort;*
> *Dull would he be of soul who could pass by*
> *This sample sad of seniority,*
> *That now in coolie quarters must support*
> *The dignity of rank. With torsos bare,*

Lieutenant-Colonels, Majors, Captains see
Sitting and staring into vacancy
Or playing Patience with a serious air.
Yet ne'er did sun on such a galaxy
Of Warriors shine in Mess or Club or Bar;
Ne'er saw I, never met a Company
So justly famous in the arts of war.
Rude homes cannot obscure their valiancy—
These are the Samurai of Singapore.

Some officers were too intent on maintaining class distinctions with the other ranks, too apathetic, or so devastated by their experiences that they lost the will to lead. Their upbringing, schooling, and years of service in the army meant that officers who had been born in the nineteenth century or during the reign of Edward VII were incapable of thinking differently in the new circumstances of Changi. The officers' ranks were still cluttered by many pre-1914-minded old gentlemen who had complete power, said Lt. John Coast. Some British commanding officers were adequate, some were excellent—but a few were vicious. They might have charm, honor, and simplicity to their credit, but such qualities were useless when dealing with the Japanese:

> On the debit side they had that narrow Regular [army] outlook, bounded by the Prep. School, the Public School and, above all, by pre-war Sandhurst, and were quite invincibly stupid; sometimes, because they just could not cope with the Nip dishonesty of mind, they behaved in a way that looked as if they were afraid. Now no one disliked these charming, empty-headed old boys as men; but as our leaders against the Nips, they were terrible. Some of them must have known their incompetency and they should have resigned in favour of younger people; this I never knew one of them to do. One of the younger element was a certain Major Woolley, who was a Major at the age of 23, and had a great deal of character and intelligence. Woolley was now ordered directly to work under the Nips; and Woolley, because he was convinced that this was weakness, flatly refused to do so. He was then court-martialled, and though he was only reprimanded, the camp authorities regarded him as an absolute four-letter man; the younger generation were very grateful to him as a balancing influence to the good.

Lt. Stanley Gimson found that some officers in the 1st Indian Heavy Anti-Aircraft Regiment were out of their depth in a situation to which they were incapable of adjusting. They had lived in a world apart, in which they each had a batman and dressed for dinner, with regimental silver on the table, and had been raised almost from school days in the military setup. That setup had run for most of their careers on regular lines with no enemies in sight.

> We had a captain, in my regiment, who was nominated for one of the overseas parties and he was told to pack up his kit and it would be collected one evening. And he came to a group of us, "What do you think, chaps, will we be changing for dinner?" And he wanted to put his "not wanted on voyage" stuff away, but his dinner jacket and black tie or his blue patrols accessible. And we indicated to him he might or might not get dinner, and he might or might not have any clothes on at the time.

Alternatively, the officers could be apathetic. At Konyu, Dunlop was horrified by the sight of the British commander and his senior officer dressed in pajamas and sarongs, "unshaven or bearded, sallow and dull of eye, full of a sort of hopeless depression." Sometimes they were simply not up to the job. George Ramsay led the thousand men of "Ramsay Force" to Burma, where they were joined by five hundred British troops from Sumatra. He found the latter "poorly officered": the officers were inexperienced and had no idea of how to control their troops, who were more "troublesome" than the Australians, Ramsay thought. Many of the British men preferred to be paraded before him when charged with disciplinary offenses. "I give them a good verbal kick in the tail, fire them or send them to detention, if I am satisfied they deserve it, and then talk to them like a Dutch uncle."

Richard Sharp, acting as adjutant to a party of 120 men after they had built the Wampo embankment, marched twelve miles to Tarsao, where they were met by a "beautiful" Indian army officer in smart uniform with polished brasses, only to find a bleak welcome:

> He was sorry there was no room for us in the camp, most unfortunately it was almost full, and we'd have to camp down in the wood—tents would be provided, of course, if we put them up—yes, it was a pity the site was so dirty, the people before us hadn't dug latrines, if we wouldn't mind digging some latrines somewhere, it would be so much nicer. Of course, we would be cooking for ourselves, their cookhouses wouldn't be able to cope, and their officers' messes were naturally designed only for small numbers. That's probably all—if you want anything, can you just ask the Sgt. Major, I'm rather busy these days, don't you know?

Sixty years later, men who were the young prisoners and who led distinguished careers after the war still vividly recall the conduct of their officers. What the celebrated artist Jack Chalker remembers most is the "eternal pettiness and bullshit and stupidity" of the British Army. Chalker did not argue with the need for discipline, intelligently implemented, only with the "demoralising" excess of it. He had been at Konyu for some months with seven British officers who had behaved bravely when a large group of officers, including brigadiers, arrived. The latter were put in a camp a short way down river:

> They ordered our officers to join them, our little group who had been with us up country, and had marched up country with us. Our own group flatly refused and said they would be staying with their men, and they were put on a court martial, as stupid as that! There were two or three high-ranking officers with the new officers' group and we hated the bloody sight of them. We all had avitaminosis, malaria, dysentery and were very ill. I was down at the water's edge with a man who could just about stand and we were trying to get some water in the 2-gallon containers and one of these idiots, I think it was a brigadier, came up and yelled at this man because he wasn't standing to attention. He was damned nearly dead and I remember telling the brigadier to get stuffed. This was the kind of lunacy we had to stomach sometimes from these idiots and we wanted nothing whatever to do with them.

Capt. John Stewart Ullman found remarkable the seeming inability of many officers to feel pity for their men:

> Pity (as I think Rousseau pointed out) is a selfish sentiment in so far as it's a reflection of the pain I myself might be feeling under those circumstances. In so far as officers would have thought, "As a prisoner I am suffering that pain too, why should I feel compassion or pity for the ORs?" Natural selfishness well buttressed by the British pre-war caste system locked the feeling well in place.

It was not surprising that the men bridled at the lack of sensitivity of some officers. Ray Parkin described how at Konyu his group of Australians went from breakfast to their evening meal without being issued a drink. They were being punished because some men had not returned a couple of tins to the cookhouse after breakfast. The officer was jeered and invited to join them at work in the afternoon sun. Then, at the evening counting parade, they suffered a long harangue from an adjutant telling them they didn't live up to his idea of parade-ground soldiers.

> Standing like a ramrod and talking like a Guards' major on a peace-time barrack square, dapper and clean shaven, in khaki drill which his batman had washed, he criticized men who had worked all day in the heat and dust. He went further and nagged them about "disgusting habits in the latrines." Now many men with dysentery spend much of their waking time in weary, weakening pilgrimages and sometimes take books for simple distraction. This was the "disgusting habits" he was alluding to. He would not be surprised, he said, if some men took their meals there!

Some of the most damning criticism was made by older officers who had served in the First World War. The Australian major Hugh Rayson was fifty-one in 1942 and had won the Military Cross in France in 1916. He noted the disloyalty of field officers to Lt. Col. A. W. Walsh, the commanding officer in Borneo. The "old school tie" brigade, the very men he expected to stand firm and set an example, repeatedly failed to do so. The officers who were most helpful were often men who had not been to a good school or university. "One recalls Ruskin's statement 'Nothing but the guilt of the upper classes, wanton, accumulated, reckless and merciless can overthrow them,'" said Rayson.

Some officers unwittingly condemned themselves from their own mouths. At Kinsaiyok some of the men were so disgusted by their food—poorly cooked, broken rice, full of dead maggots and grit, covered with a weak seaweed soup—that they took an example of it down to the "private" quarters of the most senior officer, an Englishman. Among their number was 2nd Lt. Geoffrey Pharaoh Adams, who reported the officer's reaction:

> He looked at it without speaking, turned round and walked to his bamboo table, and brought back a mess tin full of tinned pilchards in tomato sauce. "I am not complaining," he said, "I am eating well enough!" He could have said, "F—— you Jack, I'm all right!" He was, it is fair to say, a rare bird in Thailand, and his neck was only secure due to the decency and discipline of the British Tommy.

When officers at Kuching were told one morning that they were not required for work, they cheered in front of the men. "A very sorry show from a few British officers, indicative of the complete lack of interest they have in their men," Flt. Lt. Peter Lee noted. One Royal Artillery captain said that he didn't give a damn about his men—they didn't seem to care about him and would not do anything he told them. "This cannot be the type of officer they have at home," said Lee.

One dying man asked if he could see his commanding officer. It was a little awkward, said the colonel. He was playing bridge. The man died the next day. One common anecdote is of the officer whose response to the news that two fingers of a fellow officer's right hand had been shot away was "Ah well, it won't affect him—he doesn't shoot."

A few officers reveled in invitations to dine with the Japanese commanders. At Kuching Sqn. Ldr. Hardie, who sat around all day in a sarong, was nicknamed Big Chief Sitting Bull because of it, and objected to giving money to the sick, led a group of twenty-five officers to sup with the enemy. They put on their best khaki drill, polished their boots and Sam Brownes, and looked anxiously at their puttees.

> They duly turned out at 8.45 a.m., 25 in all, headed by Sqn. Ldr. Hardie and Capt. Mills, and including the Padre and the 2 Doctors, and were marched off down the road like a crowd of school-kids going off on a Sunday School outing. They returned about 1 p.m. They had been taken to a 2-storeyed wooden building near the main Jap Guard Room, and shown upstairs to a room which had been decorated with paper streamers—more Sunday School stuff—and with a long trestle table on which were bananas, pineapples, doughnuts, and toffee, coffee etc. No Jap turned up so they all moved in, being served by a native. When they had had enough they were told the charge was 75 cts. each, and marched back. Prior to going in they had had to do a mass salute for a Jap 2nd Lt. who came out specially for the purpose. I naturally did not attend. I wonder if these people ever had any pride of race: if they are typical of the 20th century Britisher, then God help us.

The division of food was a constant source of friction. One embittered soldier, shrivelled and sick, was visited by a senior officer who had just enjoyed a meal of meat with the commandant. He cursed the officer in soldier's terms: "If I fucking die, I'll fucking haunt you, you fucking bastard."

Yet only a small minority among the officers "shed all decency in their concern with self-preservation," said Gen. Clifford Kinvig, the historian of the Burma–Thailand railway. As he argued, only group cohesion could have ensured group survival. 2nd Lt. Robert Reid, who was there, agreed. Many regular officers were brainless asses, leftovers of a long-outdated social system, he said, but they were a minority and there were as many layabouts—if not more—among the men as among the officers:

> Being mixed up with the men, living with them, and since we were all in the same mess, we tried to forget about rank. The men accepted the leadership of the officers and the NCOs. They had been trained to do so. In any event, these were the best people to get things organised. That was their job. The NCOs still had a sharp edge to their tongues for anyone who stepped out of line, but rarely had to use it. The men of the Regiment were a sensible lot and as good-humoured as could be expected in these conditions. There are better ways to get things done than by issuing orders.

In conditions of such adversity, good officers did not have to pull rank to maintain order and discipline. All the accounts by men who were on Haruku speak of the good relationship between officers and men because the RAF officers believed that they had to earn respect rather than demand it. Although the officers on the island bemoaned that saluting, army punishment, and army bull had been forgotten, said LAC Don Peacock, the fact that they were no longer officers and men but fellow prisoners with a common enemy created a friendly atmosphere between ranks that more than compensated for the slavish obedience that had been lost. As Flt. Lt. Dick Philps put it, they had to behave as a coordinated group if they were to survive:

> Had there been any cracking of discipline within the camp itself, heaven knows what would have happened and it was greatly to the credit of the vast majority that there was not. It is usually considered that, to impose discipline, there must be some system of punishments. Clearly in our situation that was not possible nor, fortunately, was it necessary. The Japanese had informed us that anybody requiring punishment was to be handed over to them. This was quite unthinkable, so discipline was maintained by a combination of two things: the fact that nearly everybody realised that they had to conform if the camp was to run at all and perhaps an appreciation by the men that the officers, insofar as they had authority, were trying to help. Order had to be kept by the officers without any divine right of authority at all. Perhaps the most vitally important factor was that we knew each other, liked each other and stood together.

Capt. John Barnard in Thailand was critical of some officers but believed that most of the men appreciated that they were better off living with officers in the camp than if the officers were separated from them. Officers could help the men financially and act as at least a slender buffer between them and the Japanese. There was some respect for rank among the Koreans, and officers who had learned some Japanese were especially helpful. Morale was kept higher, sickness reduced, and many lives saved because officers were allowed to stay with their men, said Capt. William Drower.

Nor was a decent officer's lot an easy one, as Sgt. Peter Hartley discovered in Sumatra when he had to take over as "honcho" of a British working party:

> The prisoner "honcho" was directly responsible to the Japanese for the organisation and control of his men. He had to receive the instructions and see that they were carried out. He had to try to intercede for his men if they fell foul of a Jap, and by doing so usually succeeded in diverting the wrath upon himself. If he carried out his task of overseer too efficiently he was resented and unpopular with his own men; if he was inefficient he was up against the might of the Japanese. The fact that he did not actually wield a hammer or shovel himself was in fact small reward for the responsibility and consequent mental strife which he had to endure. Few honchos succeeded in getting through a day without being slapped by a Jap or sometimes badly beaten up. The Japanese took a childish delight in humiliating an officer or NCO in front of his men.
>
> During my short period in charge of this party I experienced enough of these disadvantages to assure myself that slave labour was preferable to the honour of being honcho. My first major proof of this came when I saw a Jap attacking one of my men with a shovel. The Jap swung the shovel, edge on, at the man's head, missing him by only a hair's breadth. I had no time to stop and consider the consequences; murder was about to be done. I caught hold of the Jap's arm as he was aiming a second blow, but I never did know what happened after that, nor how I got back to the camp. I was conscious only of the bandage on my head and later still of the fact that I was scarred for life.

Officers who broke under the strain or who were not resisting the Japanese sufficiently strongly were quietly removed. One colonel was threatened with a medical finding of insanity if he didn't tender his resignation. Officers who were caught dealing in rackets were brought before courts-martial. A lieutenant at Chungkai was charged with conspiring to steal quinine, dismissed from the service, and sent to live with the other ranks.

But there were also many outstanding officers who rose above their circumstances, cared for their men, insisted on military discipline, dealt diplomatically or forcefully with the Japanese, and above all showed guts, courage, and leadership. The Australian commander "Black Jack" Galleghan was as belligerent with the Japanese as he sometimes was with his own men. At Changi, he told the Japanese guards that they were a disgrace to their emperor for wearing untidy uniforms and dirty boots. Instead of beating him, the Japanese asked if the tailor in Galleghan's battalion, a Sgt. Galbraith, could repair the uniforms. Galleghan agreed and when the job was done the Japanese lined up, uniforms neatly pressed, boots shining, while the vanquished Australian officer inspected the victorious sons of Hirohito and took their salute. How his men must have been cheered by that spectacle. He also insisted that they should be clean shaven—no sloppy beards—and neatly dressed. When told there were no razors, he ordered his officers to make them out of vehicle springs and scrap steel.

Seen sixty years on, Alec Guinness's Col. Nicholson seems a caricature of the pre-war army officer, but the sense of dignity such officers conveyed inspired their men, as 2nd Lt. George Grigs found at the end of a Thailand march:

> We had little in the way of footwear or clothing left and disease and death had already sadly thinned our ranks. I was nominally in charge (under a Korean guard) of a party of thirty or so ORs involved in a march up country from one camp to another—no great distance, this time, but we were suffering from severe undernourishment and the inevitable fall in morale that accompanies such conditions. As we drew near to our destination, word reached us that the senior British officer in the camp was our (1st Cambs, that is—of which there were several ORs in my party) own 2nd I/C, Major Victor Mapey, and that he would be on the outskirts of the camp to greet us. We—all of us—decided that this would be a splendid opportunity to show the "Nips" that though they treated us as coolies we still had some pride; so we formed ourselves into a column of threes—slightly below parade ground standard, it's true—and as we drew abreast of Major Mapey my "E-e-e-y-y-e-s RIGHT" brought a response which no parade ground could have bettered. I'm pretty sure that the Major's eyes were as suspiciously damp as my own, though, and our grime had nothing to do with "square-bashing."

Fusilier Harry Howarth marched on another occasion where an officer inspired his men:

> We made our way across the Bangkok Plain, the Colonel at the head of the column holding a great staff wholly compatible with his large distinctive stature like some latter day Moses leading his people out of the desert. We were in a frightful state as we approached the Nonk [Nong] Pladuk camp. Looking down the ranks I could see blood staining many a pair of shorts, and periodic exits from the ranks for individuals to relieve themselves by the wayside. All our faces were ashen with a yellow malarial tinge and we were in the last stages of exhaustion when a remarkable thing happened. The Colonel gave the word of command from the front of the column, "March to attention the Fifth." At this command the shambling disorganised rabble became soldiers again and began to march in step as soldiers. It was a complete metamorphosis and in that instance the real meaning of the toast "The Regiment" became apparent to me. In that moment on that road I learnt the true meaning of *esprit de corps.* It was one of the truly great moments of my life. One second after that word of command, from being greatly respected, Colonel Flower became greatly loved.

Such officers earned and deserved the respect in which they were held. They also knew instinctively what they had to do and helped hundreds of men to survive. Cary Owtram, the commander of Chungkai, which had five hundred officers and sometimes ten thousand prisoners in total, was determined that the men should regain and retain their self-respect. The simplest things mattered. Owtram started a barber shop in his battalion and all the men were shaved free of charge and as often as they wished. In December 1942 he noted that there were no more beards. "When a man starts to grow a beard because he has no razor he begins to lose self-respect."

Good officers stood up to the Japanese. There was a "mutiny" at Nong Pladuk in September 1942 after Sgt. Bhumgara was beaten unconscious with a heavy piece of bamboo. Maj. Eddie Gill, the senior British officer, and Maj. Paddy Sykes, commanding officer of the 54th Infantry Brigade Company, RASC, agreed that the "moment of truth" had arrived and that they should resist the Japanese brutality. They told the commandant that unless the offending guard was punished, apologized, and was removed from the working party, the men would not work the next day. When the men fell in the next morning and Sykes and Gill were ordered to give the command to go out to work, they refused. They were marched off to the "no-good house." Other officers stood firm and also refused to give the order to work. Japanese guards trained rifles and machine guns on the men. After about an hour some groups decided that the officers would be released only if they relented and went to work. But five hundred men still refused to move unless ordered to do so by their officers. They were then stood to attention in three ranks facing the sun, with the officers formed up in three ranks a hundred yards ahead of them. The men, mostly naked to the waist, were scorched by the sun. They had to relieve themselves where they stood until the Japanese brought a spade so that holes could be dug. The other ranks were released at about 6 P.M. after repeated appeals from Capt. Ewart Escritt, Sykes's second in command, and Lt. Burt Briggs, who had been away from the camp at roll call. Only after several more hours was a compromise negotiated with the Japanese command. An apology was given for the beating and Gill and Sykes were assured that it would not happen again. It was agreed that the men would obey commands if given through their officers. The officers were finally dismissed at 2 A.M. The satisfaction of the ordeal for 2nd Lt. Robert Sutcliffe was that their mutiny had caused the British lion's tail to twitch for the first time since Singapore. But Gill and Sykes had also visibly, publicly, stood up for their men. According to Escritt, another by-product was a mutual increase in respect between officers and men.

Francis Dillon was one of the British officers who was admired not only by his men but by the Japanese, because he instinctively understood the Japanese game. John Stewart Ullman, the interpreter with F Force, thought that how prisoners fared depended on two signals: their understanding of their duties to the Japanese—obeisance, observance of the rules, and devotion to work—and their ability to exhibit the virtues of the "Way of the Warrior," or the code of Bushido, which overcame the shame of surrender. Dillon impressed the Japanese with both his moral courage and his attire. He dressed neatly and stood Sandhurst-style with feet apart, spine arched slightly backward. Other officers who ran disciplined camps, played the Japanese game, and were respected by the Japanese were Philip Toosey, "Knocker" Knights, and Lt. Col. Harold Lilly.

Lilly, who commanded the 1/5 Sherwood Foresters, had been a prisoner of the Germans during the First World War. Life always seemed to be better when he was around, said Sgt. J. S. Potter. "Pav" Pavillard observed Lilly making repeated representations to the Japanese, as a result of which Lilly's camp was one of the first to receive a supply of meat from the local Thais. His forceful personality soon had the Japanese in a "comparatively amenable" frame of mind, Pavillard said. On one occasion when Lilly demanded rest for his men, the Japanese said that they would kill him. "Go ahead," he told them. After they had killed him they would have to kill every man in order of seniority until there were none left to work. Nobody was killed.

At Tarsao, "Knocker" Knights calculated that the main priority of Tanaka, the chief engineer, was that the railway should be built on schedule. When the rate of progress dropped, the engineers screamed for more men and raided the hospital. Knights therefore decided to draft comparatively fit men into the hospital about ten at a time until as many as two hundred were tucked away. Tanaka arrived one morning, checked the working parade, sent for Knights, and delivered a severe reprimand, adding that he had already informed Knights that if the working parties were not kept up to strength he had no alternative but to make up the numbers from the hospital—which he now proposed to do.

> I reminded him that he had selected me to command the camp. This, I argued, implied responsibility for all internal administration, consequently, if it was his firm intention to make sick men work, then it was up to me, not him, to produce the number required. How many more men did he want? I could see he hadn't a clue to the answer, he hesitated for a while, then said, "One hundred more men." I also knew from the way he said this that he thought he had put me on the spot, and he was visibly surprised at my reply to the effect that I would produce him that number from the hospital, it still left a good number in the kitty, which I proposed to add to when the storm blew over. Tanaka appeared to be extremely pleased at my reaction; in fact it appreciably raised my stock in Japanese eyes. That was alright by me, it could result in my being given a greater measure of control, thereby avoiding bashing-up incidents, also providing opportunities of again pulling wool over the Japs' eyes if and when the opportunity occurred.

Both Knights and Lt. Stephen Abbott in Japan learned from long and hard experience when to challenge and how to negotiate a compromise. Hesitation was taken as a sign of guilt, and quick, forceful replies to questions or accusations were the best hope of winning the battles of wits. According to Capt. Philip Hall, his adjutant throughout captivity, Knights succeeded by developing an understanding of the Japanese mind, particularly the officers', and became able to distinguish their military code, dependent on all orders coming from the Emperor, from in some cases their private thoughts in matters referred to them. They developed a respect for him in his resistance to commands that would affect his men adversely, particularly the sick. They understood that Knights was trying to comprehend their military code, particularly with respect to soldiers being taken prisoner; that he always tried to maintain a military bearing; that, in common with most of the Japanese, he was a small man; and that, because of his civilian experience, he was able to judge the idiosyncrasies of Japanese officers and react to them accordingly. Unlike most senior officers in command of battalions who were regulars with an entirely military background, both Knights and Toosey had pre-war civilian backgrounds in industry and commerce. They were both appointed commander at more than one camp because the Japanese respected them.

Two officers—one British, Toosey; the other Australian, "Weary" Dunlop—have been given the best press in the past sixty years. Both men, who had successful post-war careers, also devoted the rest of their lives to helping former Far East prisoners of war. The testimony of the men who served with them, from all ranks, speaks eloquently of their inspirational leadership.

After building the bridge on the River Kwai, Toosey went on to command camps for the rest of the war, again showing his ability to act on his own initiative, sometimes against the wishes of other senior officers, to carry heavy burdens of responsibility at his own risk, and to demonstrate bravery of the highest order. When the Webber brothers, who, it will be remembered, ran the most successful radio in Thailand, moved to the officers' camp at Kanchanaburi, the Australian leader, Lt. Col. C. A. McEachern, told them the set must be destroyed. Senior officers were nervous about the reaction of Capt. Noguchi if the set were discovered, the operators tortured, and the name of an officer revealed. The Webbers were threatened with courts-martial if they refused to obey. Toosey went to see the brothers and asked them to promise that if they were caught and tortured so they had to reveal the name of the senior officer responsible, they would name him. Two officers had been killed for this offense at Kanchanaburi the previous year. The result was that the radio was kept operational for several more months.

When "Weary" Dunlop died in Melbourne in 1993 he was given a state funeral as an Australian hero. He was respected by his men, but also loved by them. "He is a symbol and a rock to me," Ray Parkin wrote in his diary after Dunlop had visited the men at Hintok. As his biographer Sue Ebury wrote, when morning after morning during the wet season of 1943 Dunlop lifted a sick man in his arms and confronted the drawn bayonets of the Korean guards demanding workers for that day with the words "This man is mine, Nippon!" he also challenged Death, the shadow who stood at his shoulder from the moment of surrender until August 15, 1945. The British aircraftman Bill Griffiths was blinded by an exploding mine and his hands were blown off. He was unable to travel, and the Japanese tried to finish him off with bayonets. Dunlop put himself between Griffiths and the Japanese and said they would have to kill him first. (Griffiths survived the war, was voted Britain's Disabled Sportsman of the Year in 1969, and unsurprisingly became

Dunlop's lifelong friend.) Through his example, as Ebury concludes, Dunlop offered his men a kind of redemption: he gave them back their self-respect through his strength and leadership, his defiance of the Japanese, his devoted medical care, and his concern for their emotional well-being; in return, they gave him a sense of his own worth. In their communal aims was their collective strength.

In his maiden speech to the Australian parliament, Tom Uren, who became a cabinet minister after the war, said that he got sentimental when he talked about "Weary" Dunlop and his fellow medical officers. He described the collective spirit—the socialism—that Dunlop and the other doctors fostered among the prisoners at Hintok:

> He was a remarkable man in many ways. He was not only a great doctor, but also a great soldier. We were known as "Dunlop Force." . . . The Japanese made our officers and medical orderlies an allowance. The non-commissioned officers and men who worked on the railway were also paid a small wage. This was a sham kept up by the Japanese to save face under the Geneva Convention. In our camp, the officers and medical orderlies paid the greater proportion of their allowance into a central fund. The men who worked did likewise. We lived by the principle of the fit looking after the sick, the young looking after the old, and the rich looking after the poor. A few months after we arrived at Hintok Road Camp a part of "H" Force, all British, arrived. They were about four hundred strong. As temporary arrangements they had tents. The officers selected the best, the non-commissioned officers the next best, and the men got the dregs. Soon after they arrived, the wet season set in, bringing with it cholera and dysentery. Six weeks later, only fifty men marched out of that camp and of that number only about twenty-five survived. Only a creek separated our two camps, but on one the law of the jungle prevailed, and on the other side the principles of socialism.

Officers did not have to believe in the principles of socialism to be good—though the behavior of the "I'm all right, Jack" officers as symbols of their class was undoubtedly a significant factor in the victory of Attlee's Labour Party in 1945. What made the men bloody-minded was seeing officers "vaunting privilege," neglecting their responsibility to ensure the survival of their men, and looking after their own safety and comfort. The Geneva Convention (which, of course, Japan did not sign) certainly said that officers should not work for the enemy, but it was provocative for sick men forced to work to see fit officers sitting around playing bridge.

The tension between officers and men in the Japanese prison camps is perhaps best defined by the different attitudes of Russell Braddon and "Black Jack" Galleghan. According to Braddon (a view that Dunlop would probably have shared), Galleghan was a conceited egomaniac who became hysterical if denied the usual military courtesies. At Changi he issued an order that other ranks with shoes should surrender them to officers because they were suitable garb only for officers. Yet Galleghan was also brave and conscientious, and often knew how to shake up the men. When they returned from Thailand, he called them together, said he knew they had had a rough time but that they must stop whining. That was salutary, Braddon admits. Galleghan was just as belligerent with the Japanese, too. He lost eighty-four pounds during captivity. He wrote his own—powerful—defense before he died in 1971:

> We were able to continue in all the years to run Changi as an army. I know that that got criticised. You've got Russell Braddon who wrote *The Naked Island*. Russell Braddon's idea of how to run that camp was that it was to be like a town council, of which the mayor would be elected and all the rest of it. After all Russell Braddon was a private. I ran it totally differently. I ran it as if we were still in the army. I remember I used to say to the troops as often as I could, "You're soldiers, and when I march you out of this camp I'm going to march you out as soldiers. I'm not going to march you out as a mob. You'll still be soldiers on the day it's over."

In his farewell message of September 9, 1945, to all AIF troops in Singapore, he said: "You finish your prisoner period as disciplined soldiers whom this Jap could not break."

But even if the majority of officers behaved as officers should, the facts about the officers' superior rate of survival remain telling. Among the Australians in F Force, 1,065 men of other ranks died, while only three officers did. In H Force, according to one account, twenty-six officers died, a death rate of 6 percent; but there were 627 deaths among British other ranks (37 percent), 165 among the Australians (27 percent) and 33 among the Dutch (7 percent).

It may not have been easy to be an officer and to be the focal point of both the frustration of other ranks and the violence of the Japanese, but it was—or at least could be for any individual officer who chose it to be—much safer.

PART
THREE

Chapter 21

THE HELLSHIPS

After the Burma–Thailand railway, the greatest death toll among the Far East prisoners of war was exacted at sea, on the ships used by the Japanese to transport the men from Singapore and the Philippines to Formosa (now Taiwan), Korea, and Japan, or between other countries and islands within the Japanese Empire. Japanese reports suggest that ten thousand eight hundred of the fifty thousand prisoners whom they transported by ship died at sea. One in three who died on ships in the Pacific War was killed by friendly fire from American or British bombers. More Americans died when the *Avisan Maru* was sunk than during the Bataan death march or the months at Camp O'Donnell, the two most infamous atrocities committed by the Japanese against the Americans. Approximately five thousand American prisoners died on the "hellships," as they came to be known. More Dutchmen died when the *Jun'ya Maru* was sunk than did in a year toiling on the Burma–Thailand railway. At 1,515, the death toll of Australians at sea was higher than anywhere except for Thailand and Borneo.

The war correspondent Rohan Rivett was one of the first prisoners to experience journeys on the hellships, on the *King Kong Maru,* which transported fifteen hundred men from Java to Singapore. At Tanjong Priok, the port of Batavia (now Jakarta), on October 8, 1942, the men were jammed into three holds where they were to remain without moving for ninety-six hours. There was no ventilation and the heat soon became intolerable. As the Japanese played under hoses for hours, the prisoners received one and a half pints of tea per man per day, but no water for drinking or washing. Buckets of rice and soya pap were lowered down to them three times a day. But if that was hard, the *Mayebassi Maru,* which took them on from Singapore to Burma, was worse. There were 1,799 prisoners in three holds:

> We had imagined that nothing could be worse than conditions on the trip up to Singapore but two minutes on the *Mayebassi* convinced us that we had been wrong. As I peered over the shoulders of those in front of me at the edge of the first hatch, I saw that two upper tiers in this hold were already occupied by Japanese troops. From the lower of these a forty-foot ladder descended to the very bowels of the vessel, where the floor space was already half covered by piles of Japanese gear, boxes, bed-rolls and other miscellaneous articles, including a tractor. The actual area of the hold was 75 feet by 48, and into this 650 prisoners were now driven. From the bottom of this pit the patch of daylight at the top of the hatch seemed as remote as the clouds from the depths of the Grand Canyon, and it was obvious that nobody would be able to lie down in comfort. A group of us climbed on top of the highest pile of gear, perhaps twenty feet above the bottom of the hold, and there we perched precariously in the pious hope that we were at least a little nearer to fresh air.

After loading the men, the ship stayed in Keppel Harbour for fifty-four hours. Rivett and his fellow Australians had considered the *King Kong Maru* an inferno. They now realized that it had been only one of the outer circles of the Japanese prisoner-of-war hell: "Now we were in the central torture chamber—the grill de luxe." The men got enough water, but the meat from the Singapore Cold Store was Australian mutton dating from 1931 and 1935, and without refrigeration it stank. The crew and guards used the men's medical supplies. The prisoners were beaten by the guards. Sometimes the sick were not allowed to go to the latrine. Seventeen days after they left Java, and after a journey on a third ship on top of a cargo of gravel, the men reached Moulmein, where they had been transported to work on the Burma–Thailand railway. Unlike fifteen hundred Dutch prisoners, however, they had not succumbed to an epidemic of dysentery. The Dutch journey had taken twenty-two days. When they left Rangoon for Moulmein, two hundred were dead and four hundred fifty could not walk.

Thousands of men suffered similar experiences throughout the three and a half years of captivity. On the *Byoke Maru* in 1944, Chief Petty Officer Ray Parkin was caught in a typhoon on his way to Japan:

> Men fell into helpless paroxysms of sickness. Stomachs contracted, rock-hard. On all fours with misery, men's backs arched: their shoulders rounded up and they collapsed on to the elbows, barely able to keep their faces clear of the deck as they retched. Chests tightened, squeezing the last gasp of breath out of them. Uncontrollably heaving, they were stricken with a horror that they would disembowel themselves through their throats. Their heads felt as if they were being pulled off like a fly's by some invisible giant's extruding fingers. Their tongues forced out, tearing at the roots. Eyes clenched, and then bulged . . . and . . . born of all this agony . . . only a thin string of slime.
>
> Looking up from the lower hold [there was] a line of helpless heads with open mouths lolling over the coaming, with wide staring eyes made unseeing by misery. The sounds were those of wordless animals, forced out—half-screech, half-scream—by the violence of the muscular contraction. There was a queer groan as the air rushed back into the deflated bodies. They moved helplessly with spasms like the reflexes of a newly dead snake thrown on hot ashes. The noise of some two hundred sick men sometimes rose louder than the storm; sometimes it mingled with the shriek of Tai-feng, the great wind, and the groaning labouring of the ship herself; sometimes it was drowned in a louder shout of the attacking wind and sea. As the men vomited, the ship bled through her plates as if a vital plasma were oozing out as she was being trampled to death by the unending horde of waves. It was as if the elements had decided that this was the hour in which life and all its works should be obliterated, and the Rule of the Insentient begin all over again.

On leaving Thailand in June 1944 on the *Hofuko Maru,* Signalman Walter Riley watched the dead tossed over the side of the ship in rice sacks. The bodies floated for a few moments before sinking, then sharks started tearing the bodies and devouring them. When the ship was sunk by an aircraft from the U.S. Navy, Riley observed survivors desperately searching for something to cling on to: "Pitiful cries for help all around me broke the eerie silence of this bizarre scene, but the spine-chilling cries were unanswered and one by one they died away as heads sank below the surface, to their watery graves in the China Sea."

Riley was beaten to a floating wooden plank by one of the Japanese guards. When he tried to scramble on, he was kicked away with curses. He eventually joined a raft. As it approached the shore, it overturned and tossed him into the raging sea, but he was saved by Filipinos who held out a bamboo pole to him. Then he collapsed on the beach. Riley had survived the shipwreck, but had not reached freedom:

> As I rolled over on to my back, I looked up to the sky and then I saw him, a strange Japanese soldier standing over me. His rifle with bayonet fixed, pointed menacingly down, the tip of the bayonet just two inches away from my naked stomach! "Christ Almighty," I croaked. I had miraculously survived two desperately close calls of death by drowning, a shipwreck, attack by dive bombers, death by disease and starvation and now my life was to end like this—by the steel of a Japanese bayonet.

Rather than being killed, though, Riley was sent to the camp at Cabanatuan in the Philippines, from which he escaped in the most audacious rescue of the war in the Far East.

The worst four months to be on a hellship were September 1944 to January 1945. In the Philippines, American bombers were making daily attacks on Manila, and the U.S. Army under Gen. Douglas MacArthur was advancing on the city. There were no markings on the ships to show that they were carrying prisoners, and American submarines patrolled the main shipping lanes from the Philippines and Taiwan to Japan. Prisoners could hear the ominous pings of submarines' sonar systems bouncing off the ships. But Japan needed manpower to work in mines and factories, so, as MacArthur advanced, Tokyo ordered that all fit prisoners in the Philippines should be shipped to Japan before they could be liberated. "Fit" was defined as being able to walk. Prisoners of all nationalities—British, Australian, American, and Dutch—were transported in the hellships, but the Americans were the only ones who became so dehumanized that they killed each other. All the worst experiences on the ships were encapsulated on the *Oryoku Maru,* when some desperate prisoners behaved like beasts.

The day that the prisoners at Manila's Old Bilibid Prison had dreaded for months began before dawn on December 13, 1944, with the ringing of a large gong at the guardhouse. It announced that they were about to start their long journey by sea to Japan. They knew that several of the ships used to transport prisoners had already been sunk by American submarines and bombers. The masts of about sixty could be seen across the bay. When they eventually sailed that evening in a convoy of merchant ships escorted by a cruiser and several destroyers, there were two sets of passengers on the seven-thousand-ton passenger liner *Oryoku Maru,* which had been armed with anti-aircraft guns. The cabins were filled with two thousand Japanese women and children, old soldiers, and diplomats escaping from the approach of the U.S. Army and the raids of American bombers. Below decks, down in the holds, were 1,619 prisoners; all were Americans, apart from thirty-seven British.

Urged on by grunting guards using rifle butts, bamboo sticks, and brooms, 718 men under the command of Cdr. Warren Portz had been jammed into the aft cargo space of Hold 5, where the only opening for light was the eight-by-ten-foot hatch. About seven hundred men under Lt. Col. Curtis T. Beecher were in the forward cargo compartment of Hold 1, a space of sixty feet by one hundred feet with a twenty-by-twenty-foot hatch. A horizontal platform had been installed about four feet from the floor to double the floor space. The most fortunate group were about two hundred men from the Bilibid hospital unit under Cdr. Maurice Joses who were put in Hold 2 amidships. Grain was stored on three sides of the hold; the floor was covered with horse manure and the stench burned their eyes. At least, however, they had more space than the other prisoners. But Lt. Junsaburo Toshino, the Japanese commanding officer, refused to turn on the cooling unit that had been used for the horses. The conditions in Holds 1 and 5 were much worse—there were no portholes and no ventilation—but when the men complained that they were too crowded and that some of them were already beginning to suffocate, Shusake Wada, the Japanese interpreter, who often acted as if he were in command, replied, "Let them die." In Hold 1 the men at the sides were forced to sit four to a row, each man's back against his neighbor's knees, which were squeezed tight together. The men in the center were forced to stand, packed like sardines against one another. If they wanted to lie down, they had to do so on their sides. The wooden "honey" buckets lowered down for use as latrines quickly overflowed, and urine and feces swilled across the floor. Their breakfast at Bilibid had been a cup of boiled rice. Now, twelve hours later, they were given buckets of rice, fish, and seaweed and a few spoonfuls of water. But as the latrine buckets were sent down at the same time as the food, the men couldn't tell which bucket was being passed to them. It was a big joke if a hand was accidentally dipped into the latrine bucket or the food bucket was used as a latrine.

By the time the *Oryoku Maru* sailed, at about 5 P.M., the temperature was over 100°F and the hold was so crowded that the men could not put their feet between people when they tried to walk. But the ship stopped at the Corregidor breakwater and did not set sail into the China Sea until 3 A.M. The men were already shouting for air and water, and some were fainting, but as the shouts grew ever louder, Wada—described by the men as the "hunchback dwarf"—responded by shutting the hatch on Hold 5. Soon the men were screaming. Wada complained that their cries were disturbing the women above them and threatened to instruct the guards to fire on them, but the men became tormented by thirst and heat and began to fight among themselves. As they struggled to get to the front of the hold under the hatch, men were stepping on and punching one another. Beecher and other officers tried to calm them but were ignored by desperate men. By dawn, perhaps as many as thirty-five had already died, mostly from suffocation. But at least the ship was sailing at a speedy twenty knots and was accompanied by seaplanes. Cdr. Eugene C. Jacobs, one of the medical officers, dared to think that the *Oryoku Maru* was well protected and might survive the dash through MacArthur's blockade.

He was soon less optimistic. From about 8 A.M. until 5 P.M. the *Oryoku Maru* and the rest of the convoy were repeatedly bombed and strafed. As soon as one Japanese gun crew was killed, another appeared, then another. Above the prisoners the cabins and dining rooms were littered with the dead and dying. Another medical officer, Cdr. Thomas Hayes, noted that their blood poured across the decks and dripped onto the prisoners in the holds. The screams of the wounded ripped the air "like those of witnesses to Armageddon." Hayes was ordered to treat the wounded Japanese, working by candlelight without medicine or bandages—but he was refused permission to help any wounded prisoners. Americans were sinking Japanese ships, said Wada, who then ordered a beating of the medical officer. Toshino and Wada were so angry that they refused to give food and water to the men in the holds.

With the ship's steering gear broken, Shin Kajiyama, the captain, tried to head back to Subic Bay but ran aground three hundred yards offshore from the Olangapo Naval Station, where the Japanese passengers were unloaded shortly before midnight. The bombing of the hatches and decks had at least created more air for the prisoners, but the conditions in Holds 1 and 5 had not improved. When the hatch cover was opened, dozens of dead bodies had been passed up, and the men were still crying out for water. The scene was set for one of the most horrifying incidents of the Second World War. The claustrophobia created by the overcrowding, the heat, the lack of air, water, food, and sufficient latrine buckets, the stench and the darkness, and the repeated attacks by their own bombers drove the men up to and over the edge of insanity. With the officers powerless to maintain discipline in such conditions, the art of survival became each man for himself and survival of the fittest. There was anarchy in the holds that night, according to Maj. Dwight E. Gard:

> Men raving, crawling naked in the darkness, covered with slime—
> eels—making speeches—threatening to kill—shouting at the Nips—

> men shouting the names of their enemies (whether real or imaginary I don't know)—defecating—drinking urine—stealing canteens—slashing wrists—and drinking their own blood. Many men were murdered—some for their blood, but more had their heads battered in with canteens because they couldn't keep quiet. Major Kruvanek and I formed a team to handle insane men crawling from the rear part of the shelf. Tried to keep them from piling up and shutting off the air. Wrestled with dozens and quieted insane men but only hit one man.

The sick men were trampled to death. The bodies of the men who died of suffocation shriveled and were unrecognizable. Men crazed by thirst stole canteens to get the few drops of water that had been saved, said Maj. Calvin Ellsworth Chum. Some murdered fellow prisoners for water:

> Others slit the throats of their buddies to wet their parched lips. One man drank the contents of a bucket used as a latrine. Without light, without air, without food, without water that night of terror aboard the *Oryoku Maru* 125 caged Americans suffocated. A large number of them, however, were killed by their companions who had thirsted into insanity. One infantry captain was clubbed to death with shoes when he refused to stop yelling.

Capt. Marion Lawton remembered:

> Claustrophobia and total darkness created a terrible, terrible feeling. There was the heat. The desperate need for air. The temperature must have been near 120 degrees. There was thirst. Many of the men, those that had gotten some water, gulped it right down. They sat there in that oven in their own sweat. When all the liquid was gone, men became desperate. They went mad. Some drank urine. Some turned vampire. They tried to drink the blood of the sick men who couldn't resist. Men were murdered on that ship. The next day I was next to an old college classmate of mine. His arms were badly scratched. I asked him what had happened. He told me it was nothing. "It's more than nothing," I said. "Who did this to you?" "Well, I fought off a feller for half the night who was trying to cut me so he could drink my blood. He was mad. Finally two fellers next to me realized what was going on. One of them grabbed this guy while the other one beat him on the head with his canteen."

Some prisoners thought that they heard others plotting against them. When Dudley Hensen, the chief pharmacist's mate, stumbled through the dark to a group of officers and told them that the men in his bay were plotting to kill him, they told him he was talking nonsense and should return to his place. Next morning he was found dead, with his stomach split open. Another prisoner woke up to find five men in a circle around him, sitting naked and doubled up. They were stone cold and dead. The man beside 2nd Lt. John G. Gamble (who died later in Japan) screamed, "Somebody cut my throat." A voice said to Gamble: "Quiet, or I'll cut yours."

Another witness of the "madhouse" on board was Lt. Charles W. Burris, an Oklahoman pilot:

> A guy would say, "What are you doing? Hey, he cut me with a razor! He's drinking my blood!" That happened different times at different places. Colonel Beecher in Hold 1 had set up his command post at the bottom rung of the ladder, but he couldn't see these guys or get to them. He'd holler, "Do you know who they are?" He'd say, "Kill 'em! They're not gonna stop! Just kill 'em!" So he ordered them to be murdered, and they were murdered. He said, "Beat 'em with a shoe! Choke 'em! Do anything! But kill 'em! Make sure they're dead!" You could hear them getting a beating, and they'd scream and holler. I don't remember their words, but some of them might have been begging for mercy. They went ahead and killed them. It got so bad at one point that even the Japs yelled down and threatened to shoot down in there. Finally, they did shoot down in there and killed a few people, but it didn't help any. These guys were completely out of their heads—most of them. One ol' boy yelled, "How do you like it, Beecher? You ain't gettin' no water, either! You're gonna die like the rest of us!" He couldn't control them. Nobody could control them. The threat of death didn't even control them.

Once the civilians had been disembarked, Wada told the prisoners that they would be allowed to swim to shore in the morning. But the bombers attacked again and the ship was shaken by tremendous explosions. Planked flooring fell into the bilge, and many prisoners dropped into the bottom of the ship where they were pinned down. A steel girder supporting the hatch in Hold 5 collapsed into the cargo space, killing a number of men. Coal dust ignited and there was a dash for the ladder. According to Hayes, one guard fired into his hold, killing Capt. Ted Parker. Then a bomb hit the ship's stern and it started listing, settling lower and lower. The order was given to abandon ship. Some prisoners climbed the ladder to the deck. Pte. Lee Davis was one of them: it was a mad scramble, he said, like a bunch of rats trying to get out of a hole. He ran for the dining room to look for food, but just before he reached it, a guard sprayed the area with a machine gun. Davis turned and jumped overboard, but several men were shot by the trigger-happy Japanese guards while still on board. Some prisoners fought their way to the ship's storeroom where they looted American Red Cross parcels. One was shot dead by Toshino himself. Machine guns, lined up on the shore, fired on men in improvised rafts.

Maj. Roy Bodine was awarded America's Bronze Star medal for heroism, created by President Franklin D. Roosevelt in 1941, for his efforts to rescue his fellow prisoners that day. When men in the water started shouting that the ship was going down, he jumped into the water with two fellow prisoners, one of whom was Ensign Bob Nelson:

> I looked back at the ship and it was a mess. A big portion of the stern was blown away and the whole ship looked like a scrap heap. What a loss from the beauty we boarded. I saw an old man on a big box who could make no headway. I took him . . . to another old man on a big plank who was getting along OK. He bitched like hell but I just went ahead and put them together and he had to accept it. Nelson and I had gotten half way in. I was going slow trying to keep eyes on all around me. Bob wanted to hurry ashore as he was afraid of the effects of bombs on people in the water. Bob seemed to be OK so I gave him my 4 × 4 and took a little plank from him and said I was going back toward the ship when I saw four American planes coming over low.

Bodine encouraged timid men to jump and helped the inexperienced swimmers clutch on to planks. He then swam back to the ship to fetch his shirt and straw hat and took two pairs of shoes, fearing another march when he reached the shore. Then he jumped into the water again. "Most of the men still aboard had gone down to the lower deck so they wouldn't have to jump so far. A couple of very nice young men, fair swimmers, asked me if I could recover for them a big hatch plank, which I did, and when they started they agreed willingly to wait while I looked for some more that needed help."

As Eugene Jacobs reached the deck, three planes were diving overhead:

> I ran across the deck toward the nearest shore and jumped. Some five decks below, I struck the water with a big splash, and struggled through oceans of green water before returning to the surface and God's good air. The planes pulled out of their dives. They had dropped nothing. They circled around, dipped their wings to the waving prisoners, and disappeared. I located a piece of bamboo floating nearby and slowly paddled ashore.

> Guards both on the ship and on the shore were shooting prisoners quite freely. We were rounded up into a group, in waist-deep water, and there we remained—shivering—all day. Twice in the afternoon planes returned and bombed the ship with incendiaries. Intense fires, and later many explosions. Toward sunset, we were instructed to come ashore, each four prisoners to carry a wounded man. We were herded about half-a-mile through woods to a tennis court at the old Olangapo Naval Base. A count showed 1340 survivors. In two days we had lost 286 men.

But the ordeal of the survivors was not over yet. After five days at the naval station they were taken over two days to the jail at San Fernando, Pampanga, where they had their first hot food since leaving Bilibid—rice served on two sections of corrugated roofing. Wada asked Lt. Col. Beecher to select fifteen of the sickest men to return to Manila. This was not an act of compassion: they were loaded onto a truck and driven to a small cemetery. Some of the Japanese soldiers dug a grave, and the prisoners were forced to kneel and then were bayoneted or beheaded, one at a time. The next day the rest of the men were transported on an ammunition train, packed a hundred to each car, with the wounded sitting on the roof and ordered to wave their bandages at attacking aircraft, to San Fernando del Union on the Lingayen Gulf. Their Christmas dinner was half a cup of rice and half a cup of water.

Two days later they were marched to the beach and loaded onto two ships. Most of the men were on the ten-thousand-ton *Enoura Maru,* which was also carrying hundreds of sick and wounded Japanese soldiers. But the Japanese became so impatient at the slowness of the boarding—many Americans had to be helped up the gangplank—that about 230 men were put on the twelve-thousand-ton *Brazil Maru.* The *Enoura Maru*'s previous cargo had been horses, and the hold was covered with dung. The men were forced to clear it with their bare hands.

Eugene Jacobs and Roy Bodine kept diaries of their voyages to Japan:

> 28 December: Our hold is a dark hell, full of flies. They breed somewhere below us where we put our excreta down scuttle to hatch below. [Bodine] The Japanese soldiers are eating three meals a day. A few prisoners try to trade jewelry for food, but most of us have nothing to trade. Manure and flies very bad in hold. Blackout when I attempt to stand. One died. Wrapped him in a straw mat. Brief religious ceremony. Then slide him over the side. [Jacobs]
>
> 29 December 1944: Rain. Prisoners fought each other to get the cups and pans of their mess gear under the drippings from the hatch

covers; they got only a few drops each. Two spoons of rice. Blasts of large guns on deck at 6 p.m. We crawled off the wooden hatch-covers onto the steel deck. Depth charges exploded on each side of the ship. We could also hear the guns of other ships. After some thirty minutes of blasting, there was an enthusiastic clapping of hands on the upper decks. We were told: "The Japanese Impelial Navy has sunk an Amelican submaline." Can only lie in dark corner half stretched out and pray and think about future. Mostly about food and drink, all my favorite dishes, and as usual now I feel only like retiring to enjoy the rest of my life at a little rural house near southern city. Texas? All my ambition is gone. Just want to live to eat and enjoy raising our children, live in south-west where outdoors is close and living cheap. [Bodine]

31 December: No food. Half cup of water. Colonel Johnson asked for food. Mr. Wada answered: "No way to cook food." Colonel Johnson: "We will all die!" Mr. Wada: "Evlybody must die. This no time fol sympathy." [Jacobs]

Our five guards are eating well, but have no authority to get anything for us. Today they did give us one mess kit of their leftovers which amounted to 1/4 teaspoonful per man. [Bodine]

1 January 1945: Issued five moldy "hardtack" biscuits. The prisoners are now like animals in a cage. They are begging for cigarettes. We are given three-quarters of a cup of water (a real treat). Bitter cold. Extremely hungry. Thirsty. Our bodies are very sore. [Jacobs]

The steel deck we sleep on is like ice. Some men only have a pair of shorts, and most are barefooted. I am grateful for my khaki trousers and shoes. [Bodine]

2 January: Colonel Johnson requests food. Mr. Wada: "United States submalines sink all Japanese food ships. Vely solly." The men continue to scramble around hold, grabbing for cigarettes. Many would rather smoke than eat. It is difficult to make the Japanese believe that we are weak and starving. Beards getting very heavy. Two-thirds cup of rice; one teaspoon of dried fish. No water. [Jacobs]

5 January: As we were trying to get to sleep, several of us were showered with a liquid that tasted like battery acid. What were they up to now? The liquid proved to be the contents of a latrine bucket. The prisoner carrying it up the ladder had been too weak. He spilled it. The guards laughed at us when we asked to get some seawater to clean ourselves off. [Jacobs]

6 January: Today is about a new low, or rather last night was. A five gallon bucket of urine and feces was spilled on top of us, Jacobs,

> Shambs, Nagle and myself got the worst of it. Concentrated as hell due to little water. Burned my eyes and soaked our clothes. Nobody wanted us near them so we left on wet clothes and Nips gave us a little can of salt water to wash our faces. Probably the most miserable night I have ever had. [Bodine]

On arrival in Taiwan, the Japanese soldiers were transferred to hospitals, the British sent to prison camps, and on January 6 the prisoners on the *Brazil Maru* were transferred to the *Enoura Maru,* which now had more than twelve hundred men on board.

> 7 January: We started a hospital on the upper deck; moved in some fifty dysentery patients. Got some Japanese medicine for dysentery. Looked like pellets of gunpowder. There are four deaths. The flies are bad. [Jacobs]
>
> Last Night was hell. Swearing, kicking, fighting indescribable. Piss and shit running down from above. If this ship were sunk day or night very few would get out. Only exit is long ladder through steel pipe 3 ft in diameter for 1300 men. This morning we were given 1/2 cup of barley, 1/5 cup cabbage soup and 1/5 cup tea. 3 or 4 died last night. Flies are terrible, heavy sticky ones that cover your food black and in a few seconds come back and can't be kept out. No washing of hands or mess gear, floors sticky with faeces, long lines for latrines. It's getting hot and fetid and nauseating again. There are 6 buckets for 1000 sick men down here. I am having shits too. [Bodine]
>
> 9 January: A blinding and deafening explosion (tremendous orange flash) caused pandemonium. Hatch covers fell into the bilge, dropping many prisoners thirty or forty feet below. There were screams, cries, groans, and oaths. The air was full of dust and dirt. Wounded were soon being dragged into our improvised hospital. Many fractures, mostly badly compounded. Many shrapnel wounds. Everything covered with dirt. Just as we were getting the wounded situated in the hospital, and the dysentery cases moved out, back came the planes. Finally they went away. Several of our doctors are dead; others badly wounded. In fact there are only three of us not dead or wounded. Colonel Ronnie Craig and I set some twenty fractures with makeshift splints. Major "Mac" Williams took care of the other wounded. We soon had thirty-five dead piled up against the bulkhead (after the removal of their clothing). [Jacobs]
>
> 10 January: My attention was called to a shrapnel-made gash in the bulkhead. I looked through it into the forward hold, and witnessed a horrible sight. There were 300 mangled Americans piled some three

> deep—the result of a direct bomb hit. At the sides of the hold, a few wounded were standing or sitting, motionless and dazed. The Japanese would not let us enter the forward hold to help. [Jacobs]

About two hundred fifty prisoners were killed in this raid by American bombers, including nearly all of the medical officers, and another two hundred injured. The few medical staff who survived tried to help the sick and wounded but their appeals for medicine and bandages were ignored. Men sat on piles of dead bodies. When two Japanese medical officers arrived on board on January 11, they dealt with a few wounds and then left the ship. One vomited when he saw the thousands of flies, bodies, broken arms and legs, dried blood, and excreta. The latrines were overflowing but Wada refused permission to empty them. Over two days the corpses were taken ashore, given a farewell salute, and burned at a crematorium.

On January 13, the nine hundred men who had survived were moved back to the *Brazil,* which set off the next day in a convoy across the East China Sea for Japan. Each bay in the aft hold was about ten by twelve feet, with less than four feet of headroom for thirty men who sat with their legs stretched out or lay down with their knees drawn up. The terror now was not the heat but the cold as the ship sailed north and snow fell into the hold. Forty-seven men died on the first day at sea. The shivering men took their clothes.

> 15 January: Men are dying continually. Just haul them up and throw them over. There is going to be a terrible death rate on this ship yet. Got to get clothing and bedding or we all will die. I found a ragged shirt that had been used to wipe up filth and when I went on deck to latrine took a chance and rinsed it in dirty water at rail. [Bodine]
>
> 17 January: Rex and little Van Horn both died last night. Rex practically in my arms. He was very affectionate, wanted his face against me and told me to hold his hand; and asked me four or five times to help him make an Act of Contrition. He is one man that died like a Christian in all this cursing mob. I have his ring I will try to take home for him. [Bodine]
>
> 18 January: Stealing is terrible. Jerk mats off sick. Steal canteens from under your head. Have to keep everything tied on to you or inside your clothes. [Bodine]
>
> 24 January: Got up in middle night and tried to get water from winches. Finally got a half canteen and drank a cupful but got beaten with gun butt three times. Black as spades and little can be seen. Guard huddles in little shack. If I'd been alone I'd been OK but others kept drawing his attention to me. It's a good way to be shot but worth it. [Bodine]

26 January: Cold. Many dying: only three chaplains alive out of twenty-three starting trip. Medical services have completely evaporated. Major "Mac" Williams only medic still on his feet. Passed another convoy going south. [Jacobs]

27 January: No chow or water in a.m., but chow small amount in p.m. Suffered agony all night. Soiled pants moderately 2 times. No control due to lost fat. Father Cummings died. I'm the only one left from my foot locker. About 40 died. Not buried today. Hope ends soon. [Bodine]

Two days later the *Brazil* docked at Moji, near Fukuoka on Kyushu. At last the men's journey in three hellships was over. Their journey from Manila had taken forty-six days. The exact toll is not known, but only about five hundred of the 1,619 men who left the Philippines had survived; another eight men died in the local hospital. After six weeks in the camps near Omuta and Fukuoka, another 235 had died. More than eight out of ten of the original party were therefore dead within three months.

INTERLUDE

A Happy Ending

When the *Rakuyo Maru,* sailing from Singapore to Taiwan with 1,248 British and Australian prisoners, was hit by two torpedoes on September 12, 1944, 971 of the prisoners were killed. The captain, crew, and guards abandoned ship in lifeboats, leaving the men to fend for themselves. The survivors threw rafts, hatch covers, and rubber blocks into the sea, helped the sick off the ship, and took to the water. Destroyers picked up the Japanese survivors, while the prisoners took over the lifeboats. Two days later, 136 were rescued by Japanese ships and returned to captivity.

But for 159 men the sinking of the *Rakuyo Maru* was to have a happier ending. One was the Australian NCO J. W. Turner, who watched from a raft as the ship sank, just before sunset, twelve hours after it was torpedoed. With Pte. David Flinn and Frank Jesse, he had earlier returned to the ship and found water and food. They teamed up with two other rafts, and, not realizing that the nearest land was three hundred miles away, the eighteen survivors decided to head west for the China coast.

Their combined weight meant that the rafts were always two feet under the water.

> What with the terrific heat of the sun, the drinking of salt water and the exposure to the elements, it was not long before many men became delirious. I was frightfully sunburned and lost a complete layer of skin after our rescue. One POW killed a Jap in the water after taking his flask of saki, drank it and drowned himself. In the afternoon of the fourth day the sea became very rough and a typhoon sprang up, causing men who were too weak to hold on to float off the rafts and drown. I could not get the ghastly thought of sharks out of my mind, and as we drifted away from the floating oil I kept a sharp lookout for them. A Japanese who had tied himself to a raft had half his arm and neck bitten by a shark. On the second day a Jap destroyer picked up all the remaining Japanese in the water, leaving us to the mercy of the sea. This Jap destroyer weaving in and out among our rafts was hailed by our lads, who asked what was to become of them. The Japs grinned derisively and with their thumbs pointed to the bottom of the ocean. The two and half years of POW life, plus the horrors of the torpedoing, had not broken the ever-present spirit of the Aussies and Englishmen who immediately began to sing "Rule Britannia." I know of a case of several Japanese being killed by some of our fellows prior to the destroyer arriving.

Some of the men lost their reason and started seeing visions. They tried to leave the raft and had to be pulled back, but as they grew weaker the fitter men couldn't help them and they died. One Roman Catholic handed his life jacket to a man who did not have one, took out his rosary beads, said goodbye, and jumped into the water. On the fourth day, almost at the end of their tether, and with only five of the original eighteen still alive, they sighted a submarine, with men standing on deck pointing machine guns at them. "We could see they were not Japs and thought perhaps they were Germans. Picture our surprise and joy on hearing them call out 'Take it easy you guys and we will soon have you aboard.' We were taken aboard about an hour before dark on 15 September."

Turner was one of seventy-three prisoners saved by the USS *Pampanito,* one submarine in a wolfpack that also included the USS *Growler* and the USS *Sealion II,* which had fired the torpedoes that sank the *Rakuyo Maru.* Another eighty-six men were rescued by the *Sealion,* the *Queen Fish,* and *Barb.* (The *Pampanito* had sunk another ship, the *Kachidori Maru,* in the convoy, killing 460 British prisoners.)

The men had been lucky not to be shot. At first, cruising just below the water with the periscope showing, the *Pampanito*'s lookouts had thought that the men, who were covered with oil, were Japanese. And the men could not call out because their throats were so dry. Lt. Cdr. Paul E. Summers, the captain, had given the order to kill them, but one of the crew noticed the fair hair of an Australian and called to the crew to hold their fire. The crew dived into the sea with ropes to attach to the rafts so that they could be brought alongside the submarine and carefully lifted aboard. Others came on top to help. If a Japanese plane had attacked they would have been left on deck as the *Pampanito* dived to avoid attack. Turner was taken aboard for questioning while the rest were held back by machine gun. When the men climbed aboard the *Pampanito,* they were a "pitiful sight," according to its patrol report. They were stripped, the heavy coating of oil and muck removed from them, and then given a piece of cloth moistened with water to suck on. Many had lashed themselves to the rafts and had nothing but life belts with them. They all showed signs of pellagra, beri-beri, immersion, salt-water sores, ringworm, and malaria.

The war—and captivity—was now over for Turner and the other survivors who had been saved by the Americans:

> We were given water and hot soup in limited quantities. The oil washed off our bodies, bathed and cleaned by members of the crew. We were all in a state of collapse and were dressed in clean clothes and put to bed. We were nursed and looked after from the time we came aboard until we left the sub, as well as our own mothers would have done. After a 4-hour watch on deck, members of the crew who were due for a rest gave up their beds to us and cared for us and our wants such as cocoa, soup and water. For the first couple of days we were not allowed to eat any solid food, but were given liquids, fruit juices and vitamin tablets. The majority of us had festered sores and bad sunburn which was treated by a very capable doctor who worked on us for 48 hours without sleep.

In fact, the man who treated them was not a doctor—submarines did not carry doctors—but a pharmacist first class, Maurice L. Demmers, who worked until he was close to total exhaustion. "As I examined and treated each one I could feel a deep sense of gratitude, their faces were expressionless and only a few could move their lips to whisper a faint 'thanks,' " Demmers said after the war. "It was quite gratifying to see the happy expressions on their faces when they left the ship." Only one of the rescued men, John Campbell, died.

The *Pampanito* steamed for Saipan. It arrived on September 20, when the men were greeted by cameras and flashlights and given oranges, apples, and ice cream, their first for nearly three years. After a spell in the hospital they traveled to Australia, where they revealed to the world for the first time the horrors of the Burma–Thailand railway.

Chapter 22

JAPAN

The men who were sent to Japan in 1944 were hoping for better lives away from Burma, Thailand, and the Philippines. Their journeys in the hellships were their first shock. The second was that conditions in Japan, for most, were even worse than they had so far experienced. The Australian medical officer Capt. Ian Duncan thought that Japan was the worst of all the places where he was a prisoner. Duncan was second in command to Dr. Thomas Hewlett, the American commander at Fukuoka Camp 17 at Omuta on Kyushu, where the "king rats" of the U.S. "mafia" flourished. In September 1944 there were 814 American prisoners in the camp who were then joined by 907 British, Australian, and Dutch. The Americans, who had arrived in 1943, and the Australians worked in coal mines. The British worked in a zinc foundry, and the Dutch in coal stalls or loading coal onto ships.

At other camps in Japan the men worked in coal and nickel mines, steel plants, rolling mills and foundries, and shipyards. At Wakayama near Osaka, the heat in the copper mine was so great that the prisoners could work only for short periods before losing consciousness. They had the same starvation rations and equally brutal guards as in Thailand and Burma, and had to endure the worst winter in fifty years, with temperatures falling to minus 20°F.

Those who had been in Burma and Thailand thought that the work was harder than building the railway. One prisoner sent to work at the zinc smelter was 2nd Lt. Geoffrey Pharaoh Adams:

> Huge crucibles were filled with zinc ore and placed in the furnaces, which were heated overnight to 1200 degrees. At this temperature the ore is a liquid; it is poured into hoppers and taken away to be refined, rolled and stamped. The heat in front of the banks of retorts was searing; behind each stood a large water tank into which the workers jumped every few minutes so that their clothes did not singe on their backs! The foreman said that most of the men had worked a lifetime there but some were being recalled to the colours to replace casualties. The British POWs were going to take their places. The whole factory conjured up visions of Dante's Inferno, and our hearts sank. Each *buntai,* or section, would look after a bank of retorts, which they could empty after the night's firing. Then they would clean out the furnaces and equipment, refill the retorts with ore, and leave all ready for the smelting process during the night.

In summer the temperature in the furnace rooms where the men worked with the same inadequate protection as the Japanese was more than 120°F. The heat put them off their food and they rapidly weakened as they worked, as did the Japanese, in twelve-hour shifts, with a changeover shift of eighteen hours every five days.

Pte. Roy Whitecross worked in the coal mine, fifteen hundred feet below ground level, where the coal dust hung in the air like "black fog" and the men were dirty beyond description, and then on the coal dump. The work on the dump was digging channels into the burning coal and earth to allow seawater to flood the area and put out the fire:

> We were not allowed to work in overcoats. The icy wind moaned around us as we dug into the ground that was frozen on top but down deeper was red hot and when opened to the air frequently broke into flames which gave off clouds of black smoke. Sometimes the depth of the channel shielded us from the fiendish wind, and the heat of the burning ground kept us warm for a little while. At other times our backs would be stiff and numb from the cold wind, while our faces and hands were burnt from the red-hot rocks. These frequent and sudden changes from heat to cold opened up cracks in my soft hands and in the bitter wind it felt as though my hands were being flayed with whips of wire.

The men mined coal for twelve hours a day, with a thirty-minute lunch break and a day off every ten days, on some coal seams that American miners would never even attempt to exploit, according to Staff Sgt. Harold

Feiner. They had to wade in streams and drag beams up to nine feet long while crawling on their knees through tiny laterals.

> We didn't wear clothes in the mine. It was generally very hot. In winter this was sometimes good. But we had sores over our bodies and the sweat would burn the hell out of us. Our eyes would burn and it would get into our genital area and we would scratch all over. Our faces were black. We used to always say, "Jesus, will we ever get the coal dust out of our bodies?" It was ingrained everywhere. All black. Our eyes were black, our ears. Any crevice would be black. We were given baths, but we never got clean.

The conditions in the mine were so grueling—and often dangerous—that a man counted himself lucky if he was injured and had to have a leg amputated. He hobbled around the camp but was released from "underground slavery." Others were tempted to follow his example. A few were lucky, according to Roy Whitecross, but the mutilated bodies of others went to the crematorium. As the winter wore on the sufferings increased. Without warm clothes or footwear, the freezing march to and from the mine became intolerable for many:

> It was bad enough to trudge through powdery snow which could be shaken from clothes and feet in the shelter of the mine change house, but it was infinitely worse when the snow gave way to rain and the badly drained roads near the camp were covered with a foot or more of icy slush. It was understandable that men who had endured these conditions for two winters came to the end of their physical resources, and looked about for some method of release. There was only one way out—get hurt in the mine, preferably an accident which would be sufficient to warrant admission to the camp hospital. With a fortitude borne of sheer desperation, men deliberately loosened huge outcrops of rock in the walls and let them crash down on their legs.

Ian Duncan kept detailed medical records at Fukuoka and noted the psychological problems that the men suffered as a result of the work and the beatings. After working in Thailand on the railway or on airstrips in the Philippines, they were suddenly put to work as miners and confronted with the hazards of collapsing walls and ceilings or blast injuries, and were therefore faced continuously with the threat of sudden injury or death. No effort was made to provide rest or relaxation when they weren't working: they were harassed by guards during rest periods; on rest days there were inspections; and they were not allowed organized sports or entertainment. In the mine they were punished by civilians, some after they had been injured. They lived in a state of continuous apprehension, and their "distorted psychology" created a malingering attitude that was manifested in feigned minor illnesses as well as deliberate self-injuries. According to Thomas Hewlett, men prevented chronic ulcers from healing by applying lime from the latrines to them. For a price, the "Bone Crusher" would inflict a broken arm or leg. "Such breaks were unlike those accidentally incurred, so his work was recognized immediately. Usually his patients ended up on the honey bucket detail."

A sentence of solitary confinement in Japan did not mean the intolerable heat of the "no-good house" in Thailand but the intolerable cold of the *aeso,* the icebox, in the Japanese guardhouse, where the temperature was just above freezing and several men died. One victim was the nineteen-year-old Australian Pte. David Runge. When he was overheard telling the newest Australian arrivals at Fukuoka not to work too hard, he was beaten by the guards and forced to kneel on the cold concrete floor. After thirty-six hours he developed gangrene in both feet. He was taken to the hospital, where Ian Duncan amputated both feet. Roy Whitecross was in the dispensary after the operation and saw one of the guards, nicknamed the "Sailor," laughing happily and calling to two of his pack who happened to pass by the windows:

> They all looked into the box the Sailor was carrying and joined his laughter. Idly I wondered what could be so funny. Another guard was called in. He, too, joined in the giggling. Stooping, he lifted out two legs that had been amputated just below the knees. As I turned away, nauseated at their inhuman callousness, I noticed the deep, red gashes where Captain Duncan had attempted to stop the spreading gangrene.

As well as the icebox there was the sweatbox, which was L.Bdr. Art Benford's punishment at Fukuoka when he was found talking during *tenko* (the daily roll calls). He was beaten by guards and dragged to the open door.

> Two of them picked me up and threw me into the dark interior, where I slammed against the rear wall and fell to the ground. My face was pressed against the ground which was sodden with urinal and excreta scrapings. I was wretched and my vomit added a further element to the disgusting stink which prevailed the air in my prison. The "sweat box," constructed of steel and measuring four feet square and four feet high, was designed to prevent the occupant lying down or standing, so he was for most of the

> time sitting on the putrid floor. I was enveloped by a darkness so intense that I could feel it and I was scared to move for fear of what I might encounter on the floor. I tasted blood through swollen split lips and the pains in my body merged into a huge beating pulse. In my weakened state I had wet my sacking trousers and I laid there too tired and weak to shift my position. The noise made by the opening of the door invaded my senses and though no word was spoken I knew that food had been placed on the floor. I squirmed around in the confined space until my hands contacted two Jap half mess tins. One was half full of ice-cold water and the other contained a cold "pap" that was sticky to my fingers. I swallowed a draught of water which left behind a freezing column from throat to belly. The "pap" was marginally less cold but I knew that to give myself every chance of surviving I must eat and drink every morsel they placed before me.
>
> When the door opened again hands groped for me in the darkness and pulled me from the sweat box, hoisted me to my feet and frogmarched me to the front of the guard room where I was tied to a post. About an hour elapsed before I realised that every Jap who passed by struck me at least once, and this gave me the translation to a notice in Japanese fixed to the pole above my head. . . . At one time, during the three days' punishment, with variations at the whim of each guard, I reached a point where I could no longer maintain the "brave" front I had shown to the Japs. I slumped in my bonds in utter dejection and misery. Contrary to my expectations, from that moment onwards the blows hurt less, the cold seemed less intense, and my mind became clearer. The remaining period of my incarceration became easier to bear, and when finally we were released I was considerably stronger than I had been expected to be.

The prisoners were also subject to routine brutality. One was executed for trying to learn to read Japanese and then his body was used as the target for a bayonet drill by the guards: when it was examined there were more than seventy-five stab wounds. Another was starved to death for stealing food; it took sixty-two days.

At Aomi, twenty-six of a party of ninety-five men working in a limestone quarry died. In spite of repeated requests, no officer had been allowed out of the camp to see the conditions until Lt. Stephen Abbott, the British commanding officer, was allowed to visit them and work with them. Conditions at the quarry were even worse than he had expected. The men worked in pairs—first hacking at the cliff face with pickaxes, then raking the broken rock into a large bin, lifting it to shoulder level, and emptying the contents into a small railway truck. When the truck was full, the men pushed it about a quarter of a mile up a slope to the crushing machine. Each pair of men had to quarry and transport tons of rock each day. They were dying from exhaustion and working in fear of falling rock and stone. There was not even an established system for lookouts to watch the quarry face and give any warning of an avalanche.

When Abbott went to complain to Lt. Yoshimura the next day, he realized why he had been allowed to visit his men. He was about to be humiliated:

> "Insolent captive! So you have come to complain—despite my past warnings! How dare you presume so in your arrogance! You captives need a lesson: and you will be example."
>
> He drew his sword, took a pace forward, and screamed at me to kneel before him. The sword whistled and I felt the blade touch the top of my hair.
>
> "Your forehead on the ground! Say prayers if you wish."
>
> This time I thought the end really had come: Yoshimura could surely not draw back now without an unacceptable loss of "face." And so it seemed. He shouted to the interpreter to stand back and brought his sword down again—this time striking the straw mat within an inch of my head. I did not move; and, absurdly, I remember feeling astonishment at my total lack of fear. Perhaps it was because I had become hardened to the sight and thought of death. Then he struck again—this time cutting the cloth from my right shoulder and grazing the skin. He screamed hysterically—as if he had lost all self-control.
>
> At that moment I realised that this was no execution. It was a sadistic pretence with the purpose of frightening me and giving unnatural pleasure to our commandant. If he intended to kill me he would have done so at the first blow. The performance was deliberate and premeditated. I decided, wisely, to stay in my humiliating posture. The ugly pantomime continued for several more minutes, with more shouts and blows: then it stopped and I was ordered to stand up. Yoshimura was breathing hard. His face was flushed with the exertion.
>
> "You still have complaint to make?"
>
> "Yes. I still wish to talk about the quarry."
>
> I spoke without thinking and my voice seemed firm and clear. Heaven knows why: perhaps it was my own sense of drama and theatrical training. I was outwardly calm and felt as if nothing in the world could ever frighten me again. All this was a flash in the pan, but it helped in the moment of crisis. Yoshimura was obviously taken aback and listened in silence to what I had to say. Unhappily, it had no influence on the main issue.

> "What are the lives of a hundred captives when thousands of brave Japanese are dying each day for the Emperor."
>
> This was his heartless retort to the last protest I ever made to Yoshimura. That evening Yogi gave me a written order to read to everyone in the camp:
>
> "So many injuries has increased at every workshop recently. This is due to the carelessness of every worker while they are working. Of course it is caused by deficiency of strain in spirit. If workers should suffer any injuries by the deficiency of spirit they will not in future be allowed to receive medical treatment."

In the next two weeks a sergeant was killed and two men had legs amputated after accidents. The death toll rose to forty. But Yoshimura got an unexpected comeuppance when a new quarry was opened, and he was invited to detonate the first charge at a ceremonial parade. The prisoners, who had been confined to the camp, heard a loud explosion. That night Abbott was summoned to Sgt. Sumiki, the assistant commandant, who spoke English:

> "Mr. Abbott—I have to tell you of a terrible tragedy at the quarry this morning." He looked down and slapped the scabbard of his sword several times. I wondered what was coming next. "In this disaster many people were killed." He hesitated for a moment. "Among them was our brave Commander—Lieutenant Yoshimura."
>
> My heart leapt: but I forced down my relief, tactfully shook my head and repeated his words "terrible tragedy."
>
> Sergeant Sumiki raised his eyes to mine: then, quite suddenly, he burst into laughter, gave me a hearty thump on the shoulder and cried out, "You lie! You very pleased. Me, too, very pleased!"

It wasn't only the prisoners in Japan who worked in mines. Signalman Arthur Titherington and his fellow prisoners at Kinkaseki in Taiwan were put to work in an underground pit of caves, tunnels, and crevices: "a world of utter darkness, lit only by the flickering of carbide lamps, where desperate souls hacked, scraped and filled trucks." It was a copper mine where sweat poured down their naked bodies while the honchos with their hammers forced them on to "ever more impossible" labors. Each man had to shift nine to fifteen tons a day, and after 814 days at the mine Titherington was half his normal weight of about 168 pounds. When the men were moved to a new camp in March 1945 only eighty-nine of the 524 men who had arrived at Kinkaseki were still alive.

The new camp was in the mountains at Kukutsu. The men were given three months to clear land which had become virtual jungle and plant sixteen thousand sweet potato plants. Those months became the worst phase of their captivity. They were never hungrier, worked harder, or were beaten more, said Sgt. Jack Edwards. The former crop of tea plants had run riot and the land was covered with a tall, sharp-leaved grass which had grown to a height of up to nine feet. The top of each leaf was as sharp as a razor, said Titherington. It cut the men's half-naked bodies with a painful slashing motion. Men fell to the ground exhausted but the guards beat them on, shouting, "Speedo, speedo"; two or three brutal beatings occurred every day in June. Their rice rations were cut to 250 grams per man, and they were soon suffering from extreme malnutrition. Only on July 20, less than a month before Japan surrendered, did they receive Red Cross parcels—stamped "Bermondsey 1942"—each of which was shared among four men.

The best place to be a prisoner in Japan was at the officers' camp at Zentsuji on Shikoku Island. A showcase camp, Zentsuji was regularly visited by senior Japanese representatives of the Red Cross and international delegates. The Australians who arrived on July 17, 1942, found that their rooms were in two-story barracks. They were each provided with a mattress and pillow filled with rice husks, two blankets, three bowls, a spoon and fork, toothbrush and tooth powder, soap, a pencil, and a notebook. Americans, who had arrived earlier, had erected mosquito nets over the sleeping platforms. Their evening meal was bread, soup, hamburgers, an apple, and sweet buns. There were three thousand books in the library, and language courses were offered in English, Dutch, Spanish, French, German, Russian, Malayan, Hindustani, Italian, and Japanese. They could buy shirts in the canteen and up to twenty packs of cigarettes a month. They were even allowed to walk outside the camp. Two English-language newspapers were delivered to their rooms. The Zentsuji prisoners received many more letters than those held elsewhere.

But conditions deteriorated as the number of men in the camp grew from about two hundred in 1942 to seven hundred in 1944 and eight hundred in 1945. Newspaper deliveries were stopped, there was less on offer in the canteen, weekly baths were banned, the cigarette ration was cut, lectures were restricted to ten men, inspections increased, and morning parades were called. But the ordeal of captivity at Zentsuji remained much easier than elsewhere in Japan. By April 1944, according to the Red Cross, each man had received nine food parcels. The raisins, chocolate, and milk powder in the parcels saved the lives of many prisoners, even though the Japanese stopped many from reaching them. About ten thousand parcels arrived at

Zentsuji in October 1944, but the Japanese could not be persuaded to give regular extra rations to men who were seriously ill with malnutrition, taking many of the parcels for their own consumption. Similarly, when the men killed fifty of their chickens in October 1944, the Japanese took fifteen for themselves.

Only ten or eleven men died at Zentsuji, some as a result of their treatment before they arrived. The Australian historian Hank Nelson estimates the death rate at under 1 percent—compared, for Australians, with an average of 36 percent in other Japanese camps. As he writes, "there was no gross brutality, no beheadings, no cholera and no men were worked to death." The Zentsuji officers' camp, however, was exceptional. The prisoners who labored in Japan and Taiwan believed that their experience was even more horrifying than that endured by those who worked on the Burma–Thailand railway.

INTERLUDE

The "Jap-happy"

Many of the rare photographs of the men show them naked except for what looks like a loincloth. As their clothing wore out during captivity, they had to make do with whatever was at hand, as 2nd Lt. Jim Richardson recalled:

> We started off with whatever equipment we happened to possess when Singapore fell. Clothing which wore out was not replaceable. After a couple of years or so many of us had few respectable clothes. What we did have we conserved and cobbled up with rough mending until the "garments" literally fell apart. So it was by no means uncommon to see ragged-arsed other ranks and officers working along the rail track. Soon we copied an item of Nip wear. This is the very simple and totally functional "Jap-happy." It is a length of cotton material with a tape to tie around one's waist. It hangs down one's bum; is pulled up between the legs and tucked into the waistband. It is easy to wash

and very comfortable. It is easy to remove in the performance of the all too frequent natural functions. The Japs wore it as we, under normal circumstances, would wear a jockstrap or other underwear. As sole garment it was economical. The only hazard was for those more liberally endowed than the average: a vital possession might come adrift.

Chapter 23

HARUKU

The 2,071 British and Dutch prisoners who disembarked on May 4, 1943, on the small coral Spice Island of Haruku, south of Ceram in the Molucca Archipelago, were to suffer as cruel an ordeal as any endured by the prisoners of the Japanese. They had been sailing from Java for more than two weeks when they arrived toward midnight in a drenching downpour. They were ferried some of the way to the island in canoes and then waded ashore and stumbled through jungle undergrowth, lit by an occasional candle stuck in a coconut palm, to their camp a hundred yards away in a nutmeg grove. Only one or two huts had been partially built, and the open trench latrines that had been dug between them were overflowing with water. The men slept on the muddy ground.

There were about thirty sick men who were driven with the medical staff into a bamboo hut, about sixty yards long, with no sides and a perforated roof. They lay on mats on the waterlogged floor, but water flowed everywhere and the mats soon became pulp. Only one candle was available, which the Japanese took for themselves, and the medical officers were unable to attend to the soaked patients. The next morning the sick were moved to a similar hut, but the conditions remained abysmal. The floor was covered with tree roots and scored by small water channels and there was a slope of about three and a half feet down which water poured. Even with assistance, many of the sick could not get up: there were no bedpans and many fouled themselves during the night.

The whole camp was a quagmire, "ankle-deep" in mud, said Flt. Lt. Alastair Forbes, one of the medical officers. Each hut was in a similar condition. The cookhouse and firewood were sodden, so the luckiest men didn't get their first meal until twenty-four hours after they had arrived, but feeding had to be organized in shifts and some went thirty-six hours without food. That first meal, a small helping of manioc root and meat stew, would be their best meal for months. The only drinking water came from rain, or from the river that bordered the camp, which had to be boiled before consumption. When the first hut was completed, it was fenced with barbed wire and used as a hospital. Many men were already suffering from dysentery, fouling the ground and creating a plague of flies, but the Japanese refused a request to build latrines over the sea. The sea belonged to the Emperor, they said: "Nobody had to do that sort of thing" on Hirohito's property.

The dysentery cases, who badly needed more latrine trenches nearby, had not yet been isolated, said L.Cpl. James Home, who had been in Douglas Bader's 242 Squadron before sailing to the Far East. Each day the area became more fouled:

> A bamboo rail was placed along the length of these trenches for the sick to hold on to—but on more than one occasion a weakened man could not hang on, and would fall into those filthy trenches with their seething masses of large fat maggots. All this happened in full view of everyone else and we found it impossible to imagine anything more revolting and degrading, but it was all part of the exercise to humiliate us. In order to try and control the developing epidemic, we needed much more time and some help, yet the criminal lack of response from the Japs escaped all logic. A week or two longer [to prepare latrines] would have paid real dividends for everyone in the long term. From this time forward the Japs were totally responsible for the deaths that followed so unnecessarily on Haruku.

The simplest actions helped to spread the disease. The men could not wash their hands when they tied their bootlaces or rolled a cigarette. Yet by then touching their mouths they risked dysentery, for which the only treatment was seawater diluted with rainwater and used as a purgative.

Haruku had been chosen by the Japanese as the site of an airfield that would offer air protection to shipping and increase their ability to use the Flying Fortresses they had captured from the Americans to attack Australia, six hundred miles directly south. It was destined to become a paradigm of the worst Japanese prison camps. Obstinate and brutal commanders, determined to build an airfield for the Emperor whatever the human cost and guided by the spirit of Bushido, resisted every proposal to ameliorate the men's conditions. Unusually, however, it was a camp where the British officers—all from the RAF—understood that they had no divine right of authority and did not insist on the privileges of rank.

The refusal of the Japanese commanders to act on the prisoners' proposals to improve conditions had fatal consequences. The death toll at Haruku was one of the highest suffered in Japanese hands between 1942 and 1945. According to Sqn. Ldr. W. Pitts, the British commanding officer, the treatment meted out to the prisoners was "barbarous and inhuman." The Dutch medical officer, Dr. Rudi Springer, thought that the Japanese were out for "wilful murder." When they told the Japanese about their fear of an epidemic of dysentery, they often received the answer, "Nice when dead."

The horror of Haruku was compounded by the character of the main guards, Sgt. Mori and his toady, the Korean camp interpreter, Kasiyama—known as "Tokyo Taff." The lazy camp commandant, Lt. Kurashima, abdicated command of the camp to Mori and Kasiyama—who became known to the prisoners as "Blood" and "Slime" (the primary symptom of dysentery, which was to be the biggest killer of the men, is diarrhea made up of blood and mucus from the intestines). Mori, a hero of the war with China in the 1930s, was also known to fellow soldiers as "Bamboo Man"—he had filled sections of bamboo with dynamite and used them as hand grenades. He stood only five feet five inches, but terrorized the prisoners and enjoyed beating them before an audience. No Japanese or Korean dared to challenge him. Kasiyama was subservient, sneaky, and treacherous. He crept around outside the men's huts, listening to their conversations and reporting back to Mori. When, on one occasion, Mori decided that there would be an evening's entertainment, most of the men were so tired that they stayed in their huts. He sent Kasiyama to round up the prisoners. He slashed the walls of their huts with his bamboo pole, yelling, "Come out and be happy or I will punish you."

Flt. Lt. Leslie Audus described how Mori used a cudgel of split bamboo to beat his victims unmercifully. Kasiyama used a doubled-up length of rope for the same purposes, "like a crazy man." At the first *tenko* (roll call) after Mori was told that his quota of prisoners could not be met because so many men were ill, the officers were lined up alongside the men and slapped about the head. James Home explained precisely what this entailed:

> Being "slapped" by the Japs should not be confused with the playful slaps that may be exchanged by Westerners. It consisted of a clenched fist thrown from the thigh with maximum force ending up on the face or skull with rapid repetitive movements. Beatings came along regularly

> and cost very little, as cheap as a bat of an eyelid sometimes. If you were unable to take the beating, or went down purposely thinking your attacker would desist, you had made your first mistake, for then the boot would go in with obvious joy. If you could avoid flinching or showing any sign of distress you may "save face," which, however you understand it, was their second commandment.

Home also described what happened when Mori and Kasiyama turned their attention to the sick:

> All the sick who could stand, including those with leg ulcers, chest problems, severe neuritis, beriberi and the many symptoms of malnutrition, were on parade. It was no use leaving anyone behind in a hut hoping to cover for them, as the guards would be flying around, joyfully looking for victims as they brandished their personal length of bamboo. Mori and Kasiyama, in their usual bawdy fashion, went viciously along the Tenko lines hitting over the head anyone they considered fit enough to reach the drome. Only when their quota was finally reached would they dismiss the Tenko.

The Japanese never went sick, the medical officers were told. It was work or starve. Those who could walk could work. When five men out at work were thrown bananas by the natives, a guard found the skins. Four owned up but one denied eating a banana. The four who had admitted to the "crime" were made to kneel on sharp-pebbled ground from morning until 6 P.M. without food or drink and hit with a rifle butt if they tried to relax. When the men returned from work, according to Leslie Audus, a hundred of them were formed into a ring:

> The man who denied eating the banana was brought to Mori. First he lacerated his cringing victim's limbs with a sharp-edged bamboo stick and then whipped off his canvas army belt and lashed him as he lay squirming and bleeding on the ground. After that the other malefactors were "corrected" by making them run the gauntlet of the ring of prisoners, each one having to give them a slap. If the slap was not hard enough, the "slacker" himself was whacked with a bamboo stick and told to try again.

The indifference of Dr. Shimada, the Japanese medical officer who visited the camp periodically, allowed free rein to the callousness of Mori and Kasiyama. According to Alastair Forbes, Shimada saw his main responsibility as lecturing the prisoners on the spirit of Bushido. The surgical equipment provided was poor and instruments were often broken or incomplete: "The receipt of half a dozen bandages, a small quantity of iodoform and some sterile normal saline was cause for rejoicing."

The men learned what Operation Haruku was on May 10 when twelve hundred of them were marched two miles in two working parties of six hundred each to the site of the airfield. They were halted between two huge humps of coral at the top of a hill. The hill faced a valley, on the other side of which, roughly five hundred yards away, was another hill of about equal size. They were dubbed the "camel's humps." Among the men was Pte. Tony Cowling:

> A nice view, but where was the land that we were to make into an airstrip? You could have bowled the whole 600 over with a blade of couch grass when the guards produced 300 household hammers and chisels and ordered us to cut the tops off the hills and carry the debris into the valley. This was how to build an airstrip Japanese style? A truck arrived with hundreds of little baskets. These little wicker baskets were about 24 inches wide, 18 inches from back to front, and had a carrying handle on either side. Their load capacity must have been all of 25 to 30 pounds. These were unloaded and the men without hammers and chisels started carrying baskets full of our scrapings to dump in the valley.
>
> The Japanese had brought us all this way in a hellship to work like coolies constructing an airstrip in the most primitive manner conceivable. We were obviously an expendable commodity. Their contempt for us was plain. It was clear that they were going to get the maximum work for the minimum expenditure. I realized that my life was at stake. Our captors did not have a conscience. This was truly survival of the fittest or even more primitive—straight survival—for whom amongst us was fit? That night our "meal" consisted of 20 one-pound cans of meat, a few vegetables and some rice to be shared by 2071 hungry, half-starved male adults. The rice, half cooked, measured out to half a billy-can each. The hell of Haruku had started.

Work on the airfield was hard, especially for men who were not used to manual labor, said Leslie Audus. The shadowless, shimmering surface of the projected airfield was baking hot when scorched by the tropical sun but unpleasantly bleak when it rained. It was so hot that between 11 A.M. and 3 P.M. Airman James "Freddie" Chandler tied handkerchiefs round each knee and over the backs of his hands. His feet and lips swelled "unmercifully," but he thought that the psychological effect of getting away from the camp, even to do such grueling work, was doing more good than anybody realized: "It was easy to lie back in hospital and become a mass of vermin and eventually die. But by getting out in the sun and facing up to the work and getting the benefits of the extras provided, there was at least a ray of hope."

Men injured their feet on the coral and became cripples, but still they had to work. The meals of rice pap twice a day were wholly insufficient to maintain the men's health. Medicine ran out after May 15. By May 20, fifteen men had died and only six hundred men were fit for work—and many of those were sick but had been passed as fit by Mori. The sick were constantly "tormented" by thirst, said Audus. There were too few tins, too few men employed to bring water from the river, and too few fires to boil it.

There was also a plague of flies: "In the hospital huts one heard the buzzing of millions of flies accompanied by the groans and hiccups of the mortally sick men," one doctor noted. "Maggots crawl over befouled sleeping places and over the exhausted men." The flies were so tormenting that Mori made the sick hand in twenty-five of the insects before they were allowed food; in June the target was increased to a hundred. Soon there were twelve hundred cases of dysentery. By the end of May, only twenty-seven days after arriving on the island, the first symptoms of pellagra—sores on the mouth and in the throat—caused by a deficiency of nicotinic acid in the men's diet, began to appear. Men with scurvy (from a lack of vitamin C) were bleeding from the nose and gums; stomach pains were universal. Sixty-five men had died—their stomachs were the size of a three-year-old child's.

On returning to camp, the routine was to form a burial party and to bury the men who had died the previous night and that day. The carpenter was kept busy making bamboo coffins, but they became too expensive for the Japanese and soon the dead had to be buried in rice sacks. They were carried in a coffin shoulder-high from the hospital morgue to the swamp that was the cemetery. Then the coffin was opened and the burial party removed the sack-covered body. Tony Cowling described what happened next:

> The graves were shallow, as slightly below the swampy surface was the coral rock. It invariably fell on the sick in camp to dig the graves. Normally only one man can dig a coral grave at a time as this involved swinging a pickaxe, so it becomes a drawn-out, difficult task. It was absolutely impossible for a sick man to dig six feet down in coral in one day. It was imperative to bury the dead the same day, as the heat, flies and rotten condition of their bodies meant that deterioration had already set in when they were

> hoisted shoulder-high. Many of us on the burial parties had the experience of a liquid flowing slowly out of the coffin and over our shoulders.
>
> The gravediggers could not keep up with demand for new graves so a common grave became the accepted way to lay to rest those that had succumbed during the last 24 hours. A grave for ten, twelve, or fourteen was to be expected at the height of the dysentery epidemic. Normally a guard would attend the burial ceremony—not out of respect for the dead but to guard the burial party as the cemetery was outside the camp barbed wire. Many times when we had been kept working until after dark it was the guard's job to light the way to the cemetery with a candle in one hand and rifle in the other.
>
> Occasionally Sergeant Mori would come to the cemetery, sometimes solemn, sometimes drunk. On these occasions he was a menace as he would brandish his sword, yelling at the top of his guttural, syphilitic voice at all within earshot. His actions confirmed the persistent rumours that he had syphilis. The doctors confirmed that his behaviour was entirely in keeping with the advanced stages of syphilis. On one occasion he was so drunk that he vomited into the grave as the body was lowered to its final resting place.

The doctors were in despair. There was no cooperation from the Japanese, who insisted on controlling everything, even the diet of the sick, who were supposed to be kept alive on rice porridge. Men who were convalescing craved food but were allowed no extra rations. Avitaminosis and emaciation increased. "One gets a premonition of death on a grand scale," one doctor wrote in his diary:

> Quite a lot of men show strong retrogression in their field of vision. The "blurred vision" which we saw in Surabaya deteriorates here into total blindness. Some have small sores on the eye, very painful and certainly ascribable to vitamin lack. Since they cannot see they can no longer catch flies although every patient, no matter how sick, is required to catch flies or else he gets no food. It is heart-rending to see these skeletons of young men sitting with an improvised fly-swatter in one hand, a little container for the corpses in the other.

Men were also blinded by the intense glare of sunlight reflecting off the coral as they worked on the airstrip.

The dysentery epidemic reached its peak in June, when forty-two men died during the first week; by the end of the month, 189 were dead. In the eight huts allocated to the sick, the doctors played a "grim game of ludo," with their patients as the counters. To be switched to Huts 1 or 2, where the most severe cases were treated, amounted to a death sentence. Aware that men entered the dysentery hut at one end and usually left for the mortuary at the other, LAC Fred Ryall made the "most important decision" of his life: he discharged himself, even though he was desperately ill. His decision meant that he was deemed fit for work. He crawled on the coral on his hands and knees because he was too weak to stand. A friend gave him a sip of water from his precious flask, an act of compassion, Ryall believed, that saved his life.

Years later, men who survived Haruku could still recall the scenes they saw in Hut 1. One visitor was James Home:

> The "death hut" stank to high heavens as all the patients were at the dying stage or no-hopers. The orderlies continued to lift "skeletons with skin" over wooden buckets or else they slipped a tin plate under a body that could not be moved. Having washed a body and its sleeping space, the emaciated man was rested for only a very short period of time before the same operation began all over again throughout the length of the hut. There was little wonder no Jap ever stepped foot inside. Their crass brutality did not provide them with that sort of courage, and they found it easier to kill than to save life. At night that hut was allowed one hurricane-type lantern but oil for it was severely rationed, so that when the moon was bright the oil had to be saved. At night it was difficult to judge whether a man had died without clambering up onto the bamboo shelf and looking directly into his face.
>
> There is little wonder they called it the "death hut"—bodies were laid on the bamboo shelves covered in their own excreta. They had ulcerated legs and many other sores, mouths wide open with dozens of horse flies and bluebottles in attendance. Maggots would often emerge from each and every orifice, crawling over their bodies, and all the men could do was lay there in filth and cry out for help. These were men who not many months before were perfectly healthy and happy "middle- or working-class" people and they were now being needlessly murdered by the Japs who never came forward with constructive help of any sort.

Mori, however, would not allow a separate working party for the hospital huts. Orderlies finishing their grueling night duty were ordered to join airstrip working parties and missed their sleep. The Japanese, Mori argued, were working twenty-four hours a day, so why shouldn't the prisoners? But with thirteen hundred men sick, Mori could not find the workers he needed to finish the airfield: on one day in June only 120 were fit enough for work. Mori raided the huts where the least sick men were housed and chose ninety-five of the 157 men for so-called light duties. As usual, the Japanese medical officer did not object.

Escape was out of the question: the local population was too frightened of the Japanese, there was no access to boats and nowhere to go to. As Flt. Lt. Dick Philps said, Haruku was not like Germany, where some escapes were successful. "There was only one way out of the camp and that was in a coffin. Death was the only escape."

By now food was the men's only topic of conversation (women had taken a back seat to hunger), and they were reduced to raiding the jungle for roots and leaves to supplement their rice, which they at least could flavor with the local nutmeg and mace, and vegetable soup. Yet, although they were constantly hungry, as they marched back to camp scrawny, half naked, cold, and wet, they sang "Colonel Bogey" and other RAF favorites to lift their spirits.

Mori devised a cunning tactic to exploit their hunger and his need for workers. He opened a shop—but only workers could buy the fruit, eggs, dried fish, and cigarettes it sold. He also doubled the rations and introduced pay of ten cents a day for workers—which didn't buy very much—but cut the supply of fruit to the hospital huts. The sick, he reasoned, would soon be induced to volunteer for work. LAC Peacock was one prisoner who decided to join the airfield party, even though he had malaria:

> The shop opened, when it opened at all, immediately after the working parties had been counted and dismissed. The Nips intended to see that it was the workers who got the goodies. But prices were very high for ten-cents-a-day men and customers tended to be those who had made money in strictly illegal deals with natives or Nips, or by smuggling contraband into camp. Faced with the sort of problem that no doubt sometimes baffles Chancellors of the Exchequer today, the Nips tried another way of channelling rewards to deserving mouths. No purchases were to be made without a special ticket issued only to workers. To qualify for one of these much-sought-after tickets you had to be on an outside working party at the time some sort of supplies turned up for the shop and, most important, while the Gunzo [Mori] was in a generous frame of mind. Whether or not there would be an issue of tickets became a burning issue of the working day. We even had a little song about it, sung to the tune of the Nips' lights-out bugle call. Unfortunately it is not fit to repeat. Of course the tickets didn't defeat the camp tycoons. They had more than enough cash to buy up the tickets as well as the tobacco.

The number of fatalities continued to mount. By the beginning of July, two hundred had died. When Mori was feeling generous, he would allow purchases for the hospital. But when one doctor got some eggs, Mori distributed one egg to ten patients. Dr. Shimada told the medical officers that if they had no medicines, they must treat the sick with "spirit." In Japan nobody died of dysentery, he said. So the misery—"filth, disease, emaciation and death," as Audus put it—continued. By the end of July, 243 men were dead.

When Mori had sent all the men who transported food and water to the hospital to work on the airfield in August, one doctor wrote eloquently in his diary:

> Now even more difficulties have been placed in our way, notwithstanding the fact that the state of the sick is becoming simply frightful. Extreme emaciation down to skin and bone, numerous infected wounds, skin parasites, pellagra, mental disturbances, gross filthiness, chronic diarrhoea, impaired movement even to the extent of complete paralysis, swollen stomachs and legs due to the enormous accumulation of water, that is the human suffering here, the like of which beggars description. Many howl with pain and abject misery under these hopeless conditions. The fact that there is still a young British soldier who begs me shortly before his death to tell his mother that he "died like a soldier" testifies to the strength of spirit which exceeds all comprehension.
>
> We have nowhere near enough ordinary bandaging material and we experience increasing difficulties in treating innumerable tropical ulcers, infected sores, fungal infections and skin lesions. We just have available a little iodoform, a mixture of tooth powder, aspirin, boric acid and ichthyol and also a little dermatol. The tropical ulcers have gradually become so extensive that we have to admit men to hospital for treatment. Then for a few days they can be tended with bandages soaked in a solution of rivanol, chloramine or potassium permanganate. The only salves, which we sometimes receive in the form of boric and ichthyol ointments [used to treat skin complaints] are presumably made up in unpurified lard so that when we use them eczema is often the result.

The doctors improvised. One "concoction," used to coat ulcers, was made from Japanese tooth powder, coconut oil, and chalk. It formed a hard seal but it was sometimes necessary to keep the patient off his feet. Surgery was often then possible, using a deep incision near the ulcer to drain off stagnant blood; borassic powder was used as an antiseptic. Some men had to have this treatment ten times, but once the battle against infection was won, recovery, as with appendicitis and war wounds, was often rapid. Nonetheless, by September 5, the death toll was 284.

But it was also in September that Mori finally authorized the building of a bamboo jetty out to sea to serve as a latrine—a request first made by Pitts when they had arrived four months earlier. The "super-loo" was a major landmark in the history of Haruku, said Leslie Audus: its effect on morale could not be overstressed. "Compare the pleasure of squatting over gently lapping water and gazing out over the blue sea to the beautiful, jungle-covered island of Ceram, with the revulsion and misery of similarly squatting over a trench filled with a stinging writhing soup of yellow faeces and fly maggots."

Don Peacock was another satisfied customer:

> The opening of this masterpiece was a great occasion for the Gunzo. He looked on with pride as the first customers arrived and crouched on their haunches over the holes like a troop of bare-bottomed monkeys. The British clutched bunches of leaves; the more practical Dutch each carried a bottle of water suspended from a finger with a piece of string. The Gunzo appeared to consider for a moment these primitive Western ideas of hygiene, then he strolled benignly along the line of squatting men presenting each with a square of Nip toilet paper. As he stood back to see his gifts put to good use, each man, British and Dutch alike, carefully folded up the precious piece of paper and stowed it carefully away. The British used their leaves, the Dutch their water. The Gunzo scratched his head and walked away. Every scrap of paper on the camp, including even the odd Bible, had been used to roll the local tobacco into cigarettes. Toilet paper was certainly much too valuable to be used on backsides.

As Audus observed, if it hadn't been for the "short-sighted bloody-mindedness" of the Japanese, the dysentery epidemic could have been averted and the airfield finished earlier.

The arrival of a party of mostly Dutch prisoners from Amahai in Ceram in October had several effects on Haruku. It also had an effect on the men from Amahai, who were shocked by what they saw, as one naval officer recorded:

> When we came into the camp through the dank steaming jungle a clammy fear gripped us. There was something indefinably cruel in all the trees and climbing plants which grew over them . . . threatening to engulf the damp palm-frond huts of the camp to form a green hell. It was forbidden for the healthy to go into the dysentery huts; a sort of

> parody of a rule of hygiene, but one day a sailor came and asked me, "Will you go to visit our big marine sergeant for a while? He would be so happy to see you before he goes." I slipped into the hut of the "serious dysentery cases" and there, naked, lay a man I once knew as a strong robust chap. Only the eyes were still alive. Maggots crawled over the immeasurably befouled baleh-baleh [bamboo sleeping-platform] and over his dying body. It was impossible for the two orderlies to clean those Augean stables, and it was no use contemplating more orderlies. Everyone had to go to the airfield. Mori took good care of that.

Overcoming their sense of shock, the Amahaiers determined to improve the morale of the Haruku men. They decided to work hard on the airfield so that it was completed quickly, encouraging the Haruku men to hold on in the hope of returning to Java. They sang and whistled as they marched to the airfield and their attitude impressed the guards as well as the Haruku old-timers. The guards saw the work accelerating and behaved somewhat more reasonably, said Audus, while the original Haruku men felt themselves challenged and uplifted.

At the time of the Amahaiers' arrival the dysentery epidemic on Haruku was largely over and the main killers were now the vitamin-deficiency diseases beri-beri and pellagra. Optical neuritis was also still causing partial or even complete blindness. On November 25 a party of sick men, "emaciated, naked and several unable to speak or see properly," and "in rags," left Haruku for Java. The Japanese had at last taken notice of Pitts's appeals to evacuate them from the island. They traveled to Ambon, where many were transferred to the 4600-ton *Suez Maru,* which sailed on November 25 with about 550 British and Dutch prisoners from Haruku and Ambon. Four days later the American submarine *Bone Fish* torpedoed the ship. Seven Japanese were rescued; everyone else died, some machine-gunned in the sea by an escorting Japanese corvette. Another 280 sick Haruku men, who sailed the same day, arrived in Java on December 21. Twenty died on the journey.

Meanwhile, the arrival of the Amahaiers with their determination to work had spurred Mori to improve the camp. New roads with storm gullies, new huts, a new hospital with three wards, and a parade ground were built by officers and men classified as "sick-in-quarters." Nursing became easier. The men were also allowed to build fires in their huts and could cook food. There were about eight acres of gardens which grew tomatoes, maize, katella (manioc), sweet potatoes, lambok, and other vegetables. The Japanese took the vegetables; the men were given the katella leaves. The men also dug a twenty-foot well which then had to be lined with stones and boulders brought back from every visit to the river. If they failed to bring a load back, they were made to return and as a punishment to hold the boulder over their heads.

To speed the construction of the runway, the Japanese started to use explosives and then secondhand bombs, as Fred Ryall recalled:

> We would have to make four, five or six holes in a section of coral with our chisels, putting into each a charge of dynamite and a fuse. When the Jap guard had retreated to a safe distance, he gave the order to light the fuse. We would then retreat as quickly and as far as possible, waiting for the explosions and hoping against hope there would be five. If it were only four, it was our job to go back and investigate. Even dynamite did not shift the coral in great quantities and captured Dutch bombs were introduced. We had to dig holes to take the bombs, set the fuse and retire. This, and the introduction of some sort of mechanical digger, eventually enabled the work to be finished—and within days of finishing the work the Allies came over and bombed it, so we were back again to fill in the craters.

The sight and drone of Flying Fortresses provoked mixed reactions. They meant—cheeringly—that the Americans were closing in. "But hearing allied aircraft only made the men's plight seem more pitiable," said Freddie Chandler. "It seemed unlikely that they would know of our existence, and to be in such need of everything and then to hear a plane and think of the crew and where they were going, and above all, what they would eat, was enough almost to drive one into a frenzy of starvation."

By mid-January 1944, there was no more dysentery and only one or two men were now dying each week. However, on May 5, a year and a day after their arrival on Haruku, the bombers were the only "bringers of hope," said Audus. There had been no fruit or fish in the shop for a week and avitaminosis was increasing again. There were no medicines. Most of the men wore only a "Jap-happy."

When asked to become a medical orderly, Tony Cowling agreed eagerly. It was an opportunity to help his fellow prisoners rather than the Japanese. A new world was revealed to him as he saw patients with advanced beri-beri, ulcers, and malaria, and men who had lost their sight because of malnutrition and the glare of the sun. He was most shocked by his first visit to Hut 1:

> I walked down the centre aisle with scrawny lifeless bodies on either side of me. Men who were only skin and bone with puny little bits of flesh hanging where muscles should be. I was devastated. Had I made the right

> decision to work for my buddies? I soon realized that it was far more important for me to be in here, regardless of the conditions, rather than out in the sun and rain working for an enemy that wanted to starve me to death. When I had finished taking in my new surroundings I mentioned to the doctor that one of the men had a scrotum swollen and heaving. I asked him what this condition was. The poor devil had been given up for dead in an effort to save other more promising lives. Flies had laid eggs in a cut on his scrotum and now maggots were developing inside this man. Other men, who by sheer willpower had overcome fantastic odds, had been in the ward for a long time, lying curled in the foetal position for lack of space. Now the ligaments behind their knees had shortened so that they were incapable of walking. In fact they could not straighten their legs, which were permanently bent at the knees. The doctors had arranged for orderlies to get some rocks off the beach, string from an old rice sack and assemble a weight tied to the patient's legs and strung over a bar at the foot of the bamboo. The constant weight of the rock would supposedly stretch the ligaments towards their normal position. I do not remember a single case of successful recovery. This little trip through No. 1 Ward made me aware that there is always someone worse off than you are!

According to Alastair Forbes, bedpans were useless because some patients were too weak to use one even when held by an orderly. So tin plates were placed under their buttocks, removed at regular intervals, washed, and replaced.

During their first five months on Haruku, 334 men died. After the seriously ill men left, the sea latrine was constructed, yeast was produced (using the techniques described in Chapter 18), and the gardens were started, "only" fifty-two died in the last nine months. If only the Japanese had listened. Haruku was gradually closed down in July and August 1944. As the prisoners left the camp, beside the road, hidden in the bushes in the half light, the local population of Haruku had turned out and were playing a tune on bamboo pipes. It was the tune to "When this bloody war is over/Oh! How happy I shall be." Leslie Audus recalled the scene:

> One will never know whether they chose this tune because of the singularly appropriate words or whether it was a happy chance because the tune is also that of the delightful Salvation Army hymn, "Jesus Wants Me for a Sunbeam" and they had clearly been visited by Dutch missionaries. As they understood almost no English, it is probable that it was a happy accident, possibly the happiest accident of a lifetime. Or perhaps—

> engaging thought—they had heard the men singing it as they marched to work and thought we went to work singing hymns. It was clearly an act of sympathy, of solidarity, because they too had had their share of maltreatment by the Japanese. It was a touching and moving experience.

The last party of half a dozen men, commanded by Audus, departed for Ambon on August 1, and the gate of the Haruku camp was closed forever. Had all the sweat, pain, beatings, and death been in vain? Audus wondered after the war. It was unlikely that the airfield played any significant role in the Japanese war effort. Nor had the Japanese reckoned on the Americans' outflanking them in the Banda Sea. But life for prisoners of the Japanese was often a cruel lottery. Those who had survived the horror of Haruku probably blessed their good fortune. But the group who had left in November had been killed at sea in a hellship, and the gods of war had yet more to throw at the men who left in July and August in another. Five hundred went to Ambon but the rest were returned to Java, under the command of Flt. Lt. W. M. Blackwood, on the *Maros Maru,* which left Ambon on September 17.

The journey of the *Maros,* a small six-hundred-ton wooden diesel ship, took sixty-eight days. The holds were battened down so that the five hundred Dutch and British prisoners had to travel on deck, where the sick were exposed to sun and tropical storms without any cover and confined within a space that measured forty by thirty feet. Only after thirty men had died from dehydration and exposure did the Japanese allow a makeshift awning to cover the seriously ill. Staying close to land to avoid Allied bombers, the *Maros* arrived at Raha Moena in the Celebes on September 21, then sailed for Macassar the next day carrying an extra 128 prisoners who had survived a bombing on another ship. The Korean guards bathed in drums of drinking water while the men were given less than half a pint a day. The sick men cluttered the hatches and began to die even more quickly. James Home was on the ship:

> Scenes of indescribable horror continued until they became commonplace: men picked their way through the tangled mass of humanity which lay around the narrow ship; and orderlies carried the naked and wasted bodies of the dead to the side of the ship where men like Bill Lockwood and Bud Fisher of the "waxed moustache" helped to cast the weighted bodies into the sea. Tongues began to blacken, and raw shoulders peeled and bled whilst the last drops of sanity left many men as each night was filled with the tortured yells and moans of the dying. They were joined by the curses of the more able who tried so hard to gain a little rest, hoping to sleep away their worries if only for an hour.

> Some of the more chronically ill developed an awful-sounding symptom that seemed to affect a man about to die of beriberi—a loud lasting period of violent hiccuping. Another youngster, delirious and distraught with sunstroke, shouted out the thoughts of a demented and distorted mind for thirty long hours before he became too weak to utter a single word. By this time men were dying like flies in the winter, their bodies being thrown overboard at regular intervals at the rate of about eight men each day.

More men died at Macassar before the *Maros Maru* sailed on toward Java. It was then marooned at sea for forty days. The men starved in the baking heat and were parched for water. As many as twenty men died each day, most in delirium, according to Dr. Rudi Springer. There were no rocks on board to weigh down the corpses and a working party had to go ashore to collect more. Sharks followed the ship, waiting for their daily feast.

Dick Philps saw men suddenly become euphoric:

> Many sang, rather tunelessly. About a day later there was slurring of speech, dribbling at the mouth, squinting and awkwardness of movement. The patient remained fairly rational when answering questions but was otherwise (fortunately) in a happy, dreamy state. On the third or fourth day he became delirious and died. The grotesque situation, particularly at night, with several men lying around the deck singing, can't possibly be imagined. Some men just died; no special symptoms developed; they just passed away. Some even seemed to decide to die. On several occasions I saw this, once in a personal friend who, in earlier days, before all this, had been my batman. He gave up, said he was going to die and, despite my pleadings, was dead in 24 hours. Obviously malnutrition was a big factor but the will entered it as well.

When the *Maros Maru* finally arrived at Surabaya on Java on November 23, half the men had died—"murdered," said James Home, "by inhuman indifference":

> Those who survived were mere ghosts of their former selves and many were half-demented wrecks of humanity, diseased, filthy and crawling with vermin. On the given signal to offload I tried bracing myself ready to climb out of the hold and onto terra firma; knowing that something most unpleasant was happening to me, I was rather apprehensive. Could I get out of the hold? Would someone offer to help Joe haul me

> out?—I could not afford to be left in the hold. Perhaps I had become a little panicky. I tried standing on my feet only to go crashing down in a big heap on the floor; no-one needed to tell me that I was paralysed from my waist down, a symptom of beriberi.
>
> "For Christ's sake, Jim, what's the matter? We've got to get off this bloody ship," said a concerned Joe, now forgetting his own troubles.
>
> "I've had it Joe, you get out before you land in trouble."
>
> I was concerned that he would be further punished for aiding and abetting me. I had been careless enough to become useless like those Jap animals in their fields—my future may be very short. Another semi-fit lad came across as they usually did, and together they dragged and pushed me out. It hurt like hell and each movement was agony, but I was to be forever grateful to my pals.

As the survivors walked into the camp, they looked like the last inmates of Belsen on the day of their liberation, said Laurens van der Post. One of the doctors who treated them at St. Vincentius Hospital, Nowell Peach, described them as no more than "skeletons."

Almost one in two of the men who arrived on Haruku did not survive. There were 1,021 deaths among the 2,071 men—386 at Haruku itself and 635 at other camps or on ships to Java. Another hundred and fifty prisoners simply disappeared, and many others died before the end of the war.

Haruku offered another outstanding example of the heroic work of Allied medical officers in captivity. They took beatings as they defended the sick, tended to the ill and dying in hellish conditions, and used their ingenuity to overcome the lack of medicines, drugs, and equipment.

At courts-martial in Singapore in July 1946, Kurashima and Mori were sentenced to death by hanging, and the Korean guard Kasiyama to life imprisonment.

INTERLUDE

A Conjuring Trick

The prisoners relished tricking the Japanese. Their sense of mischief, especially when they baffled the guards, cheered them up and helped to lift their spirits, as Lt. Louis Baume recalled:

> Gifts from the Indians and thefts from the Japanese enabled us to fare not too badly, but stealing had reached a high level and the constant loss of supplies was a source of great annoyance to the Japanese, who threatened the severest punishment yet failed to stop the thefts or to trace the culprits. Eventually a Japanese officer was detailed to take what steps he could and his idea was to prove to the British troops that the Japanese were fully aware of the methods adopted by us and to ridicule our efforts. So the British POWs were collected on the dockside and formed up in a circle, leaving a clear space of some twenty or thirty yards for the demonstration. The Japa-

nese officer appeared on the scene carrying a wooden box of tinned milk and in the course of his demonstration deliberately dropped the box so that it burst open. Before picking it up again, he removed three tins of milk which he put under his hat on one side. He pointed out that this was a very foolish thing for the British to do, since the Japanese knew all about it, and the next man caught would be severely punished. When he turned to take up his hat, he found that the three tins of milk had disappeared from underneath it. This infuriated him so that he ordered a squad of Japanese to line up all the prisoners in three ranks. There had obviously been no way whereby the prisoners could have disposed of the milk, yet despite five searches, it was nowhere to be found. The Japanese officer then announced his intention of shooting the prisoner concerned unless he surrendered the milk but this was of no avail. Eventually in a rage he ordered the prisoners back to camp, and stood glowering by the gate as they marched through. Imagine his feelings when one of the prisoners as he passed, rolled towards the Japanese officer three tins of milk, exclaiming, "Here, Buddy, is your milk!" Before he could recover from his surprise the prisoner had disappeared from view.

Chapter 24

SANDAKAN

About 2,750 prisoners—roughly two thousand Australians and the rest British—arrived at Sandakan in North Borneo in 1942 and 1943. By the time they had finished building a military airport in September 1944, about 2,240 were still alive. Approximately 210 men had died in the previous twenty-five months, an extraordinarily low death toll by the standards of Japanese prison camps. (During that time about three hundred officers had been transferred to Kuching.) Yet over the next eleven months all but six Australians of those 2,240 men perished in one of the worst atrocities committed by the Japanese during the war. When the airport was finished and the men were of no further use to their Japanese "tyrants," they were killed as effectively and systematically as if they had been placed against a wall and shot. The method of execution the Japanese chose was starvation, said Capt. Athol Moffitt, when he prosecuted the camp commandant, Capt. Susumi Hoshijima, at a 1946 war crimes trial.

Sandakan in most ways was no different from any other Japanese prisoner-of-war camp. The men were persistently denied medical supplies, and the sick were beaten and flogged to work. If it had not been for the events of 1944 and 1945, it would be remembered mainly for the small punishment cage designed by Hoshijima in which prisoners were incarcerated, and for the torture of men who were discovered running an underground intelligence operation with the locals. One torture victim was Lt. Rod Wells, an Australian former teacher accused of having a radio, who was taken into custody by the Kempetai and kept in isolation. When his interrogator lost patience with Wells, he changed his tactic from alternating reward and punishment to just punishment—and a horrifying punishment at that:

> He asked whether I was hungry and I said I was. With that they brought in a container of raw rice. I thought it was cooked rice. He said, "Eat," and I thought he was joking because he smiled when he said it. I said I would, but I only ate a little bit because it was raw rice. With that, two of their bullies came in, held my hands behind my back, opened my mouth, poured it in by spoon, and kept tapping my head till I swallowed it. I don't know how much of it I had, probably three or four cupfuls they got down my throat. Then they brought a garden hose in, held me, pushed the hose down my neck and turned it on. They kept going until the water came gushing up.
>
> They threw me back in the cell. You can imagine the rest. About three or four hours later the pain became excruciating as the rice swelled within the stomach. I didn't know much about human anatomy then, but the rice must have somehow gone through the pylorus, the outlet from the stomach, into the small intestine, and the pain for about a day and a half was intense. Part of the bowel came out; but there was no medical attention. It bled for a while; it was painful and gradually it got better. I managed to push it back by hand. Then the interrogation continued.
>
> On another occasion the interviewer produced a small piece of wood like a meat skewer, pushed that into my left ear, and tapped it in with a small hammer. I think I fainted some time after it went through the drum. I remember the last excruciating sort of pain, and I must have gone out for some time because I was revived with a bucket of water. I was put back in the cell again after that. The ear was very painful; it bled for a couple of days, with no medical attention. But fortunately for me it didn't become infected. Eventually it healed, but of course I couldn't hear with it, and I have never been able to hear since.

Twenty-two men were interrogated during that Kempetai investigation: one died during questioning; one was acquitted. Eight, mostly local Asians but including Capt. L. C. Mathews, AIF, who was posthumously awarded the Military Cross, were executed by firing squad in March 1944. The rest were sentenced to imprisonment at Outram Road Jail, Singapore.

Hoshijima's punishment cage, placed in front of the guardhouse and exposed to the weather and mosquitoes, was four and a half feet high, four and a half feet wide, and five and a half feet long. The men could not stand up or lie down properly, and they had to crawl into it. Sentences in the cage could be for anything up to thirty days. Men were given no blanket and no mosquito net, and their only clothing was a loincloth. For the first seven days they were also given no food and were allowed out to the latrines just twice a day. They were taken out for exercise twice a day, too, when they were beaten with sword sticks. Often they had to be carried back. Sick men with their hands tied behind their backs were put in the cage. A larger cage was built later; some men were sentenced to it for the duration. According to Moffitt, one man's weight fell from 168 to 84 pounds in fifteen days. About fifteen men died or their deaths were hastened because they were put in the cages.

Hoshijima was brutal:

> For laziness or fancied laziness of one or two, whole parties of fifty and sixty would be lined up, made to stand to attention then bashed on the back, face or anywhere else with sticks, hoes, rifle butts or canes. Some were deliberately kicked in the testicles. They then were made to stand looking directly at the sun without hats or shirts, holding their hands, sometimes with weights in them, straight out in front of them. This procedure sometimes lasted for more than an hour. Officers were treated the same. Two men had their eyes knocked out, one having his eye gouged out by Hoshijima himself. Many men had teeth knocked out or jaws broken. Hoshijima did a lot of the beating himself. His favourite trick was to make an officer stand to attention and "king hit" him: after knocking him to his feet with kicks he would repeat the performance two or three times. Men were kicked on the ulcers to make them work harder or to see if they really had ulcers.
>
> The case of Corporal Darlington, the cook, is one specific case. It is quite typical. He objected to a Jap guard washing his underpants in one of the cooking utensils. The Jap beat him and he retaliated, hitting the Jap on the lip. Four Jap guards then set on him. He was made to kneel in a most painful position for an hour on a sharp triangular piece of wood with a similar piece behind his knees to prevent his relaxing. In this position he was beaten by the guards with sticks. He was kicked in the crotch. His arm was broken and he was rendered unconscious, bleeding from the head, face, arm and legs. His arms were tied and he was placed in the small cage unconscious. There he remained for forty-eight hours with only a glass of water, his broken arm tied behind his back. Witnesses say he was delirious with pain.

Conditions at Sandakan deteriorated sharply, and eventually tragically, after January 1945. The horror is illuminated only, as Moffitt put it, by the prisoners' "comradeship, sacrifice and ingenuity" amid such barbarity. After January 10, no rice was issued by the Japanese and the men were forced to rely for food on the bags of rice that they had saved to meet an emergency. During the building of the airfield they had received seventeen ounces of rice a day from the Japanese; by 1945 they were being given at first three ounces and then two ounces of rice a day. All the snakes that had overrun the camp were caught and eaten. While 210 men died between August 1942 and September 1944, in March 1945 alone 317 men died (221 Australians and 96 English). Yet, that month, there were eighty to ninety tons of rice under Hoshijima's house, some belonging to the prisoners who were by then living on potato leaves (men caught creeping through the wire to search for potatoes were flogged), watercress, potatoes, and tapioca. Thirty big medicine boxes from the American Red Cross arrived at Sandakan in 1944, but all the prisoners received were a few bandages and drugs. Many were suffering from malaria, for which they were given scant treatment, but when Sandakan was relieved by the Allies, 160,000 quinine tablets were found, enough to treat thousands of cases. Hoshijima's policy was that the sick were an encumbrance. After the airfield was built, there was no point feeding men who could not serve the Imperial Japanese Army.

By January 1945 the airfield had been bombed by the Allies and could not be used. Meanwhile, Palawan Island, to the northwest of Borneo, had been taken by the Americans. The Japanese feared that the island would be used to launch an invasion of Borneo, and they decided to move some of the prisoners to Ranau, about 170 miles away. Under Capt. Shoichi Yamamoto, the first march started on January 29. Another eight followed at daily intervals. About 470 prisoners—some 120 English and 350 Australians—set off on these marches. They struggled along narrow tracks hacked through dense jungle swamps in incessant rain and then climbed mountain passes that rose six thousand feet above sea level. They were driven on by guards who beat them to keep them moving—and by fear. If they fell behind, they were shot, bayoneted, or simply left to die.

Some of the marchers were suffering from tropical ulcers and beri-beri, and about half were walking barefoot. They were lucky if they were given five ounces of rice a day. The men had to carry their rations, ammunition, and the Japanese officers' gear, so every prisoner on the first march was carrying between forty and sixty pounds. The marchers even threw their identity discs away to reduce the burden they were carrying. Twenty-one days had been allowed for the marches, but the longest took eighteen and most only fifteen or sixteen days. It was this relentless pace that killed most of the men who died. One of those on the first march was the Australian private Keith Botterill:

> There were one or two men left behind every second or third day. Each morning those who were too sick to move would tell our Australian officer in charge that they could not move with the party and the Japanese sergeant or officer would count us and move us off. We would get along the road about 1/4 mile and then hear shots. The Japanese officer would tell our officers that they had to shoot the men who were left behind. The way I know the Japanese shot those men was that the Japanese officer told us at night. Men dropped out from the march as they became too weak to carry on and they were immediately shot. I saw four men shot when they fell out and this was done by the Japanese sergeant major.
>
> On one occasion an Australian sergeant could not carry on and fell out. He seemed to go off his head and was grabbing our sergeant major and begging him to shoot him. The Japanese officer always tried to save as many men as he could but as the sergeant was suffering from beriberi and was too weak to go any further he asked the Australian sergeant major to give him permission to shoot him. He wrote out an authority and then the Japanese handed him his revolver and told him to shoot the sergeant. This the sergeant major did. This incident occurred at the 16-kilometre peg.

This was a rare incident of Japanese sensitivity.

Men in the seventh marching party had to sleep in the open and could smell the rotting bodies of dead marchers. L.Bdr. William Moxham saw or smelled thirty or more, he said. At the halfway mark of Boto, his party left behind four men. They left two more when they next stopped and later heard shots. "Once you stopped, you stopped for good," he said. "The Japs had no time for the sick. They would not even feed them." More sick prisoners begged the Japanese soldiers to shoot them to put them out of their misery. Four marching parties stopped at Paginatan, twenty-three miles from Ranau. When they eventually set off again, according to Moxham, only thirty-three of the original 190 men were fit to move: twenty to thirty couldn't march and the rest had died.

There was a short respite—two weeks' rest—for the men who reached Ranau, but the rations were no better than they had been at Sandakan and they were given no drugs or medicine. They had no shelter from the constant rain and slept under leaves in the mud. After their "rest" period, they were put to menial work—thatching huts, gathering wood, carrying water. Within a month more than a hundred men had died from the effects of the marches. When a man woke up in the morning, he would check if his neighbor was alive. If he was dead, any belongings that were useful would be claimed.

Every morning there was a burial party: the wrists and ankles of the corpses were tied together and they were carried on a bamboo pole and put naked into six-inch-deep graves. "The only mark of respect they got, we'd spit on the body, then cover them up, the soldier's way," said Botterill.

Botterill was one of sixty survivors, the fittest, who were made to transport rice to the men and guards still at Paginatan. Each carried a 45-pound bag on the outward leg of the five-day journey. Botterill made five of these marches:

> We'd get through the flats of Ranau and start up the mountains, and then men would start to get sick and sit down. The Japanese would shoot them and divide the rice up amongst the fit men. The killing would start about five miles out of Ranau, and the second day there'd be more killing of a morning. We'd arrive at Paginatan on the third afternoon, rest up there, and head back on the fourth day. There'd be more killing on the way back, and on the fifth day, within sight of the compound, they'd still be killing us. No effort whatsoever was made to bury the men. They would just pull them five to fifteen yards off the track and bayonet them or shoot them, depending on the condition of the men. If they were unconscious it would be a bayonet. If they were conscious, and it was what we thought was a good, kind guard, they'd shoot them. There was nothing we could do.

When all the survivors of the first marches assembled at Ranau in April, they numbered about 150. By the end of June, there were only six left. The local inhabitants reported seeing men who looked like skeletons, clad in loincloth rags, with long beards. They never spoke and their heads moved from side to side as they walked.

At Sandakan, meanwhile, American bombers continued their raids, and by the end of April, thirty of the prisoners left behind had been killed or seriously injured by bombs. The camp was now overrun by rats, especially in the hospital, where the four hundred patients were too weak to fight them off. The rice ration had been cut and ten to twelve men were dying every day. During April the supply of rice and water was stopped completely and the men had to survive on the rice they had put aside, wild vegetables, and boiled swamp water. Eight men who had earlier been caught stealing rations from the Japanese store were lashed, put in the cage for twenty-eight days, and beaten every day. All died soon afterward. Another who had gone through the wire to steal tapioca and potatoes was shot in the back. By May, fewer than 830 of the twelve hundred or so who had remained at Sandakan were still alive.

Hoshijima was transferred that month and replaced by Capt. Takuo Takakuwa, whose task was to move the remaining prisoners from the camp, a mission made more urgent on May 27 when Sandakan was bombed for the first time by Allied warships. The Japanese withdrew inland, fearing an imminent invasion, and Takakuwa decided to move all the prisoners who could walk to Ranau—the 536 fittest of the 824 who were still alive. On May 29 the camps were burned down, the ammunition dumps were exploded, and ten parties of men set out. Five pigs were given to those left behind. WO Bill Stipewich was leader of the second party and later gave a detailed account of the march to a war crimes trial:

> On the fourth day men dropped off along the track. No one was allowed to stop and assist them. The men who dropped out were being beaten by the Jap guards and we would never see them again after they had dropped out of my party. On each stop I found that there were men short in my party. We averaged about six and a half miles a day. The track was deplorable—there was mud knee deep most of the way for the first part of the journey and the track led over hills that you had to crawl up and slide down. Thirteen miles was our biggest march in one day. When we moved out in the morning, there would be some men who simply could not move who would be crippled by exposure and who were in bad shape before they started. I never ever saw any of those men again that we would leave when we marched out in the morning. When we had marched about a mile or a mile and a half from our overnight staging camp we would hear rifle fire and machine-gun fire from the direction of the camp. Different guards intimated to us that it was bad to stop because if you stopped you would be "*marti,*" meaning dead. Before we continued our march every morning in the later stages certain personnel would be picked out and told they were not to continue.

Another marcher was Pte. Nelson Short:

> They marched us right through the night and in mud up to our waists, up to our necks. The guards would be singing out, "*lakas, lakas,*" go faster. We'd be marching all night till about three o'clock in the morning or something, then when they wanted a rest, they rested. When the time came to go on again, after three or four hours' rest, the men couldn't get to their feet. They became paralysed in the legs. The ones that couldn't get up, they were all put together. We went on for a distance, and all we heard was the rattle of a tommy gun; and that's what they did with them. And that's at every resting place. Blokes fell over, couldn't go on, and they just machine gunned them. It was a killing off

> party. If their mates couldn't carry on, the Australians shook hands with them and wished them well. But they knew what was going to happen. There was nothing you could do. You just had to keep going yourself, more or less survival of the fittest. There was nothing you could do.

Bill Stipewich reached Ranau on June 26. Out of the 536 who had set out, only 186 arrived. But two Australians—Bdr. Dick Braithwaite and Gunner Owen Campbell—had succeeded in escaping from the fifth party. On June 8, after a guard had flattened him with his rifle butt, Braithwaite decided he would rather die like an animal than let "those animals" finish him off. He ducked into the jungle, killed a Japanese soldier who found him by smashing his head with a branch, survived in a swamp alive with snakes and centipedes, and after six days was picked up by a boatman who took him to his local village. One night they took him by boat to Liberan Island, where the next morning they sighted two U.S. Navy boats. Waving a white flag, they sailed alongside. "What do you know? It's an Aussie!" said the captain. When Braithwaite was picked up the next morning—June 15, his twenty-eighth birthday—the sailors held a sweepstakes on his weight: it was sixty-eight pounds. He celebrated his freedom with a pint and cans of bully beef. After a week of recuperation and debriefing, at Tawitawi in the Philippines, an Australian colonel told Braithwaite they were going to look for his friends. He started crying and said, "You'll be too late." He was right.

Campbell's escape was equally dramatic. He escaped with four other men on June 7, but all of his companions had died or been killed by the time friendly natives led Campbell to an Australian special reconnaissance unit in July.

Events at Ranau and Sandakan were now moving toward their horrifying climax. At Ranau about forty men died in the first two weeks of July. The prisoners were so ill that they could not lift the corpses. It took five men to drag the dead to their shallow graves and the guards beat them as they dug the earth. They began to realize that they were all going to die or be killed as the Allies advanced. Three of the four men who then decided to escape were to be among the six survivors of the Sandakan death marches. On July 7, only five weeks before the Japanese surrender, Botterill, Moxham, Short (who spoke Malay), and Gunner Andy Anderson decided to go as a group. They set off into the jungle, survived meetings with Japanese, who thought they were still under guard, and, as they raced for cover from an American bomber, eventually ran into a local village headman, Baragah Katus. There were rewards for villagers who returned prisoners, and severe punishments for helping them. But Baragah, who had been forced to give up his farm to work for the Japanese, assured them he was a friend. He made them a shelter and gave them forty bananas. Then he left, promising to return with more food. The men then had another lucky escape. Shortly after Baragah left, they saw a Japanese soldier heading toward them. He put his head inside the hut and asked if they had a watch, questioned them about food, and then said that some prisoners had escaped. The men said that they were on a working party and waiting for their guard to return with medicine since they were ill. When he heard the sound of aircraft, the soldier fled. Botterill, Moxham, and Short escaped into the jungle again, where they were found the next day by Baragah, who warned them that the alarm had been raised. He kept them supplied with food as they moved to new hiding places. By now Botterill was swollen with beri-beri, Moxham could not walk, and Short thought he was dying. Anderson was in an even worse state, and he died on July 29.

News then reached Baragah's village that white men had been seen dropping by parachute. They were members of a small Australian commando force. Moxham wrote a letter on a page torn from a notebook which Baragah delivered to the commando force on August 17. He returned with medicines, matches, powdered milk, and a packet of Lifesavers. There was also a note which told the three men that the war was over, but that the Japanese were still hostile and they were to stay where they were. Two days later, however, another note told them to make their way to the commandos. On August 24, still afraid of being recaptured or dying, they heard trampling and crashing. They were worried that they had finally been found by the Japanese, but it was their saviors, the commandos, and Short recalled their relief:

> We looked up and there are these big six footers. Z Force. Boy oh boy. All in greens. They had these stretchers, and they put them down. "Have a cup of tea. Some Biscuits." You could see that they had seen the state we were in. This is it. Boy oh boy. This is really it. I cried, they all cried. It was wonderful. I'll never forget that as long as I live. We all sat down and had a cup of tea together. I couldn't eat biscuits or anything like that. The stomach was shrunk. Any rate, we made up for it later on. They said, "Righto, hop on the stretchers, and we'll take you up to the camp." They put Moxham and Botterill on, and I said, "No, I'm right. I'll walk the rest of the way if you just put your arm around me. I don't want to get on a stretcher." So I walked the rest of the way into camp.

They looked pitiable, said one of the rescuers, Pte. Mick "Lofty" Hodges. Botterill was the worst, "a skin-covered collection of bones," so sick that he could do nothing for himself. Hodges doubted he would last twenty-four hours. It was beyond belief, he thought, that a man could suffer so much and still be alive, even if only just. Short was swollen with beri-beri and his limbs resembled "grotesquely stuffed sausages." After their weeks in the jungle they were offered milk, sugar, biscuits, chocolate, and cigarettes. Botterill was so overwhelmed that he wept.

Bill Stipewich had also been rescued by Z Force. He had been tipped off by a friendly guard at Ranau that the prisoners were to be killed, and sneaked out of his camp with Pte. Algy Reither (who died from exhaustion after ten days) on July 28, and hid nearby. He was protected by a village chief who also sent vegetables to the camp and then sent men to contact Z Force. Thirty-two men at Ranau were still alive when Stipewich left. None survived. Campbell, Braithwaite, Stipewich, Botterill, Moxham, and Short were to be the only survivors of the men who marched from Sandakan to Ranau seven months earlier. All the 288 sick men left behind when the huts at Sandakan were burned died or were killed before the Allies arrived. All seventy-five on the second set of marches to Ranau that started at the end of May 1945 had died within the first thirty miles. By July, only fifty men were left at Sandakan, and twenty-seven of them were dying. Takakuwa ordered the execution of the other twenty-three by Formosan guards, threatening to shoot them if his order were disobeyed. There is also strong evidence from a Chinese cook, Wong Hiong, that at least one British officer was crucified. Hiong watched as the prisoner was dragged from a barbed-wire cage to a seven-foot-high wooden cross. A Japanese officer, Lt. Moritake, then approached with a stool, a knife, and a hammer:

> The Jap officer then stood on the stool with the hammer in his right hand. He then raised the prisoner's left arm and driving a nail through the palm of the left hand fixed it to the left arm of the cross which was the height of the prisoner's shoulders. When the officer commenced to pierce the palm of the prisoner's left hand with a nail the prisoner tried to wriggle and scream, whereupon Hinata held the body of the prisoner against the upright post of the cross and put a piece of cloth into the prisoner's mouth. The Jap officer then placed the stool towards the prisoner's right and nailed the prisoner's right hand to the cross in the same manner by standing on the stool. He then put the stool aside and nailed both of the feet of the prisoner with two nails to a horizontal wooden board on which the prisoner was standing. Thereafter the Jap officer again stood on the stool and fixed the prisoner's head to the cross by driving a large-sized nail through the prisoner's forehead. The Jap officer then took the knife and first cut a piece of flesh from the left side of

> the prisoner's stomach and placed the flesh on a wooden board near by. He then cut a piece of flesh from the right side of the prisoner's stomach and also placed it on the board. He then put a rubber glove on his right hand and pulled out the intestines of the prisoner which were also placed on the board. Taking the knife again, the officer then proceeded to cut bits of flesh from the prisoner's left and right thighs, both arms and neck, all of which were placed on this same wooden board.

The most likely reason for such a barbaric punishment was that the prisoner had confessed to stealing a pig because the men were starving. The message for the few remaining prisoners was that if they stole pigs, they would end up as meat. In 1947, when Australian forces dug up the area where the cross had allegedly been, they found eight nails.

According to Hiong, the last surviving prisoner at Sandakan, an Australian, was made to kneel down and a black cloth was tied over his eyes. Staff Sgt. Murozumi then beheaded him with one stroke of a sword; his body was pushed into a trench and his head then dropped in after it.

The next day, the Japanese left Sandakan.

In September 1945, Australian intelligence officers put the final death toll in the Kuching area of Borneo as: dead, 2,808; missing, probably dead, 382; alive, 1,387. They estimated that there had been between 4,590 and 4,670 prisoners on the island. On the death marches to Ranau, only 616 of the 1,645 men on the three death marches survived. Of the 2,240 men at Sandakan after August 1943, as we have seen, only six survived. But more than a thousand could have been saved if Gen. Douglas MacArthur, the commander of U.S. forces in Southeast Asia, had spared a few aircraft to go to their rescue. Freeing the prisoners had been given top priority by MacArthur, but he concentrated his efforts on the Philippines, where many Americans were held.

At Cabanatuan, where there were fewer prisoners than at Sandakan, the most audacious rescue mission of the war occurred in January. This was a month after the Japanese had herded a hundred fifty prisoners at Palawan into pits, poured aviation fuel over them, and burned them alive, the fate that awaited other prisoners as MacArthur advanced through the Philippines.

In a perilous mission, Lt. Col. Henry A. Mucci and 120 men of the 6th Rangers Battalion, all volunteers, walked thirty miles through enemy lines to liberate the prisoners at Cabanatuan. The rescue was triumphantly accomplished. All the prisoners were saved by Mucci's rangers, assisted by local resistance groups; a thousand Japanese troops perished in the fighting. One of the rescued prisoners was Signalman Walter Riley, an Englishman who had spent January 30 dodging American air raids. Suddenly, as darkness fell, there was the sound and fury of gunfire, exploding hand grenades, and hysterical shouts from the Japanese. Riley thought that the guards were about to massacre the prisoners:

> After about fifteen minutes of pandemonium on the ground above me, the firing stopped, with the exception of a single shot here and there. Then I heard someone shout, "Make for the gate! OK fellas, get going!" What was happening?—were my fellow prisoners making a break for freedom? All around me, men climbed out of the drains and in the darkness hurried out of sight, their minds concentrating on their own safety. I tried to follow them, but my legs would not provide sufficient strength to enable me to climb out of the drain. I was left alone, clawing at the sides of the trench. Panic seized me and tears of anger filled my eyes, as I saw my colleagues making good their escape. Bob was in another drain and he had lost me.
>
> In my panic and frustration I shouted frantically, but in the confusion no one appeared to have heard my cries until suddenly, out of the darkness, two enormous hands reached down, clutched the much-patched denim jacket I was wearing and literally hauled me out of the monsoon drain and stood me on my feet on the ground above! In the eerie lights of the watchtower and pillboxes, which were now ablaze, I could just discern the figure of an American soldier, his hands and face blackened, wearing jungle battledress and carrying an arsenal of weapons—revolvers, hand grenades, a stiletto and sub-machine gun! With urgency in his voice, he said to me—"OK fellah, we're springing you guys, get to hell outa here, Goddam quick!"
>
> I spluttered a few words of thanks to my saviour and followed his instructions. With the adrenalin now flowing in my blood, I dragged my feet clumsily as I headed for the main gate, and there I joined other stragglers now leaving the camp. As I stumbled through the gate I looked in the Jap guardroom, and could see in the dim light of two hurricane lamps still burning inside, the bodies of a dozen or more Japs who had been shot down in the initial attack on the camp by our liberators. Outside the camp gate, I joined the main body of released prisoners, who were being hurriedly assembled into a long column, flanked on both sides by U.S. soldiers and Filipino guerrillas.
>
> Heavy fighting could be heard to our rear some distance along the main road, so without delay we were urged to walk as fast as we could,

> away from the camp and the battle behind us. As we started to walk, I turned and looked at the prison camp which was now on fire in several places. Cabanatuan camp was being destroyed and with that destruction, the end of captivity had arrived. Freedom lay ahead, but some twenty-five miles still separated us from the safety of the American front line. We had to get through much Japanese-held territory to reach safety.

Riley had been using crutches and wondered how far his feet could take him, but with his overwhelming desire to survive he found a reserve of energy and kept dragging his numb feet in the dust of the jungle tracks, mile after mile. He was pulled through a river by clinging to a cart and then crossed a road that was flanked by Japanese soldiers:

> After a long tense wait, fearing detection of our presence, the opportunity to cross arrived. On the given signal, we began to scramble noiselessly over the metalled road surface, hardly daring to breathe. As I crawled on to the road, I could see in the dim moonlight, a few hundred yards along the road, several Jap vehicles and hundreds of soldiers. They were talking excitedly and this was to our advantage, as they were obviously unaware of our presence. With admirable stealth, we melted into the undergrowth on the far side of the road and as we advanced, we again formed into a long line, with the American soldiers and guerrillas flanking the sides and guarding the rear of the column. It had taken one hour to get all the men across the road safely.

The rescued prisoners reached a village where they were welcomed and fed crushed mangoes and bananas, sprinkled with shredded coconut—but they were still not clear of Japanese lines. It was another five miles before they finally reached the American ambulances assembled to look after them—and were filmed for news bulletins by army cameramen. Riley's desire to live had propelled him to walk almost twenty-five miles over rough ground, through jungle, and to cross a river through waist-high water. He and the other rescued prisoners were given field rations and coffee and then driven to an evacuation hospital where they were greeted by a band playing "The Stars and Stripes Forever."

> After we had alighted from the ambulances, we were immediately supplied with eating utensils and invited to collect as much food as we wished from the field kitchen. I well remember my first meal, European-style, as a free man. French fried potatoes, sweet corn and

> sausages. I took seven sausages to start with, ate them and returned for seven more. Then I returned for five more, each time taking a liberal helping of French fries and sweet corn! After consuming my fifteenth sausage I could eat no more, and I felt ill. I was not alone, as all my colleagues had reacted to the unlimited supply of this delicious food as I had done. We had been gluttonous and foolish. Little did we realise that our stomachs had contracted through three years of a semi-starvation diet of soft food and it would take some considerable time to readjust to solid food again.

The Americans at Cabanatuan were more fortunate than the British and Australians at Ranau and Sandakan. Although MacArthur's priority was the Philippines, Lynette Silver, official historian to the Australian 8th Division, has shown that an Allied plan to rescue the prisoners at Sandakan was bungled and finally canceled in April 1945 in the belief that the camp had been evacuated. She blames gross incompetence and faulty intelligence for the failure, and has shown in her book *Sandakan: A Conspiracy of Silence* that mistakes and "stupidity" at the highest level were concealed. The failure to liberate Sandakan became the Second World War's most "deadly" secret, she argues.

At a war crimes tribunal, Hoshijima and Yamamoto were sentenced to death by hanging. The nine officers in charge of each group on the first march were sentenced to death, but only one was executed; the others' sentences were commuted to life imprisonment. Takakuwa was hanged. Col. Suga, the commander of all Japanese troops in Borneo, committed suicide by cutting his throat with a table knife.

INTERLUDE

Mozart

After leaving Cambridge in 1940, David Piper joined the Indian Army and went to Malaya with the 4th/9th Jats. He was captured in Singapore, and in October 1942 shipped to Taiwan, where he was imprisoned first at Tashoku and then, from August 1943, at Shirakawa, where the conditions deteriorated until, by 1945, it was virtually a hospital camp.

> 9 July 1944: No planes, only an abortive alert. Feel stronger, almost *compos mentis.* Maybe the soup last night—sweet potatoes, pumpkin and pork. I didn't actually get any pork, but it smelt marvellous and tasted porky. The pumpkin incidentally was swill sent by the Japanese for the pigs but cunningly intercepted by the cookhouse for POW benefit. That's how we live. Nerve better to-day too. When one is in an extremity of weakness, the most surprising things happen. Crying for example. When I was still pretty bad, Windy borrowed the gramo-

phone and played two Mozart overtures and a violin concerto. The overtures re-opened the whole lovely dizzy world of possible happiness that I had forgotten, and at the first movement of the concerto I cried till my pillow was all wet, in a wallow of supreme, happy unhappiness. For about a week I was very light—I wept because the sky was so blue, for the kindness of someone who gave me a cigarette, for a memory suddenly superimposed, vivid and all-embracing, over the grey blank. It was very blank too—the future, the past, all possibilities all blotted out, God, even the need of God. Even now mostly I feel empty, as though I had lost something. But this seems a final loss compared with earlier sensations. But Mozart—O Mozart! All the Haydn's gone, the pity. But those two can redeem me from horrible depths.

After the war David Piper was director of the Fitzwilliam Museum at Cambridge, the first director of the Ashmolean Museum in Oxford, and director of the National Portrait Gallery.

Chapter 25

CHANGI 1944-45

Capt. Tom Eaton's arm was smashed by a burst of machine-gun fire on February 15, 1942, the day of surrender, and he was not finally discharged from the hospital at Changi until the end of December, when most of the prisoners had left for Burma, Thailand, and other outposts of the Japanese Empire. Eaton, a Norwich solicitor, was then messing officer to the Norfolks until August 1944: he looked after the feeding of the troops. He was one of the fortunate prisoners who remained at Changi throughout captivity. It was one of the four camps that the Japanese were prepared to show off, as he said in a letter written to his parents in September 1945: "I have been more or less my own master within the camp and for days on end I might not see a Nip except on roll-call." Most of the men and officers lived in well-constructed buildings in the most modern and well-planned barracks. They had a regular supply of water, electric light and power, a good hospital, their own gardens, a daily news service, and excellent entertainment.

Conditions at Changi were a revelation to prisoners returning from Thailand, Burma, and elsewhere. What luxury it was to sit on real chairs at a real table and be served on china plates beneath whirring fans, Lt. Robin Fletcher wrote when he arrived back at Changi from Kanchanaburi. How marvelous it was to stand beneath a cool shower. It was the prospect of returning to Changi that cheered the survivors of F Force at Tanbaya at their farewell concert, when they sang:

Changi is an Island at the south end of Malay
We used to think it Hell on earth and prayed to get away;
But since we've been to Burma, we have grown a bit more wise
Now Singapore's the promised land, Changi Paradise.

Flt. Lt. Dick Philps, who had survived Haruku, described his arrival at Changi in 1945 as lifesaving: "Wonderful Changi Jail, civilized and, by our standards, luxurious. It had houses made of brick, mains electricity, even cultural activities going on. It also had a garden, frogs and moneylenders."

But Philps's starry-eyed view of Changi Jail was not shared by the men who had moved there from Selarang a year earlier in May 1944, when the camp strength was just over ten thousand: the jail had been built to hold just six hundred. The conditions were "appalling," said Lt. Col. E. B. Holmes, who was still the men's commanding officer: "Cells for one Asiatic criminal contained three and often four men, whilst four senior officers and their batman had to live in an Asiatic prison warder's family quarter." His Australian deputy, Brig. "Black Jack" Galleghan, agreed. There was "dangerous overcrowding," he said, with well over two hundred men sleeping in each of the hundred-yard-long huts. But there was some relief when working parties left the jail.

Unsurprisingly, not everybody concurred with Holmes's assessment. Some had experienced conditions that were far worse. Sgt. John Franks, who had survived Sonkurai, was only too happy to lie on a concrete floor that was free of bugs, and to have access to a shower. Others, though, agreed with the commanding officer. Signaller Ronald Searle arrived in 1944:

> Inside the cell blocks it was suffocatingly hot and claustrophobic; at night the outside walls threw back the heat they soaked up during the day. The rows of cells, their steel doors open, gave onto three storeys of gangways linked by metal stairways. A central well, from roof to ground level, was divided at each floor by a steel mesh. Every inch of it was spread with men; the Japanese had allotted one square metre of space to each prisoner. There were four men to each cell built to hold one person: one on the central block of stone intended to serve as a bed, one each side of it on the floor between the block and the wall and one full-length along the bottom, with either his head or his feet in the lavatory hole that was, fortunately, out of action. Otherwise these stone cubicles were bare and airless, despite a small grille-covered window out of reach by the ceiling. Along the gangways outside, the grilles over the

central well were packed with sweaty bodies and those at the top could look down through the mesh at two other layers of skinny, barely human, flesh. The noise was rarely less than unbearable.

The officers were housed in nine rows of coolie quarters, in huts which held forty to fifty, and served by 260 cooks and batmen. Sgt. Tam Innes-Ker was in a ground-floor former workshop where about a hundred and fifty were quartered on the floor. Each prisoner had six feet by four feet, with a two-foot alley between ranks.

Yet, over the next fifteen months, using the experiences of the previous two years, Changi became a small city, with its own government, "schools" and "universities," churches, factories, farms and gardens, theaters, medical services, cookhouses, craftsmen, technicians, and "businessmen" who became moneylenders. Using their skills and ingenuity to overcome the conditions in which they lived, the men achieved a remarkable triumph over adversity. They made latrines, organized cookhouses, and built atap huts outside the jail. Inside they slept four or five to a cell, under the washbasins and in the corridors. Piping was stolen and showers installed in every courtyard. As Eaton wrote, necessity was the mother of invention. There was a general shop as well as metal workshops, blacksmiths, carpenters, watchmakers, nail-makers, typewriter repairs, trailer and bicycle repairs, needle manufacture, and a brush factory. Artificial limbs for the limbless with proper knee joints were made from electric-fan blades, bits of metal, and aluminum stew pans. Using timber from doors and window frames for the heads and bamboo and casuarina for the handles, between May 1944 and August 1945 Changi's brush factory made more than five thousand brooms, eight thousand toothbrushes, and three hundred pairs of clogs. Equally ingenious was the thread machine used to unthread cotton socks. The thread, starched with rice, was then used by the tailors to repair clothing and to make fresh shorts from old scraps. About half a million yards of thread were produced. There were thirty-three staff at the rubber factory, and eight tappers collected three and a half gallons of latex a day. The latex was coagulated with urine. Thousands of composition soles were made and shoes repaired. The latex was also used as an adhesive and to repair medical appliances, and was supplied to the dental clinic, the transport office, and the book-binding department. Nails made from barbed wire supplied all the needs of the island. Axe heads and wheelbarrows were forged by blacksmiths. Cooking containers, ladles, mugs, and mess tins were welded from steel lockers. There was even a distillery which produced alcohol by fermenting old vegetable peelings and sugar. The almost universal complaint of

"Changi Balls" was treated with a juice extract containing vitamin B_2 made by crushing grass.

The worst job at Changi was in the party of nine hundred men who marched off at dawn to work on flattening the area surrounding the camp so that it could be turned into a military airbase (now the site of Changi International Airport). The prisoners reshaped the landscape, removing hills and spreading them somewhere else. With only hand tools rather than trucks and bulldozers, it was an "agonisingly endless" job, said Ronald Searle. The men worked between fourteen and sixteen hours a day and returned worn out, burned black by the sun and half blinded by the intense glare thrown up from the sandy ground they were leveling. It took a year and a half to finish the job.

The six hundred men of P Party were luckier. They went each day to work at the docks or Singapore railway station, loading and unloading ships and trains, and there were opportunities to trade on the black market and to make contact with the locals, from whom they gleaned snippets of news. That news was reflected in their songs as they marched back into Changi. Another consolation was that all men on working parties received full rations.

According to Searle, the rest of the men tried to make themselves invisible but were sooner or later rounded up for some "disagreeable" task, such as acting as a "beast in harness" to haul trailers loaded with wood, a scene he captured in one of his drawings. But for many the days passed rather idly. Capt. Ronald Horner described his typical day in January 1945:

> Rising at 08.30, shave and shower before breakfast at 09.00. Usually spend morning rehearsing or on some job connected with the theatre or ward shows. Tiffin at 13.00, afternoon either lie on my bed or if there is a call, rehearsing. Shower and change between 5 and 6. Supper at 18.00. Evening spent either with a show or visiting friends or reading. Lights out at 23.00. George Booker comes round at 22.30 or thereabouts and we usually sit outside talking or smoking until midnight or later. Clothes—at night I wear a sarong and according to how chilly it is, a shirt of white flannelette as a top. By day, shorts only. By night, shirt and either shorts or slacks. Food—breakfast: rice "pap," a "doover," in other words a rissole or biscuit with a spread of blachang. Tiffin—stew and rice and 4 "doovers." Wed. and Sat. is a curry tiffin and 5 "doovers" at night.

The men soon found ways of relieving the monotony of captivity. There were church services, educational courses, a camp library, societies to discuss hobbies and sports, swimming, and an occasional game of cricket or baseball. Lt. Eric Lomax had been dying of a combination of tropical diseases and starvation at Outram Road Jail and had taken the risk of exaggerating his decline almost to the point of no return. Fortunately, the Japanese prison staff transferred him to Changi just in time. He still has some of the books that circulated in Changi at that time and which greatly aided his recovery. The tattered volumes were held together with homemade gum made from rice and water or stewed bones and patched up with cannibalized prison records:

> Charge sheets for Indian privates written in copperplate in happier colonial days became the endpapers of works by Bunyan, Blake or Defoe. The adhesive still feels solid, heavy and crude, but also very strong; I have some of these books with me now [1997]. They are the most well-thumbed, eroded books I have ever seen, worn to a softness and fragility, and made compact by sheer use, but they seem indestructible.

Lomax hadn't seen a word of print during more than seven months at Outram Road, and he found that he had nearly forgotten how to read. He was reduced to spelling out the captions and garish headlines in a bound volume of the pinup magazine *Lilliput,* and slowly copying out words from a children's spelling book: "I had lost my mind and spent days digging about for some memory of script. To my intense relief, the skill of reading came back fast."

On his first night back at Changi, Gunner Russell Braddon could have gone to lectures on skiing, contract law, communism, or tiger hunting, to four plays, two musical shows, or a violin recital by Dennis East. He went instead to the Australian concert party, still going strong after two years. Whatever the demands from the Japanese for labor, "Black Jack" Galleghan ensured that the concert party remained intact. No better investment was made on the prisoners' behalf, said Braddon:

> There are few men who were captured on Singapore in 1942 and who survived till 1945 who do not now remember and will not always remember the skill of John Wood, the songs (topical and tuneful) of Slim de Gray and Ray Tullipan, the harmony of Geoghegan and Woods and that plaintive cry of our most melancholy comic: "You'll never get off the Island." No matter how black the news nor how depressing the atmosphere, Harry Smith, universally known as Happy Harry, had only to turn his long face full at the audience and wail the apparent truism, "You'll never get off the Island," for complete hilarity to be restored.

But there was a dark side to Changi, too. Food remained an obsession, especially after February 1945, when rations were reduced by the Japanese as the

Allies advanced—a camp order that month announced that swill was not under any circumstances to be used for human consumption. The rice ration for men on heavy duty, who received the most, was cut to seventeen ounces a day, and then to nine ounces in March, and eight ounces (including two ounces of maize) in April. The men were so hungry that they ate cat stew, dog rissoles, iguana, cobra, and hermit crab; even rats. Sgt. Stan Arneil and his men had also eaten horse, yak, whale, buffalo and snake, grasses, bamboo shoots, lily roots and banana stalks, stingray, shark, and catfish to stave off their hunger. Where Capt. Charles Wilkinson messed, the pooled ration per man per day was eight ounces. Occasional Red Cross parcels were welcome but did not stretch far. Wilkinson's Red Cross ration in April 1945 was less than an ounce of jam, two and a half ounces of corned beef, one fifth of an ounce of meat paste, an ounce of condensed milk, and an ounce of fruit pudding. Lots were drawn so that the men also received one item from a selection of "comforts"—shaving cream, a razor blade, tooth powder, toothbrush, boot polish, pencils, comb, toilet paper, or a safety razor. Treats were rare. When Wilkinson had a "party" on St. George's Day, it consisted of a mug of coffee, a cheroot, and a pie made of tapioca root, a coconut, onions, blachang, and palm oil.

Without the camp gardens, which were manured by rotting grass and up to eleven thousand gallons of urine a week collected in tanks pulled on trailers, the men would have starved. In May 1945, about 1,340 were working in the 122 acres of the other ranks' gardens, which had produced eighty-four thousand tons of root and leaf vegetables and thirty-eight hundred tons of fruit. The biggest crops were Ceylon spinach, red amaranth, green byam, sweet potatoes, kangkung, brinjals, papayas, gourds, tapioca root, and some tomatoes and guavas. Between 1942 and June 1945, the Australian poultry farm also produced 39,475 eggs, which from May 1943 were distributed to the sick of all nationalities.

To help decide who should get priority for extra rations, Dick Philps and Rudi Springer, another Haruku survivor, developed the Springer-Philps test of emaciation. It was not difficult: the candidates were asked to strip completely and walk past the two doctors as they checked their buttocks, which are normally composed of fat and muscle and are therefore good indicators of emaciation. If the bulge of a man's buttocks had disappeared completely, he had few reserves of fat left. If they could see the sacrum, the bone at the bottom of the spine, normally invisible from the side, he received an extra ration. Philps defended the test's efficacy:

> This, in well-fed peacetime, may seem almost unbelievable, but it was, in fact, a very good test: it picked out those men who really could not go on

> without a little extra, but as rice was in short supply, did not let through the net anybody who could still manage. The number of men we picked out in this way neatly balanced the amount of rice we had available for extra rations.

Philps solved his own need for animal protein by killing frogs, mixing a pastry of tapioca flour, water, coconut oil, and salt, adding the frogs' arms, legs, and backs, and making frog pie. Several officers cooked curried snails; a few caught sparrows, which they dipped in oil and roasted. One officer brought down doves with a catapult.

John Franks was in charge of the jail kitchen, cooking for more than five thousand prisoners with 120 cooks. Each day he and his men cooked seven hundred gallons of porridge, five hundred gallons of a midday hash of rice and vegetables, and up to five hundred gallons of rice in the evening; they also brewed two thousand gallons of tea every day. He was determined that the food be distributed fairly, especially when he began to receive a small ration of sugar:

> We had not received any sugar from the Japanese for over two and a half years and it was more precious than gold dust. The amount was very small, it varied between 1/3 and 1/2 oz per man per day. This quantity was therefore too ridiculous to issue separately so I decided to put it into the breakfast rice; fortunately the kitchen ration store was built like a strong room and was perfectly safe. There was only one key to this room and I carried it on a chain around my waist day and night. As I was quite determined that all would receive their full entitlement at all times, I arranged for a Sergeant to wake me at 2.30 each morning; this was the time that the first shift cooked the breakfast. He accompanied me and two others to the store where the sugar was carefully weighed out, proceeded to the kitchen where equal parts were added and stirred into each boiler of rice, when I was satisfied that this had been completed I went back to bed, the proceedings having taken half an hour. The whole procedure was then repeated for the next shift; the Sergeant woke me at 4 a.m. and I returned to bed at 4.30 a.m. I carried out this routine every night for twelve months. This was very necessary as I wanted my staff to appreciate that I was prepared to put myself out at all times so that fair distribution was maintained; this was the standard that I expected my staff to follow.

Franks was determined that the men should have a good meal on Christmas Day, and secretly set aside extras and stole vegetables and beans earmarked for the Japanese. He had four thousand five hundred men to feed:

> We made pasties which looked like the genuine Cornish variety. These were filled with beans and green leaves, grown outside the gaol; other fillings were made up with rice towgay [a local bean] and soya beans. The fish rissole was flavoured with blachang and fried in palm oil; other items were baked in the ovens. At the height of the cooking the smoke-laden atmosphere of the kitchen looked like Dante's Inferno. The staff worked themselves to a standstill and I could hardly have asked for more assistance and loyalty. By the end of the day the whole staff had worked non-stop for 48 hours; every available inch of table space and every container was fully occupied. During this time 52,000 pasties and rissoles were produced and tea was provided three times during the day. Considering that this all emanated from a kitchen built and designed to cater for 750 people, it indicated how hard everyone worked and it was a very creditable performance. The look of anticipation and joy on the faces of the men when they collected the food amply repaid us for our effort.

Franks kept the Christmas menu. There was sweet porridge, rissole, and baked cheese cup for breakfast, and vegetable nasi goreng (fried rice), baked fish, a rissole, and a fried vegetable for lunch. Dinner was grander: vegetable stew, fish rissole, fried whitebait pasty, fried towgay pasty, fried jam pasty, fried savory pasty, and baked jam cup. "Not to be compared with normal rations," Franks wrote at the bottom.

But Christmas was soon over, and as rations were cut, sickness increased. Changi's archivist, Capt. David Nelson, recorded in February 1945 that the number of vitamin-deficiency cases was increasing "alarmingly" and that dysentery and malaria were all too prevalent. An estimated 80 percent of the men were suffering from pellagra, Changi Balls, edema, or beri-beri. The price of food had also become prohibitive. By April, men were dying from malnutrition and the price of food had risen by as much as 400 percent in six months: sugar was selling at $21 a pound, coconuts at $2.50, and tapioca root at $2.60. The men inevitably started trading. Nelson sold his last gold possession on the black market, his wife's wedding ring. The proceeds went to a sick officer friend who insisted on writing an IOU for seventeen pounds, payable on release. Gold, precious stones, watches, and rings were fetching "tremendous" prices on the black market as the "wily" Chinese bought such tangible assets as fast as they could, Capt. Harry Jessup observed:

> Australian pound notes are changing hands at about $80 each, with Bank of England notes calling as high as $100. A sovereign recently changed hands at $2000; unfortunately I have no such assets to dispose

of. Short pants—by no means new—are bringing about $60, and any form of cloth from which clothes can be made commands a high price. However, I am not in favour of selling clothes, although it is impossible to stop the troops doing so. Such is inflation—and, of course, it is growing worse and worse. I'm sure the Chinese must be having a high old time counterfeiting ten-dollar bills just as fast as they can obtain suitable paper. The Nips seem to have no control whatsoever over the currency, ten-dollar bills not even being numbered any more.

When Lt. Bob Skene, a famous Australian polo player, disposed of an 18-karat-gold cigarette case inscribed by the Sultan of Johore, he secured 28,000 Japanese dollars for it. The prisoners believed that the Chinese bought gold in Singapore and passed it on through Malaya, Thailand, and Indo-China to help Gen. Chiang Kai-shek fight the Japanese. The rations were so small that by now "Black Jack" Galleghan had modified his uncompromising policy of punishing traders in such items. Inflation of the Japanese dollar left the men's pay wholly inadequate for them to make any substantial benefit, he said.

After Tom Eaton sold his watch, he cashed a check for Capt. Reginald Burton at an exchange rate which enabled Burton to buy vegetables and blachang. At the end of the war, Eaton tore up the check. Other moneylenders were less generous, as Dick Philps found when he came across those who had become wealthy in unnumbered Singaporean dollars that would ordinarily be worthless:

So they devised a method of turning it into real currency. Money was needed by the other prisoners to buy extra food, and in some cases tobacco, and the businessmen made it known that they would exchange their dud dollars for pounds sterling. They would, in fact, accept undated cheques drawn on British banks, to be dated later, and pay dollars for them, intending to change them after release, provided they considered the man giving them the cheque to be a "good risk." A cheque, of course, can be written on anything: it does not require to be in the usual form provided that it contains the necessary information—any piece of paper will do. So these men were paying out dollars in exchange for cheques promising to pay them in pounds sterling, the rate of exchange decided by themselves. Whatever one feels about this conduct, it did enable me to give a cheque for £50 and receive in exchange 110 dollars, worth, in fact, a few pence each. In case I should die before the cheque could be cashed (or I should stop it), my man required a separate, witnessed agreement, which I still have.

> I notice that it is no. 36, so thirty-five people before me had entered into deals. It is dated 7 July 1945, so there were still several weeks to go and I have no doubt he did good business in that time. He might even have been sorry to see the end of the war. I had considerable unease about making this deal, simply because I was regarded by my man as a good risk, likely to have £50 in the bank, but the rank and file, probably poor risks, would, I think, not have been able to use this facility. It seemed unfair; we on the working parties had stopped thinking like this; but death appeared the alternative, even if the war finished soon. I well remember, when the deal took place, my man telling me of the great risk he was taking of never getting the cheque home, so he was sorry—"Old Boy"—that he could not give a better rate of exchange. I spent my 110 dollars on food—protein food, eggs and fish—which could be bought from the local population.

In July, Changi at last recovered from a period of serious upset among the British and Australian command that had occurred when Lt. Takahashi, the Japanese camp commandant, had announced the previous year that Lt. Col. T. H. Newey, a Singapore Volunteer, was to be the representative officer for the other ranks. Holmes and Galleghan were told that they were to have no part in administering or organizing the camp, and the officers' area was to be a separate camp with direct access to Takahashi. Newey took the appointment without referring to Holmes or Galleghan, and it was not well received. He was junior to them, and some, according to Harry Jessup, considered him "Jap-happy." There were heated exchanges among the powers-that-be, Jessup noted in his diary. This was refuted by Reginald Burton, though, who had been with Newey at Syme Road when Takahashi had been commandant. With men dying daily, even the most trivial concession from the Japanese was valuable, Burton argued. It was worth bending over backward to keep the Japanese captors good-tempered toward the prisoners. The result of an "appeasement" policy had been that Syme Road was well run, with conditions as comfortable as possible.

Another diarist, David Nelson, believed that Takahashi had upset the smoothly functioning camp administration. Holmes had run the camp with skill, understanding, and tolerance. Misdemeanors had been minor and infrequent. Each prisoner, irrespective of rank, had shared equally the meager and monotonous rations and benefited from the concerts, shows, and lectures. What irked Takahashi, Nelson thought, was Holmes's persistence in continually bringing to the commandant's notice breaches of accepted rules governing the treatment of prisoners and the employment of prisoners on military projects.

Several of his actions made Newey unpopular. A Japanese decree that rations were not to be pooled had been ignored to help the sick men, but Newey accepted it and enforced the sliding-scale rations for men on heavy duty, light duty, and no duty. Galleghan told Newey that he had no legal disciplinary authority over Australian troops, but Newey immediately moved to be allowed by the Japanese to open correction cells. He then charged and awarded punishments to men of all nationalities, including NCOs, some of forty days. Treatment in the correction cells included the typically Japanese punishment of standing for long periods. Galleghan catalogued Newey's "illegal" conduct in his postwar report on Changi.

However, on July 5, 1945, Newey was replaced by Lt. Col. Francis Dillon, the disciplinarian who had brought order to the British F Force camp at Sonkurai, and an officer admired by all the men who served with him. With Dillon in command, the atmosphere of the camp became one of cooperation with the commanders, British, Australian, and Dutch, said Galleghan. Officers were now allowed into the jail, in spite of Japanese orders to the contrary; standing in cells was abolished as a punishment by Dillon; and Newey became the subject of charges for his behavior.

Takahashi, who was generally considered a "good Nip"—less arrogant and more intelligent than most of his compatriots—was responsible for at least one notable act of compassion and generosity. Ronald Searle had become well known for his decorations for the theater and his illustrations on posters and in programs. Takahashi had asked to see Searle's drawings in July 1944. Ten months later the commandant ordered Searle and three other Royal Engineers to the Japanese Officers' Beach Club, where they were put to work. Takahashi paid occasional visits to the club but rarely paid any attention to the prisoners. One day Searle was alone when Takahashi walked into the bar, handed his sword and cap to an assistant, strolled over to Searle, who was drawing, offered him a cigarette, and lit one himself:

> His movements were, as always, unhurried and accompanied by a slightly cynical smile. But behind that bland, narrow-eyed, aristocratic reserve, he was a razor-sharp observer. Looking at me sideways for a moment with what little there was visible of his pupils, he took off his gloves, picked up my sketchbook and a pencil, said, "May I?" and began to draw the outline of a mother and child on the first blank page. Then he stopped, looked wryly at the sketch and said in his careful English: "You know, Mr. Searle, I also am an artist—a painter. I was studying in Paris when I was called to this—ah—to serve . . ."
>
> He turned over a few pages of the sketchbook with a vaguely reflec-

tive air, handed it back to me, put on his gloves again and, with his usual slight bow, left the room puffing his "Tojo special." "Oh, I forget. I intended to ask you whether you would care for these." And he laid a handful of coloured pencils and wax crayons on the bar. Finally the question was answered. I had never for one moment imagined that Takahashi's "request" to see my drawings would turn out to have been for reasons non-military, non-political, non-administrative, and non-suspicious. Or that—as in the case of the present order to idle about the beach club—he was making a quiet, unsoldierly gesture of solidarity between artists.

Fortunately for the four of us, a sentimental fantasy had interposed itself between Takahashi the civilized, cultivated painter and the sordidly real circumstances in which Takahashi the prison administrator, lord of life and death, was now obliged to exercise his talents. Our paths crossed only briefly, but the resulting rare moments of peace that he had made possible for a few of us have been long remembered. For the first time as we were taken back to prison at night, we had something to look forward to next day.

Apart from the odd courtesy, Takahashi never spoke to me again; he gave no indication that our conversation had ever taken place. A few weeks later he was suddenly taken away from the gaol and we did not see or hear of him again. Not surprisingly our work at the club came to a halt and next day we were back on the docks with others, unloading an ammunition ship.

INTERLUDE

"Don't Let This Thing Drag On Much Longer"

After the Burma–Thailand railway was completed, many officers and men returned to the hospital camp at Chungkai. The officers now had time on their hands and their main problem was filling in the long hours of the day, as 2nd Lt. J. S. Milford recorded:

> By 9.30 I am usually roused, and I go for a brisk walk of about a mile round the perimeter of the camp, before the sun is high enough in the sky to make such exercise a burden. By this time the coffee sellers are abroad in the camp, and I go forth with my pewter mug for a penn'orth of coffee and with its aid eat part or the whole of my "doover." Next, I go down with my little bucket to the river, 1/4 of a mile away, and bring back some water either for laundering some garment or for shaving, if it is my day for that. I can only afford soap and blades to perform this office for my face on alternative days. By this time it is about 11 a.m., and I

read or write or plan a little until at 11.45 it is time to join the throng surging round the library, to see if I can get hold of any decent book before one of the other sharks snaps it up. Soon after 12, I go down to the canteen for a pint of tamarind drink which has a pleasant astringent taste which I greatly like, and perhaps may also get an egg or some peanuts, but such expenditure is not lightly to be made, and I can only permit myself such luxuries perhaps twice a week.

Lunch is at one, and between that and dinner at seven is a weary tale of hours, too hot for strenuous exercise, which must somehow be filled in. Reading, writing, planning, learning, thinking, talking, playing chess or patience, are the expedients I use to bring about the defeat of our old enemy, Father Time, but in the end he has the laugh on me, for he has won from me these days, made useless where they might have been so full of joy, and he will never let me have them back again.

At 5.45 is roll-call, a purposeless formality for officers, and then I usually have a bath, either in the river, or more hygenically I think (you would too if you saw the river) from my little bucket. Dinner follows at 7 and the cookhouse staff lavish their greatest pains and most of our 2d a day subscription on this meal, after which I go for another walk round the camp, calling in on my way to visit any friends who may be in hospital, and return to the hut in time for the evening cup of coffee. Darkness comes soon after half past eight, in spite of our summer time, or "Tokio time" as the Japs invariably call it, and most of us save the Bridge fiends bring out our little wooden stools and sit around in the dusk and darkness discussing profoundly the latest rumours and gossip and telling of the times that were and those that are to be. We have little of which to complain, with Konyu and the like as our standards of comparison—but, oh God, don't let this thing drag on much longer.

Chapter 26

FREEDOM

The first truly optimistic day at Changi was November 5, 1944, when the men heard bursts of ack-ack fire. At long last the bombers overhead were American B-29s—the men counted forty-eight. Over the next four months the raids became more frequent. On February 1, 1945, Capt. David Nelson noted the "lovely sight" of an air raid with some ninety "immense machines" glistening in the sun. The raids provided proof that the Allies were winning, and that an end to their years as prisoners was in sight. The men cheered.

"The Yanks are here," the men at Kuching in Borneo shouted on March 25, 1945, when two bombers began to drop leaflets on the camp. They were the first Allied planes the prisoners had seen for nearly three and a half years. On his way from Cabanatuan to Japan in 1944, Pte. Andrew Carson's ship was bombed, but amid the pandemonium he realized that, suddenly, there were other Americans out there, fellow countrymen still free and close enough to blast the hated enemy: "Maybe, just maybe, there were other Americans out there who, somewhere, somehow, someday, would get us out of here." Carson's was just one of many examples of perilous "friendly fire" as the Allies closed in on Japan and Thailand. At Lt. Col. Philip Toosey's camp at Nong Pladuk a stick of bombs from American B-29s hit the camp instead of the Japanese marshaling yards, killing more than ninety men and wounding more than four hundred. Incidents such as these meant that whatever their suffering, the prisoners did not glory for long in the devastation wrought by the repeated attacks made by American bombers in 1945. They lived among the miles of destruction, charred ruins as far as the eye could see. Twisted metal and smoldering wood lay in black heaps, MO Ernest Norquist wrote. The stench of burned flesh and suffocating palls of smoke hung in the air. Women stood weeping with children on their backs. Ragged, tired-looking men pushed carts or carried bundles that held all their rescued earthly possessions; some didn't even have bundles. Fukuoka, for example, an industrial town on the west coast of Kyushu, where the Japanese lived in tightly packed wooden houses, was subjected to three days of fire raids in June. The fires spread into a vast conflagration, leaving the remains of humans and animals piled on the roads, the bridge, and the canal. Only gutted buildings and the camp were left standing. Low-flying Lockheed Lightnings and B-29 Flying Fortresses revisited the town in July, when the factory was decimated.

Only days later, however, were the men to realize the significance—for Japan, for them as prisoners, and for the new world order—of the raids they saw on August 9. More than seven hundred planes were counted during the day, in the prisoners' experience an all-time record. L.Bdr. Art Benford at Fukuoka watched two formations heading for Nagasaki, and saw the town come under attack:

> It was a particularly bright and clear morning and I was looking expectantly through the fold in the hills towards Nagasaki. As I watched, I witnessed something for which I could offer no explanation. A brilliant blue and white flash momentarily blotted out the town. Then a ball of fire which quickly grew in size to envelop the whole of Nagasaki appeared to be sucked in towards the centre and thrown upwards into the air. A huge reddish-brown cloud developed with a stem of darker colour reaching to the ground. The cloud grew upwards and spread, and changed colour to near white. A gigantic cloud, rising fast, reflected the fires below which had ignited instantly. I suppose the whole event had lasted less than a minute.

Benford had witnessed the dropping of the second atom bomb. The next morning the Japanese told the men at Fukuoka that the Americans had used a new type of weapon, that tens of thousands had been killed, and that if they heard an air-raid siren they were to go immediately to the shelter and cover bare skin.

Some prisoners had been only about a mile from the epicenter of the bomb. They were the 169 men at Camp 14, Saiwaimachi in Nagasaki City, who had been working at the Mitsubishi factory. They had been brought back to the camp earlier after an air-raid warning. Pte. Jack Johnson heard a plane overhead but was a long way from the air-raid shelter and stepped out to try to locate the plane and check whether he should hurry for cover:

> What I saw was apparently three white parachutes in triangular fashion at about 60 degrees elevation. Suddenly there was a brilliant flash like a photographer's magnesium flash. Instinctively I dropped to the ground beside a kerbing at the side of the alleyway. Then came the blast with a deafening bang and I felt as though I had been kicked in the guts. I found myself gasping for breath, pinned under a lot of rubble and unable to see. The world was black. Very gradually the dust started to thin out and I was able to wriggle from under the beams that had me pinned down. After emerging from beneath the debris I stood up amid the thinning dust and as it cleared I was able to see above the ruins of our camp, the only things standing being the southern brick wall, a portion of the northern wall.

When one Australian came to, his top teeth had gone through his bottom lip. But it was an indication of the men's desperation that horse meat which had been fried by the bomb constituted the best meal they had eaten for years.

Eight prisoners died and thirty others—mostly Dutch—were injured. The dead looked as though they had been smothered with custard, said Sgt. Peter McGrath-Kerr, who was trapped under rubble and dragged from the ruins with only five broken ribs, an injured hand, and cuts to his arms and face. McGrath-Kerr's comrades took him to a clear area where a Dutch medical orderly was attending to some of the injured and left him there while they searched through the ruins. They climbed into the hills and reached a bamboo grove which had been flattened by the blast, but at least offered shelter and refuge to both prisoners and Japanese. Many around them were injured, according to Jack Johnson, "some with weeping flesh where the skin was blown from their bodies and hung about them like the skin of a potato that had been boiled in its jacket." When morning came and people started to drift back to search among the ashes, Johnson and his companions had only one thought: to find food. They made their way to their former camp, located where the kitchen had been, and found some rice and soya-bean mush which was sometimes used in their soup. They wandered about in search of more provisions but gathered together at night in a clear spot beside the canal. They spent the next two nights there. Working parties were taken back to the Mitsubishi foundry each day to clean up and for the cremation of four Dutch prisoners who died at the new camp.

The first atomic bomb had obliterated Hiroshima on August 6. After Nagasaki three days later, the Japanese Government sued for peace and Emperor Hirohito took the unprecedented decision to broadcast to the nation. Within days, the lot of the prisoners held in Japan began to improve. "Things must be happening," Norquist wrote on August 15 when the day-work party returned to camp at 2 P.M. At noon the Japanese had listened to a radio speech: the guards all had sad faces and women were crying as the work party made its way back. Things certainly were happening. That night Norquist and his fellow prisoners had their best meal as prisoners, a rich meat and vegetable stew. The next day, whenever the Japanese entered the officers' bunkhouse, they bowed. Only on August 19, however, ten days after the Nagasaki bomb, were the men informed that the war was officially over and that they were once again free men. Norquist played "The Star-Spangled Banner" and "God Save the King" on the trumpet he had kept with him throughout captivity. There were smiles, shouts, and excited chatter, then the men sang "Happy Days Are Here Again," "California, Here I Come," and "God Bless America." Norquist could hardly believe that he was free: "There's something so unreal about it. I didn't expect it to come this way, somehow. There was no fire and brimstone; no bloodshed; no gunfire; no 'Yanks and Tanks'; just the simple announcement that the war was over. Peace has come to us 'peacefully'—like a dove, on quiet wings. Yet it is nonetheless glorious."

At Aomi, the handover to the prisoners was orchestrated with military precision by Lt. Stephen Abbott, the British commanding officer, who took over but treated the Japanese commandant Yosisawa with chivalry. After shaking hands with his former captor, Abbott startled him by saying he wanted a conference to discuss the changeover of administration. Abbott already had a detailed plan for organizing the camp when the war was over and he pointed through the window to the square, where a new military unit was forming up on parade under Reg. Sgt. Maj. Charlie Spencer. The Japanese were dumbfounded by this parade of potential strength and agreed to Abbott's principal demand that he should assume command. As they left his office, Yosisawa called his staff to attention. Abbott recalled:

> When he saluted I caught his eye. A flash of mutual respect passed between us. At a special parade the next day I demanded his sword in surrender. After a moment's hesitation he unbuckled it, bowed deeply, and held it out in both hands. I knew it had belonged to his grandfather and couldn't take it. I just touched the hilt as a token gesture, and surprised those around me as well as myself.

In Singapore the secret radios at Changi had enabled the men to follow the negotiations between the Allies and the Japanese on the BBC. Soon the message was passed through the ranks that the war was over. It would be some days, however, before the guards admitted the Japanese surrender.

In Thailand the men at Nakhon Nayok were the first to learn that the war was over on August 14. At Kanchanaburi two Korean guards alerted the men a day later—but they had become so accustomed to being disappointed by false rumors that they weren't sure whether the news could be believed. The next day work carried on as normal, and a party of six hundred left for a new camp. But the ever-reliable Boon Pong cycled past and said, "Peace." Outside the camp the Thais were beaming and whispering, "War over, war over." The day passed by without any official announcement and evening roll call was held as usual. But at 9:30 P.M. an "electric current" ran through the camp—all hut commanders had been summoned to the camp commandant's office. Capt. C. F. Blackater knew then that the rumors were true:

> It was then we went mad. Crowds poured out of the huts; everybody was talking, nobody listening. There came a wild rush. Hut commanders had reappeared; they could hardly reach their respective huts. Our commander managed to battle through to the sleeping-platform and climbed up. Outside the moon flooded the camp with a brilliant light, inside feeble little oil-lamps cast shadows across the central gangway, packed tight with people. There was a cry for silence, then it came: Japan has acknowledged defeat. No details. What did details matter! It was enough. The gates of hell were about to open—we would be free. No one gave an order, it was spontaneous: huts emptied again out into the moonlight, a pause, and then—"God Save the King." Not everyone who started to sing finished. I, for one, was glad of the silvered darkness—something about the size of a vegetable marrow was in my throat. "The Star-Spangled Banner" and the Dutch Anthem followed. Another little pause and—"Land of Hope and Glory" rang through the night.

It was the first time they had sung the national anthem since Christmas 1942. It had risen out of the night on a thousand voices, slow, dignified, and beautiful, said Capt. Richard Sharp. The celebrations continued for hours.

Later the band struck up in 2nd Lt. Robert Sutcliffe's Hut 6 and they roared through all the familiar songs—"Roll Out the Barrel," "There'll Always Be an England," "The QM Stores," and numerous others:

> The monkey, Jennie, was there, swinging across the bamboo struts—we freed her from her chain, too. Oh God it was good, and all the time I

> was shouting to myself: "It's true: Bob you old stiff, it's true. And you'll be back to Ruth soon, really soon—not another year or two years, but quite soon, and we've won, and . . . Thank you God." Awakened by the British reveille: enormous thrill for everyone, this replacement of the hated Japanese bugle calls by our own: last night, suddenly, the two buglers sounded the Last Post: How deeply one's feelings are caught by these things of tradition and association: That call I have heard all too often in this 3 1/2 years of POW life—funerals of men died of sickness, overwork, starvation, and most vivid and tragic, the morning when the bugler at Nong Pladuk II sounded that call of lament and honour from us to the camp NP, 1100 yards away, as they gathered the hundred bodies from the wreckage after the first night-bombing by our own planes.

In spite of the hatred for the Japanese, Sutcliffe was perhaps not the only prisoner who felt "stirrings of pity" for the "ugly little men" who had held their captives cowed and humiliated. They were now pumping their own water, and watching, subdued, as the Union Jack was run up the staff, a forewarning of the hardship that awaited them.

That sense of pity was not at first shared by Philip Toosey. At Nakhon Nayok he was summoned by Lt. Takasaki, the hated commandant at Tamarkan who had executed those who had escaped in 1943. Takasaki was now deputy to Noguchi, who was away from the camp. A new mat had been laid out in the rear of his hut and Takasaki offered Chinese tea. "Now we are friends, we can shake hands, the war is over," he told Toosey. But Toosey rebuffed him. What had happened to the men executed at Tamarkan? he demanded. Were they shot and beheaded on Capt. Noguchi's instructions, or on an order from above? Takasaki admitted it had been his own decision. Toosey refused to take tea and proposed that he should take over the camp. At a general parade of the twelve hundred officers, he then announced that the war was over. They celebrated by singing "Land of Hope and Glory," "God Save the King," and "Jerusalem," the songs the British men sang whenever they heard the news. British, Australian, American, and Dutch flags, hidden since 1942, were hoisted.

When a second parade was held the next morning, Toosey had organized guards, armed with sticks, who were manning the gate and watching Noguchi, who had now returned from a visit to Bangkok. Other detachments examined the stores for food and clothing, and a truck went to the nearest village to buy food from the funds that Noguchi had held. As Noguchi also handed over thousands of letters that had been withheld, the men at Nakhon Nayok now made similar discoveries to those that were made in almost every camp. Rohan Rivett found a letter that his wife had sent in October 1942. And it was not only letters that had been withheld: Red Cross supplies had been, too. The men had been living virtually naked but now they found "masses" of shirts, shorts, and towels, as well as sacks of sugar, bags of beans and peanuts, and crates of drugs and medical gear which might have saved hundreds of lives. There was about one parcel for every five men. Some were stamped "Bermondsey 1942."

After the singing and the cheers died down, the predominant emotion was relief. "I am no longer a chattel, a coolie, a beast of burden (oh how weary I am of being a beast of burden)," 2nd Lt. J. S. Milford wrote. "But I am not yet a British officer again, a man with duties and obligation but entitled to consideration, service and even respect. Not until I leave the army will I be a real person again instead of a number—but at least my new number will not be a prison one." For Lt. David Boddington, it meant an end to this "filth, stench, disease, brutality and concentration camp discipline" and a return to freedom, home, lights, color, and cleanliness.

Although a majority of the men had sworn they would get their own back on their guards, they mostly found that their minds were wholly taken up with the realization that they were free again. Those around Pte. Roy Whitecross at Omuta in Japan wanted to forget the past:

> To me, the Japs were beyond adequate punishment, for what punishment could be meted out to a people who had treated us as they had? It would be farcical to punish a Jap by flogging him and saying, "That is your punishment for killing my friend. This is also your punishment for bringing me to utter misery and close to death." It would be ludicrous. No. We had learned to hate with such a hatred that there could be no fitting punishment for the acts that had bred this hatred. All we wanted was to get away from them, to try to forget them, and in the security and love of our homes try to recover, physically and mentally. The Americans on the ship that took us from Japan could not understand this attitude, because they were as we had been before the war—they thought they knew what hatred was. But they had never touched such depths of emotion as we had reached. They were lucky. In reply to their demands as to why we had not taken suitable revenge, we could only shrug our shoulders and say, "You don't understand."

Ernest Norquist also had no desire for revenge: "I want to go home and try to forget about the lost years," he wrote in his diary. "Just let me be free!" He had a hot bath, got some cigarettes, and had "good burnt gravy" soup for supper. According to him, "not many" guards were killed—but some understandably were, in ambush, shot or pushed down latrines. Officers looked the other way. Japanese soldiers lined up to surrender on the island of Bougainville, off New Guinea, were machine-gunned. Australian troops meeting prisoners from Java, five of them blind, were so shocked when they subsequently landed in Borneo that they shot the Japanese they found there. One prisoner took revenge on a Japanese colonel by defecating in one boot and urinating in the other. A hated mine boss was force-fed horse dung. One punishment was to make the culprit walk between two ranks while buckets of feces and urine were poured over him. Then they were made to clear up the mess with their hands, after which the buckets were poured over them again. But most of the men did not seek that sort of revenge; they just wanted to go home.

There were also many acts of spontaneous compassion toward the defeated Japanese. After the surrender was announced at Nakhon Pathom, Lt. Col. Albert Coates immediately visited the adjoining camp, which housed many Japanese sick and wounded from Burma, and placed at the disposal of the commanding officer the British and Australian medical officers and orderlies to help alleviate their suffering. He was thanked, but the offer was declined: the officer, with tears in his eyes, said he had no authority to accept it. A train loaded with Japanese wounded arrived at Tamuang in mid-August. They had been traveling for more than three weeks and looked as wretched as the prisoners, who nonetheless unhesitatingly gave the Japanese their food. The Dutch ensign Cornelius Dirk Punt said that he felt no revenge or hatred but pride: the men had proved that they were practicing Christians, willing and able to treat the defeated enemy as fellow human beings. PO A. W. Bird started a fund to give chocolate, sweets, and chewing gum to the schoolchildren in the local Japanese village. The 482 men subscribed enough to give 1,352 children two packets of gum and a bar of chocolate each.

The men also started recalling the many sufferings they had endured. George Grigs made an "impressive" mental list of his ailments. It could have been compiled by any one of thousands of men:

> Dysentery (once), Beri-beri (twice—slight but worrying), Diarrhoea (many times), Malaria (several times), Dengue (twice), Assorted fevers (on and off), Foot Tinia (more or less permanently), Singapore Ear (so-called, occasionally), Rheumatism (intermittently), Lumbago (once—most unpleasant), and Ringworm, Tonsillitis, Conjunctivitis, Jaundice (all once), the whole lot backed up by tropical ulcers of varying severity,

> odd skin troubles, and the usual boils and sores. It looks a good deal worse than it has really been, though at times it felt dreadfully serious—especially malaria and jaundice together.

Japan surrendered unconditionally on August 14. But it was not until the twenty-third that the Japanese High Command ordered a ceasefire, and not until the twenty-eighth that the preliminary surrender document was signed in Rangoon, and Japanese commanders agreed to assist and obey the orders of Admiral Lord Mountbatten, the Supreme Allied Commander in Southeast Asia. The men were longing to return to their homes but nobody knew when the camps would be relieved by the Allies or how the Japanese would react to defeat.

Field Marshal Count Terauchi, Commander in Chief of Japan's Southern Army, refused to accept the surrender and said on August 15 that he intended to fight on. The commander of Singapore, Gen. Itagaki, refused to surrender the island, where that summer the prisoners had been digging tunnels and artificial caves in preparation for an Allied invasion or as their own graveyards. He said that he would carry on guerrilla warfare if the Allies invaded. Even after the Emperor had spoken, moreover, the Japanese were still killing prisoners. At Osaka they shot three and beheaded two of the American airmen who had been captured. At Fukuoka, another sixteen airmen were hacked to death. It was twelve days after the August 15 broadcast that the last thirty survivors at Ranau in Borneo were executed.

At Kanchanaburi, Lt. Col. Swinton, the British commander, described the situation as "delicate" and gave his personal guarantee to the Japanese that the camp would be orderly and disciplined. The Koreans had been disarmed but the Japanese still carried their weapons and kept a guard in their room by the main gate.

The "delicacy" of the prisoners' situation was revealed after the war when it was discovered that in Taiwan there was a written Japanese order of August 1 which stated that all prisoners were to be killed if Allied forces approached the area. It was feared the prisoners would revolt as soon as they thought they were likely to be reinforced. The aim, therefore, was to annihilate all the prisoners by mass bombing, poisonous smoke, drowning, or decapitation. A similar order for the prisoners in Borneo was discovered at Kuching. The prisoners were to be marched twenty miles to the mountains, shot, and burned deep in the jungle on September 15. The sick at Lintang were to be bayoneted and the camp destroyed by fire. There was a precedent for such atrocities. On Palawan in the Philippines in 1944, 150 prisoners had been herded into air-raid shelters, doused with petrol, and set alight. When they tried to escape they were gunned down or killed with clubs and bayonets.

Across the Far East the prisoners now had to be recovered, restored to health, and returned home: men were still dying at a rate of fifteen a day. The task was a testing responsibility for Mountbatten. When Japan surrendered he was overseeing an area of more than a million square miles with a population of nearly 130 million. There was no reliable civil police force, except in Thailand, and no civil government with independent administration. The area contained nearly 750,000 Japanese, of whom some 630,000 were armed troops, and, as we have seen, it was by no means certain that they would obey the order to surrender. About 123,000 prisoners and internees had to be safeguarded under the Recovery of Allied Prisoners of War and Internees (RAPWI) program.

Three organizations played a crucial role in the work of RAPWI: E Group, which helped air crews brought down behind enemy lines and prisoners to escape; the clandestine Force 136, which had planned uprisings in the occupied territories; and the Special Operations Executive (SOE). The three organizations now worked with Mountbatten to secure the safety of the prisoners and organize their evacuation. They started by dropping leaflets on the camps: one set told the men to stay where they were; another, in Japanese, told troops that the war had ended and that they should stop fighting. One hundred and fifty tons of leaflets in fifty-eight sorties were dropped in the three days after August 28.

Captivity had been an ordeal for all the prisoners, but some were experiencing hardship beyond the everyday miseries of the prison camps when the Japanese surrendered. At Kanchanaburi the popular captain Bill Drower, who spoke fluent Japanese and had acted as an interpreter, had been in solitary confinement since May without being charged or put on trial. According to Capt. Richard Sharp, Drower had been the victim of the only serious atrocity at Kanchanaburi:

> One day a Jap private had told an officer at the pump to fill his bucket for him: and the officer, it being early morning, and he feeling awkward, told him what he could do with it. Consternation; and the officer was hauled up before Noguchi, to explain why he had refused to obey a Jap order. Bill, doing interpreting, explained it was because officers didn't like being batmen to Jap privates. That got Nog on the raw. With a bellow of rage, he broke a sword stick over Bill's head, and then laid into him, ending up by rolling with him all over the floor. With his loss of temper, he had lost face: so Bill had to pay for that too. He was made to

> stand outside the guardroom and then, in a fainting condition, thrown to the bottom of a Jap air-raid shelter where he was left to starve for days.

At first Drower was put in a narrow underground shelter without room to stand and partially filled with water. He was given no food or water for the first three days. Lizards walked along the earth roof. One night he was woken by a rat nibbling at his foot. He was then given two rice balls a day and water twice a day, but was not allowed to wash or shave. The officer cooks secreted broken-up vitamin tablets in the rice balls, which Drower thought probably saved his life. When he got malaria and blackwater fever, doctors were not allowed to visit him, and only when he was on the point of dying did Matsushita, the camp adjutant, allow Drower meat soups and vitamin tablets. Noguchi had left for Nakhon Nayok, allowing Matsushita to exercise compassion, and Drower was eventually moved to a detention cell. His treatment was a deliberate attempt at slow murder, said Rohan Rivett. He had been incarcerated for eighty days when Swinton and camp doctors hauled him from his cell. He was in a delirious and pitiable condition and would have died within a few days, but he was now carefully nursed back to health before returning to Britain. Noguchi was hanged after his war crimes trial.

The ninety-seven prisoners of the Kempetai at Outram Road Jail had suffered an equally harrowing ordeal. The guards had amused themselves by feeding the pigs and the prisoners in the same courtyard, throwing the food on the ground and simultaneously opening the doors of the cells and the pig sties. Their release had been the first demand made by Francis Dillon. When the liberating forces arrived at the jail, the prisoners did not know that the war was over. Their emotion was "heartrending," said Harry Jessup. Pte. Jack Sharpe, whose picture came to symbolize the emaciated appearance of the prisoners, weighed just fifty-six pounds and was unable to stand. On August 23, six of the former prisoners signed a statement accusing the prison commander at Outram Road of being directly responsible for the deaths of fifteen prisoners, starving inmates to death and allowing brutal warders and guards to ill-treat the sick.

Also rescued were parties of men who were still working up country in conditions similar to those of the "Speedo" period in 1943. Six hundred men had left Nakhon Pathom for the Burma–Thailand border in April, where they worked on making a road between Prachaub Kirikua and Mergui. According to one SOE operative, two hundred of the six hundred had died, and another two hundred were not expected to survive. Robert Sutcliffe described the plight of one up-country party when they arrived at Kanchanaburi:

> It was a pitiful and enraging sight. The men were in a shocking condition, emaciated, barefoot, clad in filthy rags. Apart from the awful skeletons on stretchers, very many of the "fit" had to be carried into camp. I carried an Australian in on my back who was thin and weak from dysentery, face that awful leaden hue which prolonged malaria gives to men. He kept apologising for the stink of his body, which was pretty awful. They had been sent up into Burma 6 weeks ago from the hospital camp at Nakhon Pathom; they were put to work on defensive fortifications away beyond Nikhe—about the 260 km mark; all the horrors we'd experienced two years ago were inflicted again on these men, many of whom had been up-country 3 and 4 times before. Work from 5 a.m. until 8 p.m.; food—rice and dahl. Ten per cent sick allowed, all others forced to work or stand in the sun. An Australian private . . . was found outside the camp, having collapsed on way in from a working party: he was bayoneted by the Nip guards and buried.

Claire Baker nursed some of the prisoners who had been released in Sumatra and flown to Singapore. Half were stretcher cases and most weighed no more than seventy pounds. Some wept uncontrollably; some stood at attention if spoken to. On one occasion the nurses sat down to eat with six of the men. A piece of gristle was left on the side of a plate, and one man leaned over, cut the gristle into six pieces, and shared it with his comrades. "It was a noiseless ward and not really happy, as if the patients could not express their thoughts of release," Baker said. "They had obviously thought so much about the end of hostilities that it was almost an anticlimax and their spirits had been deadened by their sufferings."

On August 28, when it was clear that the Japanese intended to obey his orders, Mountbatten ordered RAPWI into action. In Malaya there were ninety-seven Force 136 officers with fifty-two wireless sets operating in the field. E Group, Force 136, and SOE now made often dramatic entrances into the prisoners' lives. When 2nd Lt. John Fullerton walked into Kanchanaburi to buy for the canteen on August 27, he was called into the governor's house and astonished to be greeted by a self-evidently free British captain sporting a parachute badge. As Robert Sutcliffe described the meeting, the captain might have been played by David Niven:

> In great excitement John said, "By jove it's good to see you!" and got the smiling reply, "Sorry I've been so long." Over a whiskey and soda and a Players, he learnt that this laddie, Capt Newall, and his signaller, an

> Aussie Sergeant, had been dropped out of a plane 4 nights ago, landing at Ban Pong. He'd left London only 14 days ago!

The main impression of the men's rescuers was of how much they stank.

At Ubon, men of Force 136, led by Col. David de Crespigny Smiley, had already made contact with the men when Toosey arrived. They had been in the area for six months, based with the Thai army, had sent intelligence back to India by radio, watched the prisoners, and made immediate contact when the surrender was announced. They had trained fifteen hundred Thai guerrillas, and built an airstrip in the jungle on which five Dakotas had landed in one night. After the surrender they had arranged for supplies of food and drugs to be delivered to the men.

Tam Innes-Ker was astounded while he was working late in the camp office at Changi when he saw the main gate being opened for a Japanese general's car, out of which stepped two "most extraordinary sights." They were a bearded British police officer who had been hiding in the jungle, and a Chinese, both of them armed and acting truculently with the Japanese:

> They fairly laid down the law to the Nip General, having had him hauled out of bed and brought before them—I saw all this in the office. First, all guards to be withdrawn forthwith, all arms surrendered to us, all rations to be doubled at once, two powerful generating sets to be installed by 10 a.m., two transmitting sets to be produced at once—and so on. The Nip General and officers were in tears, literally, but all was produced as ordered: amongst other things, butter in 1 lb packs, which has been in the Singapore Cold Storage all those years—we each got 1 lb at once!

Airdrops of food, clothing, and medicines started after August 28. Soon afterward, 44-gallon drums on dozens of colored parachutes started cascading from the sky. They contained soup, fruit juice, sugar, milk, Nescafé, and cocoa, as well as sweets, chewing gum, cigarettes, and matches. The food and medicine came with a warning not to overeat or overmedicate, but some did. "When the Liberators dropped leaflets over Changi on 28 August, where there were now 12,000 men, even the hospital patients tottered out to look up at the sky. We all began to cry," said Ronald Searle.

However, the Liberators that now flew over the camps occasionally missed their targets or aimed too well and the cartons fell on huts. A few men were killed by the new "bombs" and some cartons were smashed on landing. When the parachutes attached to 65-gallon oil drums failed to open, the results were disastrous. At one camp, the drums hit the cookhouse, the officers' mess, a dining hall, and the latrines, killing one Korean and badly injuring four others. Leaflets confirming that the Japanese had surrendered and that they would be evacuated as soon as possible had been dropped earlier. They advised the men to stay in their camps until further orders and to list their most urgent necessities. There were also cheering messages from the pilots: "Eat up, there's plenty more where this came from," and "You eat the food, we'll xxxx the women." Another read:

> To Whom it May Concern. This gives me one of the greatest pleasures of my life to be one of the people to help my comrades directly for such a good cause.
>
> May God have mercy on you and help you safely home to your loved one. Best wishes to you all.
>
> Your buddy, Sgt. R. S. Wagner, CCS, USS *Hancock,* CV19

The messages dropped on August 31 were even more cheering: "The country's yours, boys!" said one leaflet dropped over Fukuoka.

> To the Guys below. When this is being written I am at Saipan, and am preparing for that 16-hour ride up to your location. Hope we find you alright, as our gas supply is a problem. Don't know how soon you will be out of your hole, but believe me our sole purpose is to drop you supplies, and say "hello." Hope I don't come too low and blow your shingles off. Fleet is already in Tokyo harbour. They are making landings today and commencing official occupation. It shouldn't be long now . . . Good Luck . . .

According to Chief Petty Officer Ray Parkin, men began to put on weight rapidly—too rapidly. In fifteen days some gained twenty pounds:

> Stomachs were distended, limbs were swollen. Some were caricatures of humanity. Emaciated men with puffed-up pot-bellies thrust out turning their navels inside-out. Above this taut inflation were their slatted ribs, cheekbones and hollow temples. Their shoulder-blades stuck out like featherless wings. They walked with a stately gait as if they were unnaturally pregnant. They turned corners with a circumspect manoeuvre as if they had an invisible bass drum and were afraid the wind would snatch it away.

But the airdrops meant much more than full stomachs to the men. At last the outside would know about them again. "For the past three and a half years it had never seemed to matter to anybody whether they lived or died," said Parkin. "Now they mattered. People were concerned about them. There was a surge of emotion in them that had no concise expression. It seemed that their bellies were melting within them."

When the Allies landed in Malaya on September 5, some twenty relief personnel had been flown into camps and 950 tons of supplies delivered. Mountbatten and his wife became heroes to the released prisoners, who noted their commander's charm, charisma, and lack of nonsense. Fusilier Harry Howarth was among the men when Mountbatten addressed them from a box as they sat in the dust. He seemed reluctant to start his speech, and then Howarth realized why: his eyes were full of tears and it was several seconds before he could collect himself. Then he began to speak:

> I have the Japanese general who has done this to you running around the garden at my headquarters in his bare feet between two members of the CMP. You all know what I should like to do to him for the treatment he has meted out to you. Unfortunately I am not allowed. This is the only punishment I am allowed to inflict on him. I know you have all suffered terribly and give you my word that every effort will be made to expedite your return home to your loved ones.

Mountbatten's greatest asset at this time was his wife. Wherever she went, Lady Mountbatten cheered the troops—the majority of whom hadn't seen a white woman for years—cut through red tape, and got things done. She arrived in Bangkok on September 5, ignored warnings that forty thousand armed Japanese were still at large nearby, and traveled to Nakhon Pathom the next day, sitting in the rear seat of a jeep with Lt. Col. Albert Coates. She was accompanied by a cavalcade of Japanese generals and colonels, armed Thai guards on motorbikes, and a car containing Lt. Gen. Thompson and Maj. Gen. Tyndall of the RAMC 14th Army. Coates described the exultant shouts of the men as the gates flew open and Lady Mountbatten made a triumphal tour of the camp, and then inspected the very sick, still lying on bare boards, with a kind word for each. After lunch, she addressed the men from a bamboo stage.

She went on to visit six more camps, making the same vivid impression—never forgotten—on the men as she had at Nakhon Pathom. "We were visited today by Lady Mountbatten, wearing a row of ribbons and no stockings," wrote Cpl. Albert Thompson. "Quite an agreeable dame." By the end of September, Lady Mountbatten had visited prisoners in Malaya, French Indo-China, Sumatra, and Java. She went later to Borneo, Morotai, Manila, and

Hong Kong. She found the men in "amazingly good spirits," however ill and emaciated. "The brave spirits and 'guts' have been unbelievable during all these ghastly years."

On the same day that Lady Mountbatten was in Bangkok, the men in Singapore also had a day to remember: when they awoke, the guards had disappeared and the invasion fleet had arrived. LAC Don Peacock described the sight that greeted him:

> Dark storm clouds hung low over the horizon. Beneath them the sun sparkled on an arc of white flecks stretching away to the horizon. Slowly the flecks grew into long white arrows of foam. Each was the wake of a ship. Gradually the armada took shape. Landing craft led destroyers, cruisers, troopships, the lot. More ships than Singapore had seen for many a long day. It was like the grande finale of one of those old Hollywood epics where the Army, the Navy, the Air Force and Uncle Tom Cobley and all come speeding to the rescue.

The prisoners at Kuching in Borneo were less fortunate. They knew of the surrender on August 15, leaflets were dropped on the nineteenth, and rations were increased, but on the twenty-fourth Col. Suga, the camp commandant, told them that Terauchi was fighting on. It was another eight days before Suga accepted that his war was lost, and a further eleven after that before the Australian army landed and took over Kuching. There was an emotional speech from Capt. Jennings of the USS *Barnes,* who was as moved as the men.

The prisoners in Java were in the most perilous situation, because local insurgents fighting for a free Indonesia immediately started attacking the Dutch. Mobs stormed the camp fences, and the British, who were white and therefore "Dutch," did not know who were the more dangerous, the Japanese or the Indonesians, according to L.Cpl. James Home:

> We were now seriously threatened with death at the hands of a third party with whom we had no quarrel. Outside our barbed-wire fences at all times their banners fluttered and fists threatened. Their freedom word, "*merdeka,*" mocked us as it poured from every mouth as if to say: "This is our freedom, not yours." Only the presence of our recent brutal captor stood between us.

Thankfully, on September 12 a Flying Fortress flew over the camp at Batavia and dropped leaflets telling the men that a relief party was on its way.

Although Mountbatten had received the formal surrender in Singapore on September 12, there were still isolated atrocities by the Japanese. Eleven days after the surrender, prisoners and coolies near Thakhek in Thailand were beaten and murdered until a local SOE commander, Maj. Peter Kemp, arrived. RAPWI, however, was remarkably efficient in organizing the evacuation of the men.

By the end of October, about seventy-one thousand prisoners and internees had been transported to India, Australia, and Britain, mostly by sea from Singapore, and more to the United States. Across the Far East, after three and a half years, the prisoners of the Japanese were on the journey home.

INTERLUDE

Bushido

After the war, an embittered Capt. Jacob Markowitz, one of the distinguished medical officers on the Burma–Thailand railway, described how he and his fellow prisoners experienced Bushido:

> Our captors, for nearly a century, have tried to impress the world with the high quality of their civilisation. When they took 60,000 prisoners in Malaya they had an opportunity of showing the world not only that they were excellent soldiers, but that they were decent. Instead, they have turned the word bushido into ridicule. Every Japanese, when he could mumble a few words of English, bragged of this code of the Samurai warrior, the Japanese equivalent of the European term chivalry. What, however, did we prisoners of war understand by it? In the first place, an overwhelming braggadocio and swagger, uncontaminated by such sophisticated notions as modesty, or the decent restraint of good sportsmanship.

By bushido we daily understood that a man must not be reprimanded, but smacked in the face, must not be tried in a military fashion in the guard-room, but beaten like a dog—no, not like a dog; we have never seen a dog, or for that matter any animal, beaten the way the Japanese manhandled their prisoners. By bushido we understood that a man must not merely be disciplined, but outraged as well; must never by any accident be kicked in the rump, but in the testicles. When a POW was recaptured after attempting to escape, he was charged with desertion and shot. Thus, for every infringement, fancied or real, a victim was found and the ends of justice satisfied; failing that, the whole group was punished and woe betide that group when the situation lacked a face-saving expedient, for the record of the Kempetai in extracting information from prisoners was an impressive one. By bushido, therefore, we understood the normal behaviour of our captors: remorseless, lecherous, treacherous, kindless villainy, villainy that having been done was impertinently presented to the world as chivalry.

Chapter 27

HOME AT LAST

The prisoners in Japan started their journey home in September. Some traveled through Nagasaki, where the scene of annihilation shocked them into silence. Nothing was left standing: as far as the eye could see, the area was flattened into a mass of untidy rubble. The countryside was devoid of trees. Only blackened stumps pointed skyward like accusing fingers, said L.Bdr. Art Benford. But Benford didn't regret the use of the bomb. He knew that it had saved the prisoners' lives: "We were thankful for that bomb. We had been forced to dig a huge pit which was to be our communal grave and extra machine guns had been dispersed throughout the camp. Our guards had received orders to shoot us if mainland Japan was invaded."

When the train halted, Benford and his fellow prisoners were greeted by nurses and sailors, and they got their first taste of the big hearts of the Americans. The band of the carrier *Cape Gloucester* was deployed along the dockside. To the former prisoners, they looked clean and spotless in crisp khaki drill and white uniforms. The men stood for a moment, undecided, and then they went "crazy," dancing with the nurses and sailors to "The Two O'Clock Jump":

> The dockside was in an uproar and not until the band was sent back to the ship could these bronzed and beautiful super men and women from the outside world take over. An angel in uniform spoke to me and I stared at her, unable to make my mind function, and as I stood in con-

> fused silence, the thought flashed into my mind—this was the moment and here was the evidence I had been waiting for, now I could believe the nightmare was over. These sailors were the first Americans I had encountered and I instantly liked them—they were friendly and we could not have chosen more kindly and sympathetic saviours. Rows and rows of beds filled the hangar deck, and our welfare was their only concern. We were bathed, fumigated and clothed in officers' tropical uniform, and then came the treat we had all been waiting for, our first civilized meal for three and a half years. When I walked into the mess hall I was almost overcome by the heady aroma and the mountain of fried chicken and tray upon tray of beautiful food.
>
> We filed slowly past the servery, piling our plates, the anticipation serving as an appetizer to a meal which in appearance alone was all that I had dreamed of. No more nauseating mildew rice, millet, salt plums, seaweed, cat, dog, lizard, snake and rotten duck's eggs. When I pushed back my plate, polished clean, there was no room for the tiniest morsel, and my belly was extended—for once I sat back and enjoyed the feeling.

Others gorged themselves, too. On board an American ship taking him home, Flt. Lt. Peter Lee had the breakfast he had been dreaming about for years—a plate of porridge, four fried eggs, two boiled eggs, a helping of fried ham, and two helpings of bubble and squeak, rounded off with toast and jam. His tiffin was steak and onions followed by strawberry ice cream.

When PO A. W. Bird left Wakanama on the new hospital ship USS *Sanctuary,* it sailed through the American 5th Fleet to a "tremendous" farewell. All the ships were dressed for the prisoners, with their crews drawn up on parade. The band of the *New Jersey* played "Land of Hope and Glory," and the men on the *Sanctuary* lined the decks and saluted her on their captain's command. The men left Japan feeling like heroes instead of prisoners of war, said Bird.

The journey home for some of the British went via Manila and Pearl Harbor to Vancouver, across Canada and the Atlantic to Southampton or Liverpool. The majority of British prisoners traveled home by air and sea via Rangoon, Colombo, Calcutta, and Suez. The Australians sailed south, of course, and experienced the same surprises, the same adjustments, and the same personal tragedies as the men who sailed east and west from Japan. All the way to wherever they were going, every prisoner had to adjust to freedom; the world had changed beyond their comprehension since 1942, and they had been left behind. Relations had been ruptured and some men received heartbreaking cables or letters from their wives saying they had left them, or that mothers and fathers had died before they could say goodbye. Traveling from Taiwan on the USS *Santee* was 2nd Lt. David Piper:

> We went with our earthly possessions clutched to us; pants made of flour bags, a safety-razor blade that had already served eighteen months, sheaves of rough paper covered with longingly indited imaginary menus, empty tins for putting things in; and they threw most of these into the Pacific. They dunked us in antiseptic and shaved every hair off our bodies and threw the hair in the sea. They fed us twenty-four hours a day on a soft diet scientifically calculated not to distress our starved gut. They treated us with endless kindness, amazement, and incomprehension. How could they comprehend? How could they understand the value beyond pearls that an empty coffee tin for putting things in could have for us? We could not comprehend them—even their vocabulary bristling with words we had never heard, words as simple as "jeep." They were saturated and radiant with victory, a victory to which we had contributed nothing and of which we knew very little—of the war in Europe almost nothing. They were radiantly confident in sheer health, and we went among them as shaven skeletons with distended pot stomachs; we were paupers and like paupers we were envious, mentally stripping the rich flesh from our rescuers' bodies to reduce them to our own size, to see what they would look like thin. They smelled strange, at once affluent and gross, and from this we deduced that to them we stank of prison and defeat and disease. Politely they asked us what it had been like, and we could not tell them; when we tried to tell them, they changed the subject soon enough, and soon too we learned not to try. Yet there was of course above all this a huge exhilaration, also inexpressible. Tears of sheer frustration and wonder.

The men from Taiwan feasted on the food that the Americans offered, and a few ate so much that they made themselves ill. The ship's medical officer had to use a stomach pump on two men, one of whom had eaten twelve breakfasts.

The ex-prisoners were not prepared to accept a return to stupid examples of military bull. Sgt. Jack Edwards sailed from Manila on the *Empress of Australia* on which the men, who had been in the hospital, were put on the troop deck with sling hammocks instead of in cabins with bunks. They were outraged and there was a "near riot" when they were threatened with army penalties if they strayed onto other decks. It was "bloody typical," they said. They had been captured by the Japanese, released by the Americans, and now recaptured by the British. Two men who went for a walk on the upper decks were put on a charge for being out of bounds and prejudicing good order, but their protest led to the charges being dropped. No areas were now out of bounds, they were told. For Edwards, the attitude of the ship's officers was typical of the lack of imagination and generosity toward the men from their own superiors—though there were sterling examples of a more compassionate approach. Enter Lady Mountbatten. When the *Empress of Australia* reached Singapore, she went on board and asked the "boys" if they had any complaints. They were moved to better quarters and given mattresses, and two hundred sailors due for home leave were drafted on board to look after them.

Some habits died hard. On Lt. Col. Philip Toosey's ship, the captain complained that his cabin had been rifled and all the silk stockings and other valuables he had bought for his wife stolen. Toosey responded in characteristic style, urging that he could put the matter right if allowed to command the ship until they reached Britain:

> To this he agreed so I got on the blower and I said this: "I am going to empty the alleyways for half an hour. If the Argylls do not return the silk stockings and the other things they have taken from the Captain's cabin in that time, they will get no more beer for the rest of the voyage. You know who is speaking to you and you know that I mean what I say." The booty was returned within that time.

The men who arrived at Rangoon were treated with a distantly remembered kindness. Wherever they docked they were cosseted. Soon after arriving, they were taken to a room set with tables with white cloths and flowers, with white sandwiches of butter and cheese. English girls waited on them. When one asked if they wanted anything more, only one man of the eight at the table could speak, so unused were they to the company of women. "Never were girls so beautiful, never were tablecloths whiter, never did table silver sparkle more brightly. Sandwiches and cakes were piled high in reckless abandon. It was almost too good to be true," said Gunner Stan Henderson. Then the men were taken to a hospital with rows of beds with sheets and pillowcases. "We just stood dumb, gaping, grinning foolishly," said Capt. C. F. Blackater. "It was not true. It could not be true, nothing was true. No one can pass from Hell to Paradise in 72 hours. Yet the dream went on. We had showers—clean, white water and plentiful—and then into our funny pyjamas, supper and bed."

Sgt. Tam Innes-Ker was on the first ship to arrive at Colombo. It was night when they steamed slowly past blacked-out ships. Then, at a given signal, lights flashed on, rockets exploded, and sirens blared a welcome. Innes-Ker was overwhelmed: "The tumult went on till we were well berthed. Everybody was crying. I know I was."

The next morning Lady Mountbatten arrived on board to welcome the men, after which they went ashore and were taken to a rest camp where a feast had been prepared for them.

Thousands of prisoners were arriving every day at Colombo, but each party was given a similar welcome, met by women from the army and navy, and taken off to tea parties. Sgt. A.H.B. Alexander's party was piped ashore by an Indian Army pipe band, Stan Henderson's greeted by the waving of white handkerchiefs.

Carol Broughton (née Wilson) was one of a party of Wrens who volunteered to act as hostesses when some fifteen hundred men arrived on September 20. She described the day in a letter to her mother and father:

> There was such a wonderful spirit among them and they were so thrilled to see English girls that it made quite a lump come in my throat. They were all very sallow—the skin had a grey tinge—which we learned was the result of beri-beri, and some were very emaciated and had terrible sores and scars. We heard that they were the fittest lot to come in!

The Wrens listened as the men talked of their experiences and then took them shopping for presents to take home—boxes of tea, stockings, brooches, raffia purses and handbags, and lace handkerchiefs. When the men left Colombo, they shouted, "Three cheers for the Wrens."

The first sight of home for the British was Southampton or Liverpool. When Tam Innes-Ker arrived on Merseyside, the welcome home was "fantastic." The men were greeted by the Lord Mayor, bands, senior officers, and MPs, as well as by letters and telegrams. It was two hours before they disembarked and were taken to a rest camp for documentation, new kit, and pay, through a city jammed with cheering crowds. The same scenes occurred at Southampton.

Lt. George Grigs was on the fourth ship to arrive at Liverpool on October 12. It was nearly midnight, but the route through the city was still lined with cheering crowds waving flags and setting off fireworks. "What a country this is and what a people!" he wrote in his diary. But Fusilier Harry Howarth was less impressed. There was a strange and unnatural silence on his ship as it arrived at Liverpool. Nobody spoke or waved a reciprocal greeting; nobody smiled or laughed. The ship was enveloped in a melancholy sadness. He was experiencing the emotion that was to come to many of the returning Far East prisoners of war: "We had come home and we felt as if we didn't belong. The only people who understood us were ourselves—and over the years this would become more and more true."

Some of the reunions after arrival were tear-jerking. When Chief Petty Officer Ray Parkin's comrade "John," the only naval survivor on the train, arrived in Melbourne, a special car had been sent to pick him up:

> He was taken straight to HMAS *Lonsdale,* the Melbourne depot. Within ten minutes, the Commander was shaking him warmly by the hand. "Bloody glad you're back . . . good to see you! Just step into my office, will you—I'll be with you in a few minutes." John pushed the door open and walked in. There, he saw a clean and shining boy and girl standing, with his wife's arms about their shoulders. Sitting close by, quiet and silvery, were his mother and father.

At Reading, Capt. Charles Johnson, as a former prisoner of war, was given a free taxi ride home for his reunion with his wife. The whole family had assembled to meet him: "There in the front stood a small, fair-haired boy, my son, a sight I will never forget." Maj. E. W. Swanton, who had lost seventy pounds, rang his father to tell him when he was arriving at Waterloo. He did not recognize his son and passed him by.

Sapper Lionel Morris did not know that he had been posted as "missing—presumed dead" when he reached his home in Cheshire, which he had left seven years earlier:

> My heart beat like a hammer. I rang the bell a third time. Several birds in the gabled eaves, disturbed by the unseemly din, exploded into flight and were lost in the night sky. A window opened above my head and my father's voice enquired, "Who is it?" I answered, "It is Lionel." He, somewhat bewildered, asked, "Lionel who?" "It is Lionel, your son, who else should it be?" He came down the stairs two at a time; the door flung open, and he stood gaping, unbelieving. I thought he was going to fall, but at last he got the message.
>
> "I'm all right," I said, "I've come home."

EPILOGUE

The Last Post

On May 30, 2002, as a correspondent for *The Times,* I attended a moving service at St.-Martin-in-the-Fields, London. The report that I wrote is, I hope, a suitable postscript to the Fepows' story:

> After 45 years the Last Post sounded at St.-Martin-in-the-Fields on Tuesday as members of London's Far East Prisoners of War Association laid up their standard at their final service of remembrance. The service has been held by the Fepows at St. Martin's every year since 1957 but most of the surviving Fepows are now in their eighties and they are becoming frail.
>
> "The years are passing and our members are ageing," said Fred Ryall, their chairman, who was a prisoner in Java, the island of Haruku and Singapore. "It's better to end our tradition while we can still act with dignity and are capable of organising this fitting conclusion."
>
> Each year, as the Rev. Nicholas Holtam said in his address, there have been fewer in the congregation. Those who were left grew older and age did weary them. It seemed characteristically realistic and courageously straightforward, he said, that they had decided that this service should be the last service.
>
> It was a poignant afternoon for the congregation of about three hundred, all with memories of their three and a half years of captivity under the Japanese and the cruelty and brutality they suffered at the

hands of their guards. The Fepows are from an age when men wore suits and ties and held themselves erect whatever their infirmities and had no embarrassment in vigorously singing the National Anthem. They also sang the great English hymns—"I Vow to Thee My Country," "Now Thank We All Our God," "O Valiant Hearts," and the 23rd Psalm. Mr. Ryall read "Why Are Ye Troubled?" the 24th chapter of Luke, starting at verse 38, a text used by Mr. Holtam for his address on forgiveness and repentance.

Several Fepows had said that their persecutors knew all too well what they were doing, he said. That was why they could not pray for them to be forgiven. "Just as you find it hard, some impossible, to forgive those who tortured you, so the Japanese have found it hard, some impossible, to seek remorse and repentance. It may not be possible in this life to get this sorted out any more than it has been. So today, the laying-up of the association's standard is a way of handing it all over to God with thanksgiving for what has been achieved and acceptance that we can't do everything."

As the service ended, Mary Payne, widow of the London Fepows' vice-president, read "We Will Remember Them" and the standards were committed to St. Martin's and placed beside the Association's memorial. Many would see it and marvel that the human spirit was indomitable and could not be snuffed out, said Mr. Holtam.

After a trumpeter sounded the Last Post, there were two minutes' silence followed by the Reveille and the Fepow prayer, praying that never again will man sink to such sorrow and shame: "The price that was paid—we will always remember every day, every month—not just in November." "Sunset," set to organ and cornet, sounded through the ancient church, and the Fepows, with their memories, filed out from their final service.

POSTSCRIPT

What Became of Them?

Louis Baume became chairman of the Swiss Watch Importers' Association and joint managing director of Baume, and helped to create the twenty-five-foot-tall Guinness clock for the Festival of Britain. He later bought Alpine Books in the Strand, London, became an active mountaineer, and in 1955 went to the sub-Antarctic with an expedition of cartography and exploration in South Georgia, where there is now a Mount Baume. He died in 1994.

James Bradley was awarded an MBE for his part in the escape from Sonkurai. He moved to Sussex where he ran a stud farm, built up a herd of Jerseys, and then bought a fruit farm. In 1995 he traveled to Japan to meet Hiroshi Abe, the engineer in charge at Sonkurai, when Abe showed "considerable remorse." Bradley died in 2003.

Albert Coates devoted the rest of his life to helping survivors and ensuring that frozen Japanese assets were liquidated and distributed to former prisoners or their widows. He was elected to a fellowship in the Royal College of Surgeons in 1953, knighted in 1955, and in 1962 given the highest honor that the University of Melbourne could bestow: the honorary degree of Doctor of Laws. He died in 1977.

Francis Dillon made a new and successful career as a businessman in New Delhi. He died in 1975.

William Drower became Britain's lobbyist to the U.S. Congress. After retirement, he was a fellow at the Institute of Politics at Harvard's Kennedy School of Government, a Somerset county councillor, and then chairman of the county council.

Noel Duckworth was chaplain of St. John's College, Cambridge, canon of Accra in the 1950s, and chaplain of Churchill College, Cambridge, from 1961 to 1973. He continued to coach on the towpath of the River Cam. He died in 1980.

"Weary" Dunlop devoted the rest of his life to helping the survivors of captivity and their widows. He was a regular visitor to Fepow meetings across the world. He continued his career as a surgeon, became senior consultant at the Royal Melbourne Hospital, and regularly traveled to international medical congresses. He was knighted in 1969 and made a Companion of the Order of Australia. In 1957 he dedicated the memorial at Hellfire Pass in Thailand. There is a statue of him on the grounds of the Australian War Memorial at Canberra. He died, aged eighty-five, in 1993, and was given a state funeral in Melbourne.

"Black Jack" Galleghan returned to Australia to become deputy director of the Commonwealth Investigation Service for New South Wales, commanded an Australian mission to Germany, and was president of the International Refugee Organisation, which dispatched the first 200,000 persons displaced by the war from Europe to Australia. He was knighted, and died in 1971, aged seventy-four.

Bruce Hunt was the driving force behind the establishment of the Perth Medical School and the Clinical Research Unit at the Royal Perth Hospital. He was vice president of the Royal Australasian College of Physicians and president of the Western Australian branch of the British Medical Association. He died in 1964, aged sixty-five.

Eric Lomax joined the Colonial Office in London and worked in Ghana on the Volta River Project and Tema Harbour and as assistant government agent in Sekondi. He then trained in personnel management, worked for the Scottish Gas Board, and became a lecturer. His book, *The Railway Man,* describing his experiences of captivity and his reconciliation with the man who tortured him, won Britain's preeminent nonfiction award, now known as the Samuel Johnson Prize.

Arthur Percival was flown on Gen. MacArthur's instructions to Yokohama in August 1945 to be present at the formal surrender of Japan and then at a similar ceremony in the Philippines. He retired from the army in 1946 and devoted the rest of his life to building up the Fepow organization. He was instrumental in the campaign which won nearly £5 million from frozen Japanese assets, out of which the Fepow Trust was established to help sick and needy ex-prisoners and their families. He died in 1966.

Rohan Rivett became editor in chief of the *News*, Adelaide's afternoon paper, from 1951 to 1960. When he championed the case of an illiterate Aborigine sentenced to death for murder, the sentence was commuted to life imprisonment and Rivett was acquitted of charges made against him, including seditious and malicious libel, by the state government. He later became director of the International Press Institute in Zurich. He died in 1977, aged sixty.

Richard Sharp joined the Treasury, served as private secretary to the Chancellor, Sir Stafford Cripps, became undersecretary at the Treasury, and finally took charge of the honors system as ceremonial officer in the Civil Service Department. He died in 2002.

Philip Toosey returned to Liverpool, where he became an associate of the bankers Baring Brothers. He was a Wirral JP, High Sheriff of Lancashire in 1964, president of the Liverpool School of Tropical Medicine, and president of the Fepows' Federation from 1966. He died, aged seventy-one, in 1975.

Cyril "Pop" Vardy went first to Australia, then returned to Malaya, where he was the Principal Medical Officer. He held the same post in Rhodesia and was Chief Medical Officer to the Sultan of Brunei before returning to Britain in the 1950s.

Ian Watt became an internationally acclaimed literary critic. He taught at the University of California at Berkeley, was the first dean of the School of English Studies at the University of East Anglia, and became a professor of English at Stanford. He died in 2000 at the age of eighty-three.

Cyril Wild was killed in an air crash at Hong Kong in 1946 on his return from Tokyo, where he had given evidence at a war crimes tribunal.

NOTES

ABBREVIATIONS USED:

AWM Australian War Memorial (Canberra)
IWM Imperial War Museum (United Kingdom)
TNA The National Archives of England, Wales and the United Kingdom

PART ONE

1. Surrender

3 Emperor Hirohito presided over: David Bergamini, *Japan's Imperial Conspiracy: How Emperor Hirohito Led Japan into War Against the West,* pp. 838, 842–847.

4 The task of defending: Clifford Kinvig, "General Percival and the Fall of Singapore," in Brian Farrell and Sandy Hunter (eds.), *Sixty Years On: The Fall of Singapore Revisited,* ch. 12.

4 Inspired by Hirohito: Bergamini, *Japan's,* p. 870.

5 That warrior spirit of the Japanese: Clifford Kinvig, "Allied POWs and the Burma–Thailand Railway," in Philip Towle et al. (eds.), *Japanese Prisoners of War.*

6 the British might be forced to surrender: S. Woodburn Kirby, *Singapore: The Chain of Disaster,* pp. 247–50.

6 That day a Japanese force: Bergamini, *Japan's,* p. 895.

6 Wild was with the first party: Cyril Wild, "Note on the capitulation of Singapore," in P. J. Toosey, IWM 93/14/7, PJDT-19.

7 On New Britain Island: Lionel Wigmore, *Australia in the War of 1939–45: Army (IV)*, pp. 665–73; Bill Cook, quoted in Patsy Adam-Smith, *Prisoners of War from Gallipoli to Korea,* p. 370; R. John Pritchard, Sonia Magbanu, and Donald Cameron Watt (eds.), *The Tokyo War Crimes Trials,* p. 40188.

7 The Americans on the Bataan Peninsula: Gavan Daws, *Prisoners of the Japanese,* pp. 77–80; Pritchard et al., *Tokyo War Crimes Trials,* p. 40432.

8 When Gen. Edward King had negotiated: Pritchard et al., *Tokyo War Crimes Trials,* pp. 40432, 40014.

8 One marcher was: Maj. William E. Dyess, *The Dyess Story,* pp. 70–97.

10 Staff Sgt. Samuel Moody reported: Pritchard et al., *Tokyo War Crimes Trials,* p. 40433.

10 Col. Stubbs, who was on: Ibid., p. 40434.

10 The wounded soldier D. F. Ingle: Ibid., pp. 40434–35.

10 As the men approached Orani: Stanley L. Falk, *The March of Death,* p. 126.

12 When Sgt. Earl Dodson: E. Bartlett Kerr, *Surrender and Survival,* p. 58.

13 A special correspondent of *The Times:* Published February 18, 1942.

13 Lt. Stephen Abbott had seen: *Malaya and Singapore, December 1941–February 1942,* IWM 89/15/1, pp. 10–11.

14 The fact that the European: Laurens van der Post, *The Night of the New Moon,* p. 44.

15 By May 1942, its new empire: Clifford Kinvig, *River Kwai Railway,* p. 17; Bergamini, *Japan's,* pp. 853–54.

Interlude: "We Feel Let Down Rather"

16 "So it is all over": Louis Baume, IWM 66/310/2, February 15, 1942.

2. *Changi*

18 "dirty, thirsty, sweaty": Ronald Searle, *To the Kwai—and Back,* p. 72.

18 "Where have all these sprung from?": Richard Sharp, IWM 66/240/1.

19 "As the long columns of prisoners": Stephen Abbott, IWM 89/15/1, p. 19.

19 It was easy to see: C. F. Blackater, *Gods Without Reason,* p. 24.

20 Percival was shut in a cell: Cyril Wild, quoted in James Bradley, *The Tall Man Who Never Slept,* p. 51.

20 He was punched under the jaw: Ibid.

20 It was also made brutally clear: TNA/WO32/14550: Brig. K. S. Torrance, *Major Events at Changi: 17 Feb to 16 Aug '42,* p. 2. (Also contains factual summary of events at Changi.)

21 If a sentry did not consider: H. S. Flower, IWM 86/87/1, p. 19.

21 The spectacle of a fully loaded: David Griffin, quoted in Lionel Wigmore, *Australia in the War of 1939–45,* p. 513.

22 "With a waiting list": Robert Reid, IWM 67/173/1, p. 23.

22 Hundreds of Chinese in Singapore: Pritchard, *Tokyo War Crimes Trials,* p. 40190.

22 "We are voluntarily sending out": Baume, IWM 66/310/2, February 27, 1942.

22 Within a day of the arrival: Rowley Richards and Marcia McEwan, *The Survival Factor,* p. 59.

22 the Melbourne doctor Glyn White: Adam-Smith, *Prisoners,* pp. 306–7.

23 "Bukit Timah Electric Light Company": A. E. Knights, IWM 97/23/1, 2/43–49.

24 "The feeling that British arms": Sharp, IWM 66/240/1.

25 "Various barrack blocks and latrines": W. G. Riley, IWM 86/87/1, p. 38.

25 a forestry company had been set up: F. G. Galleghan, *An Account of the Australian Experience at Changi,* AWM 541/554/11/14, part 1A, p. 8.

25 The reason, said Capt. David Nelson: David Nelson, *The Story of Changi, Singapore,* p. 14. Nelson, who was at Changi throughout his captivity, became the prison's archivist. His book is a unique account of its administration.

26 Lt. Cyril "Pop" Vardy missed: Cyril Vardy, IWM 67/166/1, p. 48.

26 "When the rations arrived": Sharp, IWM 66/240/1, pp. 3–4.

27 "Memories of fine white rice": Griffin, quoted in Wigmore, *Australia in the War,* p. 513.

27 "Breakfast. Rice with ½ sardine": Vardy, IWM 67/166/1, p. 23A.

27 Rice should not be rejected: J. Innes, IWM 88/62/1, Annex 1.

28 "It was coloured bright green": quoted in Hank Nelson, *Prisoners of War: Australians Under Nippon,* p. 23.

28 Another side effect of the lack of food: J. A. Richardson, IWM 87/58/1, pp. 93–94.

28 "Rice Balls was not an elegant term": E. S. Benford, *The Rising Sun on My Back,* ch. 3. Almost exactly the same report is in Russell Braddon, *The Naked Island,* p. 108.

29 "Ah! The exquisite sensation": Roy Whitecross, *Slaves of the Son of Heaven,* pp. 16–17.

30 "How could any man so exploit": Wallace Marsh, IWM 94/4/1, p. 32.

30 When a party of thirty-five Australians: "Typical Incidents of Ill-treatment of POWs, Singapore, 1942," in Galleghan, AWM 541/554/11/4, part 1B.

31 "As it was, it became a curse": Harry Jessup, AWM/PRO 0683, pp. 128–29.

31 "More and more working parties": J. S. Milford, IWM 67/82/1, p. 124.

31 "What a meal!": W. H. Baillies, IWM 85/36/1.

31 "Rolls, butter and marmalade too!": Denis Dodds, IWM 86/7/1, May 22, 1942.

32 "Those of us who followed this advice": A. K. Butterworth, IWM 95/17/1, p. 46.

32 "By boiling 1 lb of rice": Robert Sutcliffe, IWM 66/226/1, May 22, 1942.

33 "No money was ever better invested": Braddon, *Island,* p. 142.

33 "The rationing of a coconut": Butterworth, IWM 95/17/1, pp. 47–48.

33 Flt. Off. Denis Dodds became an enthusiastic: Dodds, IWM 86/7/1, pp. 16–19.

33 Lt. John Coast's battalion: John Coast, *Railroad of Death,* p. 45.

34 Louis Baume's party: Baume, IWM 66/310/2, April 27, 1942.

34 Wallace Marsh bought: Marsh, IWM 94/4/1, May 1, 1942.

34 The quality of the food improved: John Stewart, *To the River Kwai,* p. 36.

34 the Australians were notorious racketeers: Austin Ellerman, AWM/PRO 2080, pp. 14, 17.

35 Having cottoned on: A. E. Knights, IWM 97/23/1, 3/19.

35 "With the active co-operation": Geoffrey Pharaoh Adams with Hugh Popham, *No Time for Geishas,* p. 46.

36 involuntary subscribers to an extraordinary lottery: Hugh V. Clarke, AWM/MSS 1040.

36 "Here was the settled calm": Sharp, IWM 66/240/1, p. 12.

36 the Selarang Incident: Nelson, *Changi,* pp. 40–44; Col. E. B. Holmes, *The Selarang Incident,* Orders 2 and 3, contained in G. D. Austin, IWM 95/5/1; report by F. G. Galleghan, Appendix 2-7, SWM 54-554/11/4, part 6.

37 "The British and Australian Officers": N. G. Macauley, "Report on the Execution of Soldiers in September, 1942," September 8, 1942, in ibid.

38 "Washing was obviously": Austin, IWM 95/5/1, p. 148.

39 Capt. Harry Malet's barracks: Malet, IWM 95/9/1, September 4, 1942.

Interlude: Christmas in Captivity

41 "When I arrived at 11.45": G. J. Chambers, IWM 91/35/1, Christmas Day, 1942.

42 Horner described his Christmas meals: IWM Conshelf, p. 70.

3. *The Railway of Death*

43 The building of a railway: Kinvig, *River Kwai Railway,* pp. 40–41.

44 Muscle would replace machinery: Kinvig, "Allied POWs."

44 "In Burma all the dread agents": F.A.E. Crew, *History of Second World War: The Army Medical Services, Campaigns,* p. 22.

44 "The heap of fallen leaves": C. E. Escritt, IWM 93/7/1, XX, pp. 267–68.

45 "Serried ranges of precipitous mountains": Rohan Rivett, *Argus,* September 13, 1945.

45 Its construction would involve: Kinvig, *Railway,* p. 165.

46 Three thousand Korean and Taiwanese guards: Sybilla Jane Flower, "Captors and Captives on the Burma–Thailand Railway," in B. Moore and K. Federowich (eds.), *Prisoners of War and Their Captors on the Burma–Thailand Railway,* p. 238.

46 In all, 330,000 men labored: South East Asia Translation and Interrogation Centre, *Seatic Bulletin* 246, p. 6, in Toosey, IWM 93/14/7-39, or Escritt, IWM 93/7/1, p. 30.

47 "I hope that you will rely upon me": Nagomoto's speech is quoted in many archives, e.g., J. W. Turner, IWM 71/41/1, part 5, p. 13.

48 The "most significant collective experience": Kinvig, "Allied POWs."

Interlude: A Walk Along the River Kwai

49 "Sunday afternoon": Basil Peacock, BBC broadcast, February 8, 1967.

4. The Real Story of the Bridge on the River Kwai

Three invaluable sources are used in this chapter. The first is the voluminous archive of Brig. P.J.D. Toosey, IWM 93/14/7 (noted here as "PJDT"). The second is the large archive of C. E. Escritt, IWM 93/7/1, which also includes a transcription of Toosey's report on Thailand (noted as "Escritt"). The third is a long essay by Ian Watt, "Myths of the Kwai" (noted as "Watt"), which can be found in PJDT–7. A version of this essay was published in the Observer Magazine, *September 1, 1968 (PJDT–8). A similar account is given in "Humanities on the River Kwai," the Grace Adams Tanner lecture of April 23, 1981, at Utah State University (Watt–2).*

52 "We were travelling": Stan Henderson, *Comrades on the Kwai,* p. 22.

53 The men arrived: Lt. Col. P.J.D. Toosey, *Report on Malayan and Thailand PW Camps, with Appendices,* September 1945, PJDT–3, p. 53; Stephen Alexander, *Sweet Kwai Run Softly,* p. 106.

53 "The men just stood there": John Smyth, *The Life Story of Brig. P.J.D. Toosey* (privately printed) p. 68, PJDT–2.

55 "But the task often fell": Watt, pp. 4ff.

56 "The river had to be bridged": Philip Toosey, BBC broadcast, August 14, 1955, PJDT–1, pp. 60–61.

56 "In time with this everyone pulled": Ibid.

57 The officer's lot: Alexander, *Sweet Kwai,* pp. 113–14.

57 gouging out his eye: PJDT–0, p. 467.

57 Philip Toosey was one of the first: Watt, pp. 7–8; Alexander, *Sweet Kwai,* p. 117; Jonathan Moffatt and Audrey Holmes McCormick, *Moon over Malaya,* p. 193; J. P. Sudbury, PJDT–17, p. 38; W. M. Naylor, PJDT–16.

58 "I therefore addressed the troops": Toosey, PJDT–3.

58 the Japanese would always win: Watt, p. 7.

58 Whenever Toosey met Takasaki: PJDT–0, p. 203.

59 Toosey deliberately refused: Ibid., p. 205.

59 Boyle's appointment: Moffatt and McCormick, *Moon,* p. 193.

59 Toosey was blind to all danger: Stanley Pavillard in PJDT–34.

59 "Nowhere in the world was sadism": "Behaviour of Japanese Guards," PJDT–3, Appendix D.

59 Capt. J. Gibson observed: Gibson, IWM 66/226/1, p. 16.

60 Some of the other punishments: PJDT–3, Appendix D.

61 built a wooden cross: Fepow quoted by Moffatt and McCormick, *Moon,* p. 195.

61 "There was Lawson": PJDT–1, p. 63; PJDT–0, p. 465.

62 To try to escape from Tamarkan: PJDT–1, p. 63.

62 "lunatic fringe" of officers: Alexander, *Sweet Kwai,* p. 114.

63 At a meeting with his officers: quoted in Peter N. Davies, *The Man Behind the Bridge,* p. 109.

64 "I had had him up in front of me": PJDT–0, p. 204.

64 Toosey discovered a doctor: PJDT–0, p. 237.

65 One dish was tapioca: Watt–2, p. 2.

65 The local ladies who sold eggs: Adams, *Geishas,* pp. 61–62.

66 "Nothing excited our mirth more": Alexander, *Sweet Kwai,* p. 121.

67 As the men stood in a long human chain: Adams, *Geishas,* p. 67.

67 "a thousand stinging pinpricks": Henderson, *Comrades,* p. 44.

67 Pte. Bob Hislop: PJDT–83.

67 The men—in direct contradiction: Naylor, PJDT–16, p. 22; PJDT–0, p. 209.

68 When Dr. Arthur Moon: report by Arthur Moon in PJDT–3.

68 Toosey was horrified: PJDT–1, pp. 58–59.

69 L.Cpl. J. S. Cosford: J. S. Cosford, *Line of Lost Lives,* p. 94.

69 When Rabbi Chaim Nussbaum: Chaim Nussbaum, *Chaplain on the River Kwai,* p. 152.

70 "Dysentery cases were often fouled": Moon in PJDT–3.

70 There were dreadful sights: Blackater, *Gods,* p. 120.

71 "I was the second person": George Downes, letter to Sir John Smyth, PJDT–2.

72 He recruited Fusilier Harry Howarth: Harry Howarth, IWM 67/173/1, pp. 214ff.

72 Toosey found a savior: note on the V Organisation, Escritt–4, p. 17.

73 the "hush-hush" money: Blackater, *Gods,* p. 123.

73 Blackater supplied Simpson's: Ibid., pp. 124–25.

75 "Tamarkan was so much better": Rohan Rivett, *Behind Bamboo,* p. 260; Stan Arneil, *One Man's War,* November 26, 1943, p. 24.

76 "The spectacle was thrilling": Sharp, IWM 66/240/1.

76 "Today the American Air Force": Baume, IWM 3/4/45, 24-6-45.

76 USAF Lt. Col. William A. Henderson: correspondence and reports in Escritt–35.

77 Another witness was Capt. John Barratt: Barratt, IWM 92/14/1.

78 Many features of the film: Alexander, *Sweet Kwai,* p. 251; Watt–1, pp. 8–9.

Interlude: Boon Pong

80 Boon Pong Sirivejjabhandu: The main source is a detailed report by C. E. Escritt, IWM 93/7/1, *Note on the V Organisation,* Escritt–4.

81 Peter Heath: Escritt, *The Times* obituary, January 28, 2003.

82 Lt. Col. "Cary" Owtram regularly obtained: H. C. Owtram, IWM 66/222/1, pp. 76–78.

82 Lt. Col. "Knocker" Knights estimated: Knights, IWM 97/23/1, "Personal Experience of the V Organisation" (in Escritt–34).

82 He hid duck eggs: Coast, *Railroad,* p. 123.

82 Pavillard started with a twelve-egg omelette: Stanley Pavillard, *Bamboo Doctor,* p. 110.

82 The official report on the V organisation: Quoted in Escritt–4, pp. 7–8.

5. *"Speedo"*

84 "As the cry of 'Speedo, Speedo' went up": John Durnford, *Branch Line to Burma,* pp. 84–85.

85 Some made shoes: Pavillard, *Bamboo Doctor,* p. 112.

85 "Here the perpetual fetch and carry": Sharp, IWM 66/240/1, pp. 25–26.

86 the "stupendous" achievement of the Japanese: Coast, *Railroad,* p. 96.

86 Capt. Cyril "Pop" Vardy was amazed: Vardy, IWM 67/166/1, May 3, 1943.

86 a "remorseless invader" swept down: Rivett, *Behind Bamboo,* pp. 194–95.

87 "Wet clothes stayed wet": Coast, *Railroad,* p. 112.

87 "They ate us alive": Searle, *To the Kwai,* p. 113.

88 As dawn broke each day: Ibid., p. 110.

89 the cutting resembled Dante's Inferno: Quoted in Nelson, *Prisoners,* p. 49.

89 The men were driven by engineers: Lt. Col. H. R. Humphries, *Report on H Force,* TNA 32/14550.

91 Capt. A. K. Butterworth was with a group: Butterworth, IWM 97/17/1, pp. 60–61.

92 Dunlop earned lasting affection: Quoted by Keith Flanagan in *Hellfire, A Soldier's Story, Hellfire Pass Memorial.*

92 He kept a diary: E. E. Dunlop, *The War Diaries of Weary Dunlop.*

93 only 341 of 1,085 men had satisfactory boots: Quoted in Albert Coates, AWM 89/1695/15.

93 "In that one month, we struck the depth": Sharp, IWM 66/240/1, pp. 35–37.

94 Using the underground V Organisation: IWM 93/14/7, PJDT–4; Escritt, IWM 93/7/1.

95 a vivid *cri de coeur:* Baume, IWM 66/310/2, 14/6/43.

96 "A Nip stands at the bottom": Ibid., 18/7/43.

96 sent on a dangerous mission: Johnson, IWM 86/87/1, p. 185.

97 Burials were often denied: Baume, IWM 66/310/2, June 24, 1943.

98 A scathing report: TNA 32/14550.

Interlude: Smokey Joe's

99 "The contract": A. E. Knights, IWM 97/23/1–3/49-50.

6. Sonkurai

John Stewart Ullman wrote his book Return to the Kwai *as John Stewart. A comprehensive report, "History of F Force, April 1943–April 1944," TNA/WO32/14551/98818, with detailed appendices by fellow officers, was written by Lt. Col. S. W. Harris, the force's commander, and is used extensively here (noted as "Harris"). Another comprehensive account was written by Lt. Col. Charles Kappe, Harris's second in command. It is Appendix 1 of the report submitted by Brig. F. G. Galleghan on prisoner-of-war camps in Singapore, AWM 54/554/11/4, part 4, Appendix 1, section 3 (noted as "Kappe"). Some reports appear in both Harris and Kappe. A report by Major Bruce Hunt on the cholera epidemic is in AWM 54/554/7/4, Appendix VI, Kappe report, Appendix I, part 7. A report by Lt. Col. F. J. Dillon is in AWM 554/7/8.*

102 "We were delighted": J. N. Duckworth, "Japanese Holiday," broadcast to London, September 12, 1945.

103 George Polain, one of the Australian: Report on the work of the chaplains with F Force, in Kappe, 2B.

103 "I love this place": Stan Arneil, AWM/PRO 88/76, April 23, 1943; April 27, 1943.

103 One Japanese officer ran a brothel: Padre John Foster Haigh, IWM 66/313/1, p. 18.

104 One of the guards used a heavy steel golf club: Harris, para 15 and Appendix A, para 27.

104 Even trained infantry in good physical condition: Harris, para 24.

104 "At times in the darkness": Charles Wilkinson, IWM 81/7/1, May 26, 1943.

105 they did not forget Mother's Day: Don Wall, *Heroes of F Force,* p. 7.

105 "My mental and physical condition": Harry Silman, IWM 66/226/1, p. 5.

105 He saw the men toiling: Narrative of F Force in Thailand, April–December 1943, IWM 66/227/1.

106 Thai bandits armed with knives: Harris, para 22.

106 "The corporal approached with a large bamboo": Appendix by Bruce Hunt, in Harris, part 2; also in Kappe, part 1.

107 "Use your hands": Evidence at Tokyo War Crimes Tribunal by Cyril Wild, quoted in Bradley, *The Tall Man,* p. 61.

107 the stench was indescribable: John Franks, IWM 86/67/1, p. 39.

108 Maj. David Price: M. D. Price, IWM/P449, part II, paras 4–6.

108 They were the most "evil" breed: Franks, IWM 86/67/1, p. 40.

109 The same ordeal was suffered by the Australians: Kappe, part 2, p. 32.

109 Cholera had been diagnosed at Lower Sonkurai: A full account of the epidemic is contained in Kappe, part 4, pp. 6–15. Kappe also includes Hunt's 1943 report: AWM 54/554/7/4.

110 "Gentlemen, things are grim": Quoted by R.H.S. Kelsey in Wall, *Heroes,* p. 137.

112 "All available fit men": P. U. Coates and P. Neild, *Up Country with F Force,* IWM 93/14/7, PJDT–13, p. 7.

113 Lt. James Bradley was the only officer: Interview with author.

113 "Exhausted, starved and benumbed": Duckworth, "Japanese Holiday."

113 "Obviously obeying instructions": Harris, para 70.

114 "Long faces and embittered men live here": Haigh, IWM 66/313/1, p. 21.

114 When Capt. Bill Bishop arrived: Bill Bishop, IWM 95/9/1. p. 90.

114 The preserved meat, coarse-fibered: T. Wilson, Harris, Appendix G; *Journal of Royal Army Medical Corps,* with J. A. Reid, 89/149.

115 they looked like the mud-men of New Guinea: Stewart, *Kwai,* p. 102.

115 Adversity, said Harry Weiss: Quoted in Wall, *Heroes,* p. 53.

115 "Any profit from camp sales": Norman White, AWM/PRO 0410, July 4, 1943.

117 "It looks like a scene from a film": Harry Silman, IWM 66/226/1, p. 14.

117 "At the onset came the 'rice-water' stools": Stewart, *Kwai,* p. 96.

117 "A deathly pallor descended": John Franks, IWM 86/67/1, p. 42.

118 Hunt appealed for volunteers: Broadcast by Hunt from Singapore, September 1945, quoted in Wall, *Heroes,* pp. viii–ix.

118 "We would just slam them on": James Mudie, interview with author.

119 He kept a diary: Wilkinson, IWM 81/7/1, July 30, 1943.

120 Morale was sapped by the constant rain: M. D. Price, IWM P499.

120 "It was a vivid illustration of hope deferred": T. Wilson and J. A. Reid, *Journal of Royal Army Medical Corps,* 89/149; IWM 66/227/1.

120 the diary of . . . "Tam" Innes-Ker: IWM 84/45/1.

120 "They have lost what spirit they had": Coates and Neild, *Up Country,* p. 10.

121 one of the most audacious escapes: Bradley, *The Tall Man,* pp. 67–71.

123 Dillon had been forewarned: Don Wall, interview and correspondence with author; Wall, *Heroes,* p. 111.

124 "There were no walls": Cyril Wild, evidence to War Crimes Trial in Pritchard, *Tokyo War Crimes Trials,* p. 5466.

124 "Dogs!" he exclaimed: John Stewart Ullman, recorded in Ullman's contemporary diary made available to author.

125 "This is a hell of a bad camp": F. J. Dillon, IWM 66/214/1, pp. 280–81.

125 One of the sick men was Ken Stevens: IWM 92/35/1.

125–6 Innes-Ker's diary: IWM 84/45/1, Mrs. E. Innes-Ker, pp. 131–32.

128 "Whatever their ills": Dillon, IWM 66/214/1, pp. 282–83.

128 the prisoners had one consolation: James Mudie, interview and correspondence with author; Mudie BBC broadcast, September 13, 1945; Price, IWM P449, has detailed accounts of Mudie's radios, as does his article in the *Journal of the Royal Signals Institution,* Summer 1981, included in his IWM archive.

129 "God, how weary I am of squalor": Philippa Poole, *Of Love and War: The Letters and Diaries of Captain Adrian Curlewis,* August 30, 1943, pp. 210, 205–6.

133 "It is the only way to deal with these chaps": Silman, IWM 66/226/1.

133 Humor, such as it was: Bill Bishop, IWM 95/9/1, p. 94.

133 "He offered me a cigarette": Stewart, *Kwai,* pp. 96–97.

134 Some men simply lost the will to live: Ibid., p. 106.

135 "When a patient arrived": Robert Fletcher, "Woe to the Captive," IWM 67/176/1, p. 146.

136 A special effort, however: Ibid., pp. 167–68.

136 Duckworth would shout: Ibid., p. 168.

136 died at Tanbaya: Harris, para 91.

136 One in two of the British: Bruce Hunt, AWM 3DRL/3517/3.

136 "They were in an appalling condition": Quoted in Smyth, *Toosey,* p. 86.

136 Kanchanaburi was a grand fattening paddock: Roy Mills, AWM/PRO 88/153, December 5, 1943.

137 Wakabayashi told them that: James Mudie interview with author; Fletcher, "Woe," IWM 67/176/1, pp. 145–50.

137 One in four of the 3,122: T. Wilson and J. A. Reid, *Journal of Royal Army Medical Corps,* p. 259; IWM 66/227/1.

138 Unit spirit had helped morale: Bruce Hunt, AWM 3DRL/3517/8, article in the *West Australian.*

138 "This is just one hell of a camp": Norman White, AWM/PRO 0410, August 10, 1943.

138 Stan Arneil was worried about the Englishmen: Arneil, *War,* pp. 130, 133.

138 The British would not try: Bill Anderson, AWM/PRO 8851, p. 18.

139 "They were a city crowd": Bob Kelsey, quoted in Wall, Heroes, p. 122.

139 Stan Arneil contrasted the rations: Arneil, *War,* October 3, 1943.

139 slow-moving skeletons: David Griffin, in Wall, *Heroes,* p. 140.

140 "Where are the rest?": Leslie Greener, quoted in Adam-Smith, *Prisoners,* p. 543.

140 "a prisoners' paradise": Arneil, *War,* December 21, 1943.

140 "Were we glad to get here!": Innes-Ker, IWM 84/45/1, January 1944.

141 The death toll: "The F Force trial: Singapore Military Tribunal, 26 September–23 October 1946," quoted in McCormack and Nelson, *The Burma–Thailand Railway,* p. 103. Several reports cite slightly different numbers, but all agree on a death rate of 44 percent.

Interlude: Ave Maria

142 "We had not drunk": Fred Seiker, *Smiles: A Day in the Life of a Japanese POW on the Railroad of Death,* p. 32.

7. The Railway Opens

145 Hideguma presided at the opening ceremony: Escritt, IWM 93/7/1.

145 said Lt. John Coast: Coast, *Railroad,* pp. 144–46.

146 At Tamarkan, midway between: Rivett, *Bamboo,* p. 264.

146 The toll on human life was terrible: *Seatic Bulletin* 246, compiled by Lt. C. C. Brett, Canadian Intelligence Corps, 1946, giving history of the Burma–Thailand railway with detailed statistics, in PJDT–39 and Escritt, 31; Wigmore, *Australia in the War,* p. 588.

PART TWO

8. *Survival*

152 "It wasn't as bad as you think": Ray Parkin, quoted in Margaret Gee, *A Long Way from Silver Creek,* p. 204.

152 Lt. Eric Lomax was almost blind: Reid, IWM 67/173/1, p. 212.

152 captivity was not a perpetual regime of suffering: David Piper, *I Am Well, Who Are You?* pp. 23, 9.

153 "When starved and worked to death": Stewart, *Kwai,* pp. 164–65.

153 letters brought good and heartbreaking news: G. H. Boddington, IWM 67/148/1, October 20, 1943, p. 292.

153 "I feel sure this constant glumness": Vardy, IWM 67/166/1, p. 276.

154 "Who is our friend?": Nussbaum, *Chaplain,* p. 220.

154 There were rats everywhere: Boddington, IWM 67/148/1, p. 260; Stanley Pavillard, TNA 32/1455, sheet 6.

155 Surviving in these desperate conditions: Richards and McEwan, *Survival,* p. 131.

155 "As a doctor": Pavillard, *Bamboo Doctor,* p. 52.

155 "These days": Dunlop, *Diaries,* May 18, 1943.

157 "Difficult to understand death": Stan Arneil, quoted in Nelson, *Prisoners,* p. 56.

157 "Everywhere one looked": H. Robert Charles, *Last Man Out: Surviving the Burma Railroad,* p. 156.

157 Home had a watch: James Home, *Their Last Tenko,* pp. 44–45.

157 The same spirit inspired the men: Jack Edwards with Jimmy Walker, *Banzai You Bastards,* pp. 69–70.

158 There were a dozen men: BBC broadcast, February 11, 1954.

158 When AB Allan Gee arrived at Tamarkan: Gee, *A Long Way,* pp. 189–90.

159 "The following day": James F. Chandler, IWM 81/32/1, pp. 324–25.

159 "Then the birthday cards started to roll in": David C. Hutchinson-Smith, AWM/MSS 1534, pp. 124–25.

160 "There suddenly appeared a bedraggled little group": Reginald Burton, *The Road to Three Pagodas,* p. 105.

160 "I've travelled down some lonely roads": Duncan Butler, quoted in Adam-Smith, *Prisoners,* pp. 535–37.

161 Why was it, one Australian asked: Donald Stuart, quoted in Hank Nelson, *Prisoners,* pp. 65–66.

161 The British men who stood up best: Toosey, IWM 93/14/7, PJDT–0, p. 212.

162 "Appeals to their pride": Van der Post, *New Moon,* pp. 108–9.

162 "One could have no time for the man": Braddon, *Island,* pp. 129–30.

163 Remarkably, the men's compassion extended: Leslie Audus, *Spice Island Slaves,* pp. 195–96.

164 They dreamed of home: Ernest Norquist, "Three Years in Paradise," entry for May 8, 1943.

164 At Konyu 2nd Lt. J. S. Milford: J. S. Milford, IWM 67/82/1, November 1942, p. 294.

164 "Things like striking a match": Ken Attiwill, BBC broadcast, 23–24 February 1946.

165 When a Japanese admiral visited Kuching: George Pringle, IWM 85/36/1, pp. 272–73.

166 Singing was a huge source of solace: Stan Arneil, AWM 3DRL/369, Papers of 8th Division, file 1.

166 Col. George Ramsay, AIF, hit on a solution: George Ramsay, AWM/PRO 0079/9.

167 "It still brings tears to my eyes": Arthur Titherington, *Kinkaseki,* pp. 130–31.

167 The best night Russell Braddon remembered: Braddon, *Island,* p. 221.

167 Capt. A. K. Butterworth went into a coma: Butterworth, IWM 95/17/1, p. 70.

9. *Books*

169 tattered books changed hands: Ray Parkin, *The Sword and the Blossom,* p. 81.

169 Using a lamp made out of an old tin: A. E. Mills, BBC broadcast, February 11, 1954.

169 "If, as we hoped, we survived": Richardson, IWM 87/58/1, p. 160.

169 The British university: Memorandum, quoted in E. C. Dickson, IWM 84/29/1.

170 Among the founders: Alexander, *Sweet Kwai,* pp. 78–82.

170 a "surprising" thirst for learning: E. W. Swanton, Oral Archives, IWM, reel 1, p. 7. For the Australians: Nelson, *Prisoners,* p. 26; Wigmore, *Australia in the War,* p. 516.

171 When Stephen Alexander was reunited: Alexander, *Sweet Kwai,* p. 169.

172 E. W. Swanton's treasured 1939 *Wisden: Spectator,* February 15, 1992.

172 At Laurens van der Post's Java camp: Van der Post, *New Moon,* pp. 10–12.

172 "The whole of this side of our life": Ibid.

173 A thirst for knowledge: Ernest Gordon, *Miracle on the River Kwai,* pp. 144–45.

173 Zentsuji University: Hutchinson-Smith, AWM/MSS 1543, p. 74.

10. *Food*

175 When it came to the crunch: Piper, *I Am Well,* p. 23.

175 At Honshu in Japan: Parkin, *Sword,* p. 173.

175 Lt. Col. "Weary" Dunlop also noted: Dunlop, *Diaries,* March 3, 1943.

176 "Food. Food all the time": Pringle, IWM 85/36/1, p. 215.

176 a lump of pig fat in the stew: W. H. Baillies, IWM 85/36/1, December 11, 1944.

176 using axle grease: H.D.A. Yates, IWM, Conshelf, p. 5.

176 "We got broken rice": Quoted in Rivett, *Behind Bamboo,* p. 242.

177 The route home: Quoted in E. E. Dunlop, AWM/PRO 0926/1/74/1.

177 "the blessed food of Nippon": Edwards, *Banzai,* p. 54.

178 The men were so hungry: Don Peacock, *The Emperor's Guest,* pp. 86–87.

178 the dogs were deep frozen in the snow: Rowley Richards, quoted in Nelson, *Prisoners,* p. 184.

178 Monkeys were easy to catch: Pavillard, *Bamboo Doctor,* p. 99.

178 "Is it callous of me": Pringle, IWM 85/36/1, p. 293.

178 three kittens for their Christmas supper: Searle, *To the Kwai,* p. 158.

179 how far a chicken would go: Yates, IWM, Conshelf, p. 5.

179 Sparrows were a delicacy: Edward Burrey, AWM/PRO 662, p. 48.

179 "Dozens of little cans": Peter Hartley, *Escape to Captivity,* p. 153.

179 "Hash. Boiled vegetables": Blackater, *Gods,* pp. 147–48.

180 "Then one day the three pigs fought": Braddon, *Island,* p. 119.

181 "There were three processes": Owtram, IWM 66/222/1, p. 165.

181 Project Kedley Bean: Peacock, *Guest,* p. 113.

182 "Its beneficial results": Reginald Burton, *Railway of Hell,* pp. 151–52.

183 Red Cross parcels: Patrick MacArthur, IWM 66/218/1, May 24, 1944; Baume, IWM 66/310/2, May 18, 1944; Vardy, IWM 67/166/1, p. 298.

184 "They were crammed with food": Andrew D. Carson, *My Time in Hell,* pp. 58–59.

186 "It was a very popular job": Owtram, IWM 66/222/1, pp. 114–15.

186 As the luxuriant grass of September withered: Boddington, IWM 67/148/1, p. 380.

187 "Many doctors attribute the small death rate": John Barnard, *The Endless Years,* p. 91.

187 they lost interest in sex: Hartley, *Escape,* p. 103.

187 " 'Gentlemen,' I started": Cornel Lumière, *Kura!* p. 252.

11. Religion

189 Capt. Harry Malet celebrated: Malet, IWM 95/9/1, diary, December 25, 1942.

190 "The light leaped up": Alexander, *Sweet Kwai,* p. 157.

190 The services could not have been more moving: C. W. Johnson, IWM 86/87/1, p. 167; Sharp, IWM 66/240/1, p. 60; Hutchinson-Smith, AWM/MSS 1534, p. 96.

190 at Jesselton in Borneo: Peter Lee, quoted in Don Wall, *Kill the Prisoners!* p. 10.

190 The Roman Catholic padre at Cabanatuan: Carson, *Hell,* p. 98.

190 Even Britain's Salvation Army: Howarth, IWM 67/173/1, p. 206.

190 the first Easter Sunday was celebrated: G. J. Chambers, IWM 91/35/1, p. 12.

191 "It even had a harmonium": H. S. Flower, IWM 86/87/1, p. 20.

192 Stealing was a matter of conscience: Arneil, *One Man's War,* p. 28.

192 Sinners, however, were the subject: Philippa Poole, *Of Love and War: The Letters and Diaries of Captain Adrian Curlewis and His Family, 1939–45,* p. 135, June 21, 1942.

192 When Harry Howarth went: Howarth, IWM 67/173/1, p. 132.

192 At one Holy Communion in Singapore: Owtram, IWM 66/222/1, July 19, 1942.

192 "Unfortunately, for every 'wise man' ": Hartley, *Escape,* pp. 71–72.

193 "The communion service has again attracted": Pringle, IWM 85/36/1, p. 104.

193 Noel Duckworth, one of the heroes: *This Is Your Life,* January 12, 1959; Braddon, *Island,* pp. 113–15.

194 Similarly inspirational was Padre Alfred Webb: Stanley Gimson, interview with author.

194 the sorrows of Francis Hollis: Lionel Morris, IWM 91/18/1, p. 228.

195 the Methodist padre, Christopher Ross: Chaplain's report in Escritt, IWM 93/7/1; *Joyful News,* May 23, 1946.

196 "The menorah stands on a table": Nussbaum, *Chaplain,* pp. 62–63.

197 "But this was not whitewashed ceiling": Hartley, *Escape,* p. 116.

12. *Jungle Medicine*

198 The "hospital" at Tarsao: Vardy, IWM 67/166/1, pp. 157–58.

199 It was apparent to Lt. Col. "Weary" Dunlop: Report by Dunlop in Albert Coates's archive, AWM/PRO 89/186.

200 At Wampo, Pavillard had a cut-throat razor: Pavillard, *Bamboo Doctor,* p. 97.

200 At Lower Sonkurai, performing the same operation: Lloyd Cahill, quoted in Wall, *Heroes,* p. 58.

200 There was an emergency at Konyu: Dunlop, *Diaries,* February 18, 1943.

201 "He was a wonderful man": *Australian Women's Weekly,* October 20, 1945.

202 When another Australian doctor: Braddon, *Island,* pp. 178, 224.

202 "I never saw any of those men again": Kevin Fagan, quoted in Nelson, *Prisoners,* p. 55.

203 "I am sure it is his presence": Ray Parkin, *Into the Smother,* pp. 50–51.

203 "He was one of the most courageous men": Jack Chalker, interview with author.

204 Dunlop described some of his experiences: Dunlop, *British Medical Journal,* October 5, 1946.

205 By August 1943, at Coates's 55 Kilo camp: Quoted in Coates, AWM/PRO 89/186, pp. 10–12.

205 "I have seen some very brave men": AWM 3DRL/6610–15.

206 they suffered no subsequent disability: Coates, AWM/PRO 89/186, p. 27.

207 "Markowitz made his incision": Owtram, IWM 66/222/1, p. 126.

207 A few doctors refused to amputate: Pavillard, *Bamboo Doctor,* pp. 143–44.

208 Dutchman Capt. Henri Hekking: Charles, *Last Man Out,* pp. 104–7, 113–17, 149–60, 193.

211 Nakhon Pathom in 1944: Coates, "Nakhon Pathom Departmental Report and Statistics," in AWM/PRO 89/186; Ian L. Duncan, "Makeshift Medicine," *Medical Journal of Australia,* January 8, 1983, pp. 29–32; in AWM PR86/276; Dunlop, *BMJ.*

212 Coates performed an operation: Albert Coates and Newman Rosenthal, *The Albert Coates Story,* p. 129.

213 the solution to "Java Balls" in Borneo: Pringle, IWM 85/36/1, p. 115.

213 "After supper we were paraded naked": Anthony Cowling, *My Life with the Samurai,* pp. 116–17.

214 "Vaughan was a very reasonable young man": Thomas Hewlett, "Nightmare Revisited," speech to survivors of Bataan-Corregidor reunion, August 1978, quoted in Ian Duncan, AWM/PRO 86/276.

214 When Maj. Gen. T. O. Thompson toured: "RAPWI (16 November 1945)," appendix to report by Maj. Gen. T. O. Thompson.

13. *Smoking* Gone with the Wind

215 In Japan, for example, salt was scarce: Parkin, *Sword,* p. 174.

215 When Flt. Lt. F. C. Jackson ran out: AWM/PRO 86/144, p. 136.

215 "In the jungle it was common to hear": Rivett, *Behind Bamboo,* p. 271.

216 A copy of *Gone with the Wind:* Durnford, *Branch Line,* p. 53.

216 One soldier at Kuching: Diary of an unknown British soldier, Kuching, quoted in Wall, *Kill the Prisoners!* p. 168.

216 One man decided to "smoke" his *Belasarius:* R. L. Wild in *Blackwood's Magazine,* August 1958, p. 108.

216 Ronald Searle smoked: Searle, *To the Kwai,* p. 158.

216 One padre said he didn't object: Reid, IWM 67/173/1, p. 183.

216 "This weed is a cruel killer": Pringle, IWM 85/36/1, p. 205.

217 Capt. Harry Jessup preferred: AWM/PRO 0683, July 13, 1944.

217 At Sandakan, pipe tobacco: Lynette Silver, *Sandakan,* p. 85.

217 On Haruku, leftover leaves: Richard Philps, *Prisoner Doctor,* p. 72.

217 At Tamuang a cigarette factory: A. E. Knights, IWM 97/23/1, 4/6; A.H.B. Alexander, IWM 88/5/1, p. 48.

218 "A large bonfire had been lit": Hartley, *Escape,* p. 151.

218 "The Fifth Horseman": Quoted by Hewlett, in Duncan archive, AWM/PRO 86/276.

14. *King Rat*

219 "Although it was universally accepted": Braddon, *Island,* pp. 124–25.

220 But Clavell's King Rat: John W. Wisecup, quoted in Robert S. La Forte and Ronald E. Marcello, *The Ordeal of American POWs in Burma 1942–45: Building the Death Railway,* p. 229.

220 They were known as "The Democrats": Adams, *Geishas,* pp. 158–61, 167–71.

221 "Food was bought and sold for money": Whitecross, *Slaves,* pp. 190–91.

222 Another merciless American king rat: Daws, *Prisoners,* p. 310.

223 "New low level. Ill again": Vardy, IWM 67/166/1, p. 335.

223 The gold was sold for $200: Burton, *Three Pagodas,* p. 166.

223 The rackets were legion: Burton, *Railway,* p. 153.

224 "We entered another smaller clearing": Howarth, IWM 67/173/1, pp. 199, 213.

225 The secret of survival for the black marketeers: Interview with author.

226 "He has set up a regular shop": Fletcher, "Woe," IWM 67/176/1, p. 145–50.

226 Another racketeer was "Joe": V. K. Wright, BBC broadcast, August 22, 1958.

226 Such racketeers were the sleek and fat "nabobs": Durnford, *Branch Line,* pp. 115–16.

227 Cary Owtram's valise was ransacked: Owtram, IWM 66/222/1, p. 24.

227 "Praise be, my sadly battered": J. S. Milford, IWM 67/82/1, p. 324.

227 Some stealing, though: Pavillard, *Bamboo Doctor,* pp. 115–21.

228 Nothing was sacred: Coast, *Railroad,* p. 78.

228 When a racketeer who had looted: Pringle, IWM 85/36/1, pp. 239–41.

229 One British POW for whom stealing: Cosford, *Line,* p. 38.

229 At Zentsuji, Capt.: Hutchinson-Smith, AWM/MSS 1534, pp. 17–18.

230 The Australians had been brought up: Clarke, AWM/MSS 1040, pp. 78–79.

230 "The mystery was soon solved": Frans DuMoulin, IWM 97/6/1, p. 11.

231 Thieves who were caught: Vardy, IWM 67/166/1, p. 338.

231 It was a "desperate" act: Cosford, *Line,* p. 119.

232 "When two years later": Braddon, *Island,* p. 219.

15. *Letters*

233 Lt. Ken Tomkinson at Changi: Private memoir, p. 21.

233 Grown men wept unrestrainedly: Coast, *Railroad,* p. 112.

233 For a few brief hours: Pringle, IWM 85/36/1, p. 271.

234 "As I read on": Hartley, *Escape,* pp. 168–69.

234 Capt. Adrian Curlewis, who had: Poole, *Of Love and War,* p. 194.

235 "It's astonishing": Boddington, IWM 67/148/1, February 23, 1944, p. 226.

235 "Prisoners' Post": Peter Neild, IWM 66/221/1.

236 Maj. Compton Glossop managed: Information supplied by his family.

236 A friend of Lt. John Durnford: Durnford, *Branch Line,* pp. 93–94.

237 A friend of George Pringle: Pringle, IWM 85/36/1, pp. 278–79.

237 An even more poignant story: Boddington, IWM 67/148/1, May 8, 1943, p. xx.

16. Entertainment

Some details in this chapter were supplied by Sears Eldredge, Professor of Theater and Entertainment at Macalester College, St. Paul, Minnesota, who is researching entertainment in Japanese prisoner-of-war camps.

238 the Australian concert party: Report by Galleghan, AWM 54/554/11/4, part 1A, pp. 5–6; Nelson, *Prisoners,* p. 27; Wigmore, *Australia in the War,* p. 517.

238 The first play to be proposed: F. J. Dillon, IWM 66/214/1, p. 98.

239 "The majority of them": Ibid., p. 99.

239 "The Swiss mercenary soldier": J.A.L. Barratt, IWM 92/41/1, p. 13.

239 One of the principal singers: Haigh, IWM 66/313/1, pp. 8–9.

239 "I would willingly have donned": Adrian Curlewis, quoted in Poole, *Of Love and War,* August 3, 1942.

240 Lt. Corbin gave a (gramophone) recital: Richardson, IWM 87/58/1, p. 104.

240 It was a fine bargain: Milford, IWM 67/82/1, pp. 153–54.

240 as well as a collection of records: Leslie Audus, "Tropical Island Discs: The Story of a Collection of Gramophone Records in Japanese POW Camps," unpublished memoir.

241 "The scene was": Howarth, IWM 67/173/1, pp. 153–54.

241 Lt. Col. Cary Owtram, who commanded: Owtram, IWM 66/222/1, ch. 12.

242 He paid the orchestra special rates: Sue Ebury, *Weary: The Life of Sir Edward Dunlop,* p. 476.

242 talented female impersonators: Unpublished research by Sears Eldredge; W. G. Riley, IWM 86/87/1, p. 128.

242 "Some of them seem": Vardy, IWM 67/166/1, p. 262.

243 A set of drums: Riley, IWM 86/87/1, p. 100.

243 a double bass: Sharp, IWM 66/240/1, p. 50.

243 "The old story was completely changed": Coast, *Railroad,* p. 180.

244 "*Wonder Bar*": Robert Hardie, *The Secret Diary of Dr. Robert Hardie, 1942–45,* May 21, 1944, p. 140; Boddington, IWM 67/148/1, May 21, 1944, p. 359.

244 "As we sat on the mud": Alexander, *Sweet Kwai,* p. 186.

245 "Norman had arranged the programme": Gordon, *Miracle,* p. 160.

247 "The audience a crowd of": Durnford, *Branch Line,* p. 137.

246 "There would be the sound of footsteps": Carson, *Hell,* pp. 96–97.

246 "The tears ran down our cheeks": Vardy, IWM 67/166/1, p. 251.

17. *Sports*

247 At Chungkai there was a football pitch: Alexander, IWM 88/5/1, p. 41.

247 It was a matter of "no little surprise": Owtram, IWM 66/222/1, ch. 13.

247 Cricket was particularly popular: J. S. Potter, IWM 97/19/1, p. 8; Watt, "Myth," p. 4; Java: Don Thomas: AWM/MSS 1301, p. 26.

248 One prisoner had smuggled: Obituary of Geoffrey Edrich, *The Times,* January 30, 2004.

248 "The Australians won the toss": Titherington, *Kinkaseki,* p. 57.

248 A match at Nakom Pathom: E. W. Swanton, *Wisden Cricketers' Almanack,* 1946.

250 horseracing was the Australians' passion: George Ramsay, letter to his wife, AWM/PRO 0079/16.

250 "Bits of native sarongs": Rivett, *Behind Bamboo,* p. 164.

251 "Weary" Dunlop was a "horse": Dunlop, *Diaries,* December 25, 1944.

251 What always intrigued the diminutive Japanese: Nowell Peach, interview with author; Ebury, *Weary,* p. 343.

251 Oxford-Cambridge rugby match: Charles Fletcher-Cooke, *The Emperor's Guest,* p. 200.

252 the subject of cricket filled countless hours: Swanton, *Spectator,* February 15, 1992.

18. *Ingenuity*

253 dumb existence and grudging fortitude: Sharp, IWM 66/240/1, p. 47.

253 After the war was over, Rolex: Durnford, *Branch* Line, p. 47.

254 There were many small "factories": Knights, IWM 97/23/1, 4/7.

254 At Hintok, a water system: Wigmore, *Australia in the War,* p. 565.

255 It was a source of wonderment: Boddington, IWM 67/148/1, May 9, 1944, p. 356.

255 "Supposing I had an enamel mug": Robert Reid, IWM 67/173/1.

256 Capt. John Barnard created "quite a sensation": Barnard, *Endless,* pp. 136–38.

257 Flt. Lt. Leslie Audus, who had just emerged: Interview and correspondence with author.

19. *The "Canaries"*

260 The men in Thailand relied: Report by Jack Masefield, in R. S. Hardie, IWM 66/226/1, p. 9.

260 At Ban Pong it was the same ritual: Eric Lomax, *The Railway Man,* p. 101.

260 "The good news from the world": Rivett, *Behind Bamboo,* p. 161.

261 all wireless sets were to be: Details from "Report on Wireless News Reception, Changi," AWM 54/11/4, Appendix VIII; James Mudie: BBC talk, September 18, 1945. A detailed report on radios by Maj. Gen. M. D. Price was published in the *Journal of the Royal Signals Institution,* Summer 1981.

261 On August 16, 1942: Report by W. A. Bosley, August 15, 1945, AWM 54/11/4, Appendix VIII.

262 When John Beckett was sent: Masefield in Hardie, IWM 66/226/1, pp. 7–8.

262 "The arrangements for the operation": Ibid., p. 16.

263 the Webber brothers: Ibid., pp. 18–19; Rivett, *Behind Bamboo,* p. 296.

263 At Kuching in Borneo: Morris, IWM 91/18/1, pp. 216–17.

264 " 'Ginnie' could dimly be discerned": Pringle, IWM 85/36/1, p. 285.

264 There were several new "canaries": George Aspinall, *Changi Photographer,* p. 79.

265 "I understand that you have been": Ramsay, AWM/PRO 0079/9.

266 "A hefty Japanese sergeant": Lomax, *Railway Man,* p. 118.

266 "I was called forward": Ibid., pp. 119–20.

267 "The whole area was dark": Rivett, *Behind Bamboo,* pp. 228–29.

268 Fear of detection: Van der Post, *New Moon,* pp. 100–1.

268 tin leg: Leslie Audus, interview with author.

268 There were some sweet moments: William Drower, *Our Man on the Hill,* p. 78; Masefield in Hardie, IWM 66/226/1, p. 19.

20. *Officers and Gentlemen*

269 Men without officers were dead men: Francis Dillon, IWM 95/9/1, pp. 46–47.

269 "Weary" Dunlop led his "Java rabble": Dunlop, *Diaries,* January 7, 1943.

269 the aim of the British: Braddon, *Island,* p. 154.

270 When Chief Petty Officer Ray Parkin's: Parkin, *Smother,* p. 20.

270 "Not only could the Australians rough it": Vardy, IWM 67/166/1, p. 199.

271 "Unknown to the RSM": Pringle, IWM 85/36/1, p. 128.

271 "In those days I wore a big moustache": Donald Wise, quoted in Nelson, *Prisoners,* p. 64.

271 The Americans were equally shocked: Charles, *Last Man Out,* p. 50.

272 Many Americans interviewed after the war: La Forte and Marcello, *Ordeal,* p. 280; Robert S. La Forte, Ronald E. Marcello, and Richard L. Himmels, *With Only the Will to Live: Accounts of Americans in Japanese Prison Camps, '41–45,* pp. 232–33; Marvin Earle Robinson, *Prisoner of War Report,* p. 4.

272 "Fail to salute an officer": Pringle, IWM 85/36/1, p. 130.

272 "All the old staff wallahs": Fletcher, "Woe," IWM 67/176/1, p. 35.

273 When Lt. John Durnford arrived at Tarsao: Durnford, *Branch Line,* p. 38.

273 "To go out on working parties": Alexander, *Sweet Kwai,* p. 161.

273 "The place was full of officers": Pavillard, *Bamboo Doctor,* p. 153.

274 "Beside the wrecks": Sharp, IWM 66/240/1, pp. 44–45.

274 "Despite all their cant": Thomas Evans, IWM 85/29/1, p. 13.

274 According to Capt. Ronald Horner: IWM, Conshelf, May 21, 1942.

275 The ranks of British officers: H. S. Flower, 86/87/1, p. 34; S. J. Flower, "Captors and Captives," p. 240.

275 Among the Australians in 8th Division: McCormack and Nelson, *Railway,* p. 13.

275 As Sibylla Jane Flower, the most: Flower, "Captors and Captives," p. 240.

275 Maintaining discipline was the greatest factor: Dunlop, *BMJ,* October 5, 1946.

276 "I left this melancholy affair": Dunlop, *Diaries,* April 13, 1942.

276 One British officer who was miffed: Milford, IWM 67/82/1, p. 446.

276 "Knocker" Knights agreed: IWM 97/23/1, 3/4, p. 65.

277 "Men without socks": Arneil, *One Man's War,* April 26, 1944.

277 a parody of Wordsworth's "Upon Westminster Bridge": Fletcher, "Woe," IWM 67/176/1, p. 194.

278 The officers' ranks were still cluttered: Coast, *Railroad,* p. 72.

279 "We had a captain, in my regiment": Lt. Stanley Gimson, interview with author.

279 At Konyu, Dunlop was horrified: Ebury, *Weary,* p. 386.

279 He found the latter "poorly officered": George Ramsay, AWM/PRO 0079, letter 5 to wife from Mergui.

279 "He was sorry there was no room for us": Sharp, IWM 66/240/1, p. 27.

280 "eternal pettiness and bullshit and stupidity": Jack Chalker, interview with author.

280 "Pity (as I think Rousseau pointed out)": Correspondence with author.

281 "Standing like a ramrod": Parkin, *Smother,* p. 59.

281 Some of the most damning criticism: Hugh Rayson, AWM/PRO 0720, p. 10.

281 Some officers unwittingly condemned themselves: Adams, *Geishas,* p. 87.

281 "A very sorry show": Peter Lee, quoted in Wall, *Prisoners,* p. 25.

282 "he doesn't shoot": Quoted in Hardie, *Secret Diary,* August 18, 1944, p. 146.

282 "They duly turned out": Lee in Wall, *Prisoners,* p. 94.

282 The division of food: Richardson, IWM 87/58/1, p. 141.

282 Yet only a small minority among the officers: Kinvig, *River Kwai Railway,* p. 96.

283 "Being mixed up with the men": Reid, IWM 67/173/1, p. 36.

283 "Had there been any cracking of discipline": Philps, *Prisoner Doctor,* pp. 65–66.

283 Capt. John Barnard in Thailand was critical: Barnard, *Endless,* p. 72.

284 Morale was kept higher: Drower, *Our Man,* p. 65.

284 "The prisoner 'honcho' ": Hartley, *Escape,* p. 159.

285 "We had little in the way of footwear": George Grigs, IWM, Conshelf, p. 5.

286 "We made our way across the Bangkok Plain": Howarth, IWM 67/173/1, p. 185.

286 "When a man starts to grow a beard": Owtram, IWM 66/222/1, p. 37.

286 There was a "mutiny" at Nong Pladuk: C. E. Escritt, "The 17-hour Stand at Nong Pladuk," IWM 93/7/1, Escritt–3; Baume, IWM 66/310/2, September 8–9, 1942; Robert Sutcliffe, IWM 66/226/1, September 8–9, 1942.

287 Lt. Col. Harold Lilly: J. S. Potter, IWM 97/19/1, p. 9; Daws, *Prisoners,* p. 216; Davies, *The Man,* p. 128; report by S. S. Pavillard, TNA 32/14551, sheet 4.

288 "I reminded him": Knights, IWM 97/23/1, 3/52.

288 Knights succeeded: Philip Hall, *Kempetai on the Prowl,* foreword.

289 Toosey went to see the brothers: Davies, *The Man,* pp. 151–52.

289 "He is a symbol and a rock to me": Parkin, *Smother,* p. 188.

289 when morning after morning: Ebury, *Weary,* preface.

290 "He was a remarkable man": Quoted in McCormack and Nelson, *Railway,* p. 54.

291 Russell Braddon and "Black Jack" Galleghan: Nelson, *Prisoners,* p. 34.

291 the officers' superior rate of survival: H Force figures from L. Fernley, "Vital Statistics on H Force," IWM 88/62/1.

PART THREE

21. *The Hellships*

295 the greatest death toll: Daws, *Prisoners,* pp. 286, 297; Donald Knox, *Death March: The Survivors of Bataan,* p. 337.

296 "We had imagined": Rivett, *Behind Bamboo,* pp. 129–36.

297 "Men fell into helpless paroxysms": Parkin, *Sword,* pp. 109–10.

297 "Pitiful cries for help": Riley, IWM 86/87/1, p. 163.

298 "As I rolled over": Ibid., p. 171.

299 "Let them die": Quoted in Calvin Ellsworth Chum, *Of Rice and Men,* p. 112.

300 "Men raving, crawling naked": Dwight E. Gard, "Our Boat Trips," December 13, 1944.

301 Men crazed by thirst: Chum, *Of Rice,* pp. 114–15.

301 "Claustrophobia and total darkness": Knox, *Death March,* p. 350.

301 Some prisoners thought: A. B. Felser (ed.), *Bilibid Diary,* p. 220.

302 "Somebody cut my throat": John G. Gamble, quoted in Gard, "Boat Trips."

302 "A guy would say": Charles Burris in La Forte, *With Only,* p. 96.

302 According to Hayes: Felser, *Bilibid,* p. 223.

303 several men were shot: Pritchard, *Tokyo War Crimes Trials,* pp. 40466–69.

303 "I looked back at the ship": Roy L. Bodine, *No Place for Kindness,* p. 13.

303 As Eugene Jacobs reached the deck: Eugene C. Jacobs, "Diary of a Hell-Ship Journey," *Medical Opinion and Review,* November 1970, p. 70.

304 Eugene Jacobs and Roy Bodine kept diaries: Ibid; see also E. Bartlett Kerr, *Surrender and Survival,* ch. 12.

Interlude: A Happy Ending

310 "What with the terrific heat": J. W. Turner, IWM 71/41/1, p. 38.

311 "We could see they were not Japs": Ibid., pp. 38–39.

311 USS *Pampanito:* "The Third War Patrol, August 17–September 28, 1944," http://www.maritime.org/patrol3.htm.

312 "We were given water": Turner, IWM 71/41/1, p. 39.

22. *Japan*

314 Japan was the worst of all the places: Ian Duncan, quoted in Adam-Smith, *Prisoners,* p. 634.

314 At Wakayama near Osaka: Obituary of Kenneth Frow, *The Times,* October 1, 2003.

315 "Huge crucibles were filled": Adams, *Geishas,* p. 157.

315 "We were not allowed": Whitecross, *Slaves,* p. 203.

316 "We didn't wear clothes": Quoted in Knox, *Death March,* p. 364.

316 Ian Duncan kept detailed medical records: Ian Duncan, "Fukuoka Camp 17: Final Summary of the Medical Staff: The Psychological Problem," AWM 54/442/7/8, p. 11.

317 According to Thomas Hewlett: Thomas Hewlett, "Psychologic and Social Problems," AWM/PRO 86/276, p. 18.

317 One victim was the nineteen-year-old: Ibid.; Whitecross, *Slaves,* p. 196.

317 "Two of them picked me up": Benford, *Rising Sun,* ch. 7.

318 there were more than seventy-five stab wounds: Hewlett, "Psychologic," p. 17.

319 " 'Insolent captive!' ": S. Abbott, IWM 89/15/1.

320 "I have to tell you of a terrible tragedy": Ibid.

320 "a world of utter darkness": Titherington, *Kinkaseki,* p. 113.

320 only eighty-nine of the 524 men: Edwards, *Banzai,* p. 197.

321 the officers' camp at Zentsuji: Hank Nelson, "Humanity and Protection: The Red Cross and Australian Prisoners of War," lecture in Canberra, March 1, 2003.

Interlude: The "Jap-happy"

323 "We started off with": Richardson, IWM 87/58/1, p. 133.

23. *Haruku*

326 The whole camp was a quagmire: F. A. Forbes, "Medical Report on Certain Prisoner of War Camps in Java and the Ambon Group, April 1942–August 1945," TNA/AIR2/6955, pp. 15–16.

326 The sea belonged to the Emperor: Dr. Richard Philps, quoted in Audus, *Slaves,* p. 80.

326 "A bamboo rail was placed": Home, *Tenko,* p. 54.

326 The simplest actions: Philps, *Prisoner Doctor,* p. 40.

327 the treatment meted out to the prisoners: Sqn. Ldr. W. Pitts, "Treatment of Allied Prisoners of War on the Island of Harokoe," quoted in Lord Russell, *The Knights of Bushido,* p. 156.

327 "wilful murder": Rudi Springer in ibid., p. 156.

327 "Being 'slapped' by the Japs": Home, *Tenko,* p. 56.

328 "All the sick who could stand": Ibid.

328 "The man who denied eating the banana": Audus, interview with author.

329 "A nice view, but": Cowling, *Samurai,* pp. 89–90.

329 It was so hot: Chandler, IWM 81/32/1, pp. 242, 248.

330 "the buzzing of millions of flies": Doctor, quoted in Audus, *Slaves,* p. 87.

330 "The graves were shallow": Cowling, *Samurai,* pp. 92–93.

331 "a premonition of death on a grand scale": Quoted in Audus, *Slaves,* p. 91.

332 LAC Fred Ryall made: Interview and correspondence with author.

332 "The 'death hut' stank": Home, *Tenko,* pp. 65–66.

333 "The shop opened": Peacock, *Guest,* pp. 101–2.

334 "Now even more difficulties": Quoted in Audus, *Slaves,* p. 105.

334 The doctors improvised: Dr. Rudi Springer's diary, http://www.cofepow.org.uk/pages/asia_haruku2.htm, p. 6.

335 "Compare the pleasure": Audus, *Slaves,* pp. 109–10.

335 "The opening of this masterpiece": Don Peacock, IWM 88/33/1, p. 105.

335 "When we came into the camp": Quoted in Audus, *Slaves,* p. 114.

337 To speed the construction of the runway: Ryall, interview with author.

337 "hearing Allied aircraft": Chandler, IWM 81/32/1, p. 241.

337 "I walked down the centre aisle": Cowling, *Samurai,* p. 130.

338 "One will never know": Philps, *Prisoner Doctor,* p. 91.

339 "Scenes of indescribable horror": Home, *Tenko,* p. 92.

340 "Many sang, rather tunelessly": Philps, *Prisoner Doctor,* p. 96.

340 "Those who survived": Home, *Tenko,* p. 95.

341 they looked like the last inmates of Belsen: Van der Post, *New Moon,* p. 51.

341 no more than "skeletons": Nowell Peach, interview with author.

341 Almost one in two of the men: Charles G. Roland, "Stripping Away the Veneer," pp. 90–91.

Interlude: A Conjuring Trick

342 "Gifts from the Indians": Baume, IWM 66/310/2.

24. Sandakan

344 they were killed as effectively and systematically: Athol Moffitt, AWM/PRO 1378/1, p. 140.

345 "He asked whether I was hungry": Nelson, *Prisoners,* p. 104.

345 Twenty-two men were interrogated: Personal records of Paddy H. Funk, member of Sandakan Underground, AWM 3DRL/7408.

345 Hoshijima's punishment cage: Moffitt, AWM/PRO 1378/1, p. 147.

346 "For laziness": Ibid., p. 148.

347 All the snakes that had overrun the camp: C. R. Elliott, "The Shadow of Kina Balu: The Story of Donald V. Elliott," unpublished MS, IWM, p. 98.

347 there were eighty to ninety tons of rice: Moffitt, AWM/PRO 1378/1, pp. 144–46.

347 The marchers even threw their identity discs away: Elliott, *Shadow,* p. 105.

347 One of those on the first march: Keith Botterill, quoted in Peter Firkins, *From Hell to Eternity,* p. 174.

348 "Once you stopped": Ibid., p. 177.

349 Botterill made five of these marches: Nelson, *Prisoners,* p. 107.

349 men who looked like skeletons: Elliott, *Shadow,* p. 124.

350 "On the fourth day": Stipewich, AWM 1010/4/134, p. 7.

350 "They marched us right through the night": Nelson, *Prisoners,* p. 108.

351 two Australians . . . Campbell's escape: Firkins, *Hell,* pp. 197–203; Silver, *Sandakan,* pp. 246–54; Nelson, *Prisoners,* pp. 121–23.

352 "We looked up": Nelson, *Prisoners,* p. 123.

352 They looked pitiable: Interview with ABC, AWM 4636.

353 There is also strong evidence from a Chinese cook: Yuki Tanaka, *Hidden Horrors: Japanese War Crimes in World War II,* pp. 63–64; Firkins, *Hell,* Appendix A, Appendix B; Silver, *Sandakan,* pp. 234–35.

354 the final death toll in the Kuching: Report prepared by 9th Division Intelligence Officers, September 1945, reported in *Table Tops,* daily newspaper for Australian forces abroad, TNA/WO32/4550.

354 to liberate the prisoners at Cabanatuan: The rescue mission at Cabanatuan is the subject of *Ghost Soldiers* by Hampton Sides.

355 "After about fifteen minutes": Riley, IWM 86/87/1, pp. 186–95.

357 an Allied plan to rescue: Silver, *Sandakan,* ch. 16.

Interlude: Mozart

358 "No planes, only": Piper, *I Am Well,* p. 82.

25. *Changi 1944–45*

360 "I have been more or less my own master": Letters from Tom Eaton, September 7, 1945, and September 12, 1945, supplied to author.

361 What luxury it was: Fletcher, "Woe," IWM 67/176/1, p. 192.

361 "Changi is an Island": Ibid.

361 "Wonderful Changi Jail": Philps, *Prisoner Doctor,* p. 110.

361 The conditions were "appalling": Col. E. B. Holmes, "Interim Report on British and Australian POW Camps, Singapore Island, 17 August 1942–31 August 1945," TNA/WO97/6172, p. 7.

361 "Inside the cell blocks": Searle, *To the Kwai,* p. 132.

362 necessity was the mother of invention: Eaton, letter, September 16, 1945.

362 Artificial limbs for the limbless: Fletcher, "Woe," IWM 67/176/1, p. 209.

362 Changi's brush factory: Papers of 8th Division, AIF, AWM 3DRL/369-7/28.

362 the rubber factory: Arneil, *One Man's War,* September 13, 1944; Papers of the 8th Division, AIF, AWM 3DRL/369/5,19; Fletcher, "Woe," IWM 67/176/1, p. 209.

362 Nails made from barbed wire: Arneil, *One Man's War,* September 13, 1944.

363 "Changi Balls" was treated: Fletcher, "Woe," IWM 67/176/1, ch. 13; Arneil, *One Man's War,* September 13, 1944.

363 "Rising at 08.30": Ronald Horner, IWM, Conshelf, p. 144.

363 Lt. Eric Lomax had been dying: Lomax, *Railway Man,* p. 183.

364 "There are few men": Braddon, *Island,* pp. 164–65.

364 But there was a dark side to Changi, too: Nelson, *Story,* p. 165.

365 Sgt. Stan Arneil and his men: Arneil, *One Man's War,* March 13, 1944.

365 Wilkinson's Red Cross ration: Wilkinson, IWM 81/7/1, April 19, 1945.

365 Without the camp gardens: Arneil, *One Man's War,* March 12, 1945, and February 28, 1945.

365 the Springer-Philps test of emaciation: Philps, *Prisoner Doctor,* pp. 112–13.

366 "We had not received any sugar": John Franks, IWM 86/67/1, pp. 75–76.

367 "We made pasties": Ibid., pp. 82–83.

367 "Australian pound notes are changing hands": Harry Jessup, AWM/PRO 0683, July 10, 1945.

368 When Lt. Bob Skene: Austin Ellerman, AWM/PRO 2080, p. 24.

368 "So they devised a method": Philps, *Prisoner Doctor,* p. 112.

369 In July, Changhi at last recovered: E. B. Holmes, TWA/WO97/6172, p. 7; report by Galleghan, AWM 54/554/11/4, part 3, p. 19, part IV, pp. 22–24; Jessup, AWM/PRO 0683, July 23, 1944.

370 "His movements were, as always": Searle, *To the Kwai,* p. 173.

Interlude: "Don't Let This Thing Drag On Much Longer"

372 "By 9.30 I am usually": Milford, IWM 67/82/1, April 16, 1944.

26. Freedom

375 The first truly optimistic day: Innes-Ker, IWM 88/62/1, November 7, 1944; Nelson, *Prisoners,* p. 163.

375 "Maybe, just maybe": Carson, *Hell,* p. 165.

376 They lived among the miles of destruction: Norquist, *Prisoner,* March 10, 1945.

376 "It was a particularly bright and clear morning": Benford, *Rising Sun,* ch. 7.

377 "What I saw": Quoted in Clarke, AWM/MSS 1040, p. 120.

377 The dead looked as though: Quoted in ibid., p. 116.

378 "Things must be happening": Norquist, *Prisoner,* August 15–17, 1945.

378 "When he saluted": Stephen Abbott, IWM 89/15/1, VJ Day, pp. 59ff.

379 "It was then we went mad": Blackater, *Gods,* p. 204.

379 "The monkey, Jennie, was there": Robert Sutcliffe, IWM 66/226/1, p. 90.

380 That sense of pity: Davies, *The Man,* pp. 176–77.

380 As Noguchi also handed over: Rivett, *Behind Bamboo,* p. 315.

381 "I am no longer a chattel": Milford, IWM 67/82/1, p. 550.

381 "To me, the Japs": Whitecross, *Slaves,* p. 249.

381 "I want to go home": Norquist, *Prisoner,* August 19, 1945.

382 Officers looked the other way: These acts of revenge are discussed in Daws, *Prisoner,* pp. 337–38, 550; Jack Symon, *Hell in Five,* p. 86.

382 acts of spontaneous compassion: Coates and Rosenthal, *Story,* p. 142; Lumière, *Kura!* p. 212.

382 PO A.W. Bird started a fund: IWM, Conshelf, September 5, 1945.

382 "Dysentery (once), Beri-beri (twice)": Grigs, IWM, Conshelf, second diary, p. 8.

383 all prisoners were to be killed: *Disposal of Prisoners of War,* Tokyo document used in War Crimes Trial, in Reid, IWM 67/173/1, p. 329; Document No. 2701, in Edwards, *Banzai,* pp. 260–61; Van der Post, *New Moon,* p. 144.

384 a testing responsibility for Mountbatten: S. Woodburn Kirby, *The War Against Japan,* Vol. 5: *The Surrender of Japan,* pp. 230–49.

384 Three organizations played a crucial role: Suzanne Hall, "Politics of Prisoner of War Recovery: SOE and the Burma–Thailand Railway During World War II," *Intelligence and National Security,* 17/2, Summer 2002.

384 "One day a Jap private": Sharp, IWM 66/240/1, pp. 68–69; Drower, *Our Man,* pp. 81–83.

385 Pte. Jack Sharpe, whose picture: Obituary, *The Times,* August 30, 2002.

386 "It was a pitiful and enraging sight": Sutcliffe, IWM 66/226/1, August 23, 1945.

386 Claire Baker nursed some of the prisoners: Ms. C. M. S. Baker, IWM 96/34/1, and correspondence with author.

386 "In great excitement John said": Sutcliffe, IWM 66/226/1, August 27, 1945.

387 "They fairly laid down the law": Innes-Ker, IWM 84/45/1, p. 25.

387 "When the liberators": Searle, *To the Kwai,* p. 180.

388 There were also cheering messages: D. C. Hutchinson-Smith, "To Whom It May Concern," AWM/MSS 1534, p. 280; "To the Guys Below" in E. W. Parry, IWM 86/35/1, August 31, 1945.

388 "Stomachs were distended": Parkin, *Sword,* pp. 224–25.

389 "I have the Japanese general": Howarth, IWM 67/173/1, p. 263.

389 Coates described the exultant shouts: Coates and Newman, *Story,* p. 150.

389 "Quite an agreeable dame": Albert Thompson, AWM/PRO 89/167.

390 "Dark storm clouds hung low": Peacock, *Guest,* pp. 181–82.

390 "We were now seriously threatened": Home, *Tenko,* p. 104.

391 RAPWI, however, was remarkably: Kirby, *Surrender,* p. 249.

Interlude: Bushido

392 "Our captors, for nearly": *Journal of the Royal Army Medical Corps,* April 1946, pp. 146–47.

27. Home at Last

394 "We were thankful for that bomb": Benford, *Rising Sun,* ch. 7.

394 "The dockside was in an uproar": Ibid.

395 Flt. Lt. Peter Lee had the breakfast: Peter Lee's diary, September 13, 1945, in Wall, *Prisoners,* p. 254.

396 "We went with our earthly possessions": Piper, *I Am Well,* pp. 15–16.

396 one of whom had eaten twelve breakfasts: Titherington, *Kinkaseki,* p. 188.

396 They were outraged: Edwards, *Banzai,* p. 255.

397 "To this he agreed": Toosey archive, IWM 93/14/7, PJDT–1, p. 81.

397 "Never were girls so beautiful": Henderson, *Comrades,* p. 74.

397 "We just stood dumb": Blackater, *Gods,* pp. 213–14.

398 "The tumult went on": Innes-Ker, IWM 84/45/1, p. 29.

398 "There was such a wonderful spirit": Letter to parents, September 21, 1945.

398 "What a country this is": Grigs, IWM, Conshelf, October 13, 1945.

399 When Chief Petty Officer Ray Parkin's comrade: Parkin, *Sword,* pp. 261–62.

399 "My heart beat like a hammer": Morris, IWM 91/18/1, pp. 260–61.

BIBLIOGRAPHY

All publishers are British unless otherwise indicated.

Adam-Smith, Patsy. *Prisoners of War from Gallipoli to Korea.* Ken Fin Books (Australia), 1998.

Adams, Geoffrey Pharaoh, with Hugh Popham. *No Time for Geishas.* Leo Cooper, 1973.

Alexander, Stephen. *Sweet Kwai Run Softly.* Merriotts Press, 1995.

Arneil, Stan. *One Man's War,* Sun Books (Australia), 1982.

Audus, Leslie J. *Spice Island Slaves.* Alma Publishers, 1996.

Australian Department of Veterans' Affairs. *Stolen Years, Australian Prisoners of War.* (Australia), 2002.

Barber, Noel. *Sinister Twilight.* Collins, 1968.

Barnard, John T. *The Endless Years.* Chantry, 1950.

Barratt, Capt. John Allan Legh. *His Majesty's Service, 1939–1945.* Privately published, 1983.

Bentinck, Michael. *A Will to Live.* Privately published, 1996.

———. *Forgotten Heroes.* Privately published, 1995.

———. *My Dad, My Hero.* Privately published, 1994.

Bergamini, David. *Japan's Imperial Conspiracy: How Emperor Hirohito Led Japan into War Against the West.* William Morrow (U.S.), 1971.

Bilyeu, Dick. *Lost in Action: A World War II Account of Capture on Bataan and Imprisonment by the Japanese.* McFarland (U.S.), 1991.

Bird, Tom, ed. *American POWs of World War II: Forgotten Men Tell Their Stories.* Praeger (U.S.), 1992.

Blackater, C. F. *Gods without Reason.* Eyre & Spottiswoode, 1948.

Bodine, Roy L. *No Place for Kindness: The Prisoner of War Diary of Roy L. Bodine,* Fort Sam Houston Museum (U.S.), 1983.

Boulle, Pierre. *The Bridge on the River Kwai.* Secker, 1954.

Bowden, Tim. *Changi Photographer: George Aspinall's Record of Captivity.* ABC Times Editions, 2001.

Braddon, Russell. *The Naked Island.* Werner/Lurie, 1951.

Bradley, James. *The Tall Man Who Never Slept.* Woodfield, 1997.

———. *Towards the Setting Sun,* J.M.L. Fuller (Australia), 1982.

Burgoyne, Eric. *The Tattered Remnants.* Book Guild, 2002.

Burton, Reginald. *The Road to Three Pagodas.* Macdonald, 1963. (Republished as *Railway of Hell,* Leo Cooper, Pen & Sword, 2002.)

Caraccilo, Dominic J. *Surviving Bataan and Beyond.* Stackpole Books (U.S.), 1999.

Carson, Andrew D. *My Time in Hell: Memoir of an American Soldier.* McFarland, 1997.

Chalker, Jack Bridger. *Burma Railway Artist: The War Drawings of Jack Chalker.* Leo Cooper, Pen & Sword, 1994.

———. *Images as a Japanese Prisoner of War.* The Friends of Jack Chalker.

Charles, H. Robert. *Last Man Out: Surviving the Burma Railroad.* Crowood Press, 1989.

Chum, Calvin Ellsworth. *Under the Rising Sun.* Veterans' Publishing Co. (U.S.), 1946. (Censored by War Department.)

Clarke, Hugh V. *A Life for Every Sleeper.* Allen & Unwin, 1986.

———. *Last Stop Nagasaki.* Allen & Unwin, 1984.

Clavell, James. *King Rat.* Michael Joseph, 1962.

Coast, John. *Railroad of Death.* Hyperion, 1946.

Coates, Albert, and Newman Rosenthal. *The Albert Coates Story.* Hyland House (Australia), 1977.

Corfield, Justin. *A Bibliography of the Malayan Campaign and the Japanese Period in West Malaysia, Singapore and Borneo, 1941–45.* Edwin Mellen Press, 2001.

Cosford, J. S. *Line of Lost Lives.* Gryphon, 1988.

Cowling, Anthony. *My Life with the Samurai.* Kangaroo (Australia), 1996.

Davies, Peter N. *The Man Behind the Bridge: Colonel Toosey and the River Kwai.* Athlone Press, 1991.

Daws, Gavan. *Prisoners of the Japanese.* William Morrow (U.S.), 1994.

Drower, William. *Our Man on the Hill.* IGS Press (U.S.), 1993.

Dunlop, E. E. *The War Diaries of Weary Dunlop.* Lennard Publishing, 1986.

Durnford, John. *Branch Line to Burma.* Macdonald, 1958.

Dyess, William E. *The Dyess Story: The Eye-witness Account of the Death March from Bataan and the Narrative of Experiences in Japanese Prison Camps and of Eventual Escape.* G. P. Putnam's Sons (U.S.), 1944.

Ebury, Sue. *Weary: The Life of Sir Edward Dunlop.* Penguin Books (Australia), 2001.

Edwards, Jack, with Jimmy Walker. *Banzai You Bastards.* Souvenir Press, 1991.

Evans, Tom. "An Account of POW Life on 'The Burma Railway.'" Unpublished manuscript.

Falk, Stanley L. *The March of Death.* Hale, 1962.

Farrell, Brian, and Sandy Hunter, eds. *Sixty Years On: The Fall of Singapore Revisited.* Eastern Universities Press (Singapore), 2002.

Felser, A. B., ed. *Bilibid Diary: The Secret Notebooks of Commander Thomas Haye, POW, the Philippines 1942–45.* Archer (U.S.), 1987.

Firkins, Peter. *From Hell to Eternity.* Panther, 1985.

Firth, Douglas. *The Spirit of the River Kwai.* Privately published, 1995.

Fletcher-Cooke, Charles. *The Emperor's Guest.* Hutchinson, 1991.

Flower, Sibylla Jane. "Captors and Captives on the Burma–Thailand Railway," in *Prisoners of War and their Captors on the Burma–Thailand Railway,* ed. B. Moore and K. Federowich. Berg, 1996.

Franz, Harry. *Bamboo Treadmill.* Privately published.

Geddes, Margaret. *Remembering Weary: Sir Edward Dunlop as Recalled by Those Whose Lives He Touched.* Penguin (Australia), 1996.

Gard, Dwight E. "Our Boat Trips." Unpublished documents, Carlyle Army Base.

Gee, Margaret. *A Long Way from Silver Creek.* Privately published (Australia), 2000.

Godman, Arthur. *The Will to Survive.* Spellmount, 2002.

Gordon, Ernest. *Miracle on the River Kwai.* Collins, 1963.

Grady, Frank Dickson, and Rebecca Grady. *Surviving the Day: An American POW in Japan.* National Institute Press (U.S.), 1997.

Hall, Suzanne. "Politics of Prisoner of War Recovery: SOE and the Burma–Thailand Railway during WWII." *Intelligence on National Security* 17:2 (Summer 2002).

Hall, W. P. *Kempetai on the Prowl.* Privately published.

Hartley, Peter. *Escape to Captivity.* Dent, 1952.

Henderson, Stan. *Comrades on the Kwai.* Occasional Papers Series: No. 6, Socialist History Society.

Home, James. *Their Last Tenko.* Quoin, 1989.

James, D. Clayton, ed. *South to Bataan, North to Mukden: The Prison Diary of Brig.-Gen. W. E. Brougher.* University of Georgia Press (U.S.), 1971.

Jackson, Calvin V. *Diary of Colonel C. V. Jackson Kept During World War II, 1941–1945.* Ohio Northern University (U.S.), 1992.

Jacobs, Eugene C. "Diary of a Hell-Ship Journey." *Medical Opinion & Review,* November 1970.

———. "From Guerrilla to POW in the Philippines." *Medical Opinion & Review,* August 1969.

Jeffrey, Betty. *White Coolies.* Angus & Robertson (Australia), 1954.

Kerr, E. Bartlett. *Surrender and Survival: The Experience of American POWs in the Pacific 1941–45.* Morrow, 1985.

Kinvig, Clifford. "Allied POWs and the Burma–Thailand Railway," in Philip Towle, Margaret Kosugi, and Yoichi Kibata, eds., *Japanese Prisoners of War.* Hambledon & London, 2000.

———. *Death Railway.* Pan/Ballantine, 1973.

———. *River Kwai Railway: The Story of the Burma Siam Railroad.* Brassey, 1992.

Kirby, Maj. Gen. S. Woodburn. *History of the Second World War: The War Against Japan. Vol. I: The Loss of Singapore.* HMSO, 1957.

———. *History of the Second World War: The War Against Japan. Vol. V: The Surrender of Japan.* HMSO, 1969.

———. *Singapore: The Chain of Disaster.* Cassell, 1971.

Knox, Donald. *Death March: The Survivors of Bataan,* Harcourt Brace Jovanovich, 1984.

La Forte, Robert S., and Ronald E. Marcello. *The Ordeal of American POWs in Burma 1942–45: Building the Death Railway.* Scholarly Resources (U.S.), 1993.

La Forte, Robert S., Ronald E. Marcello, and Richard L. Himmels. *With Only the Will to Live: Accounts of Americans in Japanese Prison Camps, '41–45.* Scholarly Resources (U.S.), 1994.

Lewis, Jonathan, and Ben Steele. *From Pearl Harbor to Hiroshima & Beyond: Hell in the Pacific.* Channel 4 Books, 2001.

Lomax, Eric. *The Railway Man.* Cape, 1995.

Lumière, Cornel. *Kura!,* Jacaranda Press (Australia), 1966.

———. *Red Runs the River Kwai.* Flamingo (U.S.), 1976.

Norquist, Ernest O. "Three Years in Paradise: A GI's Prisoner-of-War Diary, 1942–45." *Wisconsin Magazine of History,* Autumn 1979.

McCormac, Charles. *You'll Die in Singapore.* Pan, 1957.
McCormack, Gavan, and Hank Nelson, eds. *The Burma–Thailand Railway.* Allen & Unwin (Australia), 1993.
McEwan, John. *Out of the Depths of Hell.* Leo Cooper, Pen & Sword, 1999.
McGowran, Tom. *Beyond the Bamboo Screen.* Cualann Press, 2000.
Mittenhall, Harry H. Mittenhall Papers, Carlyle Army Base.
Moffatt, Jonathan, and Audrey Holmes McCormick. *Moon over Malaya: A Tale of Argylls and Marines.* Tempus, 2002.
Morris, Eric. *Corregidor: The Nightmare in the Philippines.* Hutchinson, 1982.
Nelson, David. *The Story of Changi, Singapore.* Changi Museum, 2001.
Nelson, Hank, "Humanity and Protection: The Red Cross and Australian Prisoners of War." Lecture, Canberra, March 1, 2003.
———. *Prisoners of War: Australians Under Nippon.* ABC Enterprises (Australia), 2001.
Nunneley, John, and Kazuo Tamayama. *Tales by Japanese Soldiers of the Burma Campaign 1942–1945.* Cassell, 2000.
Nussbaum, Chaim. *Chaplain on the River Kwai.* Shapolsky (U.S.), 1988.
Parkes, Meg, *"Notify Alec Rattray. . . ."* Kranji, 2002.
Parkin, Ray. *Into the Smother.* Hogarth, 1963.
———. *Out of the Smoke.* Hogarth, 1960.
———. *The Sword and the Blossom.* Hogarth, 1968.
Pavillard, Stanley S. *Bamboo Doctor.* Macmillan, 1960.
Peacock, Don. *The Emperor's Guest.* Oleander, 1989.
Philps, Richard, *Prisoner Doctor: An Account of the Experiences of a Royal Air Force Medical Officer During the Japanese Occupation of Indonesia, 1942 to 1945.* Book Guild, 1996.
Piper, David. *I Am Well, Who Are You: Writings of a Japanese POW.* Delian Bower, 1998.
Poole, Philippa. *Of Love and War: The Letters and Diaries of Captain Adrian Curlewis and His Family, 1939–45.* Lansdowne Press (Australia), 1982.
Rawlings, Leo. *And the Dawn Came Up Like Thunder.* Chapman, 1972.
Richards, Rowley, and Marcia McEwan. *The Survival Factor.* Costello, 1989.
Rivett, Rohan. *Behind Bamboo.* Angus & Robertson (Australia), 1946.
Roland, Charles C. "Stripping Away the Veneer: POW Survival in the Far East as an Index of Cultural Atavism." *The Journal of Military History* 53 (1989).
Russell, Lord, of Liverpool. *The Knights of Bushido.* Cassell, 1958.
Saunders, Jack. *It Seems Like Yesterday.* Avon Books, 1995.
Searle, Ronald. *To the Kwai—and Back.* Collins, 1986.
Sides, Hampton. *Ghost Soldiers.* Little, Brown, 2001.
Silver, Lynette. *Sandakan.* Sally Milner Publishing (Australia), 1998.
Spalding, Bill. *Speedo! Speedo!: To the Limits of Endurance.* Majic Ink, 2001.
Spector, Ronald H. *Eagle Against the Sun.* Cassell, 1984.
Stewart, John. *To the River Kwai.* Bloomsbury, 1988.
Stiby, A.R.C. *Lumber Room Jumble.* Privately published, 1984.
Stubbs, Les, and Pam Stubbs. *Unsung Heroes of the Royal Air Force: The Far East Prisoners of War.* Barny, 2002.
Symon, Jack. *Hell in Five.* Privately published, 1992.
Tanaka, Yuki. *Hidden Horrors: Japanese War Crimes in World War II.* Westview Press (U.S.), 1996.
Tarling, Nicholas. *A Sudden Rampage: The Japanese Occupation of Southeast Asia 1941–45.* Hurst, 2001.
Titherington, Arthur. *Kinkaseki.* Covos Day (South Africa), 2000.

Towle, Philip, Margaret Kosugi, and Yoichi Kibata, eds. *Japanese Prisoners of War.* Hambledon & London, 2000.

U.S. Department of the Army: Office of the Provost Marshal General. *United States Prisoners of War Interned by Japan on the Four Major Islands of Japan.* U.S. Department of the Army.

Vance, Jonathan F., ed. *Encyclopedia of Prisoners of War and Internment.* ABC-CLIO (U.S.), 2000.

van der Post, Laurens. *A Bar of Shadow.* Hogarth, 1954.

———. *The Night of the New Moon.* Hogarth, 1970.

Wall, Don. *Heroes of F Force.* Privately published (Australia), 1993.

———. *Kill the Prisoners!* Privately published (Australia), 1993.

Whitecross, R. H. *Slaves of the Son of Heaven.* Dymock's, 1952. (Republished Corgi, 1961.)

Wigmore, Lionel. *Australia in the War of 1939–45: Army (IV) Japanese Thrust.* Australian War Memorial (Australia), 1957.

INDEX

ABOUT THE AUTHOR

Brian MacArthur has spent most of his career at *The Times,* where he was an executive editor during the editorships of Harold Evans, Simon Jenkins, and Peter Stothard. He was also deputy editor of *The Sunday Times,* founding editor of *The Times Higher Education Supplement* and *Eddy Shah's Today,* and editor of *The Western Morning News.*

He is the author of several books about newspapers and edited *The Penguin Book of Twentieth-Century Speeches* and *The Penguin Book of Historic Speeches.* He lives in London and Norfolk.

ABOUT THE TYPE

This book was set in Fairfield, the first typeface from the hand of the distinguished American artist and engraver Rudolph Ruzicka (1883–1978). In its structure Fairfield displays the sober and sane qualities of the master craftsman whose talent has long been dedicated to clarity. It is this trait that accounts for the trim grace and vigor, the spirited design and sensitive balance, of this original typeface.

Rudolph Ruzicka was born in Bohemia and came to America in 1894. He set up his own shop, devoted to wood engraving and printing, in New York in 1913 after a varied career working as a wood engraver, in photoengraving and banknote printing plants, and as an art director and freelance artist. He designed and illustrated many books, and was the creator of a considerable list of individual prints—wood engravings, line engravings on copper, and aquatints.